Film and Television In-Jokes

Film and Television In-Jokes

Nearly 2,000 Intentional References, Parodies, Allusions, Personal Touches, Cameos, Spoofs and Homages

by BILL VAN HEERDEN

McFarland & Company, Inc., Publishers
Jefferson, North Carolina, and London

British Library Cataloguing-in-Publication data are available

Library of Congress Cataloguing-in-Publication Data

van Heerden, Bill, 1970–
    Film and television in-jokes : nearly 2,000 intentional
references, parodies, allusions, personal touches, cameos, spoofs
and homages / by Bill van Heerden.
      p.   cm.
    Includes bibliographical references and index.
    ISBN 0-7864-0456-6 (library binding : 50# alkaline paper) ∞
    1. Motion pictures—Humor.   2. Motion pictures—Miscellanea.
I. Title.
PN1994.9.V36   1998
791.43'75—dc21   98-12991
                                                CIP

Manufactured in the United States of America

*McFarland & Company, Inc., Publishers
  Box 611, Jefferson, North Carolina 28640*

To Jenni

To Alan's friend, Bryan MacMillan

And to the one person without whose faith and support
this book would never have seen the light of day.
Thank you, Alison. You're the greatest.

Contents

Acknowledgments

If I have omitted anyone, my sincerest apologies. Your contributions are greatly appreciated. My thanks to...

Acepicture
Scott Adams
Adrienne "AYoungOne"
Meghann Ahern
Richard Akis
Colin M. Alberts
Holly Alexander
Ashley Allgood
Patricia Annino
Richard Arnold
Vicki Arnold
Michael Aulfrey
DonnaB
Mark Barr
Shawn Beach
Jen Beatty
Mr Jim Beaver
Ralph Benner
James Berardinelli
Steven M. Bergson
Zev Berkovich
Jami Bernard
Craig Bickley
Amy Bieber
Julie Bixby

Gina Blank
Dan "Saint" Bodenheimer
Lilyan Brower
Emanuel Brown
Jeremy Daniel Buhler
HeatherC
pDaleCampbell
Art Carey
Diane Carlson
Jeff Carroll
Ben Carter
Tanja Carter
Pat M. Chachich
Terry Chambers
Bryan Chaney
Murray Chapman
Ricky Cheatwood
Cliff Chen
Bruce W. Christopher
Scott Chupack
Joe Clarke
David Cleary
Anna Jeanne Conrow
Angeline Cotto-Nelson
David Cowen

Steve Cross
T. Cruise
TJ Currey
Bill Dahm
Shawn Daudlin
Father Anthony Damien
   Dauer
Jo Davidsmeyer
Bryan Davis
James Dawe
Robert J. Defendi
Patrick Delahanty
Audrey De Lisle
David Raoul Derbes
Daniel Morris DeRight
Bryan Derksen
Paul Donahue
Jerry Dreiss
Alice Dryden
Eric Mariah Mariah
   Duchin
Bobby Dupea
Winston Edmond
Helen E. Elsom
Beth "Tigger" Epstein

N.M. Federico
Alan Felsen
Mark D. Felt
Andrea Ferch
Sean "FigmentFly"
Andrew S. Fischer
Stefan Flosbach
Aurora N. Ford
MFountain
Brad Fox
Charles B. Francois
Adam Frix
John C. Fu
Victor Fujimoto
Alex Fung
Patricia E. Gallagher
William Gallagher
David Garrett
"Godfather" Geoff
John George
Christopher Gerby
Roger Gibbins
Anthony Bruce Gilpin
Camille Gleaton
Eliot Goldwarg
Chuk Goodin
Nair Hari Gopinathan
Tim Gould
Linda Grasmick
Karen Green
Aaron Greenhouse
Andreas L. Gustafsson
John Hajduk
Ed Hall
Michelle Hamilton
HappyFingr
George W. Harris
Alexander Hart
Christian Hartleben
Rob Hartmann
Erisson "E." Hastur
Richard Haussmann
Mark F. Heiman
Loren Heisey
Jack Heraty
Terry Herrin
Andrew J. Hillery III

J. A. Hitchcock
Linda Hobbet
Martin A. Hohner
Mark Holtz
Jo Horridge
Rick Howard
Alan Hunt
Danielle "JadenCat"
Julie Jekel
Neil Jones
Darryl Jorden
JsJr
Just Della
Diane Kachmar
Micheal Keane
Annie Keitz
Marty Kelley
Cary Kittrell
Eric Knoll
Michael Kotler
Joshua S. Kreitzer
Chantal Valrie Kuhn
Christian Lander
Dani Lane
Johnny Lau
Jesper Lauridsen
Andrew "Goggles Pizano"
    Lawrence
Heather Ledyit
Haynes Lee
Soo Lee
Andrea Leistra
Kathleen Lenkeit
Ian Leshin
Terri M. Librande
Charles Lindy
Marianne Lo Monaco
Louette
Mark Lowe
Scott Lucas
Cave Luther
Stephen McAuley
Lori McDowell
Shane McMordie
Scott S. Madsen
Marillia
Debbie "Kitkin" Martinez

Christina Matta
The Enigmatic Rhea
    Merana
Rachel C. Mercado
Steven Miale
Michelle "Baking
    Woman"
Nell Minow, The Movie
    Mom™
L C Moon
Ceri Alun Morgan
Dave Morrissey
Aaron M. Moy
LynnEtte Mueller
Walter Mueller
Col Needham
Suzanne Neve
Eric Newman
J. Ng
Jan Normann Nielsen
Roy O'Grady
"Agnes Tomorrow" B.
    Oltmann
Kevin "OoLaGiLi"
Steven Otte
Nicole Parrot
Amy Patrick
Michael Peiluck
Elizabeth Phillips
Chris Pierson
Dave Platt
GLen Pringle
Larissa Ranbom
Bill Ranck
Peter Reiher
Karen Rhodes
Brent Richards
Kymberlee K.-A. Ricke
Joshua Roberts
Linda Robeson
Deidre Rogers
Diana Romaine
David Romas
Diane Rosenfeldt
Alan Rosu
Dean Roth
Jay S. Rouman

Brenda Scott Royce
Barbara Ruef
St. Marc
Samantha (te7441667)
Panos Sambrakos
Ben Sandofsky
Santry
Rodney Sauer
Dan Scheraga
Michaela Schlocker
Peter Schouten
Lynn Scott
Jason Seaver
Prof. Seevots
Alan Sepinwall
David Serchay
Denis Seretis
Ivan T. Shaw
Joy Skeldon
Brad Smith
Joe Smith
Nicky Smith
Nina A. Smith
Joanne Spieker

John Spooner
Mary Spooner
Bill Steele
JMSTREEP
Tod Martin Sturgeon
Mark Suggs
Kent R. Summers
Aaron Sumner
Ferenc Szabo
Ann Teitelbaum
Julia Terho
Joseph "Coot" Thompson
Brian Tiemann
Ken Timlin
Alfred Tonna
Keith Topping
Colin "Boss Hog" Tough
Scott F. Tracy
Sue Tremblay
Scott T.S. Trimble
Ray Tsai
Steve Twohy
Autumn A. Tysko
Sean Vanderfluit

Chris Vargas
Peter Vassilakis
Albert Lee Vest
Sean Victor
Mitch Virchick
Vixen
Randy M. Wadkins
Michael Wasczcak
Sally Waters
BrYan Westbrook
Tara "Harpy" Wheeler
Wendy Westover
   Wijegunawardana
Wes Wildcat
Norman Wilner
Laura Witte
David Wohl
Fred B. Young, Jr.
Catherine Yronwode
Susan Cho Yuk
Zoomway
Lou Zucaro
and my mother, for Parker
   "McLean" Stevenson

Introduction

For centuries, artists, authors and artisans have included references, allusions or personal touches in their work, and when the art forms of film and television began to grow and develop, such references and personal touches slowly began to appear in them as well. A friend's name would be mentioned in a throwaway line, or the director of the film would appear in a small cameo role. After a while, these instances began to appear with more regularity and with greater detail. An entire army squadron would be named after the actors in a popular television show. Characters in a television series would be seen not-so-subtly using the products of the show's sponsors. A comedy routine in a film would spoof a similar sequence in another contemporary popular film. The more films and television shows produced, the greater the potential became for references back to them. However, while most art and literature of the previous era made use of more subtle forms of reference, filmmakers such as Bob Hope and Bing Crosby, the Marx Brothers, and, more recently, the Zucker brothers and Mel Brooks found that more obvious references appealed to a larger group of film viewers. Film and television writers have reached new heights in the art of referencing, occasionally using homages (for example, Clint Eastwood tossing his badge away at the end of *Dirty Harry* is a homage to a similar scene with Gary Cooper at the end of *High Noon*), but more frequently through the use of inside jokes or "in-jokes."

In-jokes are not jokes per se, but references to something outside of the context of the specific film or series. They are intentional references, or "jokes," that require some kind of explanation or inside information to understand. This can include any characters or places named after someone, any cameo appearances with special meaning, or any references to former roles, series, films, or personal information.

There is a difference between in-jokes and simple trivia. It is trivia to note

1

that the device that tells the fighter squadron to turn back in the film *Executive Decision* is called "the CRM-114." The in-joke is that this was also the name for the fictional device in the film *Dr. Strangelove* that was supposed to tell the bomber to turn back. Comparisons have also been made between the occurrences of in-jokes and mistakes in films. The one big difference is that in-jokes are intentional. I suspect that writers, directors, actors, or any originators of in-jokes sincerely want people to notice them, but are not completely sure whether anyone "catches" them or not. I received the following message from Lee Goldberg, supervising producer of the series *Spenser: For Hire*.

> We did an episode ("Sleepless Dreams") of *Spenser: For Hire* in which a brother and sister conspire to hide the fact that the brother killed their mother. Everyone in the episode was named after characters in *The Partridge Family*. We even had a character named after the show's creator. No one ever caught it.

There is a hint of disappointment in that statement. In-jokes apparently are not as much fun for their creators if they are not picked up on. In-jokes indicate a sense of playfulness on the part of the creator, as if they are daring the viewer to discover the hidden nuances in their work.

Some say that these little hidden in-jokes take something away from the viewing experience of the films, that they are reminders that the actions onscreen are not real, and that they detract from the story. In my opinion, in-jokes add to the experience. Films and television series are, above all, forms of entertainment, and seeing something that you hadn't before or knowing something new about your favorite episode or film enhances your enjoyment of the moment.

If you don't want to know that Patrick Macnee's character in *The Howling* was named after the director of *The Wolf Man*, or that Bart Simpson writes "I will not defame New Orleans" on the blackboard in the opening scene of one episode of *The Simpsons* because the city of New Orleans complained about the opening song in *The Simpsons* episode "Oh Streetcar!", but want just to watch a film or series on its own merits, then so be it. But I have discovered that film and television fans, from the truly rabid to even the most casual of viewers, get an extra little thrill when they see something or pick up on a reference that no one else in the audience does. I have read at least three different postings on the Internet from people who watched the film *Twister* and were proud to be the only one in the theater who understood (and heartily laughed at) the line "That's no moon… it's a *space station!*"—a reference to the line in *Star Wars*. Spotting an in-joke evokes the feeling of discovery and a sense of being included in something special, intermixed with a hint of superiority, knowing that you picked up on something that very few others did.

In-Jokes in Films

Abbott and Costello Go to Mars (1953)

The Venusians are played by the contestants in the 1953 Miss Universe pageant, including that year's Miss Sweden, Anita Ekberg.

Abbott and Costello Meet Frankenstein (1948)

After escaping all the Universal monsters, Bud Abbott and Lou Costello find themselves alone in a rowboat ... or so they think. A disembodied cigarette appears, and the Invisible Man speaks, voice of Vincent Price. Price had played the character in *The Invisible Man Returns* (1940), the sequel to the Claude Rains original.

Abbott and Costello Meet the Invisible Man (1951)

A photograph of Claude Rains can be seen hanging on a wall. Rains played the title role in the original, *The Invisible Man* (1933). A similar picture appeared in the film *The Invisible Man Returns* (1940), starring Vincent Price as Rains's brother.

The Abominable Dr. Phibes (1971)

There is a twist on the famous line from the film *Love Story* (1970): "Love means never having to say you're ugly" (see also *What's Up, Doc?* 1972).

The Absent-Minded Professor (1961)

Keenan Wynn stars in the film as Alonzo Hawk, and his father Ed and son Neal have small parts. Ed Wynn plays the fire chief and Neal plays one of the kids.

The Accidental Tourist (1988)

Director Lawrence Kasdan's son Jacob plays Scott Canfield. Kasdan's son Jon can also be seen in the doctor's office, and Lawrence's wife, Meg Kasdan, plays a receptionist.

Ace Ventura: Pet Detective (1994)

The name "Shady Acres Mental Hospital" is a reference to the name of director Tom Shadyac.

The Addams Family (1991)

Gomez (Raul Julia) plays with his

3

train set, and when he looks into the window of his train, a tiny little commuter looks back up at him. The commuter is played by director Barry Sonnenfeld.

The Adventures of Baron Munchausen (1989)

Robin Williams plays the King of the Moon, but the part is credited to "Ray Ditutto." The Italian phrase "Rei di Tutto" means "King of Everything," which is how the King introduces himself to the Baron.

The Adventures of Priscilla, Queen of the Desert (1994)

In the video store is a poster for "Frauds" (1993), which was also directed by Stephan Elliott and starred Hugo Weaving.

Afraid of the Dark (1991)

Director/screenwriter Mark Peploe's daughter, Lola, can be seen at both the wedding and the cemetery.

Africa Screams (1949)

The bit with the giant gorilla is a reference to the hit film "Mighty Joe Young" (1949), released earlier the same year.

After Hours (1985)

Director Martin Scorsese has a cameo as the searchlight operator in Club Berlin.

Scorsese's father, Charles, has a cameo in the film as well. Charles also receives credit as "wardrobe assistant" for the film.

Scorsese also cast his first assistant director, Stephen J. Lim, as the Club Berlin bartender.

Against All Odds (1984)

Jane Greer plays Mrs. Wyler, the mother of Jessie Wyler (Rachel Ward).

This film is based on the film "Out of the Past" (1947), and, in the previous film, Greer played Rachel Ward's role. Then, the character was named Kathie Moffett.

The Age of Innocence (1993)

Writer-director Martin Scorsese has an uncredited cameo as a photographer.

Scorsese's father, Charles, and daughter, Domenica, also have cameos in the film. Domenica Scorsese plays Katie Blenker.

Agnes of God (1985)

Director Norman Jewison's daughter, Jennifer, appears as a patient.

Airheads (1994)

Chas (Brendan Fraser) identifies a cop posing as a record exec by asking the question, "Who'd win in a wrestling match? Lemmy or God?" Lemmy is the lead singer of the hard rock group Motorhead. Later, Chas comes outside and admits his nerdy origins to his girlfriend. Members of the crowd support him, shouting out their dirty little secrets from high school. One yells, "I was editor of the school magazine!" He's played by Lemmy (and listed in the credits as "Lemmy von Motorhead").

Airplane! (1980)

Lloyd Bridges's and Robert Stack's characters are named after characters in director team David Zucker, Jim Abrahams, and Jerry Zucker's "Kentucky Fried Movie" (1977). Bridges is named "Steve McCroskey" after the guilty reporter in the courtroom scene, and Stack is named "Rex Kramer" after the thrill-seeking daredevil (and part-time airline mechanic) who risks his life by screaming one seven-letter word.

Although it was more directly inspired by the "Airport" series of films, this movie is largely a direct parody of the film "Zero Hour" (1957). In that film, the co-pilot was played by ex–football star Elroy "Crazy Legs" Hirsch. In this one, the co-pilot is played by basketball star Kareem Abdul-Jabbar. He even admits he is the basketball player.

The singing nun is a reference to Helen Reddy's singing nun in *Airport 1975* (1974).

At the start of the film, a man gets into Robert Hays's cab, and he is still waiting in the cab at the end. His last line, after the closing credits, is "Well, I'll give him another twenty minutes … but that's it." The joke here is that the man is played by Howard Jarvis, the income-tax fighter who wrote the book *I'm Mad as Hell*, about fighting the system and not being taken advantage of.

Co-directors Jim Abrahams, David Zucker and Jerry Zucker have cameos. Jerry is the ground crewman who is directing a taxiing jetliner, and David comes up to him and asks him where the coffee shop is. Abrahams plays one of the religious zealots who Kramer (Stack) fights off when he enters the terminal. Abrahams is the one who sees Kramer fighting them off, stops and decides against approaching him. He's wearing a T-shirt that reads "I Found It."

Among the jokes in the final credits (Author of *A Tale of Two Cities* … Charles Dickens) is a credit for Mike Finnel: "Generally in Charge of a Lot of Things." Finnel was an especially hard-working producers' assistant.

Airplane II: The Sequel (1982)

The opening credits crawl was inspired by the opening credits of "Star Wars" (1977), and the music heard is the theme from the series *Battlestar: Galactica*. The theme is also repeated during liftoff of the shuttle.

In the opening sequence, there is a parody of the "Phone home" line in the then-just-released "E.T., the Extraterrestrial" (1982).

The ship's computer, ROK 4000, is based on the HAL 2000 computer from *2001: A Space Odyssey* (1968). The unusual shot of Julie Hagerty's shocked face when she is told "All systems compute positive" is right out of *2001*, and so is the shot of Mr. Unger and Mr. Dunn floating through space.

As Captain Oveur (Peter Graves) tries to disconnect the malfunctioning computer, he is gassed by the computer and the theme to Graves's old series, *Mission: Impossible*, can be heard.

In the hospital, Steve McCroskey's (Lloyd Bridges) problem is said to be that "He just thinks he's Lloyd Bridges." The first time McCroskey appears, he is in bed, snorkelling, referring to Bridges's old series, *Sea Hunt*.

With William Shatner appearing as Buck Murdock, there are many references to Shatner's series *Star Trek*. On the moon's Alpha Beta Station, all the doors open and close with the familiar "Shhh" sound from the series. (The joke is, you have to make the "Shhh" sound yourself to open and close them.) Murdock is told that the station does not have a tower. "Just a bridge," bringing to mind the bridge of *Star Trek*'s USS *Enterprise*, which Murdock even sees through his periscope.

Aladdin (1992)

The stack of blocks that the Sultan plays with is sitting on a toy of the Beast from Disney's *Beauty and the*

Beast (1991). Sebastian the Crab from *The Little Mermaid* (1989) can also be seen.

The two men in the crowd that the genie pushes through are caricatures of a couple of the animators, John Musker and Ron Clements. The original plan was to use film critics Gene Siskel and Roger Ebert, but the studio could not get permission.

Alice Doesn't Live Here Anymore (1974)

Director Martin Scorsese appears in a cameo in Mel and Ruby's.

Diane Ladd's daughter, actress Laura Dern, has an uncredited bit, eating an ice cream cone at a counter.

Alien (1979)

The ship is named after the Joseph Conrad book *Nostromo*. In the novel, Nostromo is the pilot of a ship hauling ore out of a turbulent South American country. The ship in the film is also hauling ore.

The name of the shuttle *Narcissus* is taken from the Conrad novel *The Nigger of the Narcissus*. The plot revolves around a sailor who brings death on board with him.

Alien Dead (1980)

Writer-producer-director Fred Olen Ray has a cameo as a pool player.

Alien Nation: Dark Horizon (1994 TV)

At the end, Albert (Jeff Marcus) is married to May by a priestess played by Susan Appling. Appling is the wife of the film's executive producer-director, Kenneth Johnson.

Aliens (1986)

The ship, the *Sulaco*, is named after the town in Joseph Conrad's *Nostromo* (see *Alien*, 1979).

In regards to Vasquez (Jenette Goldstein), Hudson (Bill Paxton) says, "She thought they said 'illegal aliens' and signed up." This was an inside joke among the actors. Goldstein had gone to the audition thinking that the film would be about illegal immigrants. She arrived with waist-long hair and lots of makeup. Everyone else wore fatigues.

Just before the Marines are thawed out in the *Sulaco*, their names are listed on a computer screen. None of their first names are ever divulged in the film, but their first initials are all listed here, and, except for the leads (Sigourney Weaver, "E. Ripley," Michael Biehn, "D. Hicks" and William Hope, "S. Gorman"), all of the characters have the same first initial as the actors who play them. There's "A. Apone" (Al Matthews), "C. Ferro" (Colette Hiller), "J. Vasquez" (Jenette Goldstein), "M. Drake" (Mark Rolston), "D. Spunkmeyer" (Daniel Kash), "C. Dietrich" (Cynthia Scott), "R. Frost" (Ricco Ross), "T. Wierzbowski" (Trevor Steedman), and "T. Crowe" (Tip Tipping). Even Bishop (Lance Henriksen), the android, is listed as "L. Bishop." Hudson (Bill Paxton) is not listed in the manifest, but his name can be seen on the readout on his minicam: "W. Hudson," for William.

When Hudson (Paxton) finds the colonist locators on the computer, he says, "Stop your grinnin' and drop your linen!" This is a line from the AC/DC song "Shake a Leg" from the 1980 album *Back in Black*.

Bishop mentions that Ash (the android from the first film) was one of the Hyberdyne Systems 120-A/2, one letter off from "Cyberdyne." In the first draft of the script, the name Cyberdyne was used. Cyberdyne was the name of the company (short for Cyber Dynamics) that created the

Terminators in director James Cameron's film *The Terminator* (1984).

When Ripley hears that Burke doesn't want the facehuggers destroyed, she confronts him and tells him that she knows that he sent the colonists to the alien ship. He denies it, but she cites the log that she looked up in the station computer: "Directive dated 6/12/79, signed Burke, Carter J." The original film, *Alien,* opened in theatres on that date—June 12, 1979.

All You Need Is Cash (1978 TV)

The Rutles, the group in this film, are a parody of the Beatles, and one of the Beatles has a cameo. George Harrison plays the interviewer who has his microphone stolen while interviewing Michael Palin about the thefts.

Bill Murray plays American DJ Bill Murray the K, after real-life DJ "Murray the K." Murray "The K" Kaufman, a WNEW disc jockey in New York City, foresaw the mania that came with the Beatles when they first reached North America, and gained much publicity when he declared himself "The Fifth Beatle" on the air.

Alligator (1980)

Just before the baby alligator falls at the end of the film, graffiti can be seen on the wall of the sewer. It reads "Harry Lime Lives," a reference to the character in *The Third Man* (1949) who was killed in a sewer.

At the film's beginning, a 25-year veteran of the sewer department named Edward Norton is discovered missing, then killed. Ed Norton was the name of Art Carney's sewer-worker character on *The Honeymooners.*

Altered States (1980)

Screenwriter Paddy Chayefsky disowned his adaptation of his novel when director Ken Russell replaced Arthur Penn at the last minute and made radical changes. The script is credited to "Sidney Aaron," which is Chayefsky's given name.

Always (1989)

When Dorinda (Holly Hunter) returns in the plane, she is dressed like Ripley in *Aliens* (1986), and she even has a ginger tomcat, like Jones in *Alien* (1979). However, the cat's name is Linda Blair (a nod to the actress who played the demon-possessed young girl in *The Exorcist*), not Jones.

Amadeus (1984)

At the end of the film, Wolfgang Amadeus Mozart (Tom Hulce), who is too sick to continue, leaves a concert in progress. The conductor who replaces him is played by the film's music coordinator, John Strauss.

Amazon Women on the Moon (1987)

Two film reviewers named Frankel and Herbert appear in one segment. Their names are an amalgam of film reviewers Gary Franklin, Gene Siskel and Roger Ebert. They are played by "Lohman and Barkley," a Los Angeles radio team.

Henry Silva plays himself as the host of *Bullshit or Not,* a spoof on Jack Palance's series *Ripley's Believe It or Not.*

Some of the segments, directed by John Landis, feature familiar Landis in-jokes. For example:

Fred, the guy in the ads for Silly Pate, is played by film composer Ira Newborn (*The Naked Gun: From the Files of Police Squad,* 1988; *The Blues Brothers,* 1980).

The President of the Earth, seen on a viewscreen in the "Amazon Women" segment, is played by Forrest J Ackerman.

Ackerman was the creator of the first successful sci-fi/horror magazine, *Famous Monsters of Filmland*.

The man at the counter who sells Marc McClure his personalized adult video in the "Video Date" segment is played by 1960s sexploitation director Russ Meyer (*Faster Pussycat! Kill! Kill!*, 1962, *Beneath the Valley of the Ultra-Vixens*, 1979).

The customer in the drugstore where the boy goes to buy condoms is played by guitarist Steve Cropper ("Soul Man"). Cropper had previously starred in Landis's *The Blues Brothers* (1980).

The three main characters in the "Condom Man" segment are named George Bailey (Matt Adler), Violet (Kelly Preston) and Mr. Gower (Ralph Bellamy). These names come from the film *It's a Wonderful Life* (1946). In the previous film, James Stewart played George, Gloria Grahame played Violet, and H.B. Warner played Mr. Gower.

The American Friend (1977)

Director Wim Wenders appears in a cameo as a bandaged man.

Wenders also cast film directors (and bit actors) Nicholas Ray and Sam Fuller as heavies. Ray's character is named "Derwatt."

American Graffiti (1973)

The license plate number of John Milner's (Paul LeMat) car is THX 138, a reference to director George Lucas's earlier film, *THX-1138* (1971).

The American President (1995)

Lewis Rothschild (Michael J. Fox) is on the phone, trying to get Congressman Garret's vote. He snaps, and punches a conspicuously-placed can of Diet Coke across the room. Fox did ads for Coke's competitor, Pepsi, in the 80s.

An American Werewolf in London (1981)

The porno film being shown at the Eros Cinema where David (David Naughton) meets his decomposing friend Jack (Griffin Dunne) is titled *See You Next Wednesday* on the theater marquee. A poster for the film also appears in the London Underground when the man is killed (see *Schlock*, 1971).

The man who flies through the windshield of a car in Picadilly Circus and is then run over is played by director John Landis.

Landis cast Muppeteer (and future director) Frank Oz as the doctor who examines David Naughton.

America's Deadliest Home Video (1993)

The film's co-producer, Stephen Diller, has a cameo as Debbie's lover.

Eva Scott-Berry, a production assistant on the film, plays a newswoman.

Producer Michael L. Wynhoff's father, Lou, has a cameo as a security guard.

Anatomy of a Murder (1959)

Joseph Welch, who plays the judge in the film, was the famous lawyer in the Army-McCarthy hearings. At the time, Welch was a judge in real life.

...And God Created Woman (1987)

Director Roger Vadim, who also directed the original French version of this film in 1956, has a cameo as the photographer snapping pictures of Vincent Spano and Rebecca de Mornay, the "happy couple."

Andy Hardy Comes Home (1958)

Andy (Mickey Rooney) and Jane (Patricia Breslin) have a son in this film named Andy, Jr. He is played by Mickey's real-life son, Teddy Rooney.

Angels Die Hard (1970)
  Producer Charles Beach Dickerson has a cameo in the film.

Anne of Green Gables (1934)
  Actress Anne Shirley, who plays Anne (Shirley) of Green Gables, took her stage name from her character in this film. Before this film, she was known as Dawn O'Day.

Anne of the Thousand Days (1969)
  Richard Burton stars in this film, and his wife Elizabeth Taylor has an unbilled cameo in one scene as a reveller.

Another Dawn (1937)
  In the 1930s, whenever a cinema canopy was shown in a film, it usually advertised the nonexistent film *Another Dawn*. However, in 1937, when Warner Brothers was stuck for a title for their latest Errol Flynn film, they irreverently and cynically called it *Another Dawn*.

Another Stakeout (1993)
  Richard Dreyfuss won an Academy Award for his role in *The Goodbye Girl* (1977), and one of his lines in that film was, "And I don't like the panties hanging on the rod." In this film, he repeats the line while standing in front of a line of drying panties.

The Apartment (1960)
  Director Billy Wilder directed Marilyn Monroe in *The Seven Year Itch* (1955) and *Some Like It Hot* (1959). He grew to despise her demands for star treatment and her poor work ethic, and thus included the derogatory party-girl Monroe-esque character that Jack Lemmon brings home from the bar in this film.

Apocalypse Now (1979)
  Harrison Ford wears a nametag which reads "G. Lucas." George Lucas directed Ford in *American Graffiti* (1973) and *Star Wars* (1977), which made Ford famous. G.D. Spradlin's character is named R. Corman, after producer Roger Corman.
  Director Francis Ford Coppola appears as the director of the television crew filming Robert Duvall's destruction of a village.
  Coppola's nephew, Marc Coppola, appears as the Armed Forces Radio announcer.

Apollo 13 (1995)
  Jim Lovell (the astronaut played by Tom Hanks) appears as the captain of the USS *Iwo Jima*. His wife, Marilyn (played by Kathleen Quinlan), also appears as an extra in the grandstand during the launch.
  Director Ron Howard included family members in the film, as usual. His brother, Clint, is EECOM White, one of the technicians at a console in the space center; his dad, Rance, shows up as a priest watching television in the Lovell household; and, for the first time, Ron's mother Jean Speegle Howard appears, as Lovell's mother, Blanch.
  Ron Howard also cast Roger Corman as the visiting congressman who criticizes the Apollo Program's budget overruns. Corman, the king of exploitation film producers, gave Howard his first break as a director in 1977's *Grand Theft Auto*. He is notorious in the industry for slashing directors' production budgets mercilessly.

Arise My Love (1940)
  Ray Milland, asked whether he is a test pilot, says, "No, that was Clark Gable," referring to the then-recently released Gable film, *Test Pilot* (1938).

Armed Response (1986)

Writer-director Fred Olen Ray has a cameo as a soldier.

Army of Darkness (1993)

Linda, Ash's "wonderful girlfriend" in the film's prologue, is played by Bridget Fonda. Fonda was a huge fan of director Sam Raimi, and she wanted a role—any role—in this film, so Raimi added the prologue just for her.

The magic words that Ash (Bruce Campbell) must use to claim the book of the dead are "Klaatu Verata Niktu," a slight variation of "Klaatu Barada Nikto," the words used to command the robot Gort in *The Day the Earth Stood Still* (1951). Actually, the first time the wise man says it, he says "...Niktu," and Ash repeats, "...Nikto." That is, when he actually remembers the third word. The second time, when Ash uses the book to return home, the wise man pronounces the word "Nikto."

Fourteen actors are credited as playing "Fake Shemps," including Bruce's brother, Don, his father, Charlie, and Sam Raimi's brother, Ivan, who also cowrote the script (see *The Evil Dead*, 1983).

Ted Raimi, Sam's brother, has four cameos. "It used to be five," he said, "but one got cut." He's the guy Ash is telling his story to in S-Mart at the end of the film, and he also plays several roles in medieval times. He plays the terrified general with Prince Henry (Marcus Gilbert), then a brave, one-eyed general ("Aaaaar! Prince Henry! Aaaaar!"), and then one of Arthur's men—the "Cowardly Warrior." He is the bearded one who cries, "I don't want to die!" after the scout arrives, then, after Ash's pep talk, says, "You can count on my steel!" Then again, the last two characters may have been

different, which means he *did* get five roles.

The shot of Ash firing his rifle over and over at the she-demon in S-Mart while riding the display cart is right out of the opening credits of the TV show *The Rifleman*.

The Arrival (1996)

There is a voice-over of a radio announcer at the start of the film, talking about some weather conditions. The voice is that of director Dave Twohy.

Charlie Sheen has the line, "There's something to be said for abstinence." The joke here is that Sheen was one of Hollywood madam Heidi Fleiss's most visible customers.

Arsenic and Old Lace (1944)

In the scene where Mortimer Brewster (Cary Grant) is sitting on a tombstone in the graveyard outside his aunts' house, he does a double take at one of the headstones behind him, which reads "Archie Leach." Grant's real name was Archibald Leach. Furthermore, in Grant's earlier film, *His Girl Friday* (1940), Walter Burns (Grant) has the line, "The last person to say that to me was Archie Leach, just before he cut his throat!"

On Broadway, Boris Karloff played Jonathan Brewster, but he was replaced in the film version by Raymond Massey. This took a little bit of fun away from the line in the original theatrical script where Jonathan Brewster says he once killed a man "because he said I looked like Boris Karloff."

Arthur 2: On the Rocks (1988)

Cindy, Liza Minnelli's hash-slinging colleague, is played by Brogan Lane, Dudley Moore's wife.

The Asphalt Jungle **(1950)**
The colt owned by Dix (Sterling Hayden) is named Corncracker, which was also the name of another horse in one of director John Huston's films, *Three Strangers* (1946).

Assault on Precinct 13 **(1976)**
The film's editor is credited as "James T. Chance," which was the name of John Wayne's character in *Rio Bravo* (1959), the film on which this film is based. Director John Carpenter was the actual editor.

At Long Last Love **(1975)**
It was Burt Reynolds's idea to stick pieces of toilet paper over his shaving nicks in the scene where he sings the title tune. This was Reynolds's way of referring to the time he nervously cut up his face before his first screen test.

Attack of the 50 Ft. Woman **(1993 TV)**
The film showing at the drive-in when Nancy (Daryl Hannah) goes on her rampage is *Attack of the 50 Foot Woman* (1958).

Avenging Angel **(1985)**
Co-scripter Joseph Michael Cala plays a sanitarium guard in the film.
Director Robert Vincent O'Neil cast his daughter, Jessica, as Little Buck.

Baby Boom **(1987)**
The little girl in Vermont is played by Annie Meyers-Shyer, daughter of director Charles Shyer and screenwriter Nancy Meyers. The film is even dedicated to her.

Bachelor Party **(1984)**
After Cole (Robert Prescott) is stripped and dropped out a window, his naked butt is first seen, then kissed, by a man and a woman, who scream

afterwards. The man is played by co-scripter Pat Proft.

Back to School **(1986)**
Rodney Dangerfield dedicated the film to Estelle Ender, his manager and one of the film's executive producers, who died of cancer.

Back to the Beach **(1987)**
Annette Funicello gleefully feeds her son Skippy Peanut Butter, which she sold in commercials for years.

Back to the Future **(1985)**
The main street set is the same one that was used in *Gremlins* (1984).
The device in Doc Brown's (Christopher Lloyd) lab that Marty McFly plugs his guitar into is labelled "CRM-114," which was the name of the message decoder on the bomber in *Dr. Strangelove, or How I Learned to Stop Worrying and Love the Bomb* (1963). This number has been used in other Kubrick films as well (see *2001: A Space Odyssey*, 1968, and *A Clockwork Orange*, 1971).
Doc Brown, who invents a time-traveling car, has a dog named Einstein. In the film *Chitty Chitty Bang Bang* (1968), the inventor of a miracle car had a dog named Edison.
When McFly (Michael J. Fox) crashes into Farmer Peabody's barn, the farmer calls his son "Sherman." Sherman was the name of the boy time traveler on *Rocky and Bullwinkle*. The dog who ran the machine was named Mr. Peabody.
Huey Lewis, who performs the film's theme song, appears as the high school band judge with the megaphone. He rejects McFly's band because they're "just too darn loud." The joke is that it was Lewis's song they were performing.

Executive producer Steven Spielberg appears as the pickup driver who gives McFly a lift to school.

Back to the Future Part II (1989)

On the wall of television screens in the Cafe 80's restaurant can be seen episodes of *Family Ties* (starring Michael J. Fox), *Taxi* (starring Christopher Lloyd) (bottom row, second from right) and the episode of *Cheers* in which Lloyd guest starred as Shelley Long's mentor (top right corner).

In 2015, there is a marquee advertising the eighteenth sequel to executive producer Steven Spielberg's film *Jaws* (1975), with the tag line "This Time It's Really Really Personal." It is directed by Spielberg's real-life son, Max. The tag line "This time it's personal" was used for the film *Jaws: The Revenge* (1987).

Charles Fleischer, the voice of Zemeckis's Roger Rabbit, has a dual cameo. He shows up as Terry, campaigning for $100 per person to fix the clock tower in 2015, and as Terry, the mechanic who charges young Biff $302 to fix his manure-covered car in 1955.

In the window of the Blast from the Past 1980s memorabilia store (run by Judy Ovitz, wife of Creative Artists' Agency head Michael Ovitz) can be seen a stuffed likeness of director Robert Zemeckis's Roger Rabbit and two Nintendo video game cartridges based on Spielberg's *Jaws* and its sequel.

The two police officers seen after the Blast from the Past store are named Reese and Foley. Stephanie Williams plays Foley (see *1941*, 1979).

Michael J. Fox quotes a famous line from *Midnight Cowboy* (1969) as he is crossing the street: "I'm *walking* here, I'm *walking* here!"

Back to the Future Part III (1990)

The editor of Hill Valley's newspaper in 1885 is named "M.R. Gale," after *Back to the Future* trilogy screenwriter Bob Gale.

Director of photography Dean Cundey plays the photographer who takes Marty and Doc's picture in 1885.

Bad Influence (1990)

Rob Lowe plays a character who secretly videotapes a couple having sex. In real life, just before production started, the news broke that Lowe had allegedly directed his own amateur sex video. However, the film's screenwriter, David Koepp, has said that the two incidents were unrelated. "It's a really weird, wild coincidence," says Koepp. "No one believes I wrote it two years ago."

Bad Manners (1984)

Director/co-scripter Bobby Houston appears in the film as a character named "Retard."

Badlands (1973)

Martin Sheen and Sissy Spacek hold the owner of a mansion hostage. The owner's visitor is played by director Terrence Malick.

Bandits (1986)

Marie-Sophie Pochat is billed as "Marie-Sophie L." in the credits. The odd billing is due to the fact that she and director Claude Lelouch ("L." = Lelouch) were secretly involved during the picture. They were married immediately after the picture was completed.

Barbarosa (1982)

Allison and Reid Wittliff, the children of screenwriter William Wittliff, appear in the film as Emily and a cook boy.

Barfly (1987)

Writer Charles Bukowski, who was the basis for Mickey Rourke's character, appears in the bar where Rourke and Faye Dunaway meet for the first time.

Barton Fink (1991)

John Turturro plays the title role. In *Miller's Crossing* (1990) (also directed by Joel Coen), Turturro played a character who met a man at an apartment building called "The Barton Arms."

William Preston Robertson has a voice cameo (see *Blood Simple*, 1984).

Batman (1989)

The charcoal drawing of the "Bat-Man" that the newspaper reporter holds up was drawn by Batman creator Bob Kane.

The Joker's real name is revealed to be Jack Napier. His surname is in honor of Alan Napier, who played Alfred on the *Batman* television series and who died around the time the movie was being made.

Batman Forever (1995)

During the original 1960s series, *Batman*, the actors were instructed to treat the Batmobile with reverence, and not to refer to it as a "babe-magnet" or words to that effect. In this film, however, Chase Meridian (Nicole Kidman) shows interest in Batman (Val Kilmer), and he says, "It's the car, right? Women love the car."

Also in the original series, Robin had a penchant for exclaiming "Holy …" followed by any number of ridiculous combinations. In this film, upon reaching Claw Island, Robin (Chris O'Donnell) says, "Holy rusted metal, Batman!" Batman replies, "Huh?" Robin legitimizes the line by saying, "The ground, it's made of metal. And it's full of holes. You know, holey." Batman responds, "Oh."

There are references to a couple of other comic book characters as well:

When Dick Grayson (O'Donnell) tells Bruce Wayne (Kilmer) that he doesn't need his charity and he's going to go after Two-Face on his own, Wayne says, "The circus must be halfway to Metropolis by now." Metropolis was Superman's city.

Grayson suggests names for his superhero persona: "Batboy, Nightwing…" In the comic books, Dick Grayson quit being Robin and took on the identity of a character named Nightwing.

Batman Returns (1992)

Christopher Walken plays a villain named Max Schreck. Schreck was the name of the actor who played the vampire in *Nosferatu* (1922).

The sequence where the Penguin (Danny DeVito) remotely takes control of the Batmobile while Batman is driving it was inspired by a segment of a show in the original series, *Batman*, "Penguin Goes Straight." In that episode, Batman (Adam West) remotely wrests control of the Batmobile away from the Penguin (Burgess Meredith) after the Penguin hijacks the vehicle.

Battle Beyond the Stars (1980)

The film is based on *The Magnificent Seven* (1960), and Robert Vaughn, who appeared in the previous film, here plays an identical character.

Battle Cry (1955)

Actor Justus E. McQueen plays a soldier named L.Q. Jones. After this film, McQueen used the name L.Q. Jones as his stage name.

Beastmaster 2: Through the Portal of Time (1991)

Marc Singer and Kari Wuhrer drive past a movie theater which has

Beastmaster 2: Through the Portal of Time on its marquee. Singer gives it a funny look, looks to see if Wuhrer noticed, and they continue on.

Beau Hunks (1931)

Oliver Hardy joins the Foreign Legion after being jilted by his girl-friend, "Jeanie-weenie." The picture of his girlfriend is actually of actress Jean Harlow.

Composer Michael Hatley has a cameo as one of the Riffians who attack the fort at the end of the film.

Beethoven (1992)

The credits list the pseudonym "Edmond Dantes" as the film's screen-writer. This is a pseudonym used by the rather large group of comedy writers who contributed to the film's script. Edmond Dantes is the lead character in Alexandre Dumas's 1844 novel, *The Count of Monte Cristo*.

The Best Place to Be (1979 TV)

Chris Mancini appears in the film, singing his song, "Chain of Love." His father, well-known composer Henry Mancini, composed the rest of the film's music.

Being There (1979)

Every contract that Peter Sellers signed included a clause which stipu-lated that his accommodations must have the bed facing west. In the film, Chance (Sellers) says of the bed he has slept in all his life, "I like to sleep with my bed facing north." The attorney he is with says, "But this bed is facing west!"

Best Defense (1984)

After Wylie (Dudley Moore) "dis-covers" his new design, he brings his boss out to meet his wife, Laura (Kate Capshaw). She is sitting in her car, humming the theme from the *Indiana Jones* movies. Capshaw had just recently appeared in the film *Indiana Jones and the Temple of Doom* (1984).

The Beverly Hillbillies (1993)

Buddy Ebsen, who played the origi-nal Jed Clampett on the television series, shows up as the character he played on another television series, *Barnaby Jones*.

Beverly Hills Cop II (1987)

Star Eddie Murphy's uncle, Ray Murphy, Sr., plays Uncle Ray in the film.

Beverly Hills Cop III (1994)

Director John Landis has a habit of casting his fellow directors in cameos in his films. Directors in this film include:

Martha Coolidge (*Angie*, 1994; *Rambling Rose*, 1991) as the woman at the reception desk for the Security Agencies gala.

Joe Dante (*The Howling*, 1981; *Gremlins*, 1984) as the jail guard who lets Axel (Eddie Murphy) out of jail and delivers him to the FBI agent.

Arthur Hiller (*Teachers*, 1984; *Out-rageous Fortune*, 1987), then also the president of the Academy, as a patron at the bar who hears that Uncle Dave has been shot. He is the third patron seen after the amateur video shows Murphy.

George Lucas (*Star Wars*, 1977; *American Graffiti*, 1973) as a disap-pointed man with his wife who Mur-phy cuts in front of to get on the Spi-der ride at Wonder World.

Peter Medak (*Zorro, the Gay Blade*, 1981; *The Krays*, 1990) as a man on the street who tells his companion that "some black guy" just shot Uncle Dave.

George Schaefer (*MacBeth*, 1961; *Doctors' Wives*, 1971) as Mike, the man who hands Ellis DeWald (Timothy Carhart) his award at the banquet.

Barbet Schroeder (*Barfly*, 1987; *Reversal of Fortune*, 1990) as the man who asks Murphy to "please take special care" of his Porsche.

John Singleton (*Boyz N the Hood*, 1991; *Poetic Justice*, 1993) as the fireman at the end who tells Flint (Hector Elizondo) that Axel Foley shot Uncle Dave.

In addition, famed special effects pioneer Ray Harryhausen (*Jason and the Argonauts*, 1963; *Clash of the Titans*, 1981) appears as a patron at the bar who hears that Uncle Dave's been shot. He is the first patron seen after the amateur video shows Murphy.

Forrest J Ackerman also appears as a patron at the bar who hears that Uncle Dave has been shot. He is the second patron seen after the amateur video shows Murphy. Ackerman was the creator of the first successful sci-fi/horror magazine, *Famous Monsters of Filmland*.

Beware! The Blob (1972)

The Blob devours a bum who is on his way to relieve himself. This derelict is played by the film's director, Larry Hagman.

Beyond the Law (1968)

Norman Mailer, who wrote, produced, edited and directed the film, also appears as Lt. Francis Xavier Pope.

Big Business (1988)

Among the credits is the listing "Money Watchers ... Nowell Grossman, Patrick Spezialy." Director Jim Abrahams wanted a more glamourous credit for Grossman and Spezialy than "assistant accountants."

The Big Chill (1983)

Flashback scenes with Kevin Costner as Alex were filmed, but cut. That is still Costner, however, as the corpse at the beginning of the film.

When he fights off the bat, Harold (Kevin Kline) hums the theme from *Raiders of the Lost Ark* (1981), also written by Lawrence Kasdan.

Lawrence Kasdan cast some family members in the film: his son Jon plays Harold and Sarah's (Kevin Kline and Glenn Close) son, his son Jacob plays an autograph seeker, and his wife Meg is the airline hostess. Meg also composed the film's score.

The Big Easy (1987)

JFK conspiracy lawyer Jim Garrison (who was later played by Kevin Costner in *JFK*, 1991) appears as Judge Garrison.

The Big Picture (1989)

Some famous actors appear in uncredited cameos. One is Elliott Gould, who plays the lawyer in the student film. His son, Jason Gould, appears as one of the student filmmakers.

The Big Red One (1980)

All of the Nazi concentration camp guards are played by Jewish actors.

Big Trouble in Little China (1986)

Some of the lightning forms a Chinese symbol as it disappears. The symbol translates as "carpenter." This film was directed by John Carpenter.

Bikini Beach (1964)

The werewolf is played by a nonprofessional actor named Val Warren. Warren got the part by winning a make-up contest in *Famous Monsters of Filmland* magazine.

Bikini Drive-In (1995)

Director-producer Fred Olen Ray has a cameo as Randy Rocket.

Bill & Ted's Bogus Journey (1991)

Joss Ackland plays the villain De Nomolos, which is writer-producer Ed Solomon's name spelled backwards.

There are statues of David Niven and Michael Powell in heaven. Powell directed and Niven starred in the film *Stairway to Heaven* (1946), about a World War II pilot who accidentally dies and has to plead his case in heaven. In addition to the relevance of the title of the film, which was also the title of the Led Zeppelin song, often called the best rock song of all time, director Peter Hewitt has said that a lot of his favorite films involve Heaven and Hell and ghosts and angels. He has cited Frank Capra's *It's a Wonderful Life* (1946) and the film *Stairway to Heaven* as examples. In fact, set designer David Snyder said of his design of heaven, "I went back and researched films like *Here Comes Mr. Jordan* and *Heaven Can Wait,* and came up with the mystical white and lavender colour scheme."

Co-scripter Chris Matheson has a cameo at Ted's stepmother's seance. He is the one in the white button-up shirt who wants to contact Clark Gable.

Bill & Ted's Excellent Adventure (1989)

The three most important people in the future are played by three rock stars. They are Fee Waybill of The Tubes, Martha Davis of The Motels and Clarence Clemons, the saxophonist in Bruce Springsteen's E Street Band.

Birdman of Alcatraz (1962)

When Karl Malden takes over as warden of Alcatraz and takes a preliminary tour, one of the prisoners is heard to be called "Sekulovich." Malden's real name was Mladen Sekulovich, and he enjoyed sneaking his given name into many of his film and television appearances.

The Birds (1963)

Director Alfred Hitchcock leaves Davidson's Pet Shop with two white terriers as Tippi Hedren enters. The terriers, named Stanley and Geoffrey, actually belonged to Hitchcock.

The Birds II: Land's End (1994)

Tippi Hedren, the star of the original film, has a cameo as a shop-keeper.

B.L. Stryker: Auntie Sue (1989 TV)

Mitch Slade (Ted McGinley), the Ferrari-driving private detective, is an in-joke reference to Tom Selleck's *Magnum, P.I.* character. Selleck was one of this television movie's executive producers.

The Black Cat (1934)

Boris Karloff, as a devil-worshipper, recites an invocation to Satan. To please the Hays Code, the censor of the time, Latin phrases were substituted, such as "cave canem" (beware of the dog), "cum grano salis" (with a grain of salt), "in vino veritas" (in wine is truth) and "reductio ad absurdum est" (it is shown to be impossible).

Karloff's character is named after Austrian architect and set designer Hjalmar Poelzig.

The Black Hole (1979)

Dr. Reinhardt's ship is named the USS *Cygnus.* The first black hole seen from Earth was discovered in the constellation Cygnus.

Black Sunday (1977)

Director John Frankenheimer appears as the television director in the Coliseum control room.

Blackmail (1929)

Director Alfred Hitchcock can be seen being bothered by a small boy as he reads a book in the subway.

A Blade in the Dark (1983)

Director Lamberto Bava used the pseudonym "John Old, Jr." for this film, which he felt was a faceless picture that didn't really reflect his personality. This pseudonym is a homage to his father, director Mario Bava, who used the name "John Old" for some of his pictures.

Blade Runner (1982)

When Gaff (Edward James Olmos) picks up Deckard (Harrison Ford), the launch sequence on the computer is the same one used in director Ridley Scott's outer space opus, *Alien* (1979), when the escape pod separates from the mother ship. The black and white display of the VK machine was also used as a wall display in *Alien,* and the screen reading "PURGE" was also seen in the former film, when Ripley (Sigourney Weaver) sets up the pod to blast off.

Blastfighter (1984)

Director Lamberto Bava used the pseudonym "John Old, Jr." for this film (see *A Blade in the Dark*, 1983).

Blaze (1989)

The real-life Blaze Starr (played in the film by Lolita Davidovich) appears as Lily, the stripper whose shoulder Earl Long (Paul Newman) kisses backstage.

Blazing Saddles (1973)

Mel Brooks plays a governor named "Le Petomane," which was the stage name of a popular French performer (Joseph Pujol) from the beginning of the 20th century. His specialty was telling stories punctuated with flatulence.

In the shot where the showbill for "Lili von Schtupp, the Teutonic Titwillow" appears, the tune played on the honky-tonk piano in the background is "Springtime for Hitler" from Brooks's *The Producers* (1968).

"Schtup" is a Yiddish verb for "to have sex with."

Lili tells Bart (Cleavon Little) to come into her dressing room using Joel Grey's line from the film *Cabaret* (1972): "Wilkommen, bienvenue, welcome…," adding "C'mon in."

The "stinkin' badges" line is from *The Treasure of the Sierra Madre* (1948).

Everyone in the town has the surname Johnson, including Howard Johnson (John Hillerman), who owns an ice cream shop; Van Johnson (George Furth), named after the actor; Dr. Samuel Johnson (Richard Collier), named after the British author; and Olsen Johnson (David Huddleston), who is named after 1930s comedy team Ole Olsen and Chic Johnson.

On the headband of Mel Brooks's Indian chief is written "Kosher Le-Pesach" in Hebrew. This is an edible for Passover. The language the Indians speak is Yiddish.

When Mongo (Alex Karras) appears in Rock Ridge, someone exclaims, "Mongo! Santa Maria!" Conga, bongo and percussion player Mongo Santamaria is one of director Mel Brooks's favorite jazz musicians. Jazz fan Brooks even cast Count Basie and His Orchestra in the picture.

Blood Alley (1955)

This was the first film produced by John Wayne's Batjac Production Company. "Batjak" is from "Batjac," which was the name of the trading empire in Wayne's film *Wake of the Red Witch* (1948).

Blood Bath (1966)

British character actor Patrick Magee appears uncredited, covered in wax. This film also includes scenes from Magee's little-known former film, *Portrait in Terror* (1965).

Blood Salvage (1990)

Executive producers Ken Sanders and Evander Holyfield both have cameos. Sanders plays a spectator at the boxing ring and Holyfield plays the boxer. Holyfield even cast his trainer, Lou Duva, as his trainer in the film.

Blood Simple (1984)

The voice of the radio evangelist that Ray is listening to as he's driving down the road with Marty's not-quite-dead-yet body in the back seat is credited to an actor named William Preston Robertson. In just about every Coen brothers film, Robertson gets a special credit of some sort, mostly as a minor voice role. He is usually credited as "and featuring the golden throat of William Preston Robertson" or something similar.

Blue Thunder (1983)

Executive producer Phil Feldman has a cameo in the film as Colonel Coe.

Blue Tiger (1994)

The gun salesman is played, uncredited, by Michael Madsen, the brother of this film's star, Virginia Madsen.

The Blues Brothers (1980)

Many real-life blues artists have roles—Aretha Franklin plays Matt "Guitar" Murphy's wife, Cab Calloway plays Jake and Elwood's pal Curtis, Ray Charles appears as the owner of Ray's Music Exchange, James Brown plays the preacher, and John Lee Hooker and an all-star band of blues musicians play "Boogie Chillun" outside of Murphy's restaurant. Before she became popular as a solo artist, Chaka Khan (who was the lead singer for the funk-jazz group Rufus) appeared as the soloist in Brown's church choir.

As Jake (John Belushi) waits to get his belongings from the prison goods official, we see the word "Jake" tattooed on his left hand. Elwood (Dan Aykroyd) pulls up in his car, and a close-up of his hands shows the word "Elwood" tattooed on his fingers. This is a homage to the similar tattoos of "Love" and "Hate" that Robert Mitchum had on his knuckles in the film *The Night of the Hunter* (1955).

Just before Jake and Elwood crash into the shopping mall, a man in the toy store is seen with a Grover doll, asking for "a Miss Piggy." Both Muppets' voices were provided by Frank Oz, who plays Joliet's personal goods official in this film. And the man who asks for the Miss Piggy is Gary McLarty, the film's stunt coordinator.

Stephen Bishop plays the "Charming Trooper" in the car chase in the mall (see *Kentucky Fried Movie*, 1977).

The Charming Trooper's partner, who ends up sliding through the mall upside down in their car, is played by director John Landis.

The Illinois Nazis have a basis in fact. Around the time that the film was made, a Nazi group did win a court case and held a march in Skokie,

Illinois, a suburb of Chicago with a large Jewish population.

When Carrie Fisher fires her bazooka at Jake and Elwood outside of Elwood's apartment, mixed in with the bazooka sound effects are blaster fire sounds from Fisher's *Star Wars* (1977).

The desk clerk at Elwood's place is named Lloyd ("Hey, Lloyd. Anybody call for me on the phone?") and the gas station that Jake and Elwood fill up at is named "Lloyd's." Lloyd is the name of one of Aykroyd's sons. He sneaked his sons' names into many of his films.

Shotgun Britton, who plays the man who asks Elwood for the Cheez-Wiz, is also the film's makeup artist.

After Elwood's place is blown up, Jake and Elwood visit Mrs. Tarantino's house, looking for the band. Jake calls her "Mrs. Toronto?" Dan Aykroyd's hometown is Toronto.

After Murph and the Magictones finish their set, they sit down for drinks with Jake and Elwood. One of the two waitresses who brings them their drinks is John Belushi's wife, Judy Jacklin.

At Chez Paul, where Jake offers to buy "ze children," the second daughter in the family is Carrie Fisher's younger sister, Cindy Fisher.

An advertisement for the film *See You Next Wednesday* is on the billboard that the troopers hide behind (see *Schlock*, 1971).

The record company representative who offers Jake and Elroy a contract is from Clarion Records. In reality, Clarion was a budget label of Atlantic Records, who released the film's soundtrack album. The man who plays the representative is Michael Klenfner, an old friend of John Belushi's.

After Carrie Fisher fires her machine gun at Jake and Elwood in

the sewer, Elwood looks up and says, "Who *is* that girl?" This line was inspired by the line, "Who *are* those guys?" in the earlier buddy movie, *Butch Cassidy and the Sundance Kid* (1969).

As the Illinois Nazis' car flies through the air, Wagner's "The Ride of the Valkyries" is heard. The shot of the two Nazis is a parody of a famous British Air commercial which used the same music.

The song playing in the elevator at the end of the film is "The Girl from Ipanema." Landis enjoyed inserting this song into his films.

Steven Spielberg plays the Cook County small claims clerk. Later, he would cast Dan Aykroyd in *Indiana Jones and the Temple of Doom* (1984) in appreciation.

Rock musician Joe Walsh plays one of the prisoners dancing to "Jailhouse Rock" in the closing number. He helped John on the studio record for "Gimme Some Lovin'."

After the credits, there is an ad for Universal Studios with the line "Ask for Babs" (see *National Lampoon's Animal House*, 1978).

Blume in Love (1973)
George Segal's law partner, Hellman, is played by director Paul Mazursky.

Bob & Carol & Ted & Alice (1969)
First-time director (and former bit actor) Paul Mazursky has a cameo as a guest at the children's party.

Body Bags (1993 TV)
Director/co-composer/executive producer John Carpenter plays the film's host, the ghoulish coroner.

Carpenter, like many directors, has actors who he likes to cast in small roles in his films. Carpenter regulars George "Buck" Flower and Peter Jason appear in the first segment. Flower plays the bum who passes out in the restroom and Jason plays the party animal who pulls up for gas with his girlfriend.

The disheveled guy who buys a pack of Coronados in the first segment is played by horror film director Wes Craven.

Bill, the dead attendant, is played by horror film director Sam Raimi.

In the third segment, "Eye," Dr. Bregman, the doctor who tells Brent (Mark Hamill) that he has lost his eye, is played by low-budget filmmaker Roger Corman.

At the film's end, the two "real" coroners show up. One is played by Tom Arnold (*Roseanne*), and the other one, the bearded one who goes for coffee, is played by "Eye" director Tobe Hooper.

The Bodyguard (1992)

The screenplay was originally written in the '70s as a vehicle for Steve McQueen and Ali MacGraw, so star Kevin Costner got his hair cut in the style of McQueen as a tribute.

Rachel (Whitney Houston) and Frank (Costner) go to see the Japanese film *Yojimbo* (1961), which was released in the United States under the title *The Bodyguard*.

Body Heat (1981)

Director Lawrence Kasdan cast his wife Meg in the film as a nurse.

Boomerang (1992)

Producer-director team Warrington and Reginald Hudlin appear in the film as a couple of street hustlers.

Bordello of Blood (1996)

The film is very self-deprecating, and comes off as a "Dennis Miller vs. *Tales from the Crypt* episode," with Miller in his stand-up persona walking around a standard *Crypt* episode, commenting on the strange goings-on. This is most evident when Miller is walking through the power station and says, "I feel like I've walked into a bad episode of *Tales from the Crypt*."

Just before Corey Feldman gets killed, he threatens Miller by saying, "You are outta here!" When Miller was a regular on *Saturday Night Live*, he would end his Weekend Update newscast with the phrase "I am outta here."

The city founder who dies is named Gaines. His name can be seen on the outside of the mausoleum. He's named after William M. Gaines, the creator of EC Comics, the horror/sci-fi company of the 1950s, whose titles included the original *Tales from the Crypt*.

A mummy plays a card game with the Crypt Keeper. The mummy is played by Bill Sadler, who appeared in an episode of *Tales from the Crypt* called "Cutting Cards" in which he played a similar game with Lance Henriksen. Sadler also starred in the previous *Tales from the Crypt* movie, *Demon Knight* (1995).

The key that controls the vampires is the same one as in the previous film, *Demon Knight*.

Boris and Natasha (1992)

To perfect her Pottsylvanian accent, Sally Kellerman (Natasha) spent some time with the Polish house couple of John Travolta. Travolta was also given a cameo in the film as the "movie star blind date."

The Born Losers (1967)

The director, T.C. Frank, and the producer, Donald Henderson, are both actually writer-star Tom Laughlin.

Born on the Fourth of July (1989)

Director Oliver Stone has a cameo as a television correspondent.

Tom Cruise plays war vet Ron Kovic, and the real Kovic has a cameo as a wheelchair-bound war protester at a rally.

Boxcar Bertha (1972)

Director Martin Scorsese appears in the film as a bordello client.

Scorsese also named two minor characters Michael Powell and Emeric Pressberger (played by Chicken Holleman and Grahame Pitt), after the famous directors.

Boy Meets Girl (1938)

In this film, the fictitious Errol Flynn film *The White Rajah* is being premiered at the Cathay Circle Theatre in Los Angeles. The title was borrowed from an actual screenplay that Flynn once sold to Warner Bros. It was never filmed.

The Brady Bunch Movie (1995)

The original Carol Brady, Florence Henderson, plays Carol's mother, "Grandma."

In the final panel sequence, Henderson gives Carol (Shelley Long) a bottle of Wesson Cooking Oil, which Henderson endorsed on television for many years.

The original Greg Brady, Barry Williams, plays the music producer who rejects Greg's song.

The original Peter Brady, Christopher Knight, plays the coach who saves Peter from being beaten up at lunchtime.

The original Alice, Ann B. Davis, plays Schultzy, the trucker who Jan hitches a ride with. Davis also played Bob Collins's (Bob Cummings) girl Friday on the old television show *Love That Bob*. Her name on the show was Charmaine "Schultzy" Schultz.

There are some references to the original series (the voices in Jan's head, Marcia's broken nose, and so on). Some of the more obscure:

When Mike leaves for work, he kisses Carol goodbye, and she says, "Go get 'em, tiger!" As Mike walks off, she pauses a beat then says, "Tiger? Whatever happened to that dog?" Tiger was the name of the dog in the original series. During filming of an episode centred around him, Tiger accidentally got run over by a truck and killed. His trainer had to scramble to find a look-alike. He succeeded, but Tiger II couldn't act and was phased out of the show without explanation. Tiger later made an appearance in *A Very Brady Sequel* (1996).

As Greg practices his guitar in front of the mirror, Marcia comes in and says, "Greg, have you gone bananas?" The name of the musical group that the Brady kids formed on the television show was called The Banana Convention.

Holly, Peter's red-haired classmate, calls him a babe … "in a Gilligan sort of way." *The Brady Bunch*'s producer, Sherwood Schwartz, also produced *Gilligan's Island*. Peter later calls Holly "Ginger and Mary Anne combined."

After the Bradys finally decide to enter the talent contest, there is a shot of West Dale High … and the multi-coloured Partridge Family bus drives by. *The Partridge Family* was another perfect-family show in the '70s with a group of kids who sang.

Jan goes to see the school counsellor, Mrs. Cummings (famous transvestite RuPaul). As Jan leaves her office, Mrs. Cummings says, "Girl, you better work." This is a line from a song of RuPaul's, "Supermodel (You Better Work)." A clip of the song is heard just as she says the line.

The Brady Girls Get Married (1981 TV)

Mike makes a crack about *Gilligan's Island*, which was also produced by Sherwood Schwartz.

Brain Damage (1988)

Kevin van Hentenryck is seen sitting on the subway with a wicker basket on his lap. In director Frank Henenlotter's *Basket Case* films, van Hentenryck played a man who carried his deformed twin brother around in a wicker basket.

Brain Dead (1990)

Bill Pullman mentions that he went to Miskatonic University, the college where *Re-Animator* (1985) took place.

Bram Stoker's Dracula (1992)

Count Dracula (Gary Oldman) serves Jonathan Harker (Keanu Reeves) a meal, but does not join him, saying, "I never drink ... wine." This line was originated by Bela Lugosi in the original *Dracula* (1931).

Brazil (1985)

Director Terry Gilliam's first job out of college was given to him by Harvey Kurtzman, at his magazine *Help!* It was at a photo shoot for this magazine that Gilliam met John Cleese, who would later invite him to join the Monty Python comedy troupe. In this film, Gilliam named Sam

Lowry's supervisor (Ian Holm) "Mr. Kurtzman," after Harvey.

The opening theme song, which Sam also listens to in his car, was originally featured in the film "Brazil" (1944). The song is also hummed by Tuttle as he puts the panel back inside Lowry's apartment, and by Lowry as he folds up Mrs. Buttle's check and puts it in the pneumatic delivery tube. A few notes of the song are played by the keypad as Sam punches in "EREIAMJH" into Mr. Helpmann's lift.

Jack Lint's (Michael Palin) daughter, Holly, is played by director Terry Gilliam's daughter, Holly Gilliam.

Gilliam himself appears as the smoker in the shadows of the Shangri-La apartment complex, where Archibald Buttle is mistakenly apprehended. Sam Lowry (Jonathan Pryce) sees him when he comes to bring Mr. Buttle her husband's check. Lowry later slams into him in the hallway.

Dr. Chapman, the cosmetic surgeon or "acid man" who is responsible for Mrs. Terrain's deteriorating condition, is named after Gilliam's former cohort in Monty Python, Graham Chapman. Chapman actually studied to be a doctor.

Charles McKeown, who co-wrote the script, has a small part as Harvey Lime, the man in the office beside Lowry.

The sequence in which Tuttle (Robert De Niro) and Lowry escape from Information Retrieval includes a scene with soldiers marching in step and slowly lowering their rifles. This shot is a homage to a famous sequence on the steps of Odessa in Sergei Eisenstein's *Battleship Potemkin* (1925). In the original film, a distraught mother watches as her baby carriage bounces down the staircase. In this film, an operator grieves as her floor polisher bounces down the stairs.

The Breakfast Club (1985)

The guidance counsellor's desk has a name plaque on it which reads "R. Hashimoto." Richard Hashimoto was the production supervisor.

A prom queen election poster contains the name of Michelle Manning, who co-produced the film.

The parent who picks Anthony Michael Hall up at the end of the film is played by director John Hughes.

Breaking Away (1979)

In the film, Dave Stoller (Dennis Christopher) idolizes the Italian Cinzano national cycling team, so much so that he tries to speak Italian and he has his mother make pasta for him all the time. So it is appropriate that the music which is played when he is drafting the truck on his bike is Mendelssohn's *Italian Symphony* (*Symphony No. 4 in A Major-Minor*).

Breathless (1959)

The man with the dark glasses and pipe who spots Jean-Paul Belmondo in his car on the street and informs the police is played by director Jean-Luc Godard.

Breathless (1983)

Longtime art director (*Limelight*, 1952; *Bronco Billy*, 1980) and occasional director (*The Beast from 20,000 Fathoms*, 1953) Eugene Lourie has a bit part in the film, playing Dr. Boudreaux.

Brewster McCloud (1970)

Daphne Heap (Margaret Hamilton) is shown wearing ruby slippers, a reference to Hamilton's role in *The Wizard of Oz* (1939).

Suzanne's (Shelley Duvall) apartment features a poster for *MASH* (1970), which was also directed by Robert Altman.

Bride of Frankenstein (1935)

After Ernest Thesiger says, "Do you like gin?" he then says, "It's my only weakness." Thesiger said this line in his previous role for director James Whale in *The Old Dark House* (1932).

Bringing Up Baby (1938)

To get out of jail, Susan (Katharine Hepburn) pretends that she and David (Cary Grant) are gangsters. She calls him "Jerry the Nipper" and he protests, saying "Constable, she's making all this up from motion pictures she's seen!" Jerry the Nipper was the name of Grant's character in *The Awful Truth* (1937). Susan then calls the woman he was with a redheaded floozy. That woman was Grant's costar in *The Awful Truth*, redheaded actress Irene Dunne.

Broadcast News (1987)

Albert Brooks's meaty (and Oscar-nominated) role of Aaron Altman was written expressly for him by director James L. Brooks (no relation) as a way of saying thanks for his role as David, the director in Albert's *Modern Romance* (1981).

Jack Nicholson agreed to do the role in this film as a favor to director James L. Brooks, who directed his Oscar-winning performance in *Terms of Endearment* (1983). Nicholson only took credit in the closing titles so as not to take away from the real leads of the picture.

Film scorers Marc Shaiman and Glen Roven appear as the writers of the news theme.

The Brother from Another Planet (1984)

Director John Sayles plays the tall one of the two aliens in pursuit of the Brother.

Bull Durham (1988)

Another unintentional in-joke (see *Platoon*, 1986): When he is telling Susan Sarandon what he believes in, Crash Davis (Kevin Coster) says, "I believe Lee Harvey Oswald acted alone." Three years later, Costner went on to play Jim Garrison in *JFK* (1991), proving himself wrong.

Bullets Over Broadway (1994)

Cheech's dying words are a suggestion that, at the end of the play, a character should announce she is pregnant. He says, "the audience will love it..." This is how director Woody Allen ended his very popular film, *Hannah and Her Sisters* (1986).

The 'Burbs (1989)

Among Walter's (Gale Gordon) photo collection in his house is a picture of Gordon's old secretary on *The Lucy Show*, Lucille Ball.

Burglar (1987)

Director Hugh Wilson appears, as does former Monkee Mike Nesmith.

Butterfly (1981)

Co-scripter John Goff has a cameo as a truck driver.

The Cable Guy (1996)

The helicopter pilot who flies Jim Carrey to the looney bin at the end of the film is played by Bobby "Z" Zajonic. Zajonic was the actual pilot in the film and also flew choppers in *Twister* (1996), *Mission: Impossible* (1996), and many other films.

Cadillac Man (1990)

Robin Williams quotes James Dean from *Rebel Without a Cause* (1955): "I've got the bullets, god dammit!"

California Split (1974)

The film is dedicated to actress Barbara Ruick, who died during filming. She was the wife of composer John Williams.

Can You Feel Me Dancing? (1986 TV)

This film was based on the lives of Cheryl McMannis and Joe Nasser, both of whom have small roles in the film. Cheryl plays herself and Nasser plays Danny.

Canadian Bacon (1995)

The dedication at the end of the film reads "And to Johnny LaRue. Thanks to you, we got our crane shot." LaRue was a character on *SCTV* played by John Candy, who died soon after this film was made. See *SCTV* for the crane shot explanation.

Candyman (1992)

Archie Walsh is played by the film's director-screenwriter, Bernard Rose.

Cannonball (1976)

Many of director Paul Bartel's friends appear in bit parts, including directors Joe Dante and Jonathan Kaplan as gas station attendants who lend Robert Carradine their car; director Martin Scorsese as "Mafioso"; and low-budget director Roger Corman, who gave Bartel his start in film, as the district attorney who tries to stop the race at the beginning of the film.

The Cannonball Run (1981)

Playboy Seymour Goldfarb, Jr., (Roger Moore) suffers from the understandable delusion that he is movie star Roger Moore. He signs his name "Roger Moore" and reminisces about being in a series of films (James Bond) and "a very popular television series" (*The Saint*).

Goldfarb chastises his mother as being "too Jewish." Mrs. Goldfarb is played by long-time Yiddish actress Molly Picon.

When Dom DeLuise and Burt Reynolds stop for gas, DeLuise also comes out with a Big Gulp Dr. Pepper … and sings the jingle from the commercials that he did for the drink: "I'm a Pepper, you're a Pepper…"

George Furth's character, the determined "Mr. Arthur J.… uh … Foyt," is named after race car legend A.J. Foyt.

Cape Fear (1991)

Gregory Peck, who starred in the original *Cape Fear* (1962), appears as Cady's sleazy Southern lawyer. Peck owns the rights to the original, and he said that director Martin Scorsese asked him, "How about playing a cameo as a homage to the first film? We like it, we'll use some of the plot structure." Peck enjoyed it so much, he asked two others who had appeared in the original film to make cameos as well.

Robert Mitchum, who played Max Cady in the original, appears as Lt. Elgart.

Martin Balsam, who played Mark Dutton in the original, appears as the judge.

Three of Scorsese's relatives have cameos: his mother and father, Catherine and Charles, are customers at the fruit stand, and his daughter Domenica appears as Danny's girlfriend.

Caprice (1967)

Patricia (Doris Day) goes to a theatre and sees a Doris Day movie.

Capricorn One (1978)

Charles Brubaker, Jr., Brubaker's (James Brolin) son, is played by writer-director Peter Hyams's son, Chris.

The Caretaker (1963)

At the start of the film, Polly Bergen walks down the street towards a movie theater. As she walks, she passes associate producer Jerry Paris.

Carnival in Costa Rica (1947)

Leonide Massine, the film's choreographer, is the unnamed "famous dancer" with Vera-Ellen in the first production scene.

Carrie (1976)

Director—and Alfred Hitchcock buff—Brian de Palma, in addition to incorporating the "mother wielding a butcher knife" scene from Hitchcock's *Psycho* (1960), named the high school after the film's lead character—Bates High School.

The bratty kid that Carrie causes to tumble from his bike is played by de Palma's son, Cameron.

Casino (1995)

Director Martin Scorsese gave his mother a cameo as Artie Piscano's (Vinny Vella) mother.

Low-budget drive-in movie critic Joe Bob Briggs appears as the slot machine manager. He is credited as "John Bloom," which is his real name.

Casino Murder Case (1935)

William Powell can be seen talking with Philo Vance (Paul Lukas) at the auction house. Powell originated the role of Philo Vance on film in *Canary Murder Case* (1929).

Casino Royale (1967)

In Peter Sellers's hallucination, he is beset by an army of bagpipers. One stops, approaches him and says, "Excuse me. Are you Richard Burton?" Sellers answers, "No, I'm Peter O'Toole." The piper responds, "Then you're the finest man that's ever breathed. God bless you." The piper is played by an uncredited Peter O'Toole. However, the *real* in-joke is that O'Toole had a similar scene in his previous film, *What's New, Pussycat?* (1965). *What's New, Pussycat?* had the same producer as this film, and both starred Sellers and featured Woody Allen and Ursula Andress. In that film, O'Toole bumped into an uncredited Richard Burton. And the line "You're the finest man that's ever breathed" is from O'Toole's drunken scene in *What's New, Pussycat?*

As Mata Bond (Joanna Pettet) and the cab driver escape from the German spy school, she says, "This way!" and lifts open a trap door in the ground. We hear the song "What's New, Pussycat" being sung from the door. The cabbie says, "No! No! No!" and pulls her away.

The cabbie (Bernard Cribbins), by the way, actually turns out to be Carlton-Towers of the F.O. This is a reference to the earlier Sellers film *Carlton-Browne of the F.O.* (1959).

After Ursula Andress is carried off by Le Chiffre's men, Sellers runs to his driver and says "Moss! You see that car? Follow it!" The driver says "Yes sir!" and runs off. Exasperated, Sellers stares after him and says, "I'll use Fangio next time … idiot." The driver is played, uncredited, by British race car driver Stirling Moss, and Sellers's remark refers to Juan Manuel Fangio, an Argentinean racer who was the Formula-1 world champion five times in the 1950s. The inside joke here is that Fangio was Moss's teammate on the all-conquering Mercedes-Benz team for a while, and where Moss came close on several occasions to winning a championship; he never quite managed to win one, whereas Fangio was very successful.

Two regulars from Sellers's *Pink Panther* movies have cameos in the film. Actually, they had each only appeared in one *Pink Panther* film before this one, that being *A Shot in the Dark* (1964). Graham Stark (Hercule Lajoy and Dr. Balls in the *Pink Panther* films) plays the desk clerk/cashier at Casino Royale who asks for James Bond's (Sellers) autograph for his little sister. And Burt Kwouk (Kato) appears uncredited as the Chinese officer who bids 70 million tons of rice for Le Chiffre's racy photograph.

There are a few references to the "real" Bond films. The evil head of SMERSH is named Dr. Noah, after *Dr. No* (1962), and during the fight scene at the end, a window falls into a room filled with gold-encased models, reminiscent of *Goldfinger* (1964).

In the fight scene at the end, George Raft (credited as playing "Himself") is seen flipping a coin. This is a reference to his often-parodied role in *Scarface* (1932).

Raft walks up to a blond man and says, "This gun shoots backwards. I just killed myself!" The man is played by David McCallum, who starred as Illya Kuryakin in the Bond-like series *The Man from U.N.C.L.E.* The "gun that shoots backwards" gimmick is from a Matt Helm film.

Peter Sellers incorporates his Oriental, Indian and British Army Officer characters (which he also used during his days with the British comedy team The Goons) into his role in the film.

Orson Welles was in real life an avid enthusiast of magic, and at the baccarat table, he was able to lampoon his image.

When the lion jumps onto the roof of the Rolls Royce at Bond's estate, the theme of the film *Born Free* (1966) is heard. Both this theme and the themes of most of the Bond films were composed by John Barry.

In order to escape from Dr. Noah's stronghold, James Bond (Niven) has his agents fill a bag from a gas nozzle. Bond says it is "vaporized lysergic acid. It's highly explosive." Lysergic acid diethylamide is the '60s drug LSD.

As Sellers and Andress are being escorted out of Casino Royale by Inspector Mathis (Duncan MacRae), Sellers remarks, "There's something been worrying me ... you're a French officer and yet you have a Scot's accent." Mathis responds, "Aye ... it worries me too." This is a reference to the long-time practice of British actors playing characters of varying nationalities on film without changing their accent. Shades of Sean Connery's Scottish Russian in *The Hunt for Red October* (1990).

Casper (1995)

Dan Aykroyd appears uncredited as Dr. Ray Stantz from the film *Ghostbusters* (1984). He is called in to exorcise the ghosts.

Cast a Deadly Spell (1991 TV)

The main character and the head cop are named after sci-fi writers: Fred Ward as H. Philip Lovecraft and Charles Hallahan as Lt. (Ray) Bradbury.

Harry Bordon's (Clancy Brown) nightclub is called The Dunwich Room, after the H.P. Lovecraft warlock story *The Dunwich Horror*, made into a film in 1970.

Cat's Eye (1985)

The film was based on a set of Stephen King stories, and the cat in the film is chased by a rabid St. Bernard (a reference to King's *Cujo*) and is nearly run over by a red Plymouth Fury (a reference to King's *Christine*).

Cell 2455, Death Row (1955)

William Campbell stars as killer Caryl Chessman, and Campbell's brother Robert appears in a bit part.

Chances Are (1989)

The man who gives Cybill Shepherd away at the wedding is played by Cybill's real-life father, Bill Shepherd.

Charley Varrick (1973)

Director Don Siegel plays Murph, the tennis player.

The Chase (1994)

After the credits have finished, Charlie Sheen, sitting behind the wheel in a clown suit, recites the "I love the smell of napalm in the morning" speech from his dad Martin's *Apocalypse Now* (1979).

Children of a Lesser God (1986)

William Hurt and Marlee Matlin were real-life lovers while this movie was being filmed, and some of the sign language conversations between the two is not about the plot of the film, but instead is idle chitchat about their offscreen lives.

Chinatown (1974)

The thug who slits Jack Nicholson's nose is played by the film's director, Roman Polanski. Polanski reportedly really slit Nicholson's nose in the scene.

Chopping Mall (1986)

Paul Bartel and Mary Woronov appear before the opening credits as doers-in-of-swingers Paul and Mary Bland of Bartel's *Eating Raoul* (1982).

Dick Miller plays a janitor named Walter Paisley (see *Hollywood Boulevard*, 1976).

The mall's pet store is named "Roger's Little Shop of Pets," after Roger Corman's *Little Shop of Horrors* (1960). The producer of this film was Julie Corman, Roger's daughter.

The gun shop is appropriately named "Peckinpah's," after bloody good director Sam Peckinpah.

A Chorus Line (1985)

Noted choreographer Bob Fosse's daughter, Nicole Fosse, has a small part as Kristine, one of the dancing hopefuls.

A Christmas Carol (1938)

The daughter of stars Gene and Kathleen Lockhart is played by a young actress making her acting debut. It was June Lockhart, the real-life daughter of Gene and Kathleen.

A Chump at Oxford (1940)

Stan Laurel and Oliver Hardy foil a raid on the Finlayson National Bank, named after their favorite supporting player, James Finlayson.

Circuitry Man (1990)

A medic vacuums Jugs's (Garry Goodrow) mind for the police after Plughead scrambles it. He's played by co-producer Steven Reich.

Circus World (1964)

John Wayne wears his *Red River* "D" belt buckle in this film (see *Rio Bravo*, 1959).

Citizen Kane (1941)

The character of Charles Foster Kane was loosely based on William Randolph Hearst, and filmmaker Orson Welles even took the name "Rosebud" from Hearst's personal life. It was the nickname that Hearst gave to his mistress Marion Davies's clitoris.

Class (1983)

Balaban (Stuart Margolin) asks whether Mr. Burrows (Cliff Robertson) is on the board of AT&T, and his son admits that he is. Robertson is well known as AT&T's spokesman.

Cliffhanger (1993)

Finnish director Renny Harlin put his homeland's flag on one of the parachutes.

The film is dedicated to two men: Wolfgang Gulich, Sylvester Stallone's stunt double, who died in a car crash three days after filming was completed, and Fadel Kassar, father of executive producer Mario Kassar, who died of natural causes during production.

A Clockwork Orange (1971)

The soundtrack album for director Stanley Kubrick's *2001: A Space Odyssey* (1968) can be seen in a record store.

The newspaper article gives Alex's last name as "Burgess." The film was based on a book by Anthony Burgess.

Close Encounters of the Third Kind (1977)

The working title was "Watch the Skies," which was the closing line from *The Thing (From Another World)* (1951). These words can be heard in the cartoon that wakes Neary (Richard Dreyfuss).

One of Roy Neary's (Richard Dreyfuss) children is played by Dreyfuss's real-life son, Justin.

Clueless (1995)

Cher's last name is given as "Horowitz," but shown on her report card as "Hamilton." Director Amy

Heckerling's previous film, *Fast Times at Ridgemont High* (1982), featured a character named Stacey Hamilton.

Cocktail (1988)

When Tom Cruise and Lisa Baines pass the Regency Theatre in Manhattan on the way to an art show next door, the marquee on the theater reads *Barfly* (1987), another bar-based film. Oddly enough, after they are thrown out of the exhibit, it reads *Casablanca* (1942).

Cocoon: The Return (1988)

Special effects designer Robert Short, who designed and built the alien pods used in the film, also plays the scientist who takes the pods apart.

Cold Turkey (1965)

Bob Elliott (of the comedy team Bob and Ray) plays three newscasters. One is named David Chetley, after newscasting team David Brinkley and Chet Huntley, a second is Sandy van Andy (after Sander Vanocur, an NBC correspondent for many years) and the third is Paul Hardly (after Paul Harvey, a radio commentator who still has a daily syndicated show).

The Color of Money (1986)

The voice explaining nine-ball at the start of the film is director Martin Scorsese's.

One of the high rollers is played by Scorsese's father, Charles.

The Comancheros (1961)

Ina Balin's character is named Pilar Graile, after star John Wayne's wife, Pilar Palett.

Come See the Paradise (1990)

Producer Robert F. Colesberry has a cameo as a taxi driver near the end of the film.

Comfort and Joy (1984)

Mark Knopfler, lead singer of Dire Straits, wrote the soundtrack for this film, and there are lines in the film that are from an old Dire Straits song, "It Never Rains."

Coming to America (1988)

The despicable (and now down-and-out) Duke Brothers (Don Ameche and Ralph Bellamy) from director John Landis and star Eddie Murphy's earlier film, *Trading Places* (1983), show up to receive a large amount of cash from...Eddie Murphy!

A poster for Landis's *See You Next Wednesday* can be seen in the subway station where Lisa (Shavi Headley) gets off the train. The credits for *See You Next Wednesday* include Jamie Lee Curtis, who starred in Landis's and Eddie Murphy's *Trading Places* (1983) (see *Schlock*, 1971).

In the airport scene, there is a call over the P.A. system for a "Mr. Frank Oznowitz" to pick up the white courtesy phone. This is Muppeteer Frank Oz' real name (see also *Into the Night*, 1985).

Murphy's uncle, "Uncle Ray Murphy," plays Stu in the film.

Commando (1985)

The last thing that Matrix (Arnold Schwarzenegger) says to Bennett (Vernon Wells) before his plane leaves is, "I'll be back, Bennett," repeating his most famous line from *The Terminator* (1984). Bennett replies, "John? I'll be waiting, John."

Commando Squad (1987)

Screenwriter Michael D. Sonye appears in the film.

The Commitments (1991)

One of the audition songs is the title song from *Fame* (1980), which was also directed by Alan Parker.

Parker himself appears as the record producer in the studio at the end of the film. A cardboard cut-out of him can also be seen in the background in a video store, and cassettes of his films are on the shelves.

Conan the Barbarian (1981)

Franco Columbu has a small role as a Pictish scout. Columbu is a friend of Arnold Schwarzenegger's, and was his main bodybuilding rival when they were competing.

Coneheads (1993)

Dan Aykroyd's daughter and brother have cameos. His daughter, Danielle, appears as young Connie Conehead in the Coneheads' home movies. Aykroyd's brother, Peter, plays Highmaster Menthot, the Remulak resident condemned to "narfle the Garthok" for abusing the Butumius pleasure spool. He is the one who argues with Beldar about whose turn it is to die.

Prymatt and Connie watch Beldar fight the Garthok from the stands. They sit beside a Conehead woman played by Laraine Newman, who keeps marvelling at what "great seats" they have. Newman played Beldar and Prymatt's daughter in the original *Saturday Night Live* skits featuring the Coneheads. Many other *SNL* regulars appear in supporting roles as well, including Garrett Morris, Michael McKean, Jan Hooks, Jon Lovitz, Phil Hartman, Kevin Nealon, David Spade, Julia Sweeney, Adam Sandler and Chris Farley.

Connecting Rooms (1971)

Bette Davis passes a poster mentioning stage star Margo Channing. Davis played a character named Margot Channing in *All About Eve* (1950).

Conqueror Worm (1968)

Composer Paul Ferris appears in a cameo as the vengeful husband who spots Hopkins (Vincent Price) and Stearne (Robert Russell) in the Lavenham town square at the end. He is listed in the credits as "Morris Jar." Ferris's pseudonym is a pun on the name of famed composer Maurice Jarre, who worked on such films as *Lawrence of Arabia* (1962), *Dr. Zhivago* (1965), *Dead Poets Society* (1989), and *Ghost* (1990).

Coogan's Bluff (1968)

A scene of the film *Tarantula* (1955) is shown on the wall of the discotheque. *Tarantula* was the film debut of this film's star, Clint Eastwood. He had a bit part as a leader of a jet fighter squadron.

Director Don Siegel has a cameo in an elevator.

Coogan's Bluff is actually a neighborhood in northern Manhattan which is known for a steep escarpment that descends 175 feet below sea level. It is named for James Jay Coogan, a real estate merchant who owned much property in the area and even ran unsuccessfully for mayor. Included in the area of Coogan's Bluff was the Polo Grounds, home of baseball's New York Giants. Bobby Thomson's 1951 pennant-winning home run, called "the shot heard 'round the world," has also been referred to as "the little miracle at Coogan's Bluff." After the Giants moved to California, the city took over the stadium and demolished it in 1965 to make way for a public housing project. Since then, the name Coogan's Bluff fell into disuse.

Cool Hand Luke (1967)

The author of the book that the film is based on, Donn Pearce, appears as a prisoner named Sailor.

Cop and a Half (1993)

Devon Butler (Norman D. Golden) says to Nick (Burt Reynolds): "I'm your worst nightmare. An eight-year-old with a badge." This is a reference to Reggie Hammond's (Eddie Murphy) similar line in *48HRS.* (1982) that ended with "...a nigger with a badge."

The Cotton Club (1984)

Steve Vignari's gangster character, "Trigger" Mike Coppola, has the surname of the film's director, Francis Ford Coppola.

Coppola's nephew, Marc Coppola, has a small part as Husing.

The Couch Trip (1988)

Possibly as a favor to pal Dan Aykroyd and director Michael Ritchie (*Fletch*), Chevy Chase appears on a TV in a limo selling condoms.

John Williams Burns, Jr. (Dan Aykroyd), has the same prison number (74-74-505-B) as Jake Blues (John Belushi) in Aykroyd's *The Blues Brothers* (1980).

Count Yorga, Vampire (1970)

Costar Michael Macready also produced the film, and he got his father, actor George Macready, to narrate.

A Countess in Hong Kong (1967)

This was director Charlie Chaplin's final film, and he also appears in a cameo as a seasick steward.

Coupe de Ville (1990)

Arye Gross stars as Buddy Libner, and his little brother Edan plays a younger version of Buddy's little brother, Bobby (Patrick Dempsey).

The Court Jester (1956)

Danny Kaye's "pellet with the poison's in the flagon with the dragon"

routine is taken from an identical routine of Eddie Cantor's in the film *Roman Scandals* (1933).

Basil Rathbone, as Sir Guy of Gisbourne, faced Errol Flynn in a swordfight in the film *The Adventures of Robin Hood* (1938). Rathbone appears in this film as well, and duels with Danny Kaye in a parody of his previous film.

The Cowboy Way (1994)

The taxi driver is played by film composer Ira Newborn (*The Naked Gun: From the Files of Police Squad,* 1988; *The Blues Brothers,* 1980).

Creature from the Haunted Sea (1961)

Costar Edward Wain is actually Oscar-winning screenwriter Robert Towne (*Chinatown,* 1974; *The Firm,* 1993; *Mission Impossible,* 1996).

The film's director/producer, Roger Corman, has a cameo.

Creepshow (1982)

Stephen King, who wrote the stories that this film's episodes are based on, appears as hick Jordy Verrill in the second episode. Makeup expert Tom Savini appears as a garbageman.

Stephen's son, Joe King, plays the little boy who appears in the film's prologue and epilogue, reading the *Creepshow* horror comic.

The heavy ashtray which Aunt Bedelia (Viveca Lindfors) kills Nathan Grantham with in the first segment also appears in each of the other segments that follow.

Crime Without Passion (1934)

The film's writer-producer-director, Ben Hecht, has a cameo as a reporter.

Crimes and Misdemeanors (1989)

At one point, Cliff (Woody Allen) says, "I love him like a brother—David Greenglass." This sarcastic phrase was a favorite of New York liberals in the 1950s. Greenglass was the brother of Ethel Rosenberg, who with her husband, Julius, was executed in 1953 for passing U.S. atomic secrets to the Russians. Greenglass, whose evidence helped convict the Rosenbergs and who was secretly a courier for the British physicist-spy Klaus Fuchs, turned prosecution witness and got off with 15 years in prison.

Crimes of Passion (1984)

Rick Wakeman's soundtrack is based entirely on Anton Dvorak's *Symphony No. 9 in E Minor (From the New World)*, partly an in-joke on the releasing company, New World Pictures, and partly as director Ken Russell's "take" on America.

Crimewave (1985)

The opening shot is of the "Hudsucker Penitentiary." Director Joel Coen and writer Ethan Coen would later go on to use the same name in *The Hudsucker Proxy* (1994) (see also *Raising Arizona*, 1987).

Crimson Tide (1995)

"The Crimson Tide" is the nickname of the Alabama collegiate football team, and the submarine in the film is named the *Alabama*. Alabama's most famous coach, Paul "Bear" Bryant, is also referred to in the film: the captain's dog is named "Bear."

Quentin Tarantino was brought in to do uncredited "punch-ups" of the dialogue. His major contribution was the comic book bickering. The character name "Russell Vossler" is a reference to Rand Vossler, a friend of Tarantino's with whom he used to work at a video store (see *Pulp Fiction*, 1994).

Critical Condition (1987)

Screenwriters Denis and John Hamill appear in the film as maintenance men.

Cross Creek (1983)

Mary Steenburgen's husband, Malcolm McDowell, appears uncredited as famous editor Max Perkins.

Peter Coyote plays Norton Baskin, and the real Norton Baskin has a cameo as the man in a rocking chair who gives directions to Rawlings (Jay O. Sanders).

The Crow (1994)

Brandon Lee's best friend and fellow student in the martial arts, Jeff Imada, served as the film's fight choreographer. After Lee died, Imada finished his unfilmed scenes. Imada is also the Oriental gangster at the table during Top Dollar's anarchy speech who asks, "So you're saying we should just quit?"

After Draven (Lee) blows up Gideon's Pawn Shop, Officer Albrecht (Ernie Hudson) holds him at gunpoint. Albrecht is momentarily distracted by a guy stealing a TV set, and Draven disappears. The guy stealing the set is played by cartoonist James O'Barr, who created the character of The Crow in his comic books.

One of the bad guys at Top Dollar's meeting is screenwriter David Schow. He's the one who gets pulled underneath the table.

The credits contain the line "Dedicated to Brandon and Eliza." Star Brandon Lee was killed on the set shortly before filming ended. Eliza was his fiancée.

The Cry Baby Killer (1958)

Co-scripter Leo Gordon and producer Roger Corman both have bit parts. Corman plays a television cameraman on top of a van.

Cutthroat Island (1995)

Director Renny Harlin put the flag of his native Finland in a shopfront window.

Cyborg (1989)

All the main characters are named after instrument brand names or related words. The characters are Gibson Rickenbacker, Fender Tremolo, Marshall Strat, Pearl Prophet, Xylo and Roland Pick. Gibson, Rickenbacker and Fender are guitar manufacturers; a tremolo is a piece of an electric guitar used to alter the sound; Marshall makes amplifiers; a Strat (short for Stratocaster) is a type of Fender electric guitar; Pearl makes drums; Roland makes keyboards and amps; "xylo" is short for xylophone; and a pick is used to play a guitar.

Daddy's Dyin'… Who's Got the Will? (1990)

Director Jack Fisk's daughter, Schuyler Fisk, plays Sara Lee (Tess Harper) as a young girl.

Dames (1934)

During the "Dames" number, the Broadway producer (Dick Powell) doesn't want to see composer George Gershwin, but when asked by his secretary about seeing Miss Dubin, Miss Warren and Miss Kelly, he lets them enter his office. Al Dubin and Harry Warren wrote the music, and Orry-Kelly was costume designer of this picture.

Dances with Wolves (1990)

Chief Ten Bears's wife, Pretty Shield, is played by the film's language specialist, Doris Leader Charge.

The Dark Half (1993)

In the prologue of this Stephen King adaptation, young Thad Beaumont (played as an adult by Timothy Hutton) wants to become a writer and is shown writing stories. The title of his first typewritten story is "Here There Be Tygers," which was also the title of the first short story that King wrote in his career. It can be found in King's "Skeleton Crew" anthology.

Thad Beaumont's alter ego, George Stark (also Hutton) was inspired by King's one-time pseudonym, Richard Bachman. Stark was named after writer Donald Westlake's pseudonym, Richard Stark. King has called Westlake "the most civilized, urbane guy you'd ever wanna meet." Westlake publishes quirky, distinctive novels under his own name, though he once wrote a series of queasily hard-boiled novels under the name "Richard Stark."

Dark Star (1974)

One of the pieces of debris seen after the ship blows up reads "THX 1138 Toilet Tank," after the groundbreaking George Lucas sci-fi film *THX-1138* (1970).

For a brief moment, a monitor reads "Fuck you Harris," in reference to producer Jack H. Harris, whom director John Carpenter hated. Carpenter and coauthor/costar Dan O'Bannon are rumored to have sabotaged the sound so that Harris would be forced to use a good, and more expensive, production place.

Darkman (1990)

Director Sam Raimi wanted his high school buddy Bruce Campbell, who starred in Raimi's "Evil Dead" films, to play the lead role, but the producers didn't think that Campbell could handle it. Raimi still got his way, though. At the end of the film, as Darkman walks away, he assumes the face of ... Bruce Campbell, who is listed in the credits as the "Final Shemp" (see *The Evil Dead*, 1983).

The head makeup artist, Tony Gardner, himself has a cameo under makeup as the pathetic freak at the circus.

Director John Landis (*An American Werewolf in London*, 1981; *Trading Places*, 1983) also has a cameo as a physician.

Dave (1993)

In addition to the Washington and Hollywood personalities who appear as themselves, there are a number of other meaningful cameos:

Director Ivan Reitman's daughter Catherine plays the girl at Don Durenberger's Community Chevrolet who asks her mother, "That's not the president, is it?"

Reitman's son Jason plays Vice President Nance's son, who hugs his father after he is inaugurated.

Arnold Schwarzenegger, who starred in Reitman's films *Twins* (1988) and *Kindergarten Cop* (1990), appears as himself.

Bonnie Bartlett, who also starred in *Twins*, was given a one-line cameo as a member of Bill Mitchell's cabinet.

Screenwriter Gary Ross appears as one of the two policemen who pull the president and the first lady over in their car. Charles Hallahan is the one who reads the license; Ross is on the passenger side of the car.

David Copperfield (1935)

Hugh Walpole, who wrote the screenplay for this film, appears as the vicar.

Dawn of the Dead (1979)

Director George Romero plays the director in the television studio, and his wife, Christine Forrest Romero, plays the director's assistant.

The Day of the Jackal (1973)

When the Jackal (Edward Fox) is laying low in the Danish man's apartment while the Surete is hot on his trail, a news story on him comes on to interrupt a movie playing on the TV. The movie is John Huston's *Moulin Rouge* (1952). Huston was a good friend of this film's director, Fred Zinnemann.

The Day of the Locust (1975)

Long-time horror film director-producer William Castle (*The Tingler*, 1959; *House on Haunted Hill*, 1958) appears as the arrogant, cigar-chomping director.

The Day the Earth Caught Fire (1962)

While shooting an army recruitment documentary at the Clubland youth club in South London, Edward Judd met an aspiring actor named Maurice Micklewhite, who would later change his name and achieve great fame as Michael Caine. Before Caine became a well-known actor, Judd was cast as the lead in this film, and he secured a one-scene, unbilled bit part for his friend Caine. He can be seen playing a policeman, directing traffic.

The film's screenwriter, Val Guest, was once a journalist himself, so he tried to keep the newspaper office scenes as accurate as possible, setting them in the real-life London offices of *The Daily Express*. He even hired the *Express* editor Arthur Christiansen to play the editor in the movie, as well as serve as the film's technical advisor.

Days of Thunder (1990)

Aldo Benedetti, the driver who is modeled after real-life driver Mario Andretti, is played by megaproducer Don Simpson.

Dead Again (1991)

The number on Roman's (Kenneth Branagh) prison uniform, 25101415, stands for "25 October 1415," the date of the battle of Agincourt, fought by Henry V in Branagh's *Henry V* (1989).

Branagh's birthday, December 10, is shown on the first newspaper clipping in the opening sequence.

The cover of *Life* magazine in Mr. Madson's shop shows Branagh's idol Laurence Olivier in *Hamlet* (1948). Another Shakespeare reference: the name of the bridge on which Mike (Branagh) and Doug (Campbell Scott) fight is the real-life Shakespeare Bridge in Los Angeles.

At the end, Derek Jacobi leaps from the balcony to attack Branagh. This sequence is a tribute to the scene in *Hamlet* in which Olivier (as Hamlet) leaps from the balcony to attack Laertes.

In addition to Branagh and Emma Thompson's double roles, two more actors play double roles in the film. Jo Anderson plays a compassionate nun and a snooty young starlet, and the film's composer, Patrick Doyle, plays the bored-looking cop at County Hospital and a drunken guest at Otto's party who greets and kisses Margaret.

The stuttering unintentional in-joke: Derek Jacobi has said Frankie/Mr. Madson's stuttering was

not a reference to his famous role as the stuttering Claudius in the BBC production, "I, Claudius." Apparently, it was in the script before he was cast. The role was originally to have been played by Donald Sutherland.

Dead Heat (1988)

The drug company, Dante Pharmaceuticals, is named after director Mark Goldblatt's friend, in-joke specialist Joe Dante.

Dead Pigeon on Beethoven Street (1972)

Director Sam Fuller has a cameo as a U.S. senator.

Dead Poets Society (1989)

Robin Williams's advice to his students is *"Carpe diem,"* or "Seize the day." Williams starred in a film titled *Seize the Day* (1986).

The Dead Pool (1988)

The film includes the murder of a film critic known for his catchphrase, "On a scale of one to ten, ten being best…," the trademark of Los Angeles film reviewer Gary Franklin.

Slash of Guns n' Roses makes an uncredited cameo appearance. After Callahan (Clint Eastwood) visits Gennaro in prison, Slash appears in Swann's movie … firing a harpoon through a window. The Guns n' Roses song "Welcome to the Jungle" plays a major part in the film.

Deadly Blessing (1981)

Two characters go to see *Summer of Fear* (1978 TV), which was also directed by Wes Craven.

Death Machine (1994)

Characters in the film are named after sci-fi directors. William Hootkins is John Carpenter, Brad Dourif is Jack

(Joe) Dante, John Sharian is (Sam) Raimi, and Richard Brake, the lead, is Scott Ridley (Ridley Scott).

Death Race 2000 (1975)
Director Paul Bartel has an unbilled cameo as the doctor who wheels the comatose Frankenstein to the first race.

His daughter, Wendy, has a cameo as well.

Bartel also cast fellow director John Landis as a mechanic in the film.

Death Warrant (1990)
Producer Mark DiSalle has a cameo in the prison. He is the one serving food to the convicts.

Deathtrap (1982)
Director Sidney Lumet's daughter, Jenny Lumet, plays the newsboy on the stage.

The Deep (1977)
Peter Benchley, the author of the book that the film is based on, appears as the first mate who had served aboard the ship Goliath.

Deliverance (1972)
Jon Voight's son is played by director John Boorman's son, Charley.

James Dickey, who adapted the script of this film from his own novel, appears as the sheriff who shows Jon Voight, Burt Reynolds and Ned Beatty the body at the end.

Demolition Man (1993)
Sylvester Stallone is frozen in 1996, reawakened decades later, and at one point, Lenina Huxley (Sandra Bullock) tells him that she looked something up in the Schwarzenegger Presidential Library. Sly responds with disbelief and she asks him if Schwarzenegger wasn't an actor. Apparently, even though he wasn't born in the United States, Arnold became so popular that the American people changed the Constitution so that he could be president. Schwarzenegger actually has had political aspirations (see Twins, 1988).

A poster for Lethal Weapon 3 (1992) can be seen in Lenina Huxley's (Sandra Bullock) office. Both films had Mark Poll as a set designer.

The name "Lenina Huxley" is a reference to the former leader of the U.S.S.R., Vladimir I. Lenin, and Aldous Huxley, author of the futuristic novel Brave New World.

Demons (1986)
Producer Dario Argento's daughter, Fiore, plays one of the teens in the movie theater. She escapes by climbing into in air duct.

Destination Moon (1950)
Woody Woodpecker makes a special "guest appearance," describing how to fly to the moon to prospective investors in the rocket project. Producer George Pal considered Woody Woodpecker good luck and personally requested the sequence in this film from Lantz Studios.

The Devil's Daughter (1990)
The character of Romero was named after director George Romero, the writer-producer who had just co-directed Two Evil Eyes (1990) with Dario Argento.

The sect's first victim is named "Marion Crane," a reference to Janet Leigh's character in Psycho (1960).

Devouring Waves (1984)
Director Lamberto Bava used the pseudonym "John Old, Jr." for this film (see A Blade in the Dark, 1983).

Dial M for Murder (1954)

Director Alfred Hitchcock can be seen on the left side of the school reunion dinner photo on Ray Milland's wall.

Diamonds Are Forever (1971)

In Sean Connery's return to the role of James Bond, he walks into M's office for his briefing and faces lines loaded with in-jokes about his departure and comeback. Peter Franks, the diamond expert, says, "I hear you've been on holiday. Relaxing, I hope?" Bond says, "Oh, hardly relaxing, but most satisfying," referring to the fact that Connery made four non–Bond movies while gone from the series. M replies, "We do function in your absence, 007!"

Connery and Jill St. John escape from their pursuers by tipping a Mustang on its two right wheels and driving sideways through a narrow alley. However, the Mustang emerges from the alley on its two left wheels. The James Bond films are filled with inside jokes, and this stunt was filmed as an intentional continuity error. In fact, during the closeups of Connery and St. John, you can see the car lean from one side to the other as it goes through the alley.

Diary of a Chambermaid (1964)

The demonstrating fascists shout "Vive Chiappe!" a homage to the chief of the Parisian Police who prohibited showing director Luis Bunuel's earlier film L'Age d'Or (1930) after fascists destroyed the cinema where it was being shown.

Dick Tracy (1990)

Mike Mazurki has a cameo in the film. Mazurki played Dick Tracy's nemesis, Splitface, in the film Dick Tracy, Detective (1945).

Die Hard (1988)

John McClane (Bruce Willis) mentions that the terrorists have "enough firepower to orbit Arnold Schwarzenegger." Willis beat out Schwarzenegger for the part of McClane.

When L.A. police sergeant Al Powell (Reginald VelJohnson) tells Dwayne T. Robinson (Paul Gleason) that he thinks the voice on his radio belongs to a cop because he could spot a phony I.D., Robinson snaps back, "He could be a fucking bartender, for all we know!" And he once was—before his big acting break, Willis tended bar for a living.

Die Hard with a Vengeance (1995)

McClane (Bruce Willis) tells Zeus (Samuel L. Jackson) that he was working on a nice fat suspension, "smoking cigarettes and watching Captain Kangaroo." This is a line from the song "Flowers on the Wall" by the Statler Brothers. The song was playing on Willis's car radio in Pulp Fiction (1994), a film which starred both Willis and Jackson. This line is heard just as Butch (Willis) sees Marcellus Wallace walk in front of his car.

The psychologist, Dr. Fred Schiller, is named after the 18th century German poet Friedrich Schiller, who wrote the lyrics used by Ludwig van Beethoven in his Ninth Symphony, which was the music used in Die Hard (1988).

After Simon (Jeremy Irons) calls the radio talk show and says there is a bomb in a school, there is a quick shot of a fishmonger in his store. He is played by director John McTiernan's father, John McTiernan, Sr.

When McTiernan saw singer Sam Phillips on the cover of her album Martinis & Bikinis, he thought "German Terrorist," so he cast the singer in her acting debut as Katya, the silent female terrorist.

Die Hard 2 (1990)

The general is from "Valverde," the fictitious Latin American country used in *Commando* (1985).

Bruce Willis's father, David Willis, Sr., plays the tow truck driver who tows McClane's car away at the start of the picture.

Diggstown (1992)

Lou Gossett, Jr.'s, wife, Cyndi James Gossett, plays his disapproving wife in the film.

Dirty Harry (1971)

After Harry (Clint Eastwood) foils the bank robbery at the beginning of the film, he strides over to the one surviving robber. He walks away from the overturned car beside the fire hydrant, and in the background is a theater showing *Play Misty for Me* (1971), which Eastwood directed and starred in earlier that year.

Callahan, following Scorpio's directions, runs down the stairwell at Forest Hill subway station to catch the "K" car. Spray-painted in big black letters on the wall of the stairwell behind him is the name "Kyle," after Clint's son, Kyle Eastwood.

The final scene where Harry throws his badge into the river is a homage to a similar scene in *High Noon* (1952).

Director Don Siegel can be seen in one scene running down the street.

The Distinguished Gentleman (1992)

Executive producer-screenwriter Marty Kaplan appears in the film as Ned Grable.

Director Daniel Petrie, Jr. (*A Raisin in the Sun*, 1961; *Toy Soldiers*, 1991), appears as an asbestos lobbyist.

Do the Right Thing (1989)

Radio Raheem (Bill Nunn) has two sets of brass knuckles, the left one reading "Hate" and the right one "Love." Robert Mitchum had identical tattoos on his knuckles in the film *The Night of the Hunter* (1955). Raheem even paraphrases Mitchum's speech in *Night of the Hunter* about "the story of right hand, left hand."

Do You Love Me? (1946)

Betty Grable appears in a cameo as the fan who calls for Barry (Harry James) in her car at the end. Grable and James were married at the time.

Doc Hollywood (1991)

Hick Woody Harrelson and his starstruck girlfriend, Bridget Fonda, are sitting in a restaurant booth in Hollywood. She sees someone and says, "Is that a star?" Harrelson responds, "Nah, that's just Ted Danson." Harrelson and Danson starred for years in the series *Cheers*.

Director Michael Caton-Jones plays the maître d' of the restaurant at the end.

Doctor Detroit (1983)

Dan Aykroyd's brother, Peter, plays Mr. Frankman, the dim student in Cliff's class who has been in the first-year program for four years.

Dr. No (1962)

A painting of the Duke of Wellington, stolen in 1960 and never recovered, can be seen on the wall of Dr. No's headquarters.

Doctor Who (1996 TV)

The Doctor (Paul McGann) rummages through other people's lockers to find clothes after he is resurrected in the morgue. In the first one he checks, he finds a scarf just like the one worn by the Doctor as played by Tom Baker during the original series.

Doctor Zhivago (1965)

Omar Sharif appears as Zhivago and Sharif's son Tarek plays Zhivago at age 7.

Dogfight (1991)

Jonathan Demme's longtime producer, Kenneth Utt, has a cameo as the thrift shop man.

Don't Cry, It's Only Thunder (1982)

Screenwriter Paul Hensler appears in the film as Dr. Goldman.

Don't Tell Her It's Me (1990)

Director Malcolm Mowbray gave his son, Joe, a cameo in the film. He is the kid riding the bicycle.

The Doors (1991)

After the Doors arrive in New York, they drive through a crowd in a limo. Jim Morrison (Val Kilmer) sits in the back, flipping a drumstick over and over in his fingers. This was Kilmer's "signature" move, which he did for the first time in *Real Genius* (1985) with two quarters.

Young Jim Morrison, who sees the Indians on the road early in the film, is played by director Oliver Stone's son, Sean.

Stone himself plays Morrison's goateed UCLA film professor.

An agent tries to sign the band after their club gig. He has a bald, bearded sidekick who tells the band to trust him. He tells Jim, "Do yourselves a favour. Call Harry." The sidekick is played by Paul Rothchild, former promoter for the Doors. Rothchild is played in the film by Michael Wincott.

The recording engineer at Morrison's last session is played by Doors drummer John Densmore (played in the film by Kevin Dillon).

The barmaid who has the menu tattoed on her chest is played by Bonnie Bramlett, pop singer of the early seventies in the duo Delaney and Bonnie, a contemporary of the Doors.

After Jim says "fuck" on stage while singing "The End," he is yelled at to get off the stage by a bearded backstage manager. The manager is played by Eric Burdon, lead singer of the Animals.

The New Haven promoter who tells the audience to clear the aisles or else there won't be a show is played by rock promoter Bill Graham.

The Wicca priestess at the wedding ceremony between Jim and Patricia Kennealy (Kathleen Quinlan) is played by the real Patricia Kennealy.

Famous attorney William Kuntsler appears as Jim Morrison's lawyer at his trial. Kuntsler is probably best known for being the lawyer for the Chicago Seven, the organizers of the demonstrations during the 1968 Chicago Democratic convention.

Rock singer Billy Idol, who covered the Doors song "L.A. Woman," has a cameo as Morrison's friend Cat. He is the one with the broken leg at the bar.

Double Deception (1993 TV)

Noted low-budget film director Fred Olen Ray appears as a director.

The Double Man (1967)

Director Franklin J. Schaffner can be seen in a cameo at the station.

Down and Out in Beverly Hills (1986)

Director Paul Mazursky plays Sidney Waxman, Richard Dreyfuss's manager-accountant.

Downtown (1990)

Mick, Anthony Edwards's original partner, says of the violent downtown district, "Have you ever been to Diamond Street? The Terminator wouldn't go to Diamond Street!" Executive producer Gale Anne Hurd also was the executive producer for *The Terminator* (1984).

Dracula: Dead and Loving It (1995)

Madame Ouspenskaya, the woman who sells Renfield the crucifix, is played by Mel Brooks's wife, Anne Bancroft. She is named after the tiny character actress Maria Ouspenskaya. Ouspenskaya, who had the same tremor in her voice as Bancroft's character, played the gypsy woman who warned Lon Chaney, Jr., of the curse of the werewolf in *The Wolf Man* (1941).

The carriage driver at the start of the film is played by Ezio Greggio. Brooks had just appeared in a cameo in Greggio's film *The Silence of the Hams* (1994).

Dr. van Helsing (Mel Brooks) makes medical students faint during his autopsy, parodying the similar sequence in the opening credits of the television show, *Quincy, M.E.*

Dracula's line, "I never drink ... wine," is from *Dracula* (1931).

The "hat" that Dracula is wearing when he first meets Renfield (and at the ball) is a parody of Gary Oldman's hair in *Bram Stoker's Dracula* (1992).

"Yes, we have *Nosferatu* ... we have *Nosferatu* today!" is a parody of a line from the song, "Yes, We Have No Bananas."

Dracula vs. Frankenstein (1971)

After Frankenstein's monster is revived, he kills special guest star Forrest J Ackerman. Ackerman was the creator of the first successful sci-fi/ horror magazine, *Famous Monsters of Filmland*.

Dragnet (1987)

Dan Aykroyd's brother Peter plays a phony cop.

Dragon: The Bruce Lee Story (1993)

The television director of the *Green Hornet* sequences in the film is played by Van Williams, who originally played the Green Hornet.

The Drifter (1988)

Morrison, the cop on the case, is played by director Larry Brand.

Droid Gunner (1995)

Director-producer Fred Olen Ray has a cameo as a fighter pilot.

Drop Zone (1994)

Wesley Snipes's character's name is Pete Nessip. "Nessip" is an anagram of "Snipes."

The Duchess of Idaho (1950)

Red Skelton (as himself) greets Esther Williams and Van Johnson and says "you two look awfully familiar." Skelton costarred with Williams in *Bathing Beauty* (1944), and in the film prior to this one, *Neptune's Daughter* (1949), and he was good pals with Johnson.

Dune (1984)

Director David Lynch has a cameo on the spice-harvester. He is in the scene with Leto, Gurney, Keynes, and Paul touring in the ornithopter. Keynes reports wormsign to the harvester, and the man he speaks with is played by Lynch.

The script for the butchered television version of the film is credited to "Judas Booth," a combination of John Wilkes Booth (Abraham Lincoln's assassin) and the biblical figure of Judas. The director of the television version is "Alan Smithee" (see section on "Alan Smithee"). David Lynch takes full credit for the writing and directing duties on the theatrical and video versions.

Earthquake (1974)

The actor credited as playing the drunk is named Walter Matuschanskayasky. It was actually Walter Matthau, using his real name.

Easter Parade (1948)

The shedding feathered gown worn by Judy Garland in one number is an in-joke reference to Ginger Rogers's problematic gown in *Top Hat* (1935). During filming of the number "Cheek to Cheek" in *Top Hat*, Rogers's gown shed its feathers, exasperating Fred Astaire and causing delays by having to sew the feathers down. Rogers earned the nickname "Feathers" from Astaire as a result.

Easy Money (1983)

Co-scripter Dennis Blair appears as a critic in the film.

Easy Rider (1969)

Billy (Dennis Hopper) and Captain America (Peter Fonda) sell cocaine to a rich pusher who is played by record producer Phil Spector.

Easy Virtue (1927)

Director Alfred Hitchcock is seen walking past a tennis court, carrying a walking stick.

Eating Raoul (1982)

Co-scripter Richard Blackburn appears as James, from the Valley. He is the guy in the loud sports jacket who has dinner with Paul and Mary at the start of the film.

Ed (1996)

In addition to the gratuitous major league baseball cameo (Tommy Lasorda), there is a gratuitous shot of Matt LeBlanc's television series, *Friends*. Ed fools around with the channel-changer, turns on the show and sees Marcel, the friends' pet monkey.

The third out in Ed's unassisted triple play has the name "Vizquel" on his back, named after major leaguer Omar Vizquel. In addition, the Rockets rotund catcher is named Rodriguez, after Texas Rangers catcher Ivan "Pudge" Rodriguez.

Eddie (1996)

Many NBA players appear as themselves in this Whoopi Goldberg film, including Dennis Rodman, Muggsy Bogues, Larry Johnson, Olden Polynice and Vlade Divac. Some others, however, appear in cameos. In fact, the six main players on the film's New York Knicks (all of whom are fictional) are played by professional basketball players.

John Salley, then of the champion Chicago Bulls, plays Nate Wilson, the veteran with bad knees.

Rick Fox of the Boston Celtics plays sexy Terry Hastings, who is going through a divorce.

Malik Sealy of the L.A. Clippers plays egocentric superstar Stacy Patton.

Dwayne Schintzus, also of the Clippers, plays Russian Ivan Radovadovich.

Mark Jackson of the Indiana Pacers plays religious Darren "Preacher" Taylor. Incidentally, Jackson was traded to the Pacers for Malik Sealy in real life.

Greg Ostertag of the Utah Jazz plays clumsy, naive rookie Joe Sparks.

Also, Gary Payton of the Seattle Supersonics plays Rumeal Smith.

And the street guys who play pickup basketball with Stacy Patton are played by Anthony Mason, Herb Williams and John Starks, all of whom were, at the time, real-life New York Knicks.

Edge of Eternity (1959)

Director Don Siegel can be seen at the motel pool.

Eegah! (1962)

The film was made by the same people who would go on to do the musical horror *The Incredibly Strange Creatures Who Stopped Living and Became Mixed-Up Zombies* (1963). Ray Dennis Steckler, that film's director-star, has a cameo here as the man that Eegah (Richard Kiel) throws into the swimming pool.

El Dorado (1967)

John Wayne wears his *Red River* "D" belt buckle in this film (see *Rio Bravo*, 1959).

Electric Dreams (1984)

Giorgio Moroder, the film's music scorer, plays the radio station executive at the end of the film.

The Elusive Pimpernel (1950)

Robert Griffiths plays a character named Trubshawe (see *Four Men and a Prayer*, 1938).

Elvis (1979 TV)

Elvis's (Kurt Russell) dad, Vernon Presley, is played by Russell's real-life father, veteran actor Bing Russell.

The Emerald Forest (1985)

Powers Boothe's son in the film, who was raised in the jungle, is played by director John Boorman's own son, Charley.

The Empire Strikes Back (1980)

There is a reference to *THX-1138* (1971) (see *American Graffiti*, 1973). General Rieekan tells a flunky to "send Rogues Ten and Eleven to Station Three-Eight."

The bounty hunter named 4-LOM was named by Kenner Toys, who made the action figure. It stands for "For the Love of Money."

When Luke first arrives in Cloud City, he gets into a blaster fight with some stormtroopers. Leia, Chewie and C-3PO are also with the stormtroopers, along with some Imperial Commanders. Leia cries out, "Don't, Luke, it's a trap!," then is pulled away by one of the Imperial Commanders. He is played by Jeremy Bulloch, the actor behind the mask of Boba Fett.

The Enforcer (1977)

One of the detectives is played by the assistant to the producer, Fritz Manes. Manes later produced many of Clint Eastwood's films.

Enter Laughing (1967)

Rob Reiner makes his acting debut in his father Carl's autobiographical film as Clark Baxter.

The Entertainer (1960)

Reference is made to Sergeant Ossie Morris. The film was photographed by Ossie Morris.

The Entity (1983)

Director Sidney J. Furie's son, Daniel Furie, plays a student in the film.

Equinox (1971)

In this film, archaeology students search for a missing professor. The professor is played by sci-fi writer Fritz Leiber (*Night's Black Agent, The Green Millenium*).

The voice on the tape is provided by Forrest J Ackerman. Ackerman was the creator of the first successful sci-fi/horror magazine, *Famous Monsters of Filmland*.

Escape from Alcatraz (1979)

Director Don Siegel appears as a doctor.

Associate producer Fritz Manes, who produced many of Clint Eastwood's films, has a cameo as a guard.

Escape from New York (1981)

Director John Carpenter pays tribute to two contemporaries by naming two characters Romero (played by John Strobel) and Cronenberg (played by Frank Doubleday).

Kurt Russell's wife at the time, Season Hubley, makes her film debut in this movie. She is the woman who asks for a cigarette in the ruins of a Chock Full of Nuts, recognizes Snake, and is then pulled through the floor by the crazies.

Jamie Lee Curtis, who had just starred in Carpenter's *The Fog* (1980) and *Halloween* (1978), narrates the opening of the film and also provides the voice of the computer. She would do the same in the sequel 15 years later.

Escape from L.A. (1996)

Director John Carpenter's former significant other, Jamie Lee Curtis, narrates the opening of the film and also provides the voice of the computer, just as she did in *Escape from New York* (1981), 15 years earlier. However, the narration is credited to "Kathleen Blanchard."

Stunt coordinator Jeff Imada also plays Saigon Shadow.

E.T., the Extra-Terrestrial (1982)

The extraterrestrial's plant collection includes a triffid from *The Day of the Triffids* (1962).

Even Cowgirls Get the Blues (1994)

In the credits, it reads: "Dedicated to River," referring to actor River Phoenix, who had recently died of a drug overdose. River's sister, Rain Phoenix, appears in the film, and another of the film's actors, Keanu Reeves, and the director, Gus van Sant, both worked with Phoenix on the film *My Own Private Idaho* (1991).

Every Which Way but Loose (1978)

Al Silvani, who was one of the second assistant directors on the film, plays Tank Murdock's manager.

Fritz Manes, who produced many of Clint Eastwood's films, has a cameo as the bartender at the Zanzibar.

The Evil Dead (1983)

There is a ripped poster of *The Hills Have Eyes* (1978) in one scene. *The Hills Have Eyes* contained a scene with a ripped poster of *Jaws* (1975).

Twelve actors are credited as "Fake Shemps," including Ivan and Ted Raimi, brothers of the film's director. "Fake Shemp" is director Sam Raimi's term for a person who is basically an extra in any of his films. Sometimes the "shemp" may be just a hand or a stand-in. The term "fake shemp" originates from Shemp Howard, one of the later Three Stooges (Raimi is a huge fan of the Stooges). Shemp died while the Stooges were in the middle of making a number of short films, and was replaced by "fake Shemps," or stand-ins, who were used to finish his scenes. The "fake Shemps" were particularly obvious, so, as a tribute, Raimi has included credits for "fake Shemps" or similar credits in all of his films.

Evil Dead II (1987)

Freddy Krueger's glove from *A Nightmare on Elm Street* (1984) can be seen hanging on a nail on the wall near the steps in one of the cellar scenes. This was in response to the appearances of *Evil Dead* (1983) in *Nightmare* (see *A Nightmare on Elm Street*, 1984). Furthermore, the original glove from the *Nightmare* films disappeared during filming of one of the sequels.

Roc Sandstorm, Scott Spiegel, Josh Becker, Sid Abrams and Thomas Kidd are credited as this film's "Fake Shemps" (see *The Evil Dead*, 1983).

William Preston Robertson provides the narration over the main titles (see *Blood Simple*, 1984).

Director Sam Raimi's brother, Ted, plays Henrietta, the bloated corpse in the basement.

The Ewok Adventure (1984 TV)

One of the matte paintings includes Winnie the Pooh sitting in a tree.

Excuse Me, Sir (1931)

In the early 1930s, piracy of ideas was popular in the Indian film industry, and whenever director Dhiren Ganguly was questioned about the title of his upcoming movie, he would evade the question with the polite "Excuse me, sir..." before changing the subject. After a while, people started jokingly asking him when *Excuse Me, Sir* would be coming out, so he decided to give this film that title. It turned out to be one of the most successful pre–World War II Indian comedies.

The Executioner (1970)

The producers couldn't find an actor who was right for the part of a CIA agent, so it was given to one of them: Charles H. Schneer. Schneer remembers, "Since I wear glasses, I ended up doing it myself. I had one line: 'All right, fellas—*this* way.' So much for my acting career."

Executive Decision (1996)

At the beginning of the film, Kurt Russell tries to pick up a girl at a party with some hockey tickets. Then, at the end, he asks Halle Berry, "So, do you like hockey?" She answers that she's into baseball. At the time, Berry was married to David Justice of the Atlanta Braves. Incidentally, Russell had also played baseball in the California Angels organization.

The device that tells the pilots to turn back and not destroy the passenger jet is called the "CRM-114." This was also the name of a similar device in the film *Dr. Strangelove, or How I Learned to Stop Worrying and Love the Bomb* (1963).

Exit to Eden (1994)

Director Garry Marshall has cast character actor Hector Elizondo in all of his films, and in the credits of this one, Elizondo is credited as "and, of course, Hector Elizondo."

The Exorcist (1973)

Screenwriter (and author of the original book) William Peter Blatty appears as the producer of the film that Chris is acting in. He is seen talking to Burke.

The Exorcist III (1990)

Brad Dourif plays a character who is in jail. When he is asked how he is able to get in and out of jail without being seen, he replies, "It's child's play." Dourif played the evil killer who was reincarnated as the Chucky doll (also voice of Dourif) in the *Child's Play* films.

Explorers (1985)

A newspaper headline reads "Kingston Falls Mystery Still Unsolved." Kingston Falls was the town in *Gremlins* (1984), also directed by Joe Dante.

The school is named after animator Chuck Jones.

Darren's (Jason Presson) teacher is played by the film's screenwriter, Eric Luke.

The father of Starkiller's (Robert Picardo) girlfriend is played by Robert F. Boyle, who is also the film's designer.

Exposed (1983)

Writer-director James Toback plays Leo Boscovitch, Nastassia Kinski's professor/lover who she dumps at the start of the film.

Family Plot (1976)

Director Alfred Hitchcock can be seen, in silhouette, through the door window of the Registrar of Births and Deaths, talking to another man.

Fanny Hill: Memories of a Woman of Pleasure (1964)

Producer Albert Zugsmith has a cameo as a duke.

Fantasia (1940)

Mickey is an apprentice to a great sorceror named Yen Sid. Yensid is "Disney" spelled backwards.

The demon in Night on Bald Mountain was modeled after Bela Lugosi. He is named Chernobog, after the god of evil in Slavic mythology.

Far and Away (1992)

The film's screenwriter, Bob Dolman, appears as Honest Bob.

Fargo (1996)

In the scene in which Steve Buscemi returns with the money, his accomplice is watching a soap opera on television. The actor in the soap, who is only shown for a few seconds and is partially obscured by snow, is a young Bruce Campbell. This was a scene from a 1980s soap opera in which he appeared, named *Generations*. The Coen brothers wanted their buddy Campbell to be in *Fargo*, but there were no roles for him, so they threw the soap opera scene in.

The end credits do not list a name for the actor playing the victim in the field. Rather, they list the symbol similar to the one that rock star Prince changed his name to. This was meant as a joke by the writer and director. Actually, the victim was played by the Coen brothers' regular storyboard artist, J. Todd Anderson. Prince did grow up in the Minnesota area, where this film was set.

Father of the Bride (1991)

The two flower girls are played by Annie and Hallie Meyers-Shyer, daughters of director Charles Shyer and screenwriter Nancy Meyers.

Father of the Bride Part II (1995)

Annie Meyers-Shyer, daughter of director Charles Shyer and screenwriter Nancy Meyers, plays a shower guest, and her little sister, Hallie, plays Annie at the age of seven.

A Few Good Men (1992)

Two *Misery* novels, one of them *Misery's Child*, can be seen beside Danny's typewriter while he watches the ball game. *Misery* (1990) was also directed by Rob Reiner.

Aaron Sorkin wrote the screenplay,

based on his play, and he also appears in a bar in the film.

Field of Fire (1991)

David Carradine's character is named General Corman, after B-movie mogul Roger Corman, who was director Cirio H. Santiago's longtime business partner.

Finian's Rainbow (1968)

Fred Astaire has a short speech which consists, with different emphasis, of the words of one of his old songs.

Firefox (1982)

Fritz Manes, who produced many of Clint Eastwood's films, has a cameo as a captain.

Firestarter (1984)

Screenwriter Stanley Mann appears as the motel owner.

First Name: Carmen (1983)

Carmen's (Maruschka Detmers) uncle is a famous but "sick" and "washed-up" film director named Jean-Luc Godard. The part is played by the real Godard, who also directed this film.

A Fish Called Wanda (1988)

John Cleese plays a lawyer named Archie Leach, which was Cary Grant's real name.

The scene where Archie sits up in the background behind Wanda (Jamie Lee Curtis) is reminiscent of a scene in *Halloween* (1978), in which Michael Myers sat up similarly behind Curtis.

When Otto (Kevin Kline) suggests possible snitches to George, he mentions Kevin Delaney. Kevin and Delaney are Kline's first and middle names.

The Fisher King (1991)

The front window of the video store features a poster for director Terry Gilliam's *The Adventures of Baron Munchausen* (1989). A poster for Gilliam's *Brazil* (1985) also appears on the wall in the first video store scene. In fact, almost all of the posters and video boxes in the video store are from RCA/Columbia Pictures Home Video, the video division of Tri Star Pictures, which released this film.

The Flamingo Kid (1984)

Phil (Richard Crenna), the playboy, is flipping through channels, using his new toy, a remote control, and stops to watch Richard Crenna on *The Real McCoys*.

Flashback (1990)

Dennis Hopper says to Richard Masur and Michael McKean, "It takes more than going down to your local video store and renting *Easy Rider* to be a rebel." *Easy Rider* (1969) was the film that catapulted Hopper to stardom.

Flatliners (1990)

Nelson (Kiefer Sutherland) takes the first line of this movie from *Little Big Man* (1970): "Today is a good day to die." Incidentally, he also ends the film with, "It wasn't such a good day to die." Kevin Bacon also uses the phrase "hoka-hey," which is a Sioux war cry meaning "Today is a good day to die."

The Flintstones (1994)

The voice of Fred's dictabird is provided by Harvey Korman, who also provided the voice of The Great Gazoo in the original cartoon series.

Flipper's New Adventure (1964)

Ricou Browning has a bit part as Dr. Clark Burton. Browning, who also played the Creature in the *Creature from the Black Lagoon* films, was the creator of the *Flipper* films and television series.

Flowers in the Attic (1987)

In the establishing shot of the mansion, there is a shot of a maid washing a window. The maid is played by the author of the book that the film is based on, V.C. Andrews. Andrews died soon after her cameo was shot.

The Fly (1986)

At Toronto's 1983 Festival of Festivals, Martin Scorsese remarked that director David Cronenberg looked like "a gynecologist from Beverly Hills." This may be why Cronenberg cast himself as Geena Davis's obstetrician in this film's dream sequence.

The Fog (1980)

A number of the supporting characters were given the names of friends and coworkers of director John Carpenter:

Tom Atkins plays "Nick Castle," who played Michael Myers in Carpenter's *Halloween* (1978).

Charles Cyphers plays "Dan O'Bannon," a popular sci-fi writer who was the star and screenwriter of Carpenter's *Dark Star* (1973).

George "Buck" Flower plays "Tommy Wallace," who has been the production designer for numerous Carpenter films.

In addition, Darwin Johnson plays a character named "Dr. Phibes," after *The Abominable Dr. Phibes* (1971).

Follow the Fleet (1936)

There is a bugle call before one of the Fred Astaire-Ginger Rogers dance numbers (see *The Gay Divorcee*, 1934).

Foolish Wives (1922)

Mrs. Hughes can be seen reading a book with the title *Foolish Wives,* written by this film's director, Erich von Stroheim.

Footlight Serenade (1942)

Hermes Pan, the film's choreographer, dances with Betty Grable in the "Land on Your Feet" number.

For the First Time (1959)

There is a reference to a convict named Cocozza, which is star Mario Lanza's real name.

For Your Eyes Only (1981)

The opening sequence is a dig at Kevin McClory, who owns the rights to the character of Ernst Stavro Blofeld and SPECTRE. The unnamed man in a wheelchair is meant to be Blofeld, but he is never seen clearly, named in the film or even credited. The reason that the character was not identified is because of a lawsuit with McClory, who was constantly at odds with the Bond producers as to which was more important ... Blofeld or Bond. Producer Albert Broccoli knew that McClory was planning to do an unofficial remake of the Bond film *Thunderball* (1965) (which became *Never Say Never Again*, 1983) that would have included Blofeld. Broccoli wanted to kill Blofeld off before he could appear in McClory's film.

A Foreign Affair (1948)

The film's composer, Frederick Hollander, has a cameo as Erika's (Marlene Dietrich) piano player in the cabaret.

Foreign Correspondent (1940)

When Joel McCrea leaves his London hotel, he hears a driver call

Mr. van Meer. He turns, and in his reaction shot, director Alfred Hitchcock can be seen, walking towards the camera, wearing a coat and reading a newspaper.

Robert Benchley, who is cocredited with writing the film's dialogue, plays Stebbins, the London correspondent who shows McCrea around.

Forever, Lulu (1987)

Director-screenwriter-producer Amos Kollek also plays Larry, Hanna Schygulla's agent in the film.

Forrest Gump (1994)

Gary Sinise quotes a famous line from *Midnight Cowboy* (1969) as he is crossing the street: "I'm *walking* here, I'm *walking* here!"

Forrest's Chinese competitor at the ping-pong table is played by world champion ping-pong player Valentino.

Another unintentional in-joke: Lt. Dan (Gary Sinise) says to Gump (Tom Hanks), "The day you'll be a shrimp boat captain, I'll be an astronaut!" Forrest Gump does become a shrimp boat captain, and the next film for both Hanks and Sinise was *Apollo 13* (1995), where they both played astronauts. However, *Apollo 13* was not even in preproduction while this film was being shot, so the reference was purely unintentional.

42nd Street (1933)

Lyricist Al Dubin and composer Harry Warren appear as songwriters in the film.

Four Men and a Prayer (1938)

Alan Hale says that traveling around the world you meet lot of strange people, to which David Niven mutters, "Yes, I knew a fellow called Trubshawe once…" In David Niven's films after 1938, he made it a point to somehow mention the name of his good friend, British character actor Michael Trubshawe, onscreen. Niven even donated a section in his autobiography, *The Moon's a Balloon*, to Trubshawe.

Four Weddings and a Funeral (1994)

At one point, Charles (Hugh Grant) says to Carrie (Andie McDowell), "For a moment there, I thought you were Glenn Close in *Fatal Attraction*." Close dubbed McDowell's voice for *Greystoke: The Legend of Tarzan, Lord of the Apes* (1984).

Francis (1949)

The owner of Francis the talking mule in this film and its sequels is named Peter Stirling (Donald O'Connor). Peter Stirling was the real name of David Sterns, the man who created Francis.

Francis Joins the Wacs (1954)

Chill Wills, who provides the voice of Francis in all the films, also appears here as General Kaye.

Frankenhooker (1990)

Beverly Bonner reprises her role of Casey from director Frank Henenlotter's previous films, *Basket Case* (1982), *Brain Damage* (1988) and *Basket Case 2* (1990).

Henenlotter himself appears on the train that Frankenhooker takes to Manhattan. He is standing by the door holding a newspaper.

Frankie and Johnny (1991)

In one scene, Al Pacino is supposed to open a door and be surprised. *Star Trek VI: The Undiscovered Country* (1991) was being filmed in a nearby studio, so director Garry Marshall arranged for William Shatner and

Leonard Nimoy, in full Trek regalia, to be on the other side of the door Pacino opened. Watch his reaction.

Freaked (1993)

Alex Winter's bud in the *Bill and Ted* movies, Keanu Reeves, appears uncredited as Ortiz, the Dog Boy.

Freddy's Dead: The Final Nightmare (1991)

Johnny Depp appears uncredited in a television commercial. Depp played a character who was killed by Freddy when he fell asleep in *A Nightmare on Elm Street* (1984).

Freejack (1992)

Star Mick Jagger's wife, actress-model Jerry Hall, has a cameo as the newscaster who interviews Emilio Estevez in the bar.

The French Connection (1971)

Popeye Doyle's (Gene Hackman) exploits are based on the real-life experiences of policeman-turned-actor Eddie Egan. Egan appears in this film as Doyle's boss, Lt. Walt Simonson.

French Kiss (1995)

When Meg Ryan is on the train eating cheese, she makes fun of the fake orgasm scene in her previous film, *When Harry Met Sally...* (1989).

Frenzy (1972)

Director Alfred Hitchcock appears in a crowd just after the opening credits, wearing a bowler hat. Actually, he can be seen in three separate shots. As the camera first approaches the crowd, Hitchcock is seen on the left, at the back of the crowd. Shortly after that, there is a closer, left-profile view of Hitchcock in the crowd on the lower left corner of the frame. And lastly, he is seen in the same crowd, peering at a corpse floating in the Thames River. He was going to have a dummy of himself floating down the Thames for this cameo but changed his mind.

The Freshman (1990)

Victor Ray gives Clark Kellogg (Matthew Broderick) an Italian passport with the name "Rodolfo Lasparri," which was the name of a character in *A Night at the Opera* (1935).

Friday the 13th Part 3 (1982)

Director Steve Miner plays the newscaster.

Fright Night (1985)

Roddy McDowall's horror TV host is named "Peter Vincent" in tribute to two veteran horror actors: Peter Cushing and Vincent Price.

The Frighteners (1996)

When Lucy (Trini Alvarado) sees young Patricia Bradley on the video of Johnny Bartlett, Ray (Peter Dobson) picks up the video box, which is labelled *Murders, Madmen and Psychopaths*. On the left side of the cover is a picture of Pauline Parker (Melanie Lynskey) and Juliet Hulme (Kate Winslet), the two murderous girls in director Peter Jackson's *Heavenly Creatures* (1994).

Trini Alvarado's character is named Lucy Lynskey, after Melanie Lynskey. Melanie also appears in this film as the deputy who brings Lucy in for questioning.

R. Lee Ermey spoofs his role from *Full Metal Jacket* (1987) in a ghostly cameo in the graveyard.

Frank (Michael J. Fox) leaves The *Gazette* and collides with a bearded and pierced man wearing a leather jacket and a grim reaper T-shirt. He is played by director Peter Jackson.

The baby in the jumper who is carried around by the two ghosts is played by Billy Jackson, the infant son of director Peter Jackson and his wife, Fran Walsh, who was also the film's screenwriter.

From Beyond (1986)

Dr. Crawford Tillinghast (Jeffrey Combs) wears a Miskatonic U. sweatshirt. Miskatonic University is the same college where Combs's earlier film, *Re-Animator* (1985) was set.

From Dusk Till Dawn (1996)

In Quentin Tarantino's film *Pulp Fiction* (1994), the guys that Vincent and Jules kill are eating food from the fictional fast food franchise Big Kahuna Burgers. In this film, Seth (George Clooney) goes out and gets Big Kahuna burgers for Richie (Tarantino) and himself.

One of the vampires hanging from the ceiling unwraps his wings and looks very much like Dracula in *Bram Stoker's Dracula* (1992).

The crotch gun that Sex Machine (Tom Savini) wields was one of the weapons found in El Mariachi's guitar case in *Desperado* (1995), which was also directed by Robert Rodriguez.

Richie (Tarantino) gets shot through the hand. In *Desperado,* Antonio Banderas sports a scar on his left hand where he had once been shot.

From Russia with Love (1963)

In Ian Fleming's novel, the billboard that the Bulgarian assassin came through advertised the film *Niagara* (1953), and he emerged from Marilyn Monroe's mouth. However, in the film, it was changed to *Call Me Bwana* (1963), and he comes out of Anita Ekberg's mouth. The movie on the billboard was changed because *Call Me*

Bwana was produced by Bond producers Harry Saltzman and Albert "Cubby" Broccoli, and their names can be seen on the billboard.

The Front (1976)

This film, which is about blacklisted writers in Hollywood in the '50s, was written by Walter Bernstein, directed by Martin Ritt, and featured actors Herschel Bernardi, Lloyd Gough, Joshua Shelley and Zero Mostel, all of whom were blacklisted in real life.

Frozen Assets (1992)

Corbin Bernsen's mother, actress Jeanne Cooper, appears as his mother.

Full Metal Jacket (1987)

As Arliss Howard dies, an object that looks a lot like the monolith from director Stanley Kubrick's *2001: A Space Odyssey* (1968) looms in the background. However, Kubrick has said that this was not intentional. Upon viewing of the film, however, he agreed that it sure *looks* like the monolith.

Funny About Love (1990)

Director Leonard Nimoy's son, Jeff, has a cameo as one of the waiters.

Co-producer Jordan Kerner's daughter, Jeannette Kerner, appears as one of the Delta Gammas.

A Funny Thing Happened on the Way to the Forum (1966)

Michael Pertwee cowrote the screenplay for this film with Melvin Frank. Michael's brother, Jon Pertwee (best known for his portrayal of the third Doctor Who), played the slave trader Lycus in the British stage production of *Forum*, but the part was given to Phil Silvers for the movie version. During filming, however, Pertwee was asked to play the role when Silvers became ill and refused to leave his hotel room. As Jon Pertwee tells it, when Silvers found out that Pertwee was taking over the role, he made "a miraculous recovery" and immediately returned to the set. Pertwee did eventually appear in a cameo in the film. He's the man who tells Lycus (Silvers) that there is no plague in Crete.

F/X 2 (1991)

After Rollie (Bryan Brown) bugs the police station, Leo (Brian Dennehy) shows off for him behind his bar, flipping bottles and shakers around. This was a tweak at Brown's character in the film *Cocktail* (1988), where he showed Tom Cruise how to flip bottles around in the same way.

The Gambler Returns: The Luck of the Draw (1991 TV)

Numerous actors turn up as the characters that they played on television westerns of the '50s and '60s. Jack Kelly as Bart Maverick (*Maverick*) and Gene Barry as Bat Masterson (*Bat Masterson*) show up at the poker game. David Carradine as Caine (*Kung Fu*) saves the lead actors in Chinatown. Chuck Connors as Lucas McCain (*The Rifleman*), Hugh O'Brian as Wyatt Earp (*The Legend of Wyatt Earp*), Clint Walker as Cheyenne (*Cheyenne*), Johnny Crawford as Mark McCain (*The Rifleman*), James Drury as the Virginian (*The Virginian*) and Doug McClure as Trampas (also from *The Virginian*) appear as well. Brian Keith as *The Westerner* presides over a gas station in the middle of nowhere along with western fixture Dub Taylor.

Linda Evans appears in a cameo as Kate Muldoon, the character she played in the preceding film, *Kenny Rogers as The Gambler—The Adventure Continues* (1983 TV).

Ganja and Hess (1973)

Duane Jones plays a rich, decadent vampire and director Bill Gunn has a cameo as one of his victims.

The Garbage Pail Kids Movie (1987)

Director Rod Amateau's children, J.P. and Chloe Amateau, appear in the film. J.P. plays Wally.

Gardens of Stone (1987)

Rachel Feld's (Mary Stuart Masterson) parents are played by Masterton's real life parents, Peter Masterson and Carlin Glynn.

Gas Food Lodging (1992)

The letter informing Nora of Trudi's absences from school lists the name of the school principal as Allison Anders, who was the director of the film.

The name of the director of the Spanish film-within-a-film is "Carlos Colpaert." He is named after the film's executive producer, Carl-Jan Colpaert.

Gator (1976)

The man wearing horn-rimmed glasses seated to the right of Mike Douglas in the courtroom scene is Professor Watson B. Duncan III. He was the Palm Beach Junior College theater professor who steered Burt Reynolds towards an acting career.

The Gauntlet (1977)

The helicopter gunman is played by associate producer Fritz Manes, who produced many of Clint Eastwood's films.

The Gay Divorcee (1934)

The bugle call at the beginning of the "Don't Let It Bother You" dance was developed from clowning during rehearsals, and became an in-joke when used in future Fred Astaire-Ginger Rogers films.

The Gay Sisters (1945)

In 1945 there were two actors in Hollywood named Byron Barr. One of them plays a character in the film named "Gig Young," and, afterward he used the name Gig Young as his stage name.

The Gazebo (1959)

The voice on the telephone which tells Glenn Ford how to dispose of a body belongs to Alfred Hitchcock.

The General Died at Dawn (1936)

There is a scene where the general's troops stop the train, and the general (Akim Tamiroff) is sitting at the head of the car. A reporter comes up and asks him some questions and also asks for a photo. The reporter was played by John O'Hara, the novelist (Butterfield 8, 1935; Pal Joey, 1940). O'Hara got the part because he was a big movie fan. He had previously worked behind the scenes on several films. Two other reporters in this scene are played by the film's director, Lewis Milestone, and its screenwriter, Clifford Odets.

Get Shorty (1995)

When Rene Russo tells Chili Palmer (John Travolta) that he could be an actor, he agrees, but says he couldn't do something like the movie "where the three guys get left with the baby" describing the film Three Men and a Baby (1987). Travolta actually did do similar movies—Look Who's Talking (1989) and its sequels.

Director Barry Sonnenfeld has a cameo as the beefeater who opens the door of Leo's (David Paymer) limousine.

At the beginning of the film, Ray Bones makes jokes at Chili's expense. He has two toadies with him. The one on the right, who says, "That was a good one," is played by an actor named Ernest "Chili" Palmer. Palmer, a tough, streetwise Florida native, was writer Elmore Leonard's model for the original book's character. According to an article in the LA Times, he claims not to have been involved with gangsters, loan sharking, or anything of that sort. He is probably more a model from the point of view of personality and mannerisms. When the filmmakers found out from Leonard that there was a real Chili Palmer, they gave him a bit part in the film.

A line in the credits reads: "In Memory of Danny Gill." Gill was the film's special effects coordinator who died before the film was released.

The Getaway (1994)

The man who sells his truck at the end is named "Slim." In the original The Getaway (1972), this character was played by Slim Pickens.

Getting It Right (1989)

Elizabeth Jane Howard wrote the script for this film based on her book, and she also appears as a partygoer.

Ghost (1990)

Director Jerry Zucker cast his mother, Charlotte Zucker, as the bank officer.

The Ghost Creeps (1940)

The "real" ghost scenes were filmed at the last minute to parody the then-popular film, Rebecca (1940).

Ghost Dad (1990)

Diane, Elliot Hopper's (Bill Cosby) daughter, is played by Kimberly

Russell. In one sequence, Diane falls
down a flight of stairs, goes into a
coma and has an out-of-body experience. During this sequence, the
comatose Diane is played by Kimberly's younger sister Lisa while
Kimberly flies off in the out-of-body
shots. Originally, Linda (who is also
Kimberly's roommate) auditioned for
the role of Diane, but when Kimberly
saw the script and when her sister was
turned down for the role, Kimberly
called her manager and told him she
wanted to read for the part. In gratitude, she arranged for her sister to
have this bit role.

Ghostbusters (1984)

The eggs that fry themselves are
sitting next to a package of Stay-Puft
Marshmallows. There is also a large
advertisement for Stay-Puft Marshmallows (complete with the marsh-
mallow man) visible on the side of a
building.

Director Ivan Reitman's son Jason
appears as a kid at the birthday party.

Ghostbusters II (1989)

The restaurant patron who is slimed
is played by Judy Ovitz. Judy is the
wife of Creative Artists' Agency head
Michael Ovitz.

Director Ivan Reitman's son Jason
appears as a Brownstone Boy and his
daughter Catherine appears as a girl
with a puppy.

As the camera tracks along a New
York street, it moves past a theater advertising Reitman's earlier Canadian-
made horror movie, Cannibal Girls
(1973), starring Eugene Levy and
Andrea Martin (as it reads on the
marquee).

Dana's baby, Oscar, is named after
Dan Aykroyd's son.

The Godfather (1972)

The baby who is baptized at the end
of the film was actually director Francis Ford Coppola's infant daughter
Sofia, who went on to costar in The
Godfather Part III (1990).

Talia Shire, who plays Connie in all
three Godfather movies, is Coppola's
sister.

The Godfather Part II (1974)

Troy Donahue plays Merle Johnson,
the man Connie wants to marry.
Merle Johnson is Troy Donahue's real
name.

Director Francis Ford Coppola's son
Roman, who went on to do the sound
for The Black Stallion Returns (1983)
and serve as second unit director of his
father's Bram Stoker's Dracula (1992),
appears uncredited in the film as young
Sonny Corleone.

Sofia Coppola, Francis's daughter,
has a cameo in the film. She can be
seen on the boat passing the Statue of
Liberty in New York Harbor.

Coppola was given his first job in
film by low-budget director Roger
Corman, and in gratitude he cast Corman as a senator in this film. Coppola
also cast producer Phil Feldman (The
Wild Bunch, 1969) as a senator and
screenwriter/producer William Bowers
(Support Your Local Sheriff! 1969; The
Gunfighter, 1950) as the senate com-
mittee chairman.

Ed Guthman, who was a reporter at
the 1950s senate hearings, has a cameo
as a reporter at the senate hearing in
the film.

The Godfather Part III (1990)

On a newsstand on Elizabeth Street,
there is a copy of a 1979 Time magazine with the cover story "Puzo: Godfather of the Paperback Boom." Mario
Puzo wrote The Godfather.

Legendary beat poet Gregory Corso appears as an unruly stockbroker.

Not only does this film star director Francis Ford Coppola's daughter, Sofia, and his sister, Talia Shire (see *The Godfather*, 1972), but Coppola's father, Carmine, who also wrote the score for the film, appears as the bandleader.

Director Martin Scorcese's mother, Catherine, appears in a café, complaining that the neighborhood is going to hell. Scorsese's father, Charles, was an "advisor" for the film.

Boxer Anthony "The Ant" Squigliaro is played by real-life boxer Vito Antuofermo.

Godzilla, King of the Monsters (1955)

The original name of the giant lizard was "Gojira," until it was Americanized to "Godzilla." Gojira was the name of a workman at Toho Studios, which made the original film.

Gold Diggers of 1933 (1933)

A songwriter is told, "Dubin and Warren are out! You're writing the score!" Al Dubin and Harry Warren wrote the film's score.

GoldenEye (1995)

Near the end of the film, a computer screen shows the display "Pevsner Commerzbank GmBH." Tom Pevsner was the film's executive producer.

The film is dedicated to Derek Meddings, who did all the special effects with the miniatures in *Golden-Eye*. He had also done several of the other Bond movies' special effects, including the miniature poppyseed farm explosion in *Live and Let Die* (1973) and some of the footage with the Lotus Esprit in *The Spy Who Loved Me* (1977). He died of natural causes during filming.

Goodfellas (1990)

Director Martin Scorsese's mother, Catherine, plays Tommy's (Joe Pesci) mother. In the scene where she serves him and the others dinner, she did not know that Pesci's character was on his way to bury a body.

Scorsese's father, Charles, also appears, as Vinnie.

Tommy (Pesci) kills Billy Batts (Frank Vincent) by beating him. In *Raging Bull* (1980), Pesci's character nearly beats Frank Vincent's character to death.

The Goonies (1985)

At one point in the movie, Sean Astin yells, "Holy Mackenzie!" Mackenzie Astin is Sean's brother.

Near the end, Sloth pulls apart his shirt to reveal that he is wearing a Superman T-shirt underneath, and a few strains from the theme song of the film *Superman* (1978) are played. Director Richard Donner also directed *Superman*.

The town sheriff recalls some of the tall tales which Chunk has told in the past. One involves "those little green men that multiply when you throw water on them." This is a reference to *Gremlins* (1984). Both movies were written by Chris Columbus and executive produced by Steven Spielberg.

Gore Vidal's Billy the Kid (1989 TV)

Gore Vidal, who wrote the story that was the basis for this film, appears as a bearded preacher at a graveside.

Billy (Val Kilmer) flips a coin over his knuckles. This was Kilmer's "signature" move, which he did for the first time in *Real Genius* (1985) with two quarters.

Gothic (1987)

Director Ken Russell and his family can be seen on the tour boat at the end of the film.

Grand Canyon (1991)

Director Lawrence Kasdan appears as a director who tries to interest producer Steve Martin in a film.

Graveyard Shift (1990)

The film is based on a Stephen King story, and the mill where most of the action takes place is owned by Bachman Mills. When he wrote some non-horror books, King used the *nom de plume* "Richard Bachman."

The Great Muppet Caper (1981)

Some of the muppeteers have cameos:

Jim Henson appears as the man that Gonzo takes a picture of in the restaurant.

Richard Hunt plays the cab driver.

Jerry Nelson appears as a man in the park with his daughter.

The Great Race (1965)

Director Blake Edwards has a cameo in the film.

The Great Sioux Massacre (1965)

The screenwriter is credited as "Fred C. Dobbs." Fred C. Dobbs was the name of the character played by Humphrey Bogart in the film *The Treasure of the Sierra Madre* (1948). In reality, the screenwriter was Marvin Gluck. The film was based on a story by Gluck and the director, Sidney Salkow.

The Great White Hype (1996)

At the climactic fight, the Sultan (Samuel L. Jackson) greets a man with shoulder length black hair and a black suit by saying, "Vincent! How you doin', baby? You seen Jules?" This is a reference to John Travolta and Samuel L. Jackson's characters, Vincent and Jules, in the film *Pulp Fiction* (1994).

The Greatest Show on Earth (1952)

When Dorothy Lamour appears onscreen, her two costars in the *Road* movies, Bob Hope and Bing Crosby, can be seen munching popcorn in the crowd in the circus bleachers.

Greedy (1994)

The family name in the film is McTeague. *McTeague* is the name of the novel by Frank Norris that the movie *Greed* (1925) was based on.

Green Card (1990)

Executive producer Edward S. Feldman has a cameo as a taxi driver.

Gremlins (1984)

In the first scene, Randall Peltzer (Hoyt Axton) walks in front of a broken-down American Motors Gremlin, left in front of the old man's shop.

At the bar, Mr. Jones compliments Billy (Zach Galligan) on his cartoon drawing of Mrs. Deagle. Mr. Jones is played by long-time animator Chuck Jones. One of Jones's Warner Brothers cartoons is playing on the television at the time.

The films *A Boy's Life* and *Watch the Skies* can be seen advertised on a movie marquee during the opening titles. These were, respectively, the working titles of executive producer Steven Spielberg's *E.T., the Extra-Terrestrial* (1982) and *Close Encounters of the Third Kind* (1977). The name *Watch the Skies* was taken from the last line of the sci-fi film *The Thing (From Another World)* (1951).

While ripping out a telephone cord, a gremlin mumbles E.T.'s most famous line: "Phone home!"

In the final showdown with Billy at the supermarket, Stripe emerges from behind a stuffed E.T. doll.

A billboard for Rockin' Ricky Rialto

(who "whips out the oldies") is in the style of Spielberg's *Indiana Jones* movies.

Billy tells Corey Feldman that he bought a comic at Dr. Fantasy's. Dr. Fantasy is a nickname of executive producer Frank Marshall.

As Billy is walking to work at the start of the film, he greets the town doctor, saying, "Morning, Dr. Moreau." Dr. Moreau was named after H.G. Wells's famous character.

Mrs. Deagle (Polly Holliday) is a parody of the Wicked Witch of the West in the film *The Wizard of Oz* (1939).

When Billy accidentally feeds the Mogwais after midnight, one of director Joe Dante's favorite films, *Invasion of the Body Snatchers* (1956), is on television. The paranoia of *Gremlins* soon comes to resemble that of *Body Snatchers*.

Jim McKrell reprises his role (from Dante's *The Howling*, 1981) of newscaster—now field reporter—Lew Landers on TV at the end of the film.

While Randall Peltzer is talking on the phone at the convention, the machine from *The Time Machine* (1960) can be seen to his right, in the background, winding up to full power. The scene cuts to the house, and when it cuts back again, the machine is gone, leaving only a wisp of colored smoke.

Robby the Robot also appears at the inventors' convention and spouts the following lines from his scenes in *Forbidden Planet* (1956) with the cook of the C57-D: "I was giving myself an oil job"; "The question is totally without reason"; "Pardon me, sir. Stuff?"; "Thick and heavy? Would sixty gallons be sufficient?"; and "I rarely use it myself, sir. It promotes rust."

Spielberg can be seen briefly at the inventors' convention as well. He drives a futuristic wheelchair across the screen in front of Randall Peltzer.

The cocoons that the gremlins hatch from were inspired by the eggs-cocoons in the film *Alien* (1979). The latter half of the film *Alien* was based on the idea of gremlins on a B-17 bomber, transposed to a spaceship.

Gremlins 2: The New Batch (1990)

The white-haired customer at the ice cream counter in Clamp Center who asks, "there are rats?" is played by veteran film composer Jerry Goldsmith, who scored both this film and the first *Gremlins* (1984).

Alex, the guy with the ponytail behind the ice cream counter, is played by Jason Presson. Presson starred in director Joe Dante's *Explorers* (1985).

The first time Kate (Phoebe Cates) sees the hyper Mogwai, which she mistakes for Gizmo, he is perched atop an Empire State Building replica, swatting at model biplanes, bringing to mind the film *King Kong*. Makeup artist Rick Baker played Kong in the 1976 version.

Dr. Catheter's assistants are named Martin (Don Stanton) and Lewis (Dan Stanton), after the movie comedy team Dean and Jerry.

Catheter gives his secretary's used tissue to his assistant, Casper. Casper is played by the film's screenwriter, Charlie Haas.

The monkeys who get loose are named Alvin and Theodore, after the famous cartoon chipmunks.

As the hyper gremlin, in full dentist gear, approaches the bound Billy (Zach Galligan), he shrieks, "Is it safe?" This was the question that Nazi dentist Laurence Olivier asked Dustin Hoffman as he interrogated him in *Marathon Man* (1976).

Kate asks why Gizmo, dressed as

Rambo, retaliated the way he did, and Billy replies that "they just pushed him too far," which was the tag line from *First Blood* (1982).

An announcement inside the Canadian restaurant is heard: "Gretzky, party of six, eh?" a reference to Canadian hockey player Wayne Gretzky and presumably the six players on a hockey team.

Robert Prosky appears as horror movie host Grandpa Fred. He is made up to look like Al Lewis's Grandpa Munster character on *The Munsters*. Lewis used to host a similar horror movie show in his *Munsters* getup. Dante has said, "I was touring the Turner TV facilities in Atlanta once when I was scouting locations for a movie I didn't make. They had just moved a lot of stuff out of the building, and the only thing left in the basement was this crappy set which Al Lewis used on Saturday mornings for his show, where he shamelessly hammed. I thought it was kind of sad, this moth-eaten old trouper down there in the basement doing his thing, and I felt it might be an interesting character to put in this movie, because we've got this Turneresque cable network."

When Grandpa Fred sighs that there was "no moan," the director in the control booth is played by Joe Dante.

Just before Kate finds Marla (Haviland Morris) trapped in the web, she comes out of a doorway and calls, "Billy?" She is standing beside an office doorway for Vectorscope Labs, which was the name of the science lab in Dante's *Innerspace* (1987). The name beside the door: Dr. Quatermass, the name of the famous sci-fi character of film, television and books, created by author Nigel Kneale.

The first shot of the Splice O' Life

lab shows a brain suspended in liquid labelled "W.H. Donovan." This is a reference to the classic sci-fi film *Donovan's Brain* (1953).

As Dr. Catheter (Christopher Lee) enters the Gremlin-filled lab, he is carrying a pod from the film *Invasion of the Body Snatchers* (1956).

Another in the long line of unintentional in-jokes (see *Platoon*, 1986; and *Working Girl*, 1988): At the end of the film, megaentrepreneur Daniel Clamp (John Glover), based not-too-loosely on Donald Trump, becomes enthralled by a woman who works for him ("You work for me, don't you?") named Marla (Bloodstone). However, the character was named and the film shot before news of Trump's affair with Marla Maples surfaced.

Greystoke: The Legend of Tarzan, Lord of the Apes (1984)

Robert Towne's script was so rewritten and tampered with that he disowned it and insisted that the screenplay credit read "P.H. Vazak." This is the name of Towne's dog.

Groundhog Day (1993)

Director Harold Ramis appears in a cameo as a squinty doctor.

The Group (1966)

Director Sidney Lumet's father, Baruch, appears as Mr. Schneider.

Grumpy Old Men (1993)

During the "I'm Too Sexy" montage of shots, Jack Lemmon slaps cologne on his face and lets out a scream, just like Macaulay Culkin in *Home Alone* (1990).

The morning after Lemmon has sex with Ann-Margret, he does a dance in his underwear reminiscent of Tom Cruise's in *Risky Business* (1983).

Guns (1990)

Writer-director Andy Sidaris cast his son Drew as The California Kid.

The Guyver (1991)

Jeffrey Combs plays Dr. East, in contrast to the character he played in *Re-Animator* (1985), Dr. Herbert *West*.

Jimmie Walker (as Striker) spouts his famous *Good Times* catchphrase as his last line: "Dy-no-mite!"

Hairspray (1988)

Dr. Fredrickson, the psychiatrist who tries to brainwash Penny Pingleton (Leslie Ann Powers), is played by director John Waters.

Half Moon Street (1986)

When Dr. Slaughter (Sigourney Weaver) walks to the answering machine, there is a photo next to the phone which shows Weaver and her real-life father, television executive Pat Weaver.

Hallelujah, I'm a Bum (1933)

After the mayor lays a cornerstone, he reluctantly has his picture taken holding a baby. The two photographers who take his picture are played by well-known film composers Lorenz Hart and Richard Rodgers, who are also credited with writing "songs and musical dialogue" for the film.

Halloween (1978)

Director John Carpenter was raised in Bowling Green, Kentucky. In one scene, the subtitle on the screen depicts the location as "Smiths Grove, Illinois." Smiths Grove, Kentucky, is a small town of about 600 people 15 miles from Bowling Green. In another scene, a man mentions going to Russellville, which is another town near Bowling Green.

Due to its shoestring budget, the prop department had to use the cheapest mask that they could find in the costume store for Michael Myers's mask: one of William Shatner. They later spray-painted it white and teased out the hair.

The kids watch the opening of one of Carpenter's favorite films, *The Thing (From Another World)* (1951) on television. Carpenter would later remake this film in 1982 as *The Thing*.

The name of the UK distributor who handled Carpenter's early suspense film, *Assault on Precinct 13* (1976), was Michael Myers. The film bombed in the United States, but thanks to Myers's enthusiastic promotion, it was a hit in Great Britain. As a tribute (and presumably heartfelt thanks) to Myers, Carpenter named the homicidal maniac in his *Halloween* films after him.

The Hand (1981)

Director Oliver Stone has a cameo as a bum who gets killed.

Happy New Year (1987)

Claude Lelouch, who directed the film which was the basis for this one, *La Bonne Annee* (*Happy New Year*) (1973), appears as a man on a train.

Hard-Boiled (1992)

Director-screenwriter John Woo has a cameo as Mr. Woo, the nightclub owner.

Hard Core Logo (1996)

John, the bassist, says that he is getting along well with Joe and that the band should do well "unless he dies in a bizarre gardening accident." This line comes from the rock documentary spoof *This Is Spinal Tap* (1984)—one of

Spinal Tap's former drummers died in a "bizarre gardening accident."

The group's promoter, Mulligan, is played by MuchMusic VJ Terry David Mulligan.

A Hard Day's Night (1964)
John Lennon's book, *In His Own Write*, can be seen in a dressing room.

Hard, Fast and Beautiful (1951)
Director Ida Lupino has a cameo as a member of an audience.

Hard to Kill (1989)
The woman who sells O'Malley (Frederick Coffin) his Amtrak tickets is played by Catherine Quinn, who was the assistant to director Bruce Malmuth.

Harlem Nights (1989)
Eddie Murphy's uncle Ray (billed as "Uncle Ray") appears as Willie.

Harry and the Hendersons (1987)
While he roams around the city, Harry pauses to look into a woman's kitchen window. A man sees him, then yells and runs into his house. The man is played by William Dear, who co-wrote, coproduced and directed the film.

Harry and Tonto (1974)
When Harry (Art Carney) goes to Hollywood, he sees a man on the Sidewalk of Stars who suggestively lip-synchs the word "Hi." The man is played by director Paul Mazursky.

Hatari! (1962)
John Wayne wears his *Red River* "D" belt buckle in this film (see *Rio Bravo*, 1959).

Heathers (1989)
Friends Veronica Sawyer (Winona Ryder) and Betty Finn (Renee Estevez) are named after Betty and Veronica from the comic strip *Archie* and Tom Sawyer and Huck Finn.

The high school is named Westerberg High. Ryder's favorite band at the time was the Replacements, whose lead singer was Paul Westerberg.

Heavenly Creatures (1994)
Director Peter Jackson has a cameo as the bum who is kissed by Juliet outside of the theater.

Hello Again (1987)
Screenwriter Susan Isaacs appears in the film.

Hello Mary Lou: Prom Night II (1987)
Almost all of the characters with surnames have been given names of famous sci-fi and horror writers and directors:

Wendy Lyon as the lead, Vicki [John] Carpenter.

Teri Hawkes as her rival for prom queen, Kelly [Frank] Henenlotter.

Dennis Robinson as the lecherous (and burnt) teacher, Mr. [Wes] Craven.

Michael Evans as Matthew [Joe] Dante.

Larry A. Messer as Mr. [Dan] O'Bannon.

David Robertson as Mr. [Stephen] King.

Derych Hazel as Mr. [George A.] Romero.

Beth Gondak as Jess [Tod] Browning.

Richard Monette as Father [Merian C.] Cooper.

Beverly Handy as Monica [John] Waters.

John Ferguson as Eddie [Edward D.] Wood.

Hellraiser III: Hell on Earth (1992)

Screenwriter Peter Atkins appears as Rick, the barman.

Director Anthony Hickox plays one of two soldiers in the film.

Hellzapoppin (1941)

Ole Olsen and Chic Johnson see a sled on a film set and say, "I thought they burned that," referring to Rosebud in *Citizen Kane* (1941).

Elisha Cook, Jr., has the fadeout line: "You can't hurt me. I always wear a bulletproof vest around the studio." In his films, Cook would usually play weaselly little henchmen who would be dead from a gunshot by the end of the movie.

Helpmates (1932)

Stan Laurel gives his real phone number: Oxford-0614.

Her Twelve Men (1954)

Greer Garson teaches a class of 13, not 12 boys. The more appropriate original title for the play that this film was based on was "Miss Baker's Dozen."

Herbie Rides Again (1974)

Keenan Wynn appears as Alonzo Hawk, a character he played in the earlier Disney film *The Absent-Minded Professor* (1961).

Hidden Agenda (1990)

John McAllister, who plays the Sinn Fein activist, is in real life a Sinn Fein activist.

The High and the Mighty (1954)

The photo of Dan Roman's (John Wayne) dead wife is actually a picture of Wayne's third wife, Pilar Palett, whom he had just married.

High Anxiety (1977)

Mel Brooks lampoons a good number of Alfred Hitchcock's films. Included in the spoofs:

The scene in which Brooks takes a shower and is attacked by Dennis, the crazed bellhop, with a newspaper, is right out of *Psycho* (1960). After the attack, newspaper ink (instead of blood, as in *Psycho*) can be seen flowing down the drain. The camera then slowly zooms out from a closeup of Brooks's eye, as it did in *Psycho* from Janet Leigh's eye.

Incidentally, the bellhop is played by this film's co-scripter and future director (*Diner*, 1982; *Rain Man*, 1988) Barry Levinson.

Brooks agrees to meet Madeline Kahn at the North-by-Northwest corner of the Golden Gate Park, and is attacked by birds in a parody of *The Birds* (1963).

Brooks is framed for murder after a double commits murder in a scene reminiscent of the United Nations murder in *North by Northwest* (1959). When Brooks has to run from the scene of the murder, he is seen in an aerial shot that recalls the one of Cary Grant escaping in the original film.

The film's basic plotline is taken from *Spellbound* (1945), which concerns murder and trauma in a psychiatric hospital.

Brooks's fear of heights and the rickety bell tower with the spiral staircase bring to mind the film *Vertigo* (1958), but falls from heights and fears of such falls have appeared in the Hitchcock films *Blackmail* (1929), *Rebecca* (1940), *Suspicion* (1941), *Saboteur* (1942), and *North by Northwest*.

Brooks's rendering of the title song (in a style similar to Frank Sinatra) brings to mind Doris Day's Oscar-winning "Que Sera Sera" from *The Man Who Knew Too Much* (1956).

When a nervous accomplice says "I feel like I'm caught in a web" to Brooks, Brooks the director saw that there were web-shaped shadows on the wall behind him. This was not only a reference to Hitchcock's use of Expressionist imagery to suggest emotional disturbance, it was a reference to a specific shot in *Suspicion*. When Joan Fontaine suspects her husband and similarly feels like a fly caught in a trap, web-like patterns appear in the shadows behind her.

Brooks makes use (and fun) of Hitchcockian camera movements (e.g., the camera tracking slowly toward a window … which shatters as the lens hits it) and camera angles (a tense conversation is shot from below, through a glass table … but saucers, cups and trays keep obscuring the view and the camera has to adjust its position).

John Morris's score of the film is an excellent imitation of Bernard Herrmann's scores for Hitchcock's films, but perhaps the best musical joke happens when Brooks's driver (Ron Carey) tells Brooks about his predecessor and him suspecting foul play. The music suddenly surges, indicating high tension, as it did so often in Hitchcock's films, but it just turns out to be the Los Angeles Philharmonic Orchestra practicing in a vehicle alongside Brooks's car.

As Mel Brooks checks into the hotel, he finds that his room is on the 17th floor. He informs the desk clerk that he wanted something lower, and is told that they had second floor apartments, but "a Mr. McGuffin" called and told them to change it. "McGuffin" is a term coined by Hitchcock. The McGuffin is the plot element in the thriller that is of great importance to all the characters but is merely incidental to the film's audience. It is like the money that Janet Leigh steals in *Psycho* (1960), the microfilm in *North by Northwest* (1959), or the reason the birds are attacking in *The Birds* (1963): the plot revolves around it, but what it is doesn't make any difference to the viewer. This mystery man who called to change floors could also be considered a McGuffin.

The desk clerk (Jack Riley) rings for the bellboy and says, "Oh, Dennis!" exactly like Jack Benny did on his radio and television show whenever he called for singer Dennis Day.

There is also a reference to the Vincente Minnelli psychiatrist melodrama *The Cobweb* (1955). In addition to the basic premise—that of the doctors being more psychotic than the patients—one patient says he wants to change the drapes in the Psychotic Game Room, which was also a part of the storyline in *The Cobweb*.

Highlander (1986)

MacLeod (Christopher Lambert) says "It's a kind of magic" to Rachel as he leaves his antique shop to go to the final battle with the Kurgan. *A Kind of Magic* is the name of the Queen album that contains songs from the film (as well as the title of one of the songs). The Vietnam vet who tries to machine-gun Kurgan has the Queen song "Hammer to Fall" playing on his car radio.

The Kurgan's phrase "It's better to burn out than to fade away" is originally from the Neil Young song "My My, Hey Hey" from his 1979 album *Rust Never Sleeps*.

His Girl Friday (1940)

Walter Burns (Cary Grant) says, "The last person to say that to me was

Archie Leach, just before he cut his throat!" Archie Leach was Grant's real name.

Grant tries to describe a character played by Ralph Bellamy. He ends up saying that he "looks like that film actor, Ralph Bellamy."

History of the World Part 1 (1981)

In the Ancient Roman segment, Mel Brooks has to fight his black friend (Gregory Hines) to the death at the coliseum in a scene reminiscent of *Spartacus* (1960), but they escape in a scene in which white chariot horses outrun black ones, a reference to *Ben-Hur* (1959).

"The French Revolution" section has numerous references to the similar *The Three Musketeers* (1974). Spike Milligan makes a guest appearance as a filthy prisoner, parodying his cameo in *The Three Musketeers*. Also, like the previous film, there is a royal chess game with living pieces. The pieces, which are commoners here, were dogs in the original.

Hold Back the Dawn (1941)

When Iscovescu appears at the Paramount soundstage to peddle his life story to director Mitchell Leisen (who plays himself), Veronica Lake and Richard Webb are shown rehearsing a scene from *I Wanted Wings* (1941), which was also directed by Leisen. This scene was actually filmed during the production of *I Wanted Wings*.

Holiday Inn (1942)

The animated Thanksgiving sequence is a topical reference to President Roosevelt's failed attempt to change the date of the holiday.

Hollywood Boulevard (1976)

Dick Miller plays agent Walter Paisley, using the name of his character in the classic horror flick *A Bucket of Blood* (1959). He went on to use this name in later films as well.

The "actor" who cons Candy into robbing a bank is named Duke Mantee, and his partner, who doublecrosses them, is named Rico Bandello. Duke Mantee was the name of Humphrey Bogart's character in *The Petrified Forest* (1936), and Rico Bandello was the name of the gangster played by Edward G. Robinson in *Little Caesar* (1930).

Just before he is shot by the cops and his car flips over, Rico says, "Is this the end of Rico?" This was Edward G. Robinson's famous last line in *Little Caesar*.

Director Erich von Leppe (played by director Paul Bartel) is named after director Erich von Stroheim. He says he hates actresses, then screams at them, "You're cattle!" This is a reference to director Alfred Hitchcock's statement, "Actors are cattle."

The other two films being shown at the drive-in with Candy's film are called *Zombie in the Attic* and *Moonmen from Mars*. The first one is actually scenes from the Roger Corman film *The Terror* (1963), costarring Dick Miller. Paisley (Miller) even points himself out in the film. *Moonmen from Mars* also features scenes from Corman's *Battle Beyond the Sun* (1963). Low-budget filmmaker Corman gave both this film's directors, Alan Arkush and Joe Dante, their starts in film.

Screenwriter Charles B. Griffith, a longtime collaborator of Corman's, has a cameo as Mark Dentine, the washed-up '50s movie star cleaning Patrick's pool.

Forrest J Ackerman appears uncredited at the film premiere at the end. After the champagne glasses are filled, he is seen on the right side of the screen, raising his glass in a toast, "To Hollywood!" Ackerman was the creator of the first successful sci-fi/horror magazine, *Famous Monsters of Filmland*.

Robby the Robot from *Forbidden Planet* (1956) has a cameo, serving drinks at the premiere. When Paisley asks him if he has been in films, he answers, "Not recently."

Home Alone (1990)

Macaulay Culkin's brother, Kieran, has a cameo as his cousin Fuller. He also appears in the sequel.

Home Alone 2: Lost in New York (1992)

Director Chris Columbus's daughter, Eleanor, plays a little girl in the toy store.

Ally Sheedy, who appeared in producer John Hughes's earlier film *The Breakfast Club* (1985), has a cameo as a New York ticket agent.

Honey, I Blew Up the Kid (1992)

The sled Rosebud from *Citizen Kane* (1941) and the Ark of the Covenant from *Raiders of the Lost Ark* (1981) are visible in the government warehouse.

John Hora, this film's cinematographer, appears as the helicopter observer.

Honeymoon in Vegas (1992)

Sid Feder, the bald man eating his sandwich at the poker game, is played by longtime college basketball coach Jerry Tarkanian.

Betsy (Sarah Jessica Parker) is first seen talking with the mother of David, a depressed little kid who is playing a

video game. David is played by director Andrew Bergman's son, Teddy.

Hook (1991)

Set designer Norman Garwood enjoyed throwing in "little gags" while creating Pirate Town and its various store names. One example: Dick Moby's Whale Burgers, which has a sign that says "Over 80 Sold" and a "Sail Thru" lane.

When Tootles (Arthur Malet) floats out the window at the end, he says, "Seize the day!," which was the name of a 1986 Robin Williams film and also his motto for his students in *Dead Poets Society* (1989) (see *Dead Poets Society*, 1989).

Smee (Bob Hoskins) says, "Gooooood morning, Neverland!," a reference to Williams's *Good Morning, Vietnam* (1987).

The bearded pirate punished by Captain Hook is played, uncredited, by actress Glenn Close.

Hook, Line and Sinker (1969)

Peter J. Ingers (Jerry Lewis) poses as an Australian sheepherder named Fred C. Dobbs. Fred C. Dobbs was the name of Humphrey Bogart's character in *The Treasure of the Sierra Madre* (1948).

Hope and Glory (1987)

The German pilot who is shot down is played by director John Boorman's son, Charley.

Hot Shots! (1991)

The opening and closing sequences are parodies of similar scenes in *Dances with Wolves* (1990). Many of the "Indian" words spoken in these scenes are actually the names of cities, counties and lakes in Minnesota, the home of screenwriter Pat Proft. The Old

One's name is Owatonna, which is a city south of Minneapolis. Other names spoken are Minnetonka (a suburb of Minneapolis), Shakopee (a city just south of Minneapolis), Itasca (a northern county containing Lake Winnibigoshish), Orono (a city west of Minneapolis), Winnebago (a town 15 miles north of the midpoint of the Iowa border) and Minnetrista, translated as "We did" (a city southwest of Minneapolis). The Old One asks for batteries by saying "Latoya Tito Jermaine." These are the names of three of the singing Jackson family. And the word used for "She threw me a curve" is "Hershiser." Orel Hershiser is a major league baseball pitcher.

The movie is basically a parody of *Top Gun* (1986), but some other film parodies appear as well.

When Lloyd Bridges knocks Efrem Zimbalist, Jr., down a flight of stairs, Zimbalist lands in a dentist chair. The dentist asks him, "Is it safe?" This is a parody of a similar scene in *Marathon Man* (1976), with Sir Laurence Olivier as the sadistic dentist. The dentist in this film even looks like Olivier.

The scene with Ramada (Valeria Golino) and Topper (Charlie Sheen) in front of the fridge involving all the food is a parody of a similar sex scene between Kim Basinger and Mickey Rourke in the film *9 1/2 Weeks* (1986).

When the ambulance hits Dead Meat (William O'Leary), catapulting him across the crater, he cries, "Wendy! I can fly!" This is a line from *Peter Pan* (1953).

At Dead Meat's funeral, Admiral Benson (Lloyd Bridges) says that Dead Meat is dead. He adds, "So is Moe Green, Tattaglia, Barzini. The heads of all five families." This is a line from *The Godfather* (1972).

The two basketball players in the bar fight scene are Charles Barkley and Bill Laimbeer, who had a real-life feud with each other in the NBA for some time.

There are many little jokes in the final credits, as there are in the credits of most Zucker Brothers/Jim Abrahams films, but one of them in this film is notable: "Things to do after the movie—(among other things) Visit a dairy and see how milk is handled and prepared for delivery." This was a lesson learned by Evan Kim at the end of the "Fistful of Yen" portion of director Jim Abrahams's film (as writer), *Kentucky Fried Movie* (1977).

Hot Shots! Part Deux (1993)

Richard Crenna plays Col. Denton Walters, after the character he played on the 1950s television series, *Our Miss Brooks*, Walter Denton.

At one point, Topper Harley (Charlie Sheen) rides atop a boat making notes about his mission, and his voice is heard in a voice-over, all reminiscent of his dad's role in *Apocalypse Now* (1979). However, he is interrupted by his father, Martin Sheen, playing the part he played in *Apocalypse Now* (Martin appears uncredited here). They see each other, stand up, and both say, "I loved you in *Wall Street*!" Martin played Charlie's father in *Wall Street* (1987).

The "other man" in the movie, played by Rowan Atkinson, is named "Dexter Hayman," a slight variation on "Dexter Haven," who was Cary Grant's "other man" character in the famous love triangle film, *The Philadelphia Story* (1940).

The main film being spoofed here is *Rambo III* (1988) (which also costarred Crenna in a similar role), with a few other film references thrown in for good measure:

The spaghetti scene between Harley and Ramada (Valeria Golino) with the balladeers is a parody of a similar scene in *Lady and the Tramp* (1955).

The sex scene in the back of the limo spoofs the similar scene between Kevin Costner and Sean Young in *No Way Out* (1987).

Michelle (Brenda Bakke) uncrossing her legs, saying, "What are they gonna do? Arrest me for smoking?" and tying Harley to the bed with scarves during their sex scene are all references to Sharon Stone in *Basic Instinct* (1992).

Saddam Hussein freezes solid and shatters, then melts into metallic blobs and reforms just like the evil T-2000 terminator in *Terminator 2: Judgment Day* (1991).

When Hussein shatters, his little dog shatters with him, and when he reforms, bits of the dog are incorporated in with him (ears, nose), just as bits of the fly were incorporated with Seth Brundle (Jeff Goldblum) in *The Fly* (1986).

President Benson (Lloyd Bridges) throwing up on Japanese PM Soto (Clyde Kusatsu) is a reference to the real-life incident where United States President George Bush threw up on the Japanese prime minister.

The patrol boat that attacks Topper's fishing boat is called the *Behn Gazaarah*, after actor Ben Gazzara. All of the mideastern language that is spoken is gibberish with a couple of celebrities' names here and there, including "Kareem," "Al Jarreau," "Omar Sharif," and, when Topper blinds Hussein with stick-em notes, Saddam yells, "Ali MacGraw! My eyes!"

The president (Lloyd Bridges) goes scuba diving to rescue the team, bringing to mind Bridges's old television series, *Sea Hunt*. The theme from *Sea Hunt* is even heard when Benson jumps into the water.

At one point, Miguel Ferrer pops up and proclaims, "War! It's *fan*tastic!" This was the slogan used by the National Basketball Association in a series of commercials, with "The NBA" replacing "War."

House of Bamboo (1955)

Director Sam Fuller has a cameo as a Japanese cop.

The House on Skull Mountain (1974)

This black voodoo-horror film was shot in Atlanta, and Georgia senator Leroy Johnson has a cameo as the lawyer who reads the will.

House Party (1990)

Producer Warrington Hudlin and his brother, writer-director Reginald Hudlin, play the two crooks.

How to Marry a Millionaire (1953)

Lauren Bacall, who was then married to Humphrey Bogart (star of *The African Queen*, 1951), says in conversation, "That old man in *The African Queen*, I'm crazy about him."

Betty Grable fails to recognize a Harry James recording. Grable was married to James at the time.

How to Stuff a Wild Bikini (1965)

Elizabeth Montgomery appears uncredited as Big Bwana's daughter, the witch's witch. Montgomery became famous playing the witch Samantha Stevens on the series *Bewitched*.

The Howling (1981)

Director Joe Dante's mentor, B-movie director Roger Corman, appears uncredited near the beginning of the film. He goes into the telephone booth after Karen White (Dee Wallace) leaves and checks the coin return.

Corman is well-known for making films with the lowest budget possible.

Forrest J Ackerman appears uncredited as the customer in the occult bookstore who is playing with the tarot cards. Ackerman was the creator of the first successful sci-fi/horror magazine, *Famous Monsters of Filmland*.

The film's screenwriter, John Sayles, appears uncredited as the morgue attendant.

Famed animator Chuck Jones appears uncredited as the bar patron at the end who says that Karen White really turned into a werewolf.

After he is bitten by the werewolf, Bill Neill (Christopher Stone) is seen lying in bed reading *You Can't Go Home Again* by Tom Wolfe.

When Karen calls her friends, Dennis Dugan and Belinda Balaski, they are watching *The Wolf Man* (1941) on television. Another scene is shown at the very end of the closing credits.

When Dugan is talking to Balaski on the phone about Eddie Quist, a copy of Allen Ginsberg's book *Howl* is seen on the table in front of him and he is watching a cartoon version of *The Big Bad Wolf* on television.

Afterwards, he calls sheriff Slim Pickens, who is seen talking on the phone and eating Wolf brand chili.

Almost all of the film's characters are named after classic horror film directors:

Patrick Macnee plays therapist George Waggner, named after the director of Lon Chaney, Jr.'s, *The Wolf Man* (1941).

Kevin McCarthy plays "the old man," head of KDHB news Frederick W. Francis. Freddie Francis directed *Legend of the Werewolf* (1975).

Christopher Stone plays the lead, Bill Neill. R. William Neill directed *Frankenstein Meets the Wolf Man* (1943).

Belinda Balaski plays Dee Wallace's friend Terry Fisher. Terence Fisher was the director of *The Curse of the Werewolf* (1961).

Jim McKrell plays Wallace's coanchor Lew Landers. Lew Landers directed the film *The Return of the Vampire* (1943), in which the vampire, Bela Lugosi, has an assistant who is a werewolf.

Ivan Baric plays Jack Molina. Jacinto Molina was the real name of Paul Naschy, Spain's number one film star of the '70s. He was the writer, director and star of a long list of horror films, including the 3-D *Mark of the Werewolf* (1968), *Nights of the Werewolf* (1969), *The Werewolf's Shadow* (1970), *Fury of the Wolfman* (1970), *Dr. Jekyll and the Werewolf* (1971) and *Return of the Werewolf* (1980). Molina's lycanthropic character in the films was named Waldemar Daninsky, better known in his homeland as El Hombre Lobo.

When Karen returns to the news set after her experience in the X-rated theater, the announcer's voice calls out the names of the news crew, including the sportscaster, Gene Fowler. Gene Fowler, Jr., was the director of *I Was a Teen-age Werewolf* (1957).

The morgue attendant mentions that his coworker was brought in once, with water leaking from his ears. His name was Stu Walker. Stuart Walker directed *Werewolf of London* (1935).

James Murtaugh plays an encounter group participant, Jerry Warren (*Frankenstein Island*, 1981; *Man Beast*, 1955).

Noble Willingham plays a farmer at the colony named Charlie (Charles T.) Barton (*Abbott and Costello Meet Frankenstein*, 1948).

Slim Pickens plays sheriff Sam Newfield (*Dead Men Walk*, 1943).

John Carradine plays aged, despairing colonist Earle Kenton. Carradine actually worked with the real Earle Kenton in *House of Frankenstein* (1944) and *House of Dracula* (1945).

In addition, Dick Miller plays an occult bookstore owner named Walter Paisley (see *Hollywood Boulevard*, 1976).

Dante has developed a "road company" of sorts, a group of actors who regularly appear in supporting roles in his pictures. Actors in this film include Balaski, Miller, McCarthy, and Robert Picardo.

Hudson Hawk (1991)

The notes that the handcuffs make are identical to the ones heard on the red telephones in *Our Man Flint* (1965) and *In Like Flint* (1967), starring *Hudson Hawk* villain James Coburn.

Coburn plays "George Kaplan," which was the name of the fake agent in *North by Northwest* (1959).

The Hudsucker Proxy (1994)

Writer and second unit director Sam Raimi has a cameo as a brainstormer.

The Hunt for Red October (1990)

The first scene (showing that Jack Ryan is afraid of flying) and the last scene (showing him on an airplane with an oversized teddy bear) are references to the opening sequence of director John McTiernan's *Die Hard* (1988). In fact, he is the same teddy bear from *Die Hard*, "Stanley," and is listed in the credits as playing himself.

Director John McTiernan's father, John McTiernan, Sr., plays one of the military advisors.

Co-scripter Larry Ferguson appears as the Chief of the Boat on the USS *Dallas*. He is the one who tells Jonesy (Courney B. Vance), "I seen me a mermaid once..."

The Hypnotic Eye (1959)

Fred Demara plays an actor impersonating a doctor. Demara, a professional con man best known for his incredibly authentic impersonations, was known as "The Great Impostor." Tony Curtis played him in the film *The Great Impostor* (1960).

I Come in Peace (1990)

At the hospital, Smith (Brian Benben) commandeers a pay phone from a young woman. She is played by director Craig R. Baxley's daughter, Kristin.

I Confess (1953)

Director Alfred Hitchcock crosses the top of a staircase after the opening credits.

I Know My First Name Is Steven (1989 TV)

This story, starring Corin Nemec as kidnap victim Steven Stayner, is based on a real-life story. The real Steven Stayner has a cameo as a cop. He died in a motorcycle accident soon after this film was aired.

I Love Trouble (1994)

The student librarian is played by Annie Meyers-Shyer, daughter of director Charles Shyer and screenwriter Nancy Meyers. Her little sister, Hallie, also appears as a girl in a barn.

I Love You to Death (1990)

Kevin Kline's wife, Phoebe Cates, appears as one of Kline's paramours.

Director Lawrence Kasdan appears as a lawyer, and screenwriter John Kostmayer plays Benny.

Kasdan's son, Jon, appears as Dominic.

I Wanna Hold Your Hand (1978)

Victor Brandt plays the theater cop named Foley in Bob Gale and Robert Zemeckis's script (see *1941*, 1979).

If Looks Could Kill (1991)

Director William Dear has a cameo as the bomb tester.

In Like Flint (1967)

The bad guys (women, actually) devise a plot to replace the president of the United States with a look-alike. When he learns of the plot, Flint pauses and says slowly "An *actor* for a president?" The film was shot when Ronald Reagan was governor of California and was being touted as a presidential candidate.

In the Good Old Summertime (1949)

The little girl standing between Van Johnson and Judy Garland in the final scene of the film is actually a 2½-year-old actress making her film debut. It was Liza Minnelli, daughter of Garland and the film's director, Vincente Minnelli.

In the Mood (1987)

In the closing credits, it says that the real Sonny Wisecarver is alive and well in Southern California. He owns his own business. He also appears in the film as the mailman in the newsreel who gives his opinion on Wisecarver. Incidentally, the newsreel is narrated by Carl Reiner, who went uncredited.

In the Mouth of Madness (1995)

The town of Hobb's End is a reference to the film *Quatermass and the Pit* (1967). In that film, it was explained that Hobb was an old reference to the Devil, and Hobb's End was the name of the London neighborhood in the film which is visited by demons and other evil spirits. Director John Carpenter is a fan of Quatermass creator Nigel Kneale's work, and he even credited his screenplay for *Prince of Darkness* (1988) to "Martin Quatermass," but the Hobb's End reference was not his doing. Carpenter has said, "I did work on the script, bringing a clarity to certain scenes, but the references were always there. [Scriptwriter Michael] De Luca is the ultimate horror fan, the ultimate cinephile, who knows the Quatermass films inside out. If anything, he called on me to direct the picture precisely because of my own love for the same things."

In the Spirit (1990)

Coscripter Laurie Jones also plays Pamela in the film.

In This Our Life (1942)

This was director John Huston's second film, and, in the roadhouse scene, the stars of Huston's first film, *The Maltese Falcon* (1941), are seen sitting at a table. They are Humphrey Bogart, Mary Astor, Peter Lorre, Sydney Greenstreet, Ward Bond, Barton MacLane and Elisha Cook, Jr. Lee Patrick, who also starred in *The Maltese Falcon*, appears in a supporting role in this one as well.

Huston's father, Walter, appears in a cameo as the bartender. Walter also had a cameo in his son's first film.

Indecent Proposal (1993)

Diana (Demi Moore) is seen reading *The Firm*, which was to be Paramount Pictures' next big film.

The secretary at the real estate office is seen reading *Backlash*, a book which criticizes this film's director, Adrian Lyne, for his portrayal of women in previous films.

Independence Day (1996)

The Day the Earth Stood Still (1951), which was about friendly aliens arriving on Earth, is seen on the Casse family television set in the motorhome.

The opening fly-by of the alien ship was very reminiscent of the opening shot of *Star Wars* (1977). Coincidentally, this shot was also parodied in the opening shot of *Spaceballs* (1987), which starred Bill Pullman, who appears in *Independence Day* as the U.S. president.

As Russell Casse (Randy Quaid) prepares to destroy the alien ship, he tells the other fighters, "Just hold 'em off me for a few seconds…" This exact line was used in the Battle of Yavin sequence in *Star Wars*.

Jasmine (Vivica Fox) tells her stripper friend Tiffany, "I have a really bad feeling about this," just before Tiffany goes to greet the aliens. This was the lamentation of many characters in the *Star Wars* trilogy.

The field that Casse was supposed to dust was Lucas' Field, owned by Lucas, the guy who brings his dead plants to Casse's children. Lucas was named after *Star Wars* director George Lucas.

Many scenes have been pointed out as being similar to famous *Star Wars* scenes, including the escape from the mother ship at the end (the Millenium Falcon's escape from the exploding Death Star in *Return of the Jedi*, 1983) and the dogfight in the canyon (the dogfight in the asteroid belt in *The Empire Strikes Back*).

When the TV station is taking calls about the lack of television reception, one operator says, "I love *The X-Files*, too. I hope you get to watch it."

Another, more subtle *X-Files* reference: as the jets attack the alien ship for the first time, there is a screen back

at the base showing the status of 12 of them (three by four). They blink out one by one as the planes are destroyed. The third one across in the second row lasts until the very end (presumably Will Smith's plane). Its number code on the screen: 1121. This number is commonly used as an in-joke in the series *The X-Files*. It is the birthdate of creator Chris Carter's wife (November 21).

The aliens are destroyed by giving their shields a "virus." In the film *The War of the Worlds* (1953), the invading Martians are defeated because they contract a virus for the common cold, which turns out to be deadly to them.

Another *War of the Worlds* reference: In that film, the aliens are nuked (ineffectually) by a Northrop YB-49 flying-wing jet bomber. In *Independence Day*, the aliens are nuked (ineffectually) by a Northrop B-2 flying-wing jet bomber, which is a direct descendant of the YB-49.

Independence Day and *War of the Worlds* have a lot in common. The basic story of both films is virtually identical: The aliens land ships in strategic positions all across the planet, then launch a coordinated attack. Conventional weapons are used against them but prove ineffective against enemy shields. An analysis of the alien movements shows they are systematically wiping out all resistance across the planet. Nukes are eventually used on them (by a flying wing aircraft) and the effect is reported by forward observers in a protected position peering through the dust and debris. The nukes are also stopped by the shields. Finally the aliens are defeated by a virus (both films refer to cold viruses in particular).

David Levinson (Jeff Goldblum) gets into the alien ship, turns on the monitor, and a red light comes on the screen and the words "Good morning, Dave" are seen and heard. These were the introductory words said to David Bowman (Keir Dullea) by HAL the computer in *2001: A Space Odyssey* (1968). The red light looks exactly like one of HAL's "eyes" from that film.

A helicopter is sent to communicate with one of the ships using flashing lights mounted on it, bringing to mind the communication scene in *Close Encounters of the Third Kind* (1977).

After he shoots it down, Smith punches the alien and says, "Now that's what I call a close encounter," referring to *Close Encounters of the Third Kind*.

The scene in which Steve (Will Smith) first sees the saucer is, shot-for-shot, the same as the scene in *Close Encounters* where Richard Dreyfuss encounters the family on the mountain waiting to see the UFOs. Smith's slow turn to look up and over his shoulder gives it away.

The Statue of Liberty is used in early scenes to help establish the setting as the Fourth of July (engraved on its tablet), but, in the first scene of July 3, the statue is seen destroyed, bringing to mind the final scene of *Planet of the Apes* (1968).

Erick Avari, who had starred in writer Dean Devlin and director Roland Emmerich's previous film *Stargate* (1994) as the leader of the people on the alien planet, has an uncredited cameo in this picture. He is the head of the SETI team who wakes up and bangs his head on his lamp.

Veteran character actor Tracey Walter also has an uncredited bit part. He is a scientist at Area 51. He can be seen around the spaceship and in the "alien autopsy" scene.

As Goldblum and Will Smith escape the aliens' mother ship, the doors start to close and Goldblum says "Must go faster ... must go faster..." This was the line Goldblum used when he was being chased in a jeep by the Tyrannosaurus Rex in *Jurassic Park* (1993).

The "Oops!" dialogue between Goldblum and Smith in the spaceship is a direct reference to a comedy routine by Bill Cosby. Goldblum utters the line, "What you doin' sayin' 'Oops' there?" which is, word-for-word, from Cosby's routine.

The shot at the end of the film showing Goldblum and Smith walking across the desert away from their smoldering ship is very reminiscent of the scene at the end of *The Right Stuff* (1983) which showed Chuck Yeager (Sam Shepard) walking away from his downed airplane.

Rance Howard has a speaking part as the chaplain at Area 51 who marries Will Smith and his fiancée. This is possibly a reference to the priest Rance played in his son Ron Howard's *Apollo 13* (1995). In the first film, Rance had speaking lines but they were cut. His only remaining scene consisted of him sitting in the living room of the Lovell home, watching television.

The film's producers probably knew that the film's competition would include *Striptease* (1996) and *The Cable Guy* (1996): there are characters in this film who are a stripper (Vivica Fox) and a cable guy (Jeff Goldblum).

After the opening scenes on the moon, the camera cuts to SETI with a scientist playing golf, a reference to astronaut Alan Shepard's golf shot while on the moon.

During the briefing, Smith said he was eager to go "whup E.T.'s ass." This may also be a reference to the film breaking the box office records of the film *E.T., the Extra-Terrestrial* (1982), one of the highest-grossing films ever.

In the film, *Entertainment Tonight* reports on the landing of the spaceships, and the show's logo, "ET," appears prominently on the screen (a subtle reference to *E.T., the Extra-Terrestrial*).

Quaid lamenting "Looks like I picked a bad day to give up drinking" could be a reference to Lloyd Bridges's repeated lines in the *Airplane!* movies.

The first time we see Dylan, Jasmine's son, he runs past his Godzilla toys on his way to wake up his mom and Steve. The next film that director Roland Emmerich and writer Dean Devlin planned to make was *Godzilla*.

The news clips in the film appear on Sky Television and the Fox network, both owned by Rupert Murdoch, who also owns 20th Century–Fox. *Independence Day* was made by 20th Century–Fox.

Brent Spiner's character, Dr. Okun, is named after special effects artist Jeffrey Okun, who worked with Emmerich and Devlin on their previous film, *Stargate*.

Indiana Jones and the Last Crusade (1989)

As Elsa Schneider (Alison Doody) and Indy walk through the catacombs beneath the library, she spots a carving on the wall and points it out to Indy, who identifies it as the Ark of the Covenant. She asks, "Are you sure?" He answers, "Pretty sure," in reference to his adventures in *Raiders of the Lost Ark* (1981).

Indy and his father (Sean Connery) break off from the German blimp in a biplane, and Indy remarks that he knows how to fly a plane but not how to land one (from *Temple of Doom*).

When making *Star Wars* (1977), George Lucas owned a dog named "Indiana." In this film, it is revealed that Indy got his nickname from the family dog.

The dog that is barking when young Indy passes with the cross in his hand is an Alaskan Malamute, the same type of dog that Lucas's Indiana was.

Walter's (Julian Glover) wife, who tells him that his guests are asking about him, is played by Glover's wife. She is listed in the credits only as "Mrs. Glover."

Indiana Jones and the Temple of Doom (1984)

In gratitude for being cast as a small claims clerk in *The Blues Brothers* (1980), Steven Spielberg cast Dan Aykroyd as the English ticket agent who greets the heroes at the airport. Aykroyd has said that he just showed up on the set one day and asked, "What part can I play?"

Director Steven Spielberg and producers George Lucas and Frank Marshall all have cameos during the car ride from the club to the airport. Lucas and Spielberg play missionaries in long black coats and pith helmets at the airport, and Marshall plays a rickshaw driver.

The opening sequence is set in a posh Hong Kong bar, and as the cars drive by the front, its name is seen— Club Obi Wan, after the name of producer George Lucas's *Star Wars* character.

Short Round (Ke Huy Quan) is named after screenwriter Willard Huyck's dog, which was named after the orphan in the film *The Steel Helmet* (1951).

Indy, wielding his whip, meets two sword-toting guards near the rope bridge. Smiling, he reaches for his gun, so that he can simply shoot them like he did in the famous scene in *Raiders of the Lost Ark* (1981), but he realizes that he doesn't have his gun, so he has to fight them off with his whip. This was originally how the scene in *Raiders* was supposed to be filmed (see *Raiders of the Lost Ark*, 1981). So he kills off one guard, and the other runs off. With a bellow, Indy runs after him, but, seconds later, he stops with a look of surprise on his face. He turns and runs away, hotly pursued by many guards. This was a reworking of a similar scene of Ford's in *Star Wars* (1977) when, as Han Solo, he went chasing after a Stormtrooper on the Death Star.

Inner Sanctum II (1994)

Director Fred Olen Ray has a cameo as Officer Scott.

Innerspace (1987)

The patients in the doctor's waiting room are played by Joe Flaherty and Andrea Martin, Martin Short's costars from *SCTV*.

As Tuck (Dennis Quaid) is fighting with the other pilots in the kitchen at the film's start, Lydia (Meg Ryan) interviews an official in a suit. He is played by the film's screenwriter, Jeffrey Boam.

Longtime animation director Chuck Jones has a cameo in the checkout line at Jack's store. He comments on the price of aspirin.

Ozzie Wexler, the scientist who injects Dennis Quaid into Short, is played by John Hora, who was the cinematographer for many of director Joe Dante's films (*The Howling*, 1981; *Gremlins*, 1984), though not this one. His character is named after famed cinematographer Haskell Wexler.

The words "Eat Me" and "Drink Me" appear on a computer screen during reenlargement. Jack (Martin Short)

correctly identifies them as being from *Alice in Wonderland*, but his first guess is that the words are from *The Exorcist* (1973). This is a reference to the possessed Regan's constant chant of "Lick me!" in that film.

After Jack and Lydia are captured by the bad guys, Dr. Canker (Fiona Lewis) makes a phone call and Scrimshaw (Kevin McCarthy) puts his jacket on. In the background, beside the oriental chef, a pod from McCarthy's *Invasion of the Body Snatchers* (1956) can be seen on the ground.

Scrimshaw's chef is named "Murnau," after groundbreaking German film director F.W. Murnau (*The Last Laugh*, 1924).

Innocent Blood (1992)

Director John Landis has a habit of casting his fellow directors in cameos in his films. Directors in this film include:

Dario Argento (*Suspiria*, 1977; *Two Evil Eyes*, 1990) as the paramedic who tells Don Rickles that he is going to be fine.

Frank Oz (*Dirty Rotten Scoundrels*, 1988; *What About Bob?* 1991) as the pathologist who prepares to autopsy Macelli (Robert Loggia), but ends up chasing him through the hospital.

Sam Raimi (*The Evil Dead*, 1983; *Darkman*, 1990) as the man at Roma Meats, where Macelli beds down for the day in the meat locker.

Michael Ritchie (*The Bad News Bears*, 1976; *Fletch*, 1985) as the night watchman at the yard where Macelli takes LaPaglia to kill him with a garbage truck.

In addition, makeup artist/actor Tom Savini (*Dawn of the Dead*, 1979; *Friday the 13th*, 1980), who also directed *Night of the Living Dead*

(1990), appears as the news photographer in the car that Macelli's goons scare off. He later tells Anthony LaPaglia that Macelli is still alive.

Science fiction personality Forrest J Ackerman appears as the man who has his car stolen by the newly undead Macelli. Ackerman was the creator of the first successful sci-fi/horror magazine, *Famous Monsters of Filmland*.

The film's writer/associate producer, Michael Wolk, plays the surgeon who appears at the door just in time to see Rickles's head disintegrate.

The nurse who has Rickles's arm come off in her hands and then runs away screaming in an exaggerated, over-the-top manner is played by long-time horror film "scream queen" Linnea Quigley.

To salute the king of directorial cameos, Landis included Alfred Hitchcock's cameo in *Strangers on a Train* (1951), where he is loading a double bass fiddle onto a train, on the television set in Rickles's hospital room.

See You Next Wednesday is advertised on the marquee across the street from the Melody Lounge exotic dance bar. The car crash at the Shadyside gas station was filmed in Squirrel Hill, and the nearby multiplex cinema changed its marquee to *See You Next Wednesday* every night after closing. The film itself featured no footage of that theater (or the street on which it resides), although it might have been edited out (see *Schlock*, 1971).

An Innocent Man (1989)

The detective's office is a replica of the office in the sixth season episode "Find Me a Rainbow" of star Tom Selleck's series *Magnum, P.I.* The window of the office was also seen in the *Magnum P.I.* episode "Murder By Night."

Internal Affairs (1990)

Director Mike Figgis has a cameo as Hollander.

Producer Frank Mancuso, Jr., has a bit part as the radio cop.

Into the Night (1985)

Director John Landis has a habit of casting his fellow directors in cameos in his films. Directors in this film include:

Jack Arnold (*The Creature from the Black Lagoon*, 1954; *The Incredible Shrinking Man*, 1957) as a man in an elevator with a "nice dog."

Paul Bartel (*Eating Raoul*, 1982; *Lust in the Dust*, 1985) as the top-hatted doorman of the Beverly Wilshire Hotel.

David Cronenberg (*Dead Ringers*, 1988; *The Fly*, 1986) as Jeff Goldblum's group supervisor in the boardroom.

Jonathan Demme (*Philadelphia*, 1993; *The Silence of the Lambs*, 1991) as the Federal Agent (thin, wearing glasses) who shoots a terrorist and argues with Clu Gulager in the hotel room at the end.

Richard Franklin (*Cloak & Dagger*, 1984; *Psycho II*, 1983) as the aerospace engineer sitting next to Dan Aykroyd in the cafeteria.

Carl Gottlieb (*Caveman*, 1981; *Amazon Women on the Moon*, 1987) as the Federal Agent (plump, sporting a moustache) who argues with Clu Gulager in the motel room at the end.

Amy Heckerling (*Fast Times at Ridgemont High*, 1982; *Look Who's Talking*, 1989) as Amy, the waitress in the Ship's Restaurant.

Jim Henson (*The Great Muppet Caper*, 1981; *Labyrinth*, 1986) as the man who Carl Perkins tells to get off of the phone. By the way, the person Henson is talking to is named "Bert," after Henson's Muppet, voice of Frank Oz.

Colin Higgins (*9 to 5*, 1980; *The Best Little Whorehouse in Texas*, 1982) as the actor playing a terrorist at a beauty concert.

Lawrence Kasdan (*The Big Chill*, 1983; *Body Heat*, 1981) as the detective interrogating Bud Herman with his jacket slung over his shoulder.

Jonathan Kaufer (*Soup for One*, 1982) as the script clerk on the film set.

Jonathan Lynn (*Clue*, 1985; *My Cousin Vinny*, 1992) as the tailor trying to fit the four Iranians.

Andrew Marton (*The Longest Day*, 1962; *King Solomon's Mines*, 1950) as the driver ogling dirty pictures in the traffic jam at the beginning.

Paul Mazursky (*Harry and Tonto*, 1974; *Down and Out in Beverly Hills*, 1986) as Bud Herman, beachhouse owner and accused drug dealer.

Daniel Petrie (*A Raisin in the Sun*, 1961; *Fort Apache: The Bronx*, 1981) as the director of the television hostage-taking.

Don Siegel (*Invasion of the Body Snatchers*, 1956; *Dirty Harry*, 1971) as the man caught with a girl in the bathroom of the Beverly Wilshire Hotel.

Roger Vadim (*Barbarella*, 1968; *...And God Created Woman*, 1956) as Monsieur Melville, the French kidnapper.

Landis himself appears in the film as the mute member of the quartet of Iranian vigilantes.

In the airport scene, there is a call over the P.A. system for a "Mr. Frank Oznowitz" to pick up the white courtesy phone. This is muppeteer-director Frank Oz's real name.

In addition, makeup artist Rick Baker (*The Exorcist*, 1973; *Star Wars*, 1977; *Batman Forever*, 1995) appears as a drug dealer who approaches Goldblum and Michelle Pfeiffer's car on the street. The hooker who appears just before Baker is played by Pfeiffer's sister, Dedee Pfeiffer.

Screenwriter Waldo Salt (*Serpico*, 1973; *Midnight Cowboy*, 1969) appears as the derelict who tells Goldblum that his car has been towed away by the cops.

Two *See You Next Wednesday* posters are seen on the wall in the office where Ed (Goldblum) and Diana (Pfeiffer) make their phone call (see *Schlock*, 1971).

Intruder (1988)

The "head in one hand, sandwich in another" speech was previously used in *Raising Arizona* (1987).

Invaders from Mars (1986)

Jimmy Hunt, who played the little kid in the original film *Invaders from Mars* (1953), appears here as the police chief. He says, "I haven't been here since I was a kid."

The alien from the original film also appears as a prop in the school basement.

Invasion of the Body Snatchers (1956)

Charlie, the meter reader in Dr. Miles Benell's (Kevin McCarthy) basement, is played by director Sam Peckinpah (*Ride the High Country*, 1962; *The Wild Bunch*, 1969). Peckinpah, who contributed to the film's script, served as a dialogue director for director Don Siegel since Siegel's *Riot in Cell Block 11* (1954). He built up quite a reputation as a writer and director of TV westerns before he directed his first film in 1961, five years after his appearance in this one.

Invasion of the Body Snatchers (1978)

The original film's star and director, Kevin McCarthy and Don Siegel, both have cameos. Siegel appears as a cab driver and McCarthy is briefly seen, feverishly running down the street, warning passing motorists of the invasion, essentially playing the exact same character as he did in the original.

Robert Duvall appears in one shot as a priest on a swing.

Invasion of the Star Creatures (1962)

Longtime movie heavy Bruno Ve Sota directed this film and has a cameo role as well.

Invasion U.S.A. (1985)

Chuck Norris's brother, Aaron, who also received story credit for the film, has a cameo.

Irma La Douce (1963)

The pimps' union is called the Mecs' ("tough guys") Paris Protective Association, or the MPPA. MPPA also stands for Motion Picture Producers Association, an organization which gave director Billy Wilder much trouble.

Ironweed (1987)

A final credit of the film reads "In Memirium [sic]: Jon O'Connell, a Fellow Craftsman." O'Connell, the film's master set painter, was killed in a car crash.

Irreconcilable Differences (1984)

Director Charles Shyer and screenwriter Nancy Meyers cast their daughter, Annie Meyers-Shyer, as a little girl in a crowd.

It Happened in Athens (1962)

The American coach is played by Olympic runner Bob Mathias.

It's a Small World (1935)

Director William Castle has a cameo as a cop.

It's a Wonderful Life (1946)

After using a raven in his previous film, You Can't Take It with You (1938), director Frank Capra began using a raven in all of his films. It became his signature. In this film, it "starred" as Uncle Billy's (Thomas Mitchell) pet, Jimmy.

I've Heard the Mermaids Singing (1987)

Sheila McCarthy reads a review to Paul Baillargeon out of a newspaper. The name of the paper is The Toronto Globe and Star. There is no such paper, but the title is a combination of two real Canadian papers: The Toronto Star and The Globe and Mail. It's actually a mock-up paper that the prop people made from Section Two of an edition of The New York Times.

Jagged Edge (1985)

Visible in David and Jenny Barnes's bedroom is a poster for Return of the Jedi (1983), also directed by Richard Marquand.

Jason Goes to Hell: The Final Friday (1993)

Steven, the lead, is played by John D. LeMay, who had previously starred in the similarly-titled but otherwise unrelated Friday the 13th: The Series.

Officer Bish, the policeman that the Jason-possessed reporter Robert Campbell (Steven Culp) throws over the reception desk as he comes into the station, is played by the film's writer-director, Adam Marcus.

Marcus's brother, Kipp Marcus, also plays a cop in the film. He is Randy, the young deputy who is a friend of Steven's. He is the one who Steven tricks into letting him out of jail, then later beats up on the side of the road.

At the start of the film, an assistant

coroner makes fun of Jason, and is then killed by the coroner, who is possessed by Jason. The assistant coroner is played by the film's screenwriter, Dean Lorey.

The burly, bearded security guard at the hospital who calls Jason a "big ol' pussy" is played by the actor behind Jason's hockey mask, Kane Hodder.

After the Jason-possessed Robert Campbell is pumped full of bullets in the police station and left for dead, two police officers run up to him, check him out and get their heads bashed together. They are played by Los Angeles radio personalities Mark Thompson and Brian Phelps ("Mark and Brian").

The last shot features Freddy Krueger's gloved hand reaching out of the ground and pulling Jason's hockey mask down. Krueger was the antagonist of the "Nightmare on Elm Street" films, and he and Jason were considered to be the two big horror characters of the 1980s. The joke here is twofold. "A Nightmare on Elm Street 8" was supposed to be a showdown of Freddy vs. Jason, but it was never made. The last *Nightmare* film was called *Freddy's Dead: The Final Nightmare* (1991) (see this film's title), and this was the filmmakers' way of showing that Jason (and the *Friday the 13th* series of films) as well as Freddy (and the *Nightmare* series), were finally done.

Jaws (1975)

After the decision is made to keep the beaches open, Brody (Roy Scheider) and Hooper (Richard Dreyfuss) organize a task force to keep them safe. Meanwhile, a reporter in glasses walks along the sand, doing a story about "a cloud in the shape of a killer shark." The reporter is played by the

author of the book that this film is based on, Peter Benchley.

Meadows, the mayor's assistant, is played by Carl Gottlieb, who cowrote the film with Steven Spielberg.

When Mrs. Brody tries to contact her husband on the *Orca*, a man is heard on the radio, calling the ship. The radio operator's voice was provided by director Steven Spielberg.

Jesus of Montreal (1990)

Director Denys Arcand appears in the film as the judge.

The Jewel of the Nile (1985)

As Ralph (Danny DeVito) emerges into a huge crowd of swordsmen and other assorted rioters, he cracks, "Oh my God, look at this. Looks like Our Lady of Mt. Carmel schoolyard." Our Lady of Mt. Carmel was the grammar school DeVito attended in Asbury Park, New Jersey.

The Arabic speech in the climactic "stage" scene is supposedly made up of Arabic translations of the names of films of Michael Douglas's father, Kirk.

After Michael Douglas produced Diane Thomas's screenplay, *Romancing the Stone*, he expressed his appreciation by giving her a white Porsche. She died in an accident while driving the car, and so this film is dedicated to her memory.

JFK (1991)

The real Jim Garrison (Kevin Costner's character) appears in the film as Garrison's ultimate nemesis, Judge Earl Warren. Garrison had also played a New Orleans judge in *The Big Easy* (1987).

Joe Versus the Volcano (1990)

Joseph Banks (the name of Tom Hanks's character) was the name of

Captain Cook's chief botanist on his expeditions to the South Pacific in the 18th century.

Meg Ryan plays three roles in the film, and there is no real similarity between the three characters. However, the first time he meets each of these characters, even the first one, Joe (Tom Hanks) says, "You know, the first time I saw you, I thought I had seen you before."

Johnny Be Good (1988)

The NCAA investigator who follows Johnny through all the colleges is played by director Robert Downey, Sr. (*Putney Swope*, 1969; *Up the Academy*, 1980), father of the film's costar, Robert Downey, Jr.

The Joy Luck Club (1993)

Amy Tan, the writer of the book that this film was based on, appears during the first party scene, chatting with guests just beyond a doorway.

Judgment in Berlin (1988)

Sean Penn has a small role as a witness at the trial. Penn is the son of the film's director, Leo Penn.

Jumpin' Jack Flash (1986)

Director Penny Marshall cast her brother Garry as a police detective in the film.

Junior (1994)

The stewardess who asks Danny DeVito to take his seat is played by Judy Ovitz. Judy is the wife of Creative Artists' Agency head Michael Ovitz.

Film composer Ira Newborn (*The Naked Gun: From the Files of Police Squad*, 1988; *The Blues Brothers*, 1980) appears as a Lyndon executive.

Jurassic Park (1993)

Ellie Sattler (Laura Dern) says "Something went wrong" to Dr. Malcolm (Jeff Goldblum). This line was also spoken to Goldblum in *The Fly* (1986) by Geena Davis.

Just One of the Guys (1985)

The villain of this high school romance is named after Gregg Toland, who was the Academy Award–winning cinematographer of such films as *Wuthering Heights* (1939) and *Citizen Kane* (1941). Also, the name of the high school is Sturges-Wilder, referring to directors Preston Sturges and Billy Wilder.

Kalifornia (1993)

The four locations of the previous murders, all of which are shown on screen, incorporate the names of the four actors playing the leads. They are, in order: *Brad*bury Textile Warehouse, *Pitt*sburgh, Pennsylvania (Brad Pitt); the location of *Michael* Zaruba's murder spree, Novak Farm, *Forbes*, Tennessee (Michelle Forbes); *Lewis*ton Abattoir, Mt. *Juliet*, Texas (Juliette Lewis); and *David*son Mine, *Dew Cove, Ne*braska (David Duchovny).

Kenny Rogers as The Gambler—The Adventure Continues (1983 TV)

Johnny Crawford, who had starred in *The Virginian* years before, returned for this film to play Masket. He also appeared in *The Gambler Returns: The Luck of the Draw* (1991 TV) as his character from the series.

Kentucky Fried Movie (1977)

The film that Jeff Maxwell goes to see at the Rialto Theatre in Feel-Around is titled *See You Next Wednesday* (see *Schlock*, 1971).

There is also a poster for JohnLandis's

Schlock (71) behind the theater ticket booth.

Landis enjoyed putting folksinger Stephen Bishop in his films, credited as "Charming (something)." In this film, he is the "Charming Guy" who is told, "Show me your nuts."

Rick Baker plays a (possibly) impotent gorilla who destroys the set of *A.M. Today*. The gorilla is named Dino, after producer Dino DiLaurentiis, who did not get along with Baker during the filming of DiLaurentiis's *King Kong* (1976). Baker played Kong.

Master Klahn's hand, which is fitted with various attachments, is based on demented killer Patrick O'Neal's similar hand in *Chamber of Horrors* (1966). Many other film villains would go on to have similar attachments (*Innerspace*, 1987, and so on).

The segment "A Fistful of Yen" is a send-up of Bruce Lee–type kung fu films, and its name is a take-off of the spaghetti western, *A Fistful of Dollars* (1964). The segment contains many in-joke references to kung fu films of the time, including the deep scratch marks on Bruce Lee's cheeks. And, of course, the end is a *Wizard of Oz* (1939) spoof.

The "Cleopatra Schwartz" preview is a take-off of the *Cleopatra Jones* blaxploitation films of the 1970s.

"Schwartz," the rabbi, is played by Landis's publicist, Saul Kahan.

Casting director Michael Hanks also has a small role, as field reporter Ron Butler on *A.M. Today*.

Script supervisor Katherine Wooten was given a bit part as the woman who tries to wake her husband, who took Nytex P.M.

Landis's daughter, Tracy Landis, plays the girl behind the movie theater's snack bar counter.

The film's writers, Jim Abrahams, Jerry Zucker and David Zucker, who would later go on to direct such films as *Airplane!* (1980) and *The Naked Gun: From the Files of Police Squad* (1988), all have multiple cameos in the film. Steve McCrosky, the announcer in the courtroom scene, is played by Jim Abrahams. The man in the alarm-filled car is David Zucker, and the man who took Nytex P.M. and cannot wake up is Jerry Zucker. David and Jerry also appear in the courtroom sequence. David as the accused, Sheldon Grunwald, and Jerry is Theodore "Beaver" Cleaver (beside Tony Dow, who actually played Wally Cleaver on *Leave It to Beaver*). And all three, Jim, Jerry and David, play the technicians with the newscaster on television at the end of the film who watch the couple have sex.

Jerry and David also gave their mother, Charlotte, a cameo. She is the jury member who tells the court how to pronounce "heinous."

Forrest J Ackerman also appears in the jury. He's the second one in the front row. Ackerman was the creator of the first successful sci-fi/horror magazine, *Famous Monsters of Filmland*.

Key Exchange (1985)

Director Barnet Kellman appears in the film as a director.

Kika (1993)

The woman that interviews Nicholas on the television program about writers is the mother of director Pedro Almodovar.

The Killer Shrews (1959)

Baruch Lumet, the father of director Sidney Lumet, has a small part.

The Killer Who Wouldn't Die (1976 TV)

Mike Connors stars as Kirk Ohanian, a former cop who operates a charter boat service. This was supposed to be a pilot for a series called *Ohanian*. Kirk Ohanian is Connors's real name.

The Killers (1964)

The short order cook making hamburgers in the diner is played by director Don Siegel.

Kindergarten Cop (1990)

Director Ivan Reitman's son Jason appears as Jason and his daughter Catherine plays a third grade student in Penelope Ann Miller's class.

The King of Comedy (1983)

As with many of his films, director Martin Scorsese cast his family in small roles. His mother, Catherine, plays Rupert's (Robert De Niro) mother, his father Charles can be seen in a bar, his sister Cathy plays Dolores, Rupert's fan, and Scorsese himself plays the director of Jerry Langford's (Jerry Lewis) show.

Some of the "street scum" are played by Mick Jones, Joe Strummer, Paul Simonon, Dom Letts, Pearl Harbour and Ellen Foley. Jones, Strummer and Simonon were the rock group The Clash, and singer-actress Foley ("Paradise by the Dashboard Light" by Meat Loaf, *Night Court*) was Jones's girlfriend at the time. She even sang "Hitsville UK" on the Clash's album *Sandinista*. Letts and Mick Jones were original members of the group Big Audio Dynamite. Pearl Harbour and her band, The Explosions, were a popular San Francisco band in the early 1980s.

Martin Scorsese memorializes his late cook, Dan Johnson, in the credits. Johnson died of natural causes during the making of the film.

Kingpin (1996)

In a parody of Woody Harrelson's previous film, *Indecent Proposal* (1993), Chris Elliott offers Harrelson $1 million if he will let him sleep with "your friend here." Later on, Harrelson is seen covered in dollar bills, gleefully throwing them in the air, just as Demi Moore did in *Indecent Proposal*.

Randy Quaid runs away from his handlers and walks alone along the highway. Joyriding Indians zoom past and throw bags of garbage at him. The camera pans up from the trash to a profound close-up of the abject Quaid, one tear rolling down his cheek. This is a reference to the Public Service Commercials with Native American actor Iron Eyes Cody. In the commercial, Cody saw the waste the world is coming to and a lone tear trickled down his face.

During the film's climactic bowling scene, the audience becomes hushed, and suddenly an unseen character yells "Attaboy Luther!" but there is no credited character in the film named Luther. This is a reference to the Don Knotts film *The Ghost and Mr. Chicken* (1966). In that film, an unseen character yells "Attaboy Luther!" every time that Luther (Knotts) speaks in front of an audience.

Knightriders (1981)

Director George Romero's buddy, Stephen King, and King's wife, Tabitha, have cameos in the film. King is seen munching on a hoagie.

L.A. Story (1991)

Harris (Steve Martin) quotes poems that Martin previously quoted in *The Man with Two Brains* (1983).

La Bamba (1987)

Associate producer Daniel Valdez plays Lelo, and director Luis Valdez's daughter Kati appears as Ritchie's sister, Connie Jr.

Rock star Eddie Cochrane is played by Brian Setzer, lead singer of the Stray Cats.

The Ladies' Man (1961)

George Raft appears in a cameo reading the boxing magazine *Ring*. Early in his career, Raft was a professional boxer.

Ladies Who Do (1963)

The screenplay for this film was written by Michael Pertwee, and he wrote a small part for his brother, Jon Pertwee. Jon, who would later go on to fame as the second Doctor Who, appears here as Sidney Tait.

The Lady from Shanghai (1948)

There is no character in this film, male or female, from Shanghai. Director Orson Welles has said that he dreamed up the title to coax production money from studio boss Harry Cohn.

The Lady in the Lake (1946)

Crystal Kinsley, the character who never appears because she is dead, is listed as being played by Ellay Mort. "Elle est morte" is French for "she is dead."

Lady L (1965)

Writer-director Peter Ustinov has a cameo as Prince Otto.

The Lady Vanishes (1938)

Director Alfred Hitchcock appears very near the end of the movie, in Victoria Station, wearing a black coat and smoking a cigarette.

The Lair of the White Worm (1988)

As Mary (Sammi Davis) is telling Angus (Peter Capaldi) about the party at the start of the film, a neighbor passes by her farm and calls out, "Hi, Mary!" He is played by the film's director, Ken Russell.

The Langoliers (1995 TV)

Director Tom Holland has a cameo as Harker.

Larger Than Life (1996)

The film features a parody of *She Wore a Yellow Ribbon* (1949), with Bill Murray dressed up like John Wayne, Tai the elephant playing the role of Wayne's trusty steed, and the theme from *The Magnificent Seven* (1960) playing in the background.

Last Action Hero (1993)

The words "A Franco Columbu Film" appear on the screen at the beginning of *Jack Slater IV*. Columbu is a friend of Arnold Schwarzenegger and his former main bodybuilding rival.

Joan Plowright praises Laurence Olivier's performance in *Hamlet* (1948) in Austin O'Brien's class. Plowright is Olivier's widow.

In the film, Jack Slater (Schwarzenegger) exists in a world where there is no Arnold Schwarzenegger. He goes into a video store and sees a stand-up poster for *Terminator 2: Judgment Day* starring Sylvester Stallone. Schwarzenegger says, "He's fantastic! It's his best performance ever!" (see *Twins*, 1988)

Austin O'Brien tries to prove to Schwarzenegger all through the film that they are in a movie. When they first go to the drug dealers' house, Schwarzenegger starts to walk away, then turns and says, "I'll be back. Hah!

You didn't know I'm going to say that, did you?" O'Brien replies, "That's what you always say … Everybody keeps waiting for you to work it in. It's kind of like your calling card." Also, when Schwarzenegger leaves his house to go find a cigar, he turns to say the line, but O'Brien cuts him off, "'I'll be back.' I know, I know." (see *Commando*, 1985)

O'Brien tells Schwarzenegger to watch out when he meets John Practice (F. Murray Abraham), because "he killed Mozart!" Abraham played Salieri, Mozart's rival, in *Amadeus* (1984).

Two of Schwarzenegger's former costars make very brief walk-ons outside the police station. Robert Patrick appears as the T-1000 from *Terminator 2*, and Arnold's costar in *Total Recall* (1990), Sharon Stone, appears as her character from *Basic Instinct* (1992), leaving the station and lighting a cigarette. Also, Schwarzenegger's friend and *Twins* (1988) costar, Danny DeVito, provides the voice of the cartoon cat, uncredited.

Director John McTiernan's father, John McTiernan, Sr., plays a cigar stand man.

The Last Boy Scout (1991)

The movie that Darian Hallanbeck (Danielle Harris) watches on television is *Lethal Weapon* (1987), also written by Shane Black.

Joe (Bruce Willis) mentions "reindeer goat cheese pizza," which was also mentioned by Willis in *Hudson Hawk* (1991).

Last Man Standing (1996)

Wanda, the prostitute, describes one of her old regular customers who used to come around every Friday or Saturday. His name was Clint. The film is largely based on the Clint Eastwood film *A Fistful of Dollars* (1964).

Another reference to *A Fistful of Dollars*: there is a dead horse in the middle of the street, just as in the Eastwood film.

The Last of the Finest (1990)

Brian Dennehy's daughter Kathleen appears as the lab technician who examines the burnt dollar bill with Wayne (Joe Pantoliano).

Last Resort (1986)

Martine, the resort's baby-sitter, is played by director Zane Buzby.

Last Rites (1988)

Nuzo's (Chick Vennera) daughter and son are played by writer-director-producer Donald Bellisario's children, Troian and Michaelangelo.

The Last Woman on Earth (1960)

Screenwriter Robert Towne did not have the script finished by the time filming began, so he was brought along on location to finish writing it and, at the same time, he played the second lead, Anthony Carbone's lawyer, even though he had never acted before. Towne used the pseudonym "Edward Wain" in the credits as both actor and screenwriter.

Laughter in Paradise (1951)

Screenwriter Michael Pertwee (brother of *Doctor Who*'s Jon Pertwee) has a cameo in the film as Stuart.

Laura Lansing Slept Here (1988 TV)

Annette Gomphers, one of the kids, is played by star Katharine Hepburn's real-life niece, Schulyer Grant.

Leaving Las Vegas (1995)

The smiling singer in the "Red Mutten" commercials is played by director Mike Figgis.

Legend of the Werewolf (1975)

Screenwriter Anthony Hines used the pseudonym John Elder to write this film's screenplay. "John Elder" was the name of John Wayne's character in the film *The Sons of Katie Elder* (1965).

Leon (1994)

Mathilda registers Leon and herself at the hotel as "Mr. McGuffin and daughter." This is a reference to the Alfred Hitchcock term "McGuffin" (see *High Anxiety*, 1977, for a definition).

Lethal Weapon (1987)

As insurance (in a very subliminal way) for his then-upcoming film, *The Lost Boys* (1987), director Richard Donner included in this film a theater marquee reading "*Lost Boys*–This Year's Hit." It can be seen behind Riggs (Mel Gibson) and Murtaugh (Danny Glover) after they leave Michael Hunsacker's (Tom Atkins) office.

Lethal Weapon 2 (1989)

As promotion for his cable series *Tales from the Crypt*, director Richard Donner included scenes from Robert Zemeckis's "And All Through the House" episode on the Murtaugh family television set, right before daughter Traci Wolfe's condom commercial. Incidentally, Zemeckis's wife, Mary Ellen Trainor, who starred in the *Crypt* episode, also plays the police psychologist in the *Lethal Weapon* films.

Lethal Weapon 3 (1992)

Director Richard Donner is an animal rights and prochoice activist, and placed many posters and stickers for these causes in the film. Of note are the T-shirt worn by one of Murtaugh's daughters (her idea) and an 18-wheeler with an antifur slogan on the side.

Murtaugh and Riggs drive past a cinema advertising *Radio Flyer* (1992), also directed by Donner.

Riggs interrupts what he thinks is a crime in progress, only to learn that it is just a movie being filmed. The loud-mouthed director yells at Riggs, and, to calm him down, Riggs says, "Listen, Joel," then proceeds to beat him into embarrassment, much to the delight of his crew. The director is patterned after Joel Silver, the producer of the *Lethal Weapon* films and a guy with a reputation for being tough to deal with. The director even looks like Silver, with glasses and curly black hair.

Donner's wife, Lauren Shuler-Donner, plays the nurse who takes Leo's watch off in the hospital after he has been shot.

A Letter to Three Wives (1985 TV)

Ann Sothern, who played one of the wives, Rita Phipps (here played by Michele Lee), in the original 1949 version, appears as Ma Finney.

Lianna (1983)

Writer-director-editor John Sayles also appears in the film as Jerry, the randy film teacher who is Lianna's best friend.

Licence to Kill (1989)

Pedro Armendiraz, Jr., plays President Hector Lopez, the son of Kerim Bay. Pedro Armendiraz, Sr., played Kerim Bay in *From Russia with Love* (1963).

As Bond hangs on to the tanker in the final car chase scene, Sanchez (Robert Davi) fires at him. The bullets ricocheting off of the tanker play the James Bond theme.

Life of Brian (1979)

Executive producer George Harrison of Dark Horse Productions appears as Mr. Papadopoulos, owner of "The Mount," who shakes hands with Brian and gives a very Liverpudlian "'ullo."

Lifeboat (1944)

The model in the "before" and "after" pictures in the newspaper ad for Reduco Obesity Slayer read by Gus (William Bendix) is director Alfred Hitchcock.

Light Sleeper (1991)

In one scene, John LeTour (Willem Dafoe) is shown sitting on his bed looking at old photographs and listening to some CDs. One of the CDs is the soundtrack from Dafoe's movie *Streets of Fire* (1984).

Limit Up (1989)

In one scene, trader Peter Oak (Dean Stockwell) is seen in an elevator, punching keys in his palm, then throwing up his hands in exasperation. These actions were the same ones Stockwell used in the show *Quantum Leap* after trying to get information out of Ziggy's remote device. In the film, Oak could have only been working with a calculator, but as he walks out of the elevator, his hands are empty.

The Lion King (1994)

Simba says to Scar (Jeremy Irons), "You're so weird." Scar replies, "You have no idea!" the same reply that Irons used in *Reversal of Fortune* (1990).

Zazu starts singing "It's a Small World After All," and Scar shuts him up saying, "Anything but *that*!" At Disney World, this song plays continuously ad nauseam throughout the park.

When Timon puts his arm into the hollow log to pull out some grub, one of the bugs that crawls out of the hole is wearing Mickey Mouse ears. The film was made by Disney, and this is known as a "Hidden Mickey." In many Disney films, Disney imagineers have placed hundreds of hidden, hard-to-notice "Hidden Mickey" images.

Lisztomania (1975)

The "Millionairess" and "Most Promising Actress" as addressed in the concert are none other than Madame von Meck (Isabella Tebzynska) from director Ken Russell's *The Music Lovers* (1970) and Alma Mahler (Georgina Hale) from Russell's *Mahler* (1974).

When Liszt (Roger Daltrey) changes into a dress at Princess Carolyn's (Sara Kestelman) command, he changes behind a screen which has a painting of a holy man on it, complete with halo. The man in the painting is Daltrey's pal and bandmate in the Who, Pete Townsend.

Little Women (1994)

In the end credits, the film is dedicated to Polly Klaas, the 12-year-old girl who was kidnapped from her Petaluma, California, home in 1993 and later found murdered. Winona Ryder, who spent much of her youth in Petaluma, joined in the highly publicized search effort and made a number of emotional appeals for the child's safe return.

Lobster Man from Mars (1989)

The script for this film, which had been written in 1978, was finally filmed in 1989 by Electric Pictures. Electric's first feature was *Waxwork* (1988), and several of the members of the cast and crew of that film were drafted to work on this one, including cinematographer Gerry Lively, director Anthony Hickox (who was so good in his cameo in *Waxwork* that he appears as John, the male lead in this film), and actors Patrick Macnee and Deborah Foreman.

The film's voice-over narration is provided by novelty disk jockey Barry Hansen, better known as Dr. Demento, and the king of Mars is played by the singer of the first hit novelty horror song, Bobby "Boris" Pickett of "The Monster Mash" fame.

The Lodger (1926)

At one point, director Alfred Hitchcock found himself without enough extras to complete a scene. In order for the cameras to keep rolling, he filled in as a member of a crowd watching an arrest. He can be seen wearing a cap and leaning against an iron railing. This was the first of his many cameo appearances in his films. He can also be seen in this film seated at a desk in a newsroom. Hitchcock later said that, after his fans began to expect his cameo, he tried to "just get it out of the way so that the audience can enjoy the film."

The Lonely Guy (1984)

Erica Hiller, the daughter of director Arthur Hiller, has a cameo in the bank.

The Long Kiss Goodnight (1996)

The TV in the motel room is playing a film with a title very similar to this film's: *The Long Goodbye* (1973). The title song can even be heard on the television.

The Long Riders (1980)

Ry Cooder, who composed the music for the soundtrack, appears as the saloon singer.

All four sets of character brothers are played by actual brothers. David, Keith and Robert Carradine play the Younger brothers; Stacy and James Keach play Jesse and Frank James; Randy and Dennis Quaid play the Miller brothers; and Christopher and Nicholas Guest play Bob and Charlie Ford.

The Longest Yard (1974)

Burt Reynolds's character, Paul "Wrecking" Crewe, wears jersey number 22, the number Reynolds wore as a player at West Palm Beach High School and Florida State University (see also *Semi-Tough*, 1977).

Burt's brother, Jim Reynolds, plays Ice Man in the film. However, the role is credited to "Jim Nicholson." At the time, Jim was coaching football at a high school in West Palm Beach, Florida.

As Unger (Charles Tyner) dishes out the food on make-work day by the river, he says, "Lookie, lookie, here comes Cookie!" This was the catchphrase of NFL and CFL fullback Cookie Gilchrist. The phrase originally came from a George Burns and Gracie Allen film, *Here Comes Cookie* (1935).

Look Who's Talking Too (1990)

Coscripter Neal Israel has a cameo as Dr. Ross, and his daughter Mollie plays Mikey's dream friend at the end of the film.

Lookin' to Get Out (1982)

Jon Voight coscripted, coproduced and starred in this film, and his daughter Angelina Jolie Voight also appears in the film as Tosh, Patti's (Ann-Margret) daughter. She has since dropped her last name for her current acting career, being billed as Angelina Jolie in films such as *Hackers* (1995) and *Foxfire* (1996).

Looking for Mr. Goodbar (1977)

Theresa Dunn (Diane Keaton) can be seen reading a copy of *The Godfather*. Keaton appeared in the 1972 film version of the novel and its 1974 sequel.

Lost in America (1985)

The Mercedes driver that crossing guard David Howard (Albert Brooks) gives directions to is played by executive producer Herb Nanas.

The Lost Weekend (1945)

Don Birnam (Ray Milland) is handed his hat by a woman as he leaves the bar. The arm that is shown belonged to Loretta Young.

Love Child (1982)

Director Larry Peerce's son, Matthew, has a small role. He can be seen sitting in a car.

Loving You (1957)

Elvis Presley has a scene at the end where he sings to a crowd from a stage. One of the women in the crowd—a stocky dark-haired woman sitting on the aisle seat—is his mother, Gladys. Elvis would not watch this film at all after Gladys died, because of that one scene.

Lt. Robin Crusoe, USN (1966)

Story credit for the film went to Retlaw Yensid. This is "Walter Disney" spelled backwards and was Disney's only film writing credit.

McClone (1989 TV)

In an episode of the series *The Highwayman*, a genetically designed perfect soldier named McClone goes AWOL and is pursued by evil clones and government scientists. Producer Glen A. Larson intented to continue the character in a series called *McClone* on NBC in 1989, and this pilot was even aired, but the series did not sell and was cancelled. It was to be a parody of Larson's old series *McCloud*, and he even cast *McCloud* regulars J.D. Cannon and Terry Carter as regulars.

McLintock! (1963)

John Wayne wears his *Red River* "D" belt buckle in this film (see *Rio Bravo*, 1959, 4).

Mad Love (1935)

A woman posing as a wax statue apparently comes to life, and a drunken housekeeper who sees it runs screaming into the streets, telling policemen, "It went for a little walk." This line was used by Norton, the archaeologist (Bramwell Fletcher) about the monster in director Karl Freund's *The Mummy* (1932).

Made in America (1993)

The African craft shop is on the same street as a theater advertising a Paula Prentiss retrospective. Prentiss is the wife of director Richard Benjamin.

Made in Heaven (1987)

Timothy Hutton's then-wife, Debra Winger, appears unbilled as Emmett, the masculine-looking character who "runs things" in heaven.

The film's coscripter, Ray Gideon, plays Mr. Packert, and editor Tom Walls plays C.C. Stank.

Neil Young, who wrote the music for the film, appears in a cameo as a truck driver.

Stuntman Doug DeGrazzio appears in the film.

Rock singers Ric Ocasek (of The Cars) and Tom Petty appear in cameos, as Shark, a beatnik, and Stanky.

The Madness of King George (1994)

Ian Holm, a well-known Shakespearean actor, plays a character who knows nothing about Shakespeare. When his companions are appalled that he has given the mad king, usurped by his own child, a copy of *King Lear*, Holm helplessly declares, "I didn't know what it was about." George also complains that Holm's character reads badly (which he does).

The Magic Christian (1969)

A steward brings one of the female passengers her tea, and she says, "That'll be all." He says, "Not quite, milady..." and leans over her menacingly, baring his fangs. He is played by Christopher Lee, who had starred in many films as Count Dracula, including the film he made just before his cameo in this one, *Dracula Has Risen from the Grave* (1968).

A silent, solitary drinker sits at the ship's bar. A woman comes up to him and he buys her a drink. She then breaks into song. The drinker is played by director Roman Polanski (*The Fearless Vampire Killers*, 1967; *Rosemary's Baby*, 1968), but the singer is not listed in the credits. After her song, she pulls off her wig to reveal the bald head of Yul Brynner!

The Magnificent Ambersons (1942)

The newspaper that shows the story about the explosion that injured George Amberson Minafer also has an article written by "Jed Leland," who is a character from *Citizen Kane* (1941), also directed by Orson Welles.

The Major and the Minor (1942)

It was decided to include scenes of the mother of Ginger Rogers's character. Spring Byington was the first choice, but she was appearing in another film. Rogers suggested her real mother, Lela Rogers, who got the role.

Major Payne (1994)

Screenwriter Dean Lorey has a cameo in the film as Mr. Shipman.

Making Mr. Right (1987)

Director Susan Seidelman put *The Parent Trap* (1961), the granddaddy of dual-role comedies, on a marquee, acknowledging the roots for John Malkovich's double role.

Mallrats (1995)

As Jeremy London waits for an elevator in this Kevin Smith film, the song *The Girl from Ipanema* can be heard playing in the background. This was a song that director John Landis enjoyed putting into his films. It can even be heard in an elevator at the end of *The Blues Brothers* (1980).

The Maltese Falcon (1941)

Director John Huston's father, Walter, appears in a cameo as Captain Jacobi, who stumbles into Sam Spade's office with the Falcon.

Man Bites Dog (1992)

The original title for this Belgian film about a serial killer was *C'est arrive pres de chez vous*, which translates as *It Happened Near You*. This is the title of a newspaper column in Belgium that reports bizarre and violent murders which occur locally.

Man of the House (1995)

Ben Archer (Jonathan Taylor Thomas) can be seen sitting under a tree reading a book with an ad for *The Lion King* (1994). Thomas was the voice of the young Simba in *The Lion King*.

The Man Who Fell to Earth (1976)

In one scene, rock star David Bowie and Candy Clark are singing a hymn in church and Bowie cannot carry a note.

The Man Who Knew Too Much (1956)

Bernard Herrmann, who composed the score for the film, appears as the conductor of the orchestra during the Albert Hall sequence.

Director Alfred Hitchcock can be seen from the bank watching Arab acrobats in the Moroccan marketplace (with his back to the camera) just before the murder.

The Man Who Wasn't There (1983)

Director Bruce Malmuth's son, Evan, plays a delivery boy and his daughter, Gail, appears as the tour guide.

Malmuth himself plays the fireplug crusher.

The Man with Two Brains (1983)

Director Carl Reiner cast his wife, Estelle, as the tourist in the elevator.

The Manchurian Candidate (1962)

All the members of the platoon are named after the cast and creator of the TV show *You'll Never Get Rich*, a.k.a. *The Phil Silvers Show*:

Nicky Blair plays Silvers, named after Phil Silvers.

Irving Steinberg plays (Mickey) Freeman.

John Laurence plays (Maurice) Gosfield.

Tom Lowell plays (Harvey) Lembeck.

William Thourlby plays (Jimmy) Little.

James Edwards plays Cpl. (Allan) Melvin.

John Francis plays (Nat) Hiken (the series' creator).

Maniac (1980)

Tom Savini's gory makeup is the main attraction in this film, and Savini himself has a cameo as one of the victims.

Marnie (1964)

Director Alfred Hitchcock enters from a hotel room on the left side of the corridor after Tippi Hedren passes by. He glances at the camera and suddenly looks alarmed, as if he is aware that he has just wandered into the shot, then hurries out of view.

The production company created for the film, "Geoffrey Stanley," was named after Hitchcock's pet terriers, which were seen in his film *The Birds* (1963).

Married to the Mob (1988)

Brian Hansen, a filmmaker and friend of director Jonathan Demme, died of Meningitis at 32. Demme dedicated this film to his memory.

The "Sourpuss" F.B.I. man is played by Demme's longtime producer, Kenneth Utt.

Mars Attacks! (1996)

Two directors have cameos in the film. Barbet Schroeder (*Barfly*, 1987; *Reversal of Fortune*, 1990) plays Maurice, the French president who gets zapped by the Martians, and Jerzy Skolimowski (*Moonlighting*, 1982; *The Lightship*, 1985) appears as Dr. Ziegler, who provides the translating machine.

To get into "The Kennedy Room," Jerry Ross (Martin Short) opens up a bust of JFK and presses a button, revealing a hidden door. In the television series *Batman*, Bruce Wayne (Adam West) would open the secret door leading to the Batcave by opening up a bust of William Shakespeare and pressing a button.

The spaceship sawing through the Washington Monument is a reference to a similar scene in *Earth vs. the Flying Saucers* (1956).

The Martian Chronicles (1980 TV)

One of the aliens is a dead ringer for David Bowie's alien character in *The Man Who Fell to Earth* (1976).

Martin (1978)

Cuda invites a boozy, joking priest named Father Howard to dinner, who makes it clear that he does not believe in vampires. He is played by director George A. Romero.

Maryjane (1968)

Actor Dick Gauthier, who cowrote the film's script, has a bit part.

Matewan (1987)

Writer-director John Sayles makes a brief cameo as Hardshell, the preacher.

Matinee (1993)

Kevin McCarthy and William Schallert appear uncredited as the general and the dentist in the film-within-a-film, *Mant*. Director Joe Dante is a longtime movie buff who casts popular character actors who starred in the films of his youth (particularly horror films) in his films whenever possible. McCarthy (*Invasion of the Body Snatchers*, 1956) and Schallert (*The Incredible Shrinking Man*, 1957) are two excellent examples. Also in this film are Robert Cornthwaite (*The Thing [From Another World]*, 1951) as the scientist in *Mant* and Joe Dante regular Dick Miller (*A Bucket of Blood*, 1959) as one half of a pair of thugs selling the film. The other is director John Sayles, who

wrote and had a cameo in Dante's earlier film, *The Howling* (1981).

The lead character of Lawrence Woolsey (John Goodman) is based on the real-life gimmick-crazy cigar-smoking rotund horror film producer of the 1950s, William Castle.

Maurice (1987)

Helena Bonham Carter can be spotted at the cricket match. Carter had just starred in director James Ivory's previous film, *A Room with a View* (1986).

Maverick (1994)

Danny Glover appears uncredited as a bank robber. Mel Gibson and Glover appear to recognize each other, then shake their heads, "Nah." Gibson and Glover starred in director Richard Donner's *Lethal Weapon* trilogy. Glover even uses his line from the *Lethal Weapon* films, "I'm too old for this shit."

Maximum Overdrive (1986)

Director and writer Stephen King appears as the man the ATM swears at. Incidentally, the blonde with the red headband in the pickup on the drawbridge is Marla Maples.

The Mayflower Madam (1987 TV)

The film is based on the real-life experiences of Sydney Biddle-Barrows (Candice Bergen). Biddle-Barrows also appears in this movie as her friend, Peggy Eaton.

Mean Streets (1973)

Writer-director Martin Scorsese has an uncredited cameo as the car gunman who shoots Johnny Boy.

The woman who comes to Theresa's aid when she has an epileptic fit is played by Scorsese's mother, Elizabeth.

A scene from the John Wayne movie *The Searchers* (1956) was used in this film, but Wayne was not shown in the scene. Scorsese originally wanted to use a scene with Wayne in the film *Donovan's Reef* (1963), but Wayne refused, so Scorsese substituted the *Searchers* scene. Scorsese also used certain scenes from Roger Corman's *The Tomb of Ligeia* (1964).

Meatballs Part II (1984)

Cheryl (Kim Richards) is asked if she comes from another planet (due to her lack of experience with boys). She replies that she "is ... sort of." Richards played a young alien girl stranded on Earth in two Disney movies: *Escape to Witch Mountain* (1975) and *Return from Witch Mountain* (1978).

Meet the Hollowheads (1988)

Anne Ramsey has a cameo as Station Master Babblaxe, and the flunky that she orders around is played by her brother, longtime character actor Logan Ramsey. The film is "lovingly dedicated" to Anne Ramsey, who died soon after filming was completed.

One of the policemen who brings Cindy (Juliette Lewis) back from her party is credited as "Jack Cheese," but he is actually played by Bobcat Goldthwait (see *Tapeheads*, 1988). His line "When are kids going to learn to just say no?" is right out of his standup routine.

Melvin and Howard (1980)

Paul LeMat stars as Melvin Dummar, a real person who claims to have met Howard Hughes. The real Dummar has a cameo behind an airport lunch counter.

Memories of Me (1988)

As Alan King takes Billy Crystal and JoBeth Williams on a backstage tour of a movie studio, they run into Sean Connery in full dress regalia. Connery had just wandered off the set of *The Presidio* (1988).

Merry Christmas, Mr. Lawrence (1983)

Rock star David Bowie speaks the line, "I wish I could sing."

Miami Blues (1990)

Coproducer and unit production manager Kenneth Utt has a cameo as Krishna Ramba. He is the sad-faced Krishna that Fred Ward talks to about the murdered Krishna Ravindra.

Junior goes out and buys an Uzi squirt gun, then checks into a hotel. The hotel's desk clerk is played by the film's producer, Gary Goetzman.

Midnight Kiss (1993)

Celeste Yarnell, who played a vampire named Diane LeFanu in the film *The Velvet Vampire* (1971), has a cameo in this vampire flick as Sheila, one of the film's first casualties.

Mike's Murder (1984)

At one point, Debra Winger speaks to her mother on the phone. The voice on the other side is provided by Winger's real-life mother, Ruth.

Miller's Crossing (1990)

Writing-directing team Joel and Ethan Coen gave their buddy, director Sam Raimi (*The Evil Dead*, 1983; *Darkman*, 1990), a cameo as a snickering gunman. Frances McDormand, the star of Raimi's *Darkman* and wife of Joel, also has an unbilled cameo as a secretary.

William Preston Robertson has a voice cameo (see *Blood Simple*, 1984).

Millions Like Us (1943)

Basil Radford and Naunton Wayne play characters named Charters and

Caldicott. These characters also appeared in *Night Train to Munich* (1940) and *The Lady Vanishes* (1938), films which were also written by Sidney Gilliat and codirector Frank Launder.

Mind Twister (1994)

Director Fred Olen Ray appears in the film as a photographer.

Miracle on Ice (1981 TV)

A game film of Jerry Houser being smashed into the boards is being shown on a television screen. A teammate says to Houser, "Don't tell me. *Slap Shot*." Houser was also in the hockey film *Slap Shot* (1977).

The Mirror Crack'd (1980)

Star Elizabeth Taylor's ex-husband, Senator John Warner, appears in a cameo as a fisherman.

Misery (1990)

When the sheriff goes into the general store to ask about Annie, the owner is arranging videotape boxes on a stand. One of them is *When Harry Met Sally...* (1989), also directed by Rob Reiner.

The helicopter pilot who flies sheriff Richard Farnsworth around is uncredited. He is played by director Rob Reiner, who shaved his beard for the part.

J.T. Walsh has an unbilled cameo as Colorado police chief Sherman Douglas. Sherman Douglas is also the name of an NBA player who was then a rookie with the Miami Heat.

Mr. and Mrs. Bridge (1990)

The film has a credit at the end reading "Shakespearean tutor to Mr. Newman: Sen. Bob Dole." This refers to the Kansas politician's reading of *Romeo and Juliet* to Paul Newman to assist him in his characterization of Kansas City lawyer Walter Bridge.

Mr. and Mrs. Smith (1941)

Midway through the film, director Alfred Hitchcock passes Robert Montgomery in front of his building. After Hitchcock passes him, Montgomery turns to look back as if his character recognized Hitchcock.

Mr. Baseball (1992)

Two of the *gaijin* (non–Japanese) players that Jack (Tom Selleck) is introduced to in the Japanese restaurant are "Animal" Niven and Lyle Massey. They are played by Bradley Jay "The Animal" Lesley and Leon Lee, two baseball players who never made it big in North America, but actually played for many years in Japan.

The catcher in the opening scene is played, unbilled, by TSN announcer and former Toronto Blue Jay catcher Buck Martinez.

Mr. Destiny (1990)

Michael Caine's daughter, Sari Caine, has a cameo as L.J.'s (Jim Belushi) daughter in the "alternate reality."

Larry's wife's maiden name (he asks for his secretary to look her up in the company directory) is "Ellen Ripley." Ellen Ripley was the name of Sigourney Weaver's character in the three *Alien* films.

Mr. Saturday Night (1992)

At Buddy Young, Jr.'s (Billy Crystal) last television show, he freaks out, tears up some cue cards and fires his two new comedy writers, who turn and walk away. They are played by the film's screenwriters, Lowell Ganz and Babaloo Mandel.

Lucky Zindberg, Buddy's bandleader on his television show, is played by the film's scorer, Marc Shaiman. He is the one who asks Buddy, "What's the matter, Buddy? Having a bad day?"

Buddy appears on *The Ed Sullivan Show* after the Beatles, and the audience consists of screaming teenage girls. The one wearing glasses sitting to the right of Stan (David Paymer) who goes crazy and starts shaking him is played by Billy Crystal's daughter, Lindsay.

Mistress (1992)

When Marvin (Robert Wuhl) finds out that Eli Wallach's girlfriend doesn't want to be in his film, he gets mad and says, "Here I am giving her a chance to be in a *real film* … I'm not saying it's gonna be *Batman 3* …" Wuhl appeared as Alexander Knox in the original *Batman* (1989).

Coming out of Rabotta's, Marvin and his wife meet Evan Wright (Robert De Niro) and his family, including his daughter, Raphaela, who has a few lines ("I like the food here …"). She is played by writer-director Barry Primus's daughter, Raphaela Rose Primus.

At the party, George (Eli Wallach) talks with a woman with short brown hair. They go into the house while talking about tiles, and she asks, "Where is Macedonia?" She is played by Roberta Wallach, the daughter of Eli Wallach and Anne Jackson.

Mixed Nuts (1994)

The landlord's name is Tannenbaum, which is German for "Christmas tree." After he is shot, his body is disguised as a Christmas tree.

Mo' Better Blues (1990)

Joie Lee (Spike's sister) is given away at the wedding by her real-life father, Bill Lee.

Producer Monty Ross has a cameo as one of the patrons at the club.

Modern Romance (1981)

Director-star Albert Brooks's brother Bob Einstein plays the pushy salesman at Sports Locker. Einstein was a regular on *The Smothers Brothers Show* as Officer Judy and produced *Bizarre*, but is probably better known as Super Dave Osborne. The family name is "Einstein," which explains why Albert changed his last name.

Another of Albert's brothers, Cliff Einstein, has a cameo in the scenes set in the recording studio. He plays the music mixer, the bald man sitting to the left of the head mixer, who gets up and goes to his car during the break.

David, the director of the film that Brooks is editing, is played by real-life director-screenwriter James L. Brooks (*Terms of Endearment*, 1983; *I'll Do Anything*, 1994)—no relation to Albert. He would later return the favor by casting Albert in his Oscar-nominated role of Aaron Altman in *Broadcast News* (1987).

As Kathryn Harrold comes into David's party, she recognizes a man named Harvey. He introduces her to a man named Ed and the three of them duck into a room and do some cocaine. Harvey is played by Harvey Skolnik, and Ed is played by longtime television comedy writer-producer Ed. Weinberger (*The Associates*, *The Cosby Show*), who won numerous Emmys while collaborating with James L. Brooks on the shows *Taxi* and *The Mary Tyler Moore Show*.

Albert Brooks and Harrold arrive at the party and a man named Jerry asks where the bathroom is. Cropped off of the frame on the television-video version, he is played by Jerry Belson, a television writer who is a friend of

James L. Brooks and who later collaborated with him on (and won Emmys for) *The Tracey Ullman Show*.

Monkey Business (1931)

Sam Marx, father of the Marx Brothers, can be seen in two scenes, once on the ship and once on the dock. He can easily be seen as the Brothers get up off the stretchers as they leave the ship—he is a dapper man with a moustache and straw boater hat in the middle of the screen.

Moon Over Parador (1988)

At the start of the film, Jack Noah (Richard Dreyfuss) is told that there was a role in a Neil Simon play that was perfect for him. He asks who got the part, and is told Mandy Patinkin. It is later established that Noah was well-received in *Evita*, and, in this film, Noah plays another Central American dictator, Alphonse Simms. Mandy Patinkin is known for his portrayal of real-life South American dictator Che Guevara in the Broadway production of *Evita*. This scene was also filmed in the lobby of the Joseph Papp Public Theatre, where Patinkin often performs.

Jonathan Winters tells a long story concerning an English pirate who founded the country of Parador to explain why Alphonse Simms has an Anglo-Saxon surname. The reason for it in the film was that it was shot in Brazil, and the director needed a shot of a crowd of Brazilian extras chanting Simms's name. When the crowd is calling out "Simms! Simms!" they are actually chanting "Sim!," which is "yes" in Portugese, the language of Brazil.

As Dreyfuss (an actor playing an actor playing a president) walks by a noisy helicopter, he is asked questions by reporters. He smiles, shakes his head and pretends he cannot hear them. This was a favorite ploy of actor-turned-president Ronald Reagan.

Dreyfuss plays the real Simms as well as Jack Noah, but in the shots which contain both Noah and Simms, Dreyfuss's twin brother Lorin Dreyfuss plays Simms.

Director Paul Mazursky appears in drag, uncredited, as Alphonse Simms's mother.

Paul's wife Betsy Mazursky appears at a buffet table and asks, "*Por favor*, is it safe to eat this lettuce here?"

Paul's daughter, Jill Mazursky, plays the assistant director of the second film crew, who yells at everyone to be quiet.

The producer of the second film is named "Menachem," after low-budget film producer Menachem Golan, who frequently films in South and Central America.

Moonraker (1979)

Drax's Venice laboratory has an electronic lock on it. The sequence which unlocks the door is the hailing tune from *Close Encounters of the Third Kind* (1977).

Moonstruck (1987)

Nicolas Cage plays Ronny, a man with only one arm. In Cage's previous role in *Peggy Sue Got Married* (1986), Cage's character begged Peggy to marry him, saying he doesn't know what the future might bring—and that he might lose his arm.

Moonwalker (1988)

The villain's name is Frank Lideo. One of the film's executive producers is Michael Jackson's longtime manager, Frank DiLeo.

More American Graffiti (**1979**)

Harrison Ford, who had appeared in the original *American Graffiti* (1973) before hitting it big, has an uncredited cameo in this film as a motorcycle cop.

The Morning After (**1986**)

At the end of the film, a line reads, "Our Thanks to David," an acknowledgement of screenwriter David Rayfiel's extensive contributions to the script, which was only credited to James Hicks.

Moscow on the Hudson (**1984**)

Robin Williams, Maria Conchita Alonso and Cleavant Derricks go see director Paul Mazursky's *An Unmarried Woman* (1978) (on a double bill with James Toback's *Exposed*, 1983). Alonso gives it a "ten out of ten," but Williams calls it "decadent."

Mazursky himself appears as Dave, the man who gives Alejandro Rey a dollar after Rey staggers off of a raft from Cuba.

Mazursky's wife, Betsy, has a cameo as the manager of Bloomingdale's who doesn't want Williams defecting in her store.

Rey's son, Brandon Rey, has a small part in the diner on Independence Day.

Moses the Lawgiver (**1975 TV**)

Burt Lancaster plays Moses and his own son, Will, plays Moses as a young man. William Lancaster is best known as the writer of the film *The Bad News Bears* (1976).

Mother (**1996**)

The song that John Henderson (Albert Brooks) listens to as he drives is called "Mrs. Henderson" in a parody of the Simon and Garfunkel song "Mrs. Robinson" from *The Graduate* (1967).

Mother, Jugs & Speed (**1976**)

The ambulance-chasing lawyer comes into Harry's (Allen Garfield) office, and Harry tells him that a woman named Mrs. Natasha Gurdin got her hand caught in a garbage disposal. Natasha Gurdin was the real name of actress Natalie Wood.

Moving Violations (**1985**)

Director Neal Israel and his brother, coproducer Robert Israel, appear as a couple of commuters at a bus stop who watch the puppet stand roll by.

Mrs. Doubtfire (**1993**)

When the family is looking for Mrs. Doubtfire's replacement, the last name that they cross off of their list of applicants is "Paula DuPree." DuPree was the film's associate producer.

Mrs. Doubtfire loses her teeth in the drink at the restaurant and says, "carpe diem" ("seize the day") (see *Hook*, 1991).

Mrs. Parker and the Vicious Circle (**1994**)

Writer Robert Benchley is portrayed in this film by Campbell Scott. Benchley's real-life grandson, author Peter Benchley, plays Frank Crowninshield.

The Muppet Movie (**1979**)

The film is dedicated to ventriloquist Edgar Bergen, who also makes a cameo appearance in the film and who was an inspiration to Muppets creator Jim Henson.

The Muppets Take Manhattan (**1984**)

Director John Landis often cast Muppeteer Frank Oz in his films (*The Blues Brothers*, 1980; *An American Werewolf in London*, 1981; and so on), so Oz cast Landis in this film as the movie executive that Kermit gives his script to.

Murder **(1930)**

Director Alfred Hitchcock is seen walking past the house where the murder was committed, about one hour into the movie.

Murder at the Gallop **(1963)**

Miss Marple's (Margaret Rutherford) assistant, Mr. Stringer, is played by Rutherford's real-life husband, Stringer Davis.

Murder on Flight 502 **(1975 TV)**

Star Robert Stack's wife and daughter have bit parts in the movie. His wife Rosemary plays Dorothy Saunders, and his daughter Elizabeth appears as Marilyn Stonehurst.

Murphy's Romance **(1985)**

Columbia Pictures, which made this film, was at the time owned by Coca-Cola, and they included a lot of Coke product placement in their films. A double whammy appears in this film. The boy goes into his local grocery store and asks if they are hiring anyone, and behind him there can be seen a Coke sign. The camera cuts to the owner, who tells him, "We don't have any jobs for you right now," and behind the bad man are two Pepsi signs.

Co-scripter Irving Ravetch plays a customer in the store.

My Blue Heaven **(1990)**

FBI agent Barney Coopersmith goes undercover as a Canadian named "Dickie," a name that he hates. In reality, Coopersmith is played by a Canadian named "Dickie" (Rick Moranis).

This film was made by Warner Bros. and a theater in the background of one scene advertises Warner's upcoming Clint Eastwood film, *White Hunter,*

Black Heart (1990), which was released later that year.

My Brilliant Career **(1979)**

Director Gillian Armstrong has a cameo as a backup singer in the cabaret.

My Favorite Brunette **(1947)**

Ronnie (Bob Hope) goes into private dick Sam McCloud's office and says to him, "All my life, I wanted to be a hard-boiled detective like Humphrey Bogart or Dick Powell … or even Alan Ladd!" Just as Hope says this, McCloud turns around, revealing himself to be Alan Ladd (he appears uncredited).

Hope plays golf with a sanitarium inmate, and the inmate says that George Washington has the room next to his and keeps him awake all night by playing Yankee Doodle on his fife—off key. Hope responds, "Why don't you tell Petrillo about it?" James Caesar Petrillo was the head of the American Federation of Musicians in the 1940s and 1950s. He led the union's members into a very controversial and longlasting recording ban from 1942 to 1944, then again in 1947. He was vilified by the press and became a common target for the comedians of the day for his alleged iron-handed leadership style.

McCloud (Hope) is referred to as "a Harvard man." He replies, "I am not. Fairmount High. Cleveland." This was Hope's actual high school.

Willie (Lon Chaney, Jr.) bends the bars on Hope's window apart, and Hope happily ushers him out, saying, "You're great! I'll buy you a rabbit later." This is a reference to Chaney's role as Lenny in *Of Mice and Men* (1939), in which he repeatedly asked Burgess Meredith, "Tell me about the rabbits, George."

Hope tries to keep the incriminating record away from the bad guys, and, while doing so, he discovers a bottle of booze in the chandelier and says, "Aha! Ray Milland's been here!" This is a reference to Milland's Academy Award–winning role as an alcoholic in *The Lost Weekend* (1945).

At the end of the film, the governor tells the executioner that Hope's execution is off. He calls, "Harry!" The executioner turns around … and it is Bing Crosby (whose real first name is Harry), Hope's occasional partner, who appears uncredited. He says, "Off? Off?," and stomps off. Hope remarks, "Boy, he'll take any kind of a part."

My Favorite Spy (1951)

Bob Hope holds up a skull and says, "Looks like a fella I know who sings…," a friendly jab at his occasional cohort in film, Bing Crosby.

My Favorite Year (1982)

This film is supposedly based on a true incident when Mel Brooks (here, the character of Benjy Stone) was assigned to watch Errol Flynn (Alan Swann) when Flynn was scheduled to appear on Sid Caesar's (King Kaiser) *Your Show of Shows*. Brooks, like Benjy, worked as a writer on the show, and changed his name when he entered show business. Brooks's real name is Melvin Kaminsky.

Myra Breckinridge (1970)

The film is based on Gore Vidal's 1968 novel, in which Myra is the result of a sex change operation. Before the change, she was a dedicated young film critic named Myron. Myron is played in the film by real-life film critic Rex Reed.

The Naked Gun: From the Files of Police Squad (1988)

Among the typically humorous closing credits are the following examples: After a listing for "Weird Al" Yankovic, who appears in the film, is a credit for "'Weird Leslie' … Leslie Maier." Before becoming an assistant to the executive producers of the film, Maier worked as Yankovic's publicist. At her request, the producers wrote a role for her former client and gave her a cameo as his publicist.

The credits also read: "Produced By … Robert Weiss," "Mr. Weiss's Wardrobe … Andrea Thau," "Mr. Weiss's Divorce Attorney … Marsha Durko." Thau is Weiss's cousin, but she has no ties with the fashion industry and the wardrobe job did not exist. On the other hand, Weiss did get divorced during the filming of the movie, and Durko was his attorney.

The Naked Gun 2½: The Smell of Fear (1991)

In the middle of the panic at the end of the film, Lloyd Bochner, clutching a book with the title *To Serve Man*, cries "It's a cookbook!" This is taken from the famous *Twilight Zone* episode "To Serve Man," in which Bochner appeared.

The Naked Gun 33⅓: the Final Insult (1994)

The cover of the issue of *Playboy* that Papshmir (Raye Birk) is reading in his Lear jet features Anna Nicole Smith. Smith plays Tanya Peters in the film.

Naked Obsession (1991)

Director Fred Olen Ray (*Hollywood Chainsaw Hookers*, 1988; *Bikini Drive-In*, 1995) has a cameo as the MC of the Ying Yang strip club.

The Nasty Rabbit (1965)

Assistant cameraman Laszlo Kovacs (who went on to serve as cinematographer on many films) appears as the Idiot.

National Lampoon's Animal House (1978)

Babs (Martha Smith) becomes a tour guide at Universal Studios at the end of the film. The credits for this film (and other John Landis films) include an advertisement at the end for a tour at Universal Studios which says, "Ask for Babs." As of 1989, Universal Studios no longer honor the "Ask for Babs" promotion, which was either a discount or free admission to visitors who said the phrase.

Stephen Bishop appears as "Charming Guy," the member of the frat house singing "I gave my love a cherry" in the stairway (see Kentucky Fried Movie, 1977).

In director John Landis's earlier film, Schlock (1971), the Schlockthropus, a "missing link"–type creature, falls in love with a girl named Mindy, played by Eliza Garrett. Garrett appears in this film as the girl who consoles Otter (Tim Matheson) when he hears of his "girlfriend's" death. Later, when asked what she is studying, she replies, "Primitive cultures," a reference to Schlock.

National Lampoon's Loaded Weapon 1 (1993)

The first time Samuel L. Jackson sees Emilio Estevez in the nonsmoking squad room, Estevez starts to light up a cigarette. Jackson yells, "Cigarette!" and leaps on him. This scene is a parody of Riggs and Murtaugh's initial meeting in Lethal Weapon (1987) where Murtaugh sees Riggs's gun and yells, "Gun!"

Dr. Leecher (F. Murray Abraham) is a send-up of Dr. Hannibal Lecter (Anthony Hopkins) from The Silence of the Lambs (1991).

Erik Estrada and Larry Wilcox show up in a shootout at the Squealer's Hotel as their characters from the show CHiPs. Estrada even sits upon a motorcycle.

The interrogation of Miss Demeanor (Kathy Ireland) is a take-off on the similar scene with Sharon Stone in Basic Instinct (1992).

The comparing of injuries between Estevez and Ireland is a spoof of a scene in Lethal Weapon 3 (1992).

The headbanging drive-away at the film's end to the tune of "Bohemian Rhapsody" by Queen was taken right out of Wayne's World (1992).

Natural Born Killers (1994)

Director Oliver Stone inserted footage from many films as a critique of violence in the media. One of the clips is from Midnight Express (1978), which Stone wrote the screenplay for.

Navy SEAL's (1990)

At the end of the film, as Charlie Sheen is hiding in the ruins, he is spotted by a local. Sheen listens to him say something, then turns around and shoots him. He then says, "Boring conversation ... leader, we're gonna have company," to Michael Biehn. This line was taken from Star Wars (1977), when Han Solo comes to the Death Star to rescue the princess. He speaks to an Imperial worker over a microphone, then blasts it and says, "Boring conversation anyway ... Luke, we're gonna have company!"

Never a Dull Moment (1968)

Director Jerry Paris has a cameo as a police photographer.

Never Love a Stranger (1958)

John Drew Barrymore plays the lead, Francis Kane. Francis Kane was the real name of Harold Robbins, who wrote the novel upon which the film is based.

Never Say Never Again (1983)

The film's title was originally to be *Warhead* but it was changed, becoming an in-joke about Sean Connery's refusal to ever play 007 again after completing *Diamonds Are Forever* (1971). He was eventually paid $5 million, which made him the highest paid British actor at the time. At the end of the film, Rowan Atkinson asks Bond to reconsider leaving. Bond (Connery) says, "Never." Domino (Kim Basinger) asks, "Never?" and Connery turns and winks at the camera.

New York Stories (1989)

In director Francis Ford Coppola's segment of the film, "Life without Zoe," he cast his father, Carmine, as a street musician. Carmine also serves as a composer of many of his son's films.

Night and the City (1992)

Screenwriter Richard Price plays a doctor in the film.

The man in the fedora seated beside Robert De Niro in the bar is played by famed boxing personality Bert Randolph Sugar.

A Night in Casablanca (1946)

Harpo repeatedly plays the number 5 on the roulette wheel and wins so much money that he breaks the bank. This is a reference to the then-recently-released *The Big Sleep* (1946), in which Vivian Sternwood Rutledge (Lauren Bacall) won $28,000 at roulette by betting on the number 5.

Night of the Creeps (1986)

All the main characters (and even some minor ones) are named after horror movie directors.

Steve Marshall plays the kid with the crutches, John Carpenter "J.C." Hooper (John Carpenter, Tobe Hooper).

Jason Lively plays his pal, Christopher Romero (George Romero).

Jill Whitlow plays Cynthia (David) Cronenberg, the girl who Chris falls for.

Tom Atkins plays the cop on the case, Roy (James) Cameron.

Wally Taylor plays Detective (John) Landis.

Bruce Solomon plays Sgt. (Sam) Raimi, the desk sergeant who calls Detective Cameron.

Robert Kino plays Mr. (Steve) Miner, the security guard at the lab.

One of the frat brothers is named (Sean) Cunningham. He's the one taking names as the fraternity members board the bus.

As the call comes over the radio that the two cops have the zombie cornered, a policeman is telling Cameron where all the cops are, and he mentions "Officer (Joe) Dante."

Even the school newspaper, which is shown after the first body is found outside of the sorority, is called the (Wes) *Craven Clarion*.

Dick Miller makes a special appearance as Walter Paisley, the cop at the armory, possibly a two-part in-joke referring to his role as the gun dealer in *The Terminator* (1984) (see *Hollywood Boulevard*, 1976).

The film is so self-deprecating that when Detective Cameron finds out that the lab is a cryogenics lab, he asks, "What is this, a homicide or a bad B movie?"

Night of the Living Dead (1968)

Director George A. Romero has a cameo as the interviewer in Washington, D.C.

Night on Earth (1991)

The name "Helmut," which belongs to the New York taxi driver (Armin Mueller-Stahl), is taken from a member of the crew of director Jim Jarmusch's *Down by Law* (1986).

The names of the Helsinki taxi driver ("Mika") and the unlucky guy ("Aki") come from directors Mika and Aki Kaurismaki, friends of Jarmusch.

A Night to Remember (1943)

The line "Still here, Miss Evans?" is a reference to one of the two ladies in first class who did not make it off of the *Titanic*.

Night Train to Munich (1940)

Basil Radford and Naunton Wayne play characters named Charters and Caldicott. These characters also appeared in *The Lady Vanishes* (1938), which was also written by Sidney Gilliat and Frank Launder. They appeared later in *Millions Like Us* (1943) as well.

A Nightmare on Elm Street (1984)

There is a ripped poster of *The Evil Dead* (1983) visible. Also, the movie Nancy (Heather Langenkamp) watches to stay awake is *The Evil Dead* (see *The Evil Dead*, 1983).

A Nightmare on Elm Street 3: Dream Warriors (1987)

The scene in which Neil Gordon (Craig Wasson) is thrown into a grave and partially buried by the skeleton of Freddy is a reference to *Body Double* (1984), in which Wasson's character is similarly buried alive.

1941 (1979)

John Candy plays a soldier named Foley and Mickey Rourke plays one named Reese. These are the names that director-screenwriter Robert Zemeckis and screenwriter Bob Gale use for any police or government agents in the films that they have written.

An airplane crashes into the "Hollywood" sign, destroying the "land" part. This is a reference to the story of when the sign did actually read "Hollywoodland" in the early days of Hollywood. The sign was erected in 1923 as a promotional gimmick to launch a 640-acre subdivision in the area called Hollywoodland. By 1949 the sign had become an eyesore—the "H" had blown down, the remaining letters had holes in them from missing panels and the paint was badly peeling. The Hollywood Chamber of Commerce then decided to restore the sign to read "Hollywood." However, there are many legends rampant about how the last four letters of the sign "mysteriously disappeared."

Ninotchka (1939)

The posters for this film, Greta Garbo's first comedy, contained the line "Garbo Laughs!" This was a reference to the advertising used for Garbo's first talkie, *Anna Christie* (1930), which used the ad line "Garbo Talks."

Nobody's Perfekt (1981)

First-time director Peter Bonerz also appears in a cameo.

No Justice (1989)

Director Donald Farmer (*Vampire Cop*, 1990; *Red Lips*, 1995) has a cameo as a reporter.

No Surrender (1985)

Rock musician Elvis Costello appears as a magician who is all thumbs, a reference to Costello's own lack of dexterity is playing the guitar. He even wears his trademark top hat.

No Way Out (1987)

The film is dedicated to its British cinematographer, John Alcott, who died of a heart attack after the film was completed.

North (1994)

Alan Rachins makes a cameo appearance as his character from *L.A. Law*, defending North's parents.

As Graham Greene and North fish through the floor of his igloo, they whistle the theme to *The Andy Griffith Show*. The show used to begin with the whistled theme as Griffith and his son walk along with fishing poles.

Among North's prospective parents are Kelly McGillis and Alexander Godunov in their Amish roles from *Witness* (1985).

The last set of parents and family that North "auditions" is a jumble of references to old-time perfect television families. They are Ward (*Leave It to Beaver*) and Donna (*The Donna Reed Show*) Nelson (*Ozzie and Harriet*), with children named Bud (*Father Knows Best*) and Laura (*The Dick van Dyke Show*). Ward calls his daughter "Kitten" (*Father Knows Best*), and they own a sheepdog (*My Three Sons*) named Oliver.

Bruce Willis, who first appears dressed as a rabbit, drives North home in a Volkswagen Rabbit.

North by Northwest (1959)

Roger O. Thornhill (Cary Grant) claims that the "O" stands for "nothing." This is a reference to movie mogul David O. Selznick, who also claimed that his "O" did not stand for anything. Actually, Selznick's "O" stood for "Oliver."

Director Alfred Hitchcock misses a bus during the opening credits.

North to Alaska (1960)

John Wayne wears his *Red River* "D" belt buckle in this film (see *Rio Bravo*, 1959).

Northern Pursuit (1943)

Errol Flynn tells the heroine that she is the only girl he has ever loved, then turns to the camera and says, "What am I saying?" In 1942, during the filming of this movie, Flynn was in the middle of a scandalous rape case. He was charged with the statutory rape of two teenage girls on his yacht. There was even a youth organization formed to support him, The American Boys Club for the Defense of Errol Flynn (ABCDEF). Flynn was acquitted.

Norwood (1970)

Jack Haley, Jr., directed this film, and his dad, Jack Haley, Sr., appears as Joe Namath's dad.

Nothing but Trouble (1991)

Star Dan Aykroyd's brother, Peter, has a cameo as Mike, the doorman.

Notorious (1946)

At a big party in Claude Rains's mansion, director Alfred Hitchcock can be seen drinking champagne and then quickly departing.

Nuns on the Run (1990)

The first time that we see gang boss Case (Robert Patterson), he is relaxing in the back of his bar, watching *The Long Good Friday* (1980) on television. Both gangster films were made by George Harrison's Handmade Productions.

The flight attendants at the end of the film, played by Eric Idle and Robbie Coltrane in drag, are listed in the credits as being played by Brian Hope and Charlie McManus. These are the names of Idle's and Coltrane's characters.

Nuts (1987)

Coscripter Darryl Ponicsan appears in the film.

O Lucky Man! (1973)

Director Lindsay Anderson has a cameo as the talent scout who slaps Mick (Malcolm McDowell).

Old Explorers (1990)

Coproducers David Herbert and Tom Jenz appear in the film as policemen.

Writer-director-producer William Pohlad cast his son, Christopher, as Billy Watney.

The film is based on James Cada's play of the same name, and Cada has a cameo as the watch commander.

The Old Man and the Sea (1958)

The book's author, Ernest Hemingway, appears in an uncredited bit part in this film.

On Deadly Ground (1994)

After he beats up an Inuit-hating oil worker, Forrest Taft (Steven Seagal) asks him, "What does it take to change the essence of a man?" This question is very similar to one that was posed (and answered) by Kelly LeBrock in an aftershave commercial. LeBrock was married to Seagal at the time.

On Her Majesty's Secret Service (1969)

At the end of the opening sequence, James Bond (George Lazenby) saves a beautiful girl who then runs away from him. Bond sighs, "This never happened to the other fellow." Lazenby was the first actor to take on the role after Sean Connery, and this was a reference to the original Bond, Connery.

On the Town (1949)

Frank Sinatra is subjected to good-natured kidding about his real-life marriage to Ava Gardner.

On the Waterfront (1954)

Fred Gwynne testifies at a hearing and gives his name as Mladen Sekulovich, which is the real-life given name of Gwynne's costar, Karl Malden.

Once Bitten (1985)

Director Howard Storm's sons, Anthony and Casey Storm, appear in the film as a couple of kids.

Once Upon a Crime (1992)

Director Eugene Levy has a cameo in the film as a cashier.

One Froggy Evening (1955)

The building in the closing scenes is named the Tregoweth Brown building, a reference to film editor Treg Brown.

One from the Heart (1982)

Director Francis Ford Coppola's parents, Carmine and Italia Coppola, can be seen in an elevator in the film. Carmine also serves as composer of many of his son's films.

One in a Million: The Ron LeFlore Story (1978 TV)

James Luisi plays Jimmy Karalla in this telefilm, and the real Jimmy Karalla also has a cameo as a heckler.

One of Our Aircraft Is Missing (1942)

Director Michael Powell appears in a cameo as a dispatching officer.

One on One (1977)

Barry Brunz, Robby Benson's alumni big brother, is played by director Lamont Johnson.

One, Two, Three (1961)

C.R. McNamara (James Cagney) threatens a girl with a grapefruit, reminiscent of his mushy scene in *Public Enemy* (1931) with Mae Clark.

Cagney also says, "Mother of mercy, is this the end of Little Rico?" This is a parody of Edward G. Robinson's line in *Little Caesar* (1930), which was "Mother of mercy, is this the end of Rico?"

Only the Lonely (1991)

To try to make peace with Maureen O'Hara, Ally Sheedy agrees to go see a film with her and John Candy. The film they wind up going to see is *How Green Was My Valley* (1939) starring Maureen O'Hara.

Operation Kid Brother (1967)

This film stars Sean Connery's younger brother, Neil, as a spy, along with James Bond film regulars Bernard Lee (M) and Lois Maxwell (Moneypenny). In this film, Lee plays Neil's boss, Commander Cunningham, and Maxwell plays Cunningham's secretary, Max. Adolfo Celi, who was Emilio Largo in *Thunderball* (1965), appears as Thair, the villain, and the love interests are played by Daniela Bianchi, who appeared in *From Russia with Love* (1963) and Yashiko Yama from *You Only Live Twice* (1967).

The Osterman Weekend (1983)

Director Sam Peckinpah's daughter Kristen appears as Dick Tremayne's (Dennis Hopper) secretary.

Out of the Dark (1988)

A credit in the film reads "In Loving Memory of Divine." It was the last role for actor Harris Glenn Milstead, a.k.a. Divine.

Outland (1981)

Marc Boyle plays a character named Spota. Director-screenwriter Peter Hyams has included a character named "Spota" in many of his films since *The Hunter* (1980), which he wrote.

The Outsiders (1983)

The letter jacket that the "soc" at the concession stand is wearing as he challenges Darrel (Patrick Swayze) is a jacket from the high school that author S.E. Hinton attended.

Overboard (1987)

Sheriff Earl is played by actor Bing Russell, who is Kurt Russell's dad.

Pacific Heights (1990)

Director John Schlesinger can be seen getting on the hotel elevator.

Pack Up Your Troubles (1932)

Composer Marvin Hatley has a cameo as a soldier in the battlefield scene. He had previously played another soldier in the earlier Laurel and Hardy film, *Beau Hunks* (1931).

Pale Rider (1985)

Executive producer Fritz Manes, who produced many of Clint Eastwood's films, has a cameo as a stage rider.

The Paradine Case (1947)

Director Alfred Hitchcock is seen leaving the train at Cumberland Station, carrying a cello.

Pardon Us (1931)

Producer Hal Roach and director James Parrott have cameos in the film. After Oliver Hardy is recaptured, he is marched along. Roach is marching right in front of Hardy, and Parrott is beside Hardy.

Party Camp (1987)

One of the kids at the camp is the son of director Gary Graver. He is the pudgy kid at the shooting range with the shooting instructor, Dyanne (Jewel Shepard).

Passenger 57 (1992)

FBI agent Dwight Henderson is played by Robert Hooks, father of director Kevin Hooks.

Pastime (1991)

Roy Dean (William Russ) and Tyrone (Glenn Plummer) walk down a dark alley, and Russ mentions a couple of pitchers' names: Paige, Newcombe, Feller and Spahn. Don Newcombe and Bob Feller are among six ex–major leaguers who appear in cameos at the first game in the movie:

Duke Snider sits in the stands, eating hot dogs with his daughters.

Don Newcombe raises the flag for the national anthem.

Ernie Banks, Harmon Killebrew, Bob Feller and Bill Mazeroski can be seen standing in the stands during the national anthem.

The Pawnbroker (1965)

Director Sidney Lumet's father, Baruch, appears as Mendel.

Peeping Tom (1960)

Mark's (Karlheinz Boehm) father is played by director Michael Powell. In the scenes showing Mark as a child, Mark is played by Powell's son, Columba Powell.

Pee-wee's Big Adventure (1985)

Phil Hartman and Michael Varhol, who cowrote the film with Paul Reubens (Pee-wee), both have cameos.

Hartman, in his film debut, plays a reporter and Varhol plays a photographer.

Peggy Sue Got Married (1986)

Peggy Sue's (Kathleen Turner) bratty younger sister, Nancy, is played by director Francis Ford Coppola's daughter, Sofia Coppola.

The People vs. Larry Flynt (1996)

Following in the footsteps of Jim Garrison in JFK (see JFK, 1991), the real Larry Flynt appears as the judge who sentences Flynt (Woody Harrelson).

The Perfect Weapon (1991)

There is a line in the credits dedicating the film "to Ed Parker and the spirit of Kenpo." Parker is a martial arts teacher who teaches the art of Kenpo. The film's star, Jeff Speakman, was a pupil of Parker's.

A Perfect World (1993)

Butch (Kevin Costner) and Philip visit a Friendly Department Store, outside of which there is a poster for Costner's Bull Durham (1988).

Pete 'n' Tillie (1972)

Walter Matthau takes his girl to a cinema showing Lonely Are the Brave (62), one of his earlier films.

Pet Sematary (1989)

The book's author, Stephen King, appears as the minister at little Gage's funeral.

The Phantom (1996)

While Kit (Billy Zane) speaks with the spirit of his father (Patrick McGoohan) in the back seat of the cab, Al the cabbie (John Capodice) looks back at him warily. Kit then speaks to Al, and Al replies with, "You talkin' to me now?" This line comes from Robert De Niro's cabbie character in the film *Taxi Driver* (1976).

Phantom of the Paradise (1974)
The studio owner, Philbin (George Memmoli), is named after Mary Philbin, the star of *The Phantom of the Opera* (1925).

The original record label was called "Swan Song Records," but all references had to be optically removed, because the real Swan Song Records, which handled such acts as Led Zeppelin, sued. Ergo there are wavy lines around the logos.

After Beef is killed, Swan talks to Phoenix (Jessica Harper) in her dressing room. There is an article clipped to the mirror with the headline, "Harper's Bizarre." It is an actual review of the work of Jessica Harper.

Philadelphia (1993)
Tom Hanks's father is played by the Reverend Robert Castle, who was the subject of director Jonathan Demme's *Cousin Bobby* (1991). He is Demme's cousin.

Low-budget moviemaker Roger Corman, who gave Demme his start in film, has a cameo as Mr. Laird.

Demme's long-time producer, Kenneth Utt (here serving as executive producer) has a cameo in the jury.

Pillow Talk (1959)
Rock Hudson poses as an effeminate man to try to get to know Doris Day better. This was a ploy Hudson often used in his films to gain the confidence of prospective lovers. The in-joke, which was well-known by the gay community in Hollywood, was that this was a gay man (Hudson, who didn't publically reveal himself to be a homosexual until much later) playing a straight man pretending to be gay.

Pimpernel Smith (1941)
Screenwriter Roland Pertwee has a cameo as Sir George Smith.

Pink Cadillac (1989)
Clint Eastwood and Bernadette Peters sit at a table in a Las Vegas club that features a stand-up comic in the background doing an Elvis Presley impression. The comic is played by Jim Carrey, who had previously appeared in Eastwood's *The Dead Pool* (1988) and became a good friend of Eastwood's.

Eastwood pulls into a gas station and asks the attendant if he is seen a strawberry blonde in a pink Cadillac. The attendant looks up from the windshield he is cleaning and says, "Only in my dreams." The attendant is played by rock singer Bryan Adams.

The Pink Panther Strikes Again (1976)
As former Chief Inspector Dreyfus (Herbert Lom) fades out of sight at the end, he is gleefully playing an organ, a scene reminiscent of Lom's 1962 version of the film *The Phantom of the Opera.*

Planes, Trains and Automobiles (1987)
At the beginning of the movie, Neal Page (Steve Martin) races another man for a taxi. He is played by Kevin Bacon, in a cameo. Later, Neal phones his wife to tell her that he has been delayed, again, and in the background, you can hear the fight from *She's Having a Baby* (1988) between Bacon and Elizabeth McGovern, when she screams that she doesn't like his friend's girlfriend. Both films were directed by John Hughes.

Platoon (1986)
Director Oliver Stone can be seen giving orders in a bunker. A Viet Cong

soldier with a bomb strapped to his back runs in and blows them all up.

After Sgt. Elias (Willem Dafoe) complains about having to take inexperienced men on a dangerous mission, O'Reilly (John C. McGinley) observes, "He's been here two years and he thinks he's Jesus fucking Christ." Two years later (1988), Dafoe appeared as Jesus in *The Last Temptation of Christ*, in which it was implied that Christ did have sex.

Play Misty for Me (1971)

Don Siegel, who had directed many of the films of this film's director-star, Clint Eastwood, has a cameo as Murphy, Dave Garver's bartender friend.

The Playboys (1992)

Screenwriter Shane Connaughton plays the customs officer.

The Player (1992)

The opening tracking shot (which lasts, uncut, for six-and-a-half minutes) includes dialogue from Fred Ward about famous long tracking shots in older movies, particularly the opening shot of Orson Welles's *Touch of Evil* (1958), and how they are never done any more. Fifteen takes of this shot were made, five were printed, and the tenth one was used in the film. In fact, you can see the actual slate, and hear "Take ten" at the very beginning of the shot.

Cher appears at the awards ceremony in a bright red dress, despite the invitation specifying "black and white only." In real life, Cher never wears red.

This film's screenwriter (and producer) Michael Tolkin appears in the film with his brother Stephen as Eric and Carl Schecter. They try to sell Griffin (Tim Robbins) a script just after he gets back from the police station.

The Playgirl and the War Minister (1962)

This was the American title of the British film *The Amourous Mr. Prawn*, which was about a general's wife who opened their official home to paying guests. However, there is no playgirl or War Minister in the film. It was so titled because of the popularity of the Profumo Scandal at the time, which concerned an affair between England's war minister and playgirl Mandy Rice-Davies. The affair was the subject of the film *Scandal* (1989).

Point Break (1991)

One of the places that Utah (Keanu Reeves) follows Bodhi (Patrick Swayze) to is Patrick's Roadhouse. Swayze previously starred in the film *Road House* (1989).

Point of No Return (1993)

During the escape, the last guard at the gate is played by cinematographer Michael Watkins.

Director John Badham has a cameo as a room-service waiter.

Poltergeist (1982)

The movie on television in the bedroom is *A Guy Named Joe* (1943), a film about a pilot who returns to the world as a ghost. Steven Spielberg (who cowrote and coproduced) first saw it on television when he was 14, and it was one of the first films to make him cry. He later remade the movie as *Always* (1989).

Poltergeist III (1988)

The film is dedicated to Heather O'Rourke, who played the little girl in all three *Poltergeist* films. O'Rourke died at the age of 12, just after filming this movie. Ironically, the actors who played her siblings from both of the previous films also passed away.

Porky's II: The Next Day (1983)
Coscripter Roger Swaybill plays a busboy in the film.

Posse (1993)
Jimmy Love is played by noted television producer Stephen J. Cannell (*The A-Team*).

Possessed by the Night (1994)
Writer-director Fred Olen Ray has a cameo as a waiter.

Predator 2 (1990)
The skull of a creature that resembles the ones in the *Alien* movie series is on the wall in the Predator's trophy room. Prior to this movie, DC Comics put out a popular series, *Alien vs. Predator*. Furthermore, the story for this film is very similar to an early draft of the film *Alien³* (1992), in which the aliens landed on Earth.

The Presidio (1988)
James Hooks Reynolds plays a character named Spota. Director Peter Hyams has included a character named "Spota" in many of his films since *The Hunter* (1980), which he wrote.

Pretty Maids All in a Row (1971)
Gene Roddenberry wrote and produced the film, and Roddenberry's daughter Dawn has a small role.

Roddenberry also cast James Doohan in this film. Doohan had played Scotty in Roddenberry's *Star Trek* some years before.

Prince of Darkness (1988)
The credits list "Martin Quatermass" as the screenwriter, but it was actually director John Carpenter. The

pseudonym is a homage to Professor Quatermass, a famous character in sci-fi created by British writer Nigel Kneale. However, producer Larry Franco has denied that this is a pseudonym for Carpenter, possibly because of the negative reaction that the film received. The press kit for the film contains the following biography of the screenwriter: "Martin Quatermass, born in London, England, is a former physicist and brother of Bernard Quatermass, the rocket scientist who headed the British Rocket Group during the 1950s. Quatermass graduated from Kneale University with a degree in theoretical physics. *Prince of Darkness* is his first screenplay, and he assures that all the physical principles used in the story, including the ability of subatomic particles to travel backward in time, are true. Author of two novels, *Schrodinger's Revenge* and *Schwarzchild Radius*, he currently lives in Frazier Park, California, with his wife, Janet."

The Princess Bride (1987)
The cap that director Rob Reiner (as filmmaker Marty DeBergi) wore in his film *This Is Spinal Tap* (1984) can be seen hanging on a peg behind the headboard of Fred Savage's bed (next to the devil mask).

Christopher Guest (as Count Rugen) does his imitation of Henry Daniell in the film *The Sea Hawk* (1940).

Prison Ship (1984)
The voice of the mouse robot is provided by writer-director-producer Fred Olen Ray.

Private Investigations (1987)
Director-screenwriter Nigel Dick appears in the film as a photographer.

Problem Child (1990)

Director Dennis Dugan has a cameo as the "All-American Dad."

The Professional (1994)

Gary Oldman states to a drug dealer that he "knows" Beethoven. Oldman played Ludwig van Beethoven in his previous film, *Immortal Beloved* (1994).

Prom Night III: The Last Kiss (1989)

The sex ed teacher is played by director Ron Oliver. He also did the voice-over one-liners.

Psycho (1960)

Director Alfred Hitchcock can be seen through Janet Leigh's window as she returns to her office. He is wearing a cowboy hat.

Hitchcock's daughter, Patricia, also appears as Leigh's married coworker, Caroline.

Psycho II (1983)

Screenwriter Tom Holland plays Deputy Norris.

Psycho IV: The Beginning (1990 TV)

Director Mick Garris was very eager to direct this film when he heard of the story, and campaigned for it. Director John Landis really wanted Garris to direct the film as well, so he called up executive producer Hilton Green, star Anthony Perkins and MCA to get him the job. In return, Garris cast Landis as Mike Calvecchio, the producer of Fran Ambrose's radio talk show.

In the December 1990 issue of *Cinefantastique*, it was reported that Hilton Green (who was the producer of *Psycho II*, 1983, and *Psycho III*, 1986, and the assistant director on Alfred Hitchcock's original *Psycho*, 1960), has a bit part as the mayor of Fairville (actually Fair*vale*); that this film's coproducer, George Zaloom, appears as an orderly in the mental hospital; and that Garris himself has a cameo as a fireman. However, Green and Garris are not listed in the credits, and no mayor is shown. The only shot of a fireman is a very brief glimpse at the end, and Zaloom is credited as playing a janitor, but no janitor is seen in the film, either.

Garris did give his wife a part, as in his other films. Cynthia Garris appears as Ellen Stevens, Fran's technician in the booth with Landis.

Many lines and camera shots are taken right out of *Psycho* (1960). During the fireworks, Norman (Henry Thomas) says that his mother is in bed and that she "hasn't been herself lately." Also, after Norman kills his girlfriend, he cries, "Mother! Oh, God, mother ... Blood! Blood!" These lines were also in the original film.

Norman peeks through a hole in one of the cabins at someone in the shower (in this case his mother's boyfriend), as in the first film. In the most stylish reference to *Psycho*, Norman (Anthony Perkins) cuts his thumb and puts it under the kitchen tap. He watches the blood go down the drain in a shot exactly like the one from the shower scene in *Psycho*.

Pulp Fiction (1994)

The marquee where Butch (Bruce Willis) is boxing advertises the following fights: "Coolidge vs. Wilson" and "Vossler vs. Martinez." The first is a reference to the presidential election race of Calvin Coolidge and Woodrow Wilson. The second is a reference to Rand Vossler and Jerry Martinez, two friends of director Quentin Tarantino from when he worked in a video store.

The motorcycle (or "chopper") that Bruce Willis rides away from the pawn shop is named "Grace," which some people have interpreted as a religious message. In reality, Tarantino's ex-girl-friend's name is Grace. He dated her when he was working at Video Archives, before fame and fortune, and they got back together again before he began making *Pulp Fiction*.

During World War II, Little Butch's grandfather got his watch out of the war by giving it to a gunner named Winocki. In the film *Air Force* (1941), John Garfield gives a dog to a Marine to get it out of harm's way. Garfield's name in the film was Winocki.

Marcellus Wallace and Vincent Vega get their names from characters in "Reservoir Dogs": Marcellus Spivey was Mr. White's former fence, and Vic Vega was Mr. Blonde's real name.

In Tarantino's *Reservoir Dogs* (1992), Mr. Pink (Steve Buscemi) gives a long speech about not tipping waitresses. Buscemi has a cameo in *Pulp Fiction* as the waiter in Jack Rabbit Slims dressed as Buddy Holly. Vincent says he is "not much of a waiter."

Lance (Eric Stoltz) shows three types of heroin to Vincent. One is called "Bava." This is a reference to Mario Bava, who directed such cult horror films as *Danger: Diabolik* (1967) and *The Evil Eye* (1962).

Jimmy (Tarantino) wears a T-shirt bearing the logo of *Orbit*, a local alternative newspaper in Detroit. Tarantino did an interview with this paper when he was promoting *Reservoir Dogs* (1992).

Puppet Master (1989)
Director David Schmoeller also wrote the script, but used the pseudonym "Joseph G. Collodi." Carlo Collodi was the name of the Italian author who wrote *The Adventures of Pinocchio*

in 1883, another story of puppets coming to life.

The film's prologue is set in the Bodega Bay Inn. Bodega Bay was the setting of the Alfred Hitchcock film *The Birds* (1963).

The Puppet Masters (1994)
When Sam (Eric Thal) goes to Neil Jarvis's apartment and finds the eggs, he rings the super's doorbell. The name at the top of the apartment's doorbells is "J. Hegedus." James C. Hegedus was the film's art director.

Q & A (1990)
Director Sidney Lumet's daughter, Jenny, plays Nancy Bosch.

Coproducer Burtt Harris plays Phil.

The Quest (1996)
Roger Moore introduces himself as "Dobbs, Lord Dobbs," parodying his James Bond character.

The Quick and the Dead (1995)
Director Sam Raimi's pal Bruce Campbell is credited as "Wedding Shemp," but his part was cut from the film (see *The Evil Dead*, 1983).

Quiz Show (1994)
When Van Doren (Ralph Fiennes) is asked about the names of the kings of numerous countries (and he deliberately flubs the name of the King of Belgium), one of the questions concerns Iraq. Van Doren says, "Yes, I remember from reading the *Seven Pillars of Wisdom*." In the PBS film *A Dangerous Man: Lawrence After Arabia* (1992 TV), Lawrence (Fiennes) writes the *Seven Pillars of Wisdom*.

Quo Vadis? (1951)
Peter Ustinov, as Nero, says as he dies, "Is this the end of Nero?," echoing Edward G. Robinson's line at the

end of *Little Caesar* (1930), "Is this the end of Rico?"

Elizabeth Taylor was originally scheduled to star in this film, but had to bow out. At one point during filming, she visited the set and appeared as an extra, as one of the Christians being herded into the Coliseum.

The Rabbit of Seville (1950)

A signboard lists the opera's featured cast as Michele Maltese and Carlo Jonzi, references to the cartoon's writer, Michael Maltese, and director, Charles "Chuck" Jones.

Radio Flyer (1992)

A poster for *X-15* (1961), also directed by Richard Donner, is visible outside the movie theater.

Radioland Murders (1994)

The film is dedicated to the memory of actress Anita Morris, who died soon after her scenes were shot.

Raging Bull (1980)

Director Martin Scorsese has a cameo as a Barbizon stagehand, and his father, Charles, plays Charlie, the man with Como.

Raiders of the Lost Ark (1981)

Indy (Harrison Ford) is saved from an angry horde of Hovito Indians by a seaplane bearing the call letters OB-CPO, a reference to producer George Lucas's *Star Wars* characters, Obi-Wan Kenobi and C-3PO.

The Nazi pilot in the desert who takes aim at Indy during his fistfight is played by producer Frank Marshall.

In one of the Indy series' most popular scenes, Indy is challenged by a large swordsman, who swings his scimitar around in grandiose fashion. A big fight scene is anticipated, but Indy just draws his gun and shoots him. Ford got dysentery while on location, and was feeling awful when they were trying to shoot the scene. The way it was originally scripted, Indy and the guy with the sword were supposed to face off and Indy was supposed to beat him with the whip. After multiple takes that did not work right, Ford decided to just pull the gun and shoot, so he could end the scene and go collapse.

Rain Man (1988)

Autistic savant Raymond Babbitt (Dustin Hoffman) memorizes a phone book up to and including the names of Marsha and William Gottsegen, who are Hoffman's real-life in-laws.

At the end, the hospital sends a doctor to interview and evaluate Raymond. The doctor is played, uncredited, by director Barry Levinson.

The Rainbow (1989)

Glenda Jackson here plays the mother of the character she portrayed in *Women in Love* (1969).

Raising Arizona (1987)

The film's directors, Joel and Ethan Coen, cast their lawyer, Peter Benedek, as the prison counsellor advising convicts on their future "careers."

The acronyms "P-O-E," "E-O-P" and "O-P-E," spray-painted in the washroom, are references to Sterling Hayden's carvings in *Dr. Strangelove, or How I Learned to Stop Worrying and Love the Bomb* (1963).

Factory workers can be seen wearing overalls bearing the name "Hudsucker Industries." Director Joel Coen would later go on to use the same name in his *The Hudsucker Proxy* (1994) (see also *Crimewave*, 1985).

Gale (John Goodman) and Evelle Snopes (William Forsythe) take their surname from the stories of William Faulkner. The white-trash Snopes family appears in several Faulkner novels, beginning with *The Hamlet*.

William Preston Robertson has a voice cameo (see *Blood Simple*, 1984).

Real Genius (1985)

After Mitch (Gabe Jarrett) spills all his papers on some steps and Jonathan Gries helps him pick them up, he walks up to Chris (Val Kilmer) in a classroom. Kilmer is flipping two quarters over the knuckles of both of his hands. This "knuckle flip" became Kilmer's "signature" move and he has used it in many of his later films.

Rear Window (1954)

Director Alfred Hitchcock can be seen winding the clock on the mantlepiece in the songwriter's apartment. The songwriter is played by real-life songwriter Ross Bagdasarian, who created the characters of David Seville and Alvin, Simon and Theodore, the Chipmunks.

Rebecca (1940)

Near the end of the film, George Sanders argues with a policeman who accuses him of illegal parking. Director Alfred Hitchcock walks past in the background. This is shortly after the scene with Sanders in the phone booth. There is an often-published studio photo that shows Hitchcock just outside the booth while Sanders is using the phone, but that scene does not appear in the film.

Red Heat (1988)

Viktor Rosta's (Ed O'Ross) brother, who Arnold Schwarzenegger shoots dead on the stairs, is played by Gabor Koncz, Hungary's leading action movie star.

Reds (1981)

Harvard Lampoon veteran George Plimpton plays a magazine publisher who rejects the articles submitted by John Reed (Warren Beatty). In real life, John Reed was himself a member of the *Harvard Lampoon*.

The Ref (1994)

This film was written by Richard LaGravenese, whose screenplay for *The Fisher King* (1991) was selected by film critic Gene Siskel as the worst Academy Award nomination of 1991. So, in this film, the military school commandant is named "Siskel" and even looks a little like him. The character is blackmailed by one of his students, who has photos showing "Siskel" with topless dancers.

Jeremiah Willard is played by Jonathan Demme's longtime producer, Kenneth Utt.

The Reivers (1969)

William Faulkner, on whose novel the film is based, named the Memphis whorehouse "Binford's" after notorious Memphis movie censor Lloyd T. Binford.

Repo Man (1984)

The Repo Man's Code is a parody of Isaac Asimov's *Laws of Robotics*.

The announcement "Paging Dr. Benway" is heard in the hospital, and the name "Bill Lee" is mentioned. These were both characters in William S. Burroughs's book *Naked Lunch*.

Lite (Sy Richardson) gives Otto

(Emilio Estevez) a book called *Diuretics* to "help change your life." This is a reference to L. Ron Hubbard's *Dianetics*.

The movie was made by Edge City Productions. Edge City is a recurring theme in Tom Wolfe's *Electric Kool-Aid Acid Test*. Also, the destination placard on the bus that Otto takes back to his folks' house reads "Edge City."

Writer-director Alex Cox has a cameo in the film.

Repulsion (1965)
Director Roman Polanski appears as a spoons player.

Reservoir Dogs (1992)
Suzanne Celeste, who plays the lady that Mr. Orange (Tim Roth) shoots, was Roth's dialogue coach. Roth insisted that she take the role because she was so hard on him.

In a flashback scene, Mr. White (Harvey Keitel) is asked about "Alabama." This is a reference to Patricia Arquette's role in screenwriter Quentin Tarantino's *True Romance* (1993). In that film's original ending, Alabama ends up a widow and turns to crime with Mr. White.

The Return of Frank James (1940)
John Carradine, who plays "that dirty little coward, Bob Ford," dies in this film to please the Hays Code. The film is a sequel to *Jesse James* (1939), also starring Henry Fonda. In the previous film, Ford (Carradine) shoots Jesse James (Tyrone Power) in the back, and gets away with very little retribution following his crime. The Production Code of the day would not allow such an act to go unpunished, so he was brought back for the sequel (this film) and made to pay.

The Return of Sherlock Holmes (1987 TV)
The book that Ms. Houston (Lila Kaye) is reading at her desk was written by Jessica Fletcher. Jessica Fletcher was the name of the crime-solving mystery writer played by Angela Lansbury in the series *Murder, She Wrote*.

Return of the Jedi (1983)
Three of Jabba's henchmen are named Klaatu, Barada, and Nikto, after the famous phrase from *The Day the Earth Stood Still* (1951).

Lando's copilot, Nien Numb, supposedly speaks a Kenyan dialect, and one of his lines is apparently translated as "A thousand herds of elephants are standing on my foot."

Chewbacca and two Ewoks take over an AT-ST manned with two Imperial commandos. One of the two is the film's director, Richard Marquand. The other is Frank Marshall, producer of the occasional George Lucas film.

Return of the Living Dead (1985)
A policeman pulls up to the cemetery in a van, gets out, and has his brains eaten by zombie Trash (Linnea Quigley). The cop is played by director Dan O'Bannon.

Return of the Living Dead Part II (1988)
One of the zombies looks remarkably like Michael Jackson in full *Thriller* gear, and, after being electrified, its hair catches on fire (referring to Jackson's accident during filming of a Pepsi commercial).

The Return of the Man from U.N.C.L.E. (1983 TV)
George Lazenby appears briefly and helps Napoleon Solo (Robert Vaughn) out of a jam. Lazenby is driving an

Aston-Martin with the license plate "JB-007," but is never actually called James Bond. Lazenby played Bond in *On Her Majesty's Secret Service* (1969).

Return of the Pink Panther (1975)

A number of international assassins try to kill Clouseau at Oktoberfest (and fail), and it is mentioned at one point that only the Russian and Egyptian assassins are left. As soon as this is mentioned, there is a cut to an elevator opening and out steps the Egyptian assassin, the uncredited (and Egyptian) Omar Sharif.

Revenge of the Creature (1955)

In all the *Creature* pictures (*The Creature from the Black Lagoon*, 1954; *The Creature Walks Among Us*, 1956; and this one), the Creature is played by underwater swimming expert Ricou Browning. In this picture, Browning also has a cameo out of costume as a scientist. He assists John Agar and Lori Nelson in examining a shark on a table in the laboratory.

Star John Agar said that he had a wonderful time making the picture, and that his wife Loretta joined him on location. Agar has said, "as a matter of fact, she had a little part in the picture. Remember the scene at the lobster house? After that, there's a shot of a guy and a girl in a boat; the girl's Loretta."

Ricochet (1991)

Mary Ellen Trainor reprises her role of reporter Gail Wallens, whom she played in *Die Hard* (1988).

The Right Stuff (1983)

Beeman's, the gum that is chewed in the film, is the lucky gum of pilots. It was also used in *The Rocketeer* (1991).

Brigadier General Chuck Yeager (who is played in the film by Sam Shepard) appears as the bartender at the bar the test pilots frequent.

Rio Bravo (1959)

This was the first film in which John Wayne wore his *Red River* "D" belt buckle. The letter "D" is for Dunson (Wayne's character in *Red River* was named Tom Dunson) and the two wavy lines represent a river. This was given to him by director Howard Hawks in commemoration of the brand used in *Red River* (1948). Wayne went on to wear this belt buckle in various other films.

The River (1984)

Director Mark Rydell's daughter Amy appears as young Betty Gaumer.

The River Wild (1994)

Roarke (Joseph Mazzello) wears a Ministry cap through part of the film. Ministry performed some of the songs on the film's soundtrack.

Road Show (1941)

Shemp Howard appears in a cameo as Moe Parker. The character was named after Howard's brother and fellow Stooge, Moe Howard.

The Road to Utopia (1945)

Bob Hope says that Bing Crosby's voice is "just right for selling cheese," which is what Crosby used it for on his then-popular radio show.

At one point, Bob and Bing are sledding and happen to glance at a far-off mountain. Suddenly, stars appear above it, mimicking the logo of Paramount, who made the picture. Hope says to the camera, "It may only be a mountain to you, but it's bread and butter to me."

Roberta (1935)

During the song "I Won't Dance," Ginger Rogers sings to Fred Astaire about "doing the Continental," a reference to the dance in their previous film, *The Gay Divorcee* (1934). The two then strike a pose from that number while the band plays a riff.

There is a bugle call before one of Fred Astaire and Ginger Rogers's dance numbers (see *The Gay Divorcee*, 1934).

Robin Hood: Men in Tights (1993)

Robert Ridgely reprises his role of the hangman from director Mel Brooks's *Blazing Saddles* (1974).

King John (Richard Lewis) asks Robin (authentic Brit Cary Elwes) why the people would follow him. Robin smirks and says, "Because ... unlike some other Robin Hoods, I can speak with an English accent." One of the criticisms of Kevin Costner's role in *Robin Hood: Prince of Thieves* (1991) was that his English accent was horrible.

Ah Choo's pep talk ("We didn't land on Sherwood Forest ... Sherwood Forest landed on us!") is a parody of Denzel Washington's similar speech in *Malcolm X* (1992).

At the end of *Robin Hood: Prince of Thieves*, Sean Connery made an unbilled cameo as King Richard. In this one, Patrick Stewart makes a similar cameo.

As Richard kisses Maid Marian, the Rabbi (Mel Brooks) looks over his shoulder and says, "It's good to be the king." This was the phrase Brooks kept saying as the king in the French Revolution segment of *History of the World—Part 1* (1981).

RoboCop (1987)

Screenwriter Ed Neumeier named the gang's weaselly second-in-command Emil Antonowsky (played by Paul McCrane)—his full name is seen on the library computer screen with which RoboCop interfaces. However, Neumeier refuses to admit that this was a reference to Universal Studios marketing president Marvin Antonowsky.

RoboCop 2 (1990)

In the scene where RoboCop is being reprogrammed by Dr. Juliette Faxx (Belinda Bauer), the following hex numbers scroll quickly up the screen: "50 45 54 45 20 4B 55 52 41 4E 20 49 53 20 41 20 47 52 45 41 54 20 47 55 59." Converted to ASCII text, it reads: "Pete Kuran is a great guy." Kuran was the film's special effects photographer.

Among RoboCop's new directives ("Don't walk across a ballroom floor swinging your arms") is DIRECTIVE 262—"Avoid Orion meetings." Orion was the film's production company. The line was sneaked in by Kuran, who said, "I just sort of put it in. I figured somebody at home might see it and be amused."

Leadperson David Hack's name can be seen in some graffiti painted on a wall.

The Rock (1996)

Sean Connery is asked where he got his training and with a smile, he replies "British Intelligence." This is a playful reference by Connery to his days as James Bond.

When Goodspeed (Nicolas Cage) introduces himself as "Stanley Goodspeed," Connery says, "But of course you are!" This was the line Connery used in the Bond film *Diamonds Are Forever* (1971) when Plenty O'Toole (Lana Wood) introduced herself to Bond.

The Rocketeer (1991)

The villain's henchman, Lothar (Tiny Ron) is made up to look exactly like old-time tough-guy actor Rondo Hatton.

The model that Cliff (Bill Campbell) glides away on to make his escape from the FBI is reminiscent of Howard Hughes's Spruce Goose, a huge plane made entirely of wood which most people doubted would ever fly. This explains his "Son of a bitch *will* fly!" comment. At the time the film was made, Disney owned the original Spruce Goose, and they supposedly placed this part in the film as a promotion for that attraction, which was one of only two money-losing Disney attractions in the United States (the other was *The Queen Mary*).

Cliff chews gum through the movie for luck, and at the end, Hughes throws him a pack of Beeman's gum and says, "Don't ever fly her without this." Beeman's is the lucky gum of pilots. It was also used in *The Right Stuff* (1983).

As Neville Sinclair (Timothy Dalton) flies away from the exploding blimp in the jet pack, he says, "I'll miss Hollywood." Cliff replies, "I don't think so." Sinclair then proceeds to crash into the "Hollywoodland" sign, destroying the letters "land" (see *1941*, 1979).

Dave Stevens, the creator of the *Rocketeer* comic book, appears as the commanding officer in the Nazi black and white test flight movie.

Rocky (1976)

A streetcorner quartet can be seen singing the song "Take Me Back." In reality, the group was called The Valentines, and its lead singer was Sly's brother, Frank Stallone.

When he was a struggling actor, Stallone lived on Balboa Boulevard in Los Angeles. He used the name of this street for Rocky's surname.

In 1975, Sylvester Stallone appeared in an episode of *Police Story* where he played a cop named Elmore Quincy Caddo. In one scene, he asked his partner to call him by his nickname— "Rocky." This was the inspiration for his character's first name in this film.

Rocky V (1990)

Director John G. Avildsen cast his two sons, Chris and Jonathan, as the two druggies.

The Rocky Horror Picture Show (1975)

Eddie (Meat Loaf) has the words "Love" and "Hate" printed on his knuckles. This is a reference to *The Night of the Hunter* (1955), in which Robert Mitchum had the same words on his knuckles.

The film's crew had an Easter egg hunt on the set one day, and three of the eggs can be seen in the film. One is under Frank's throne, one appears instead of a light in the main room, and one can be seen as the group goes up in the elevator to the lab.

The Rookie (1990)

As Charlie Sheen comes into the dry cleaner that serves as a front, he says, "Candygram for Mr. Mongo." This was a line said by Sheriff Bart (Cleavon Little) to fool Mongo (Alex Karras) in the film *Blazing Saddles* (1973).

Romeo and Juliet (1996)

There are many references to the works of Shakespeare:

A familiar red-and-white "Enjoy Coca-Cola" logo is morphed into a sign reading "Wherefore L'amour." There is a hot dog stand named

Rosencranzky's, after the character of Rosencrantz in *Hamlet*.

The run-down theater in Verona is called the Globe. The London theater in which Shakespeare's plays were originally performed was called the Globe.

"The Merchant of Verona Beach" is named after *The Merchant of Venice*.

"Out, Out Damn Spot Cleaners" is from a line of Lady Macbeth's in *Macbeth*.

Rope (1948)

Director Alfred Hitchcock's trademark profile can be seen briefly on a flashing neon sign in the view from the apartment window. In fact, it is actually a sign advertising the "Reduco" product that was the subject of his cameo in *Lifeboat* (1944). However, it is virtually impossible to read the word "Reduco" by watching the film on video or laserdisc, and it is very difficult even in a theater. The problem is that the sign is not in focus due to the limited depth of field provided by the movie camera. However, in Patrick Humphries's *The Films of Alfred Hitchcock* there is a still photo that is just barely sharp enough to make out "Reduco"—especially if one knows it is there. Some sources say that Hitchcock has a flesh-and-blood cameo, crossing a street, but the neon sign is in fact his only appearance in this film.

Rosemary's Baby (1968)

Producer William Castle has a cameo as a man in a phone booth.

Rosemary (Mia Farrow) meets a woman in her laundry room (played by Angela Dorian) and remarks that she looks like actress Victoria Vetri. The joke here is that Dorian actually *is* Vetri, a former *Playboy* Playmate and star of *When Dinosaurs Ruled the Earth*

(1970), who had just changed her name to Angela Dorian.

Rough Cut (1980)

The script is credited to "Francis Burns," but it was actually written by Larry Gelbart, using Larry Linville's character's name in Gelbart's series *M*A*S*H* as a pseudonym.

Roxanne (1987)

This movie is a remake or update of the story of Cyrano de Bergerac. Steve Martin's character, C.D. Bales, has the same initials as de Bergerac.

Rude Awakening (1990)

In this 1960s-based film, there are three '60s survivors seated at a table in the background of Ronnie Sunshine's Nouveau Woodstock restaurant: Dr. Timothy Leary, proponent of hallucinogenic drugs; former Black Panther Bobby Seale; and '60s activist Jerry Rubin.

The voice of the "smoked" fish was provided by director Aaron Russo.

Rumble Fish (1983)

The film is based on a book by S.E. Hinton, who also appears in a bit role in the film.

Director Francis Ford Coppola's son, Gio, appears in a small role.

Runaway Brain (1995)

There is a character named Dr. Frankenollie, and besides the obvious Frankenstein reference, it was also a reference to legendary Disney animators Frank Thomas and Ollie Johnston.

Runaway Daughters (1994 TV)

Low-budget filmmaker Roger Corman, who gave director Joe Dante his start in film, has a cameo as Mr. Randolph.

The Running Man (1987)

Just before Ben Richards (Arnold Schwarzenegger) is whisked down the tube, he turns to Killian (Richard Dawson) and says, "I'll be back." Killian replies, "Only in a rerun" (see *Commando*, 1985).

Schwarzenegger's friend and chief competitor from his bodybuilding days, Franco Columbu, appears as a 911 security officer.

Ruthless People (1986)

Codirectors Jerry and David Zucker's mother, Charlotte Zucker, has a cameo as the judge at Sam Stone's bail hearing.

The Ryan White Story (1989 TV)

The real Ryan White plays a fellow patient of Ryan's (Lukas Haas).

Saboteur (1942)

Robert Cummings and the saboteurs drive into New York and pull up in front of a line of stores. On the far left of the screen, in front of the picture window of Cut Rate Drugs, director Alfred Hitchcock can be seen very briefly.

Saint Jack (1979)

Eddie Schuman is played by the film's director, Peter Bogdanovich.

Salem's Lot (1979 TV)

James Mason plays the vampire's aide, and Mason's wife, Clarissa Kaye, has a small part as a female vampire.

Samson and Delilah (1984 TV)

Victor Mature, who played Samson in the original 1949 film, here plays Samson's father.

The Sand Pebbles (1966)

The end credit "Diversions by Irving Schwartz" was a tribute to a mysteri-

ous, unknown correspondent whose letters proved to be morale boosters for the cast and crew during difficult location shooting in Hong Kong and Taiwan.

Saturday Night Fever (1977)

When John Travolta comes out in his underwear, he cries out, "Al Pacino! Attica! Attica!" This is a reference to *Dog Day Afternoon* (1975), where Pacino plays a bank robber whose whole plan goes awry. At one point in the movie, Pacino goes outside the bank, and yells "Attica! Attica!" at the police, taunting them about the Attica uprising some years before.

say anything... (1989)

When Lloyd (John Cusack) drives along 45th Street in Seattle, he passes the Guild 45th Theater, which is showing Cusack's *Tapeheads* (1988).

Scanners (1981)

In the credits, there is a listing for "Assistant to Mr. Heroux [the film's producer, Claude Heroux]—Kim Obrist." Kim Obrist is the name of the film's female lead character.

Scared Stiff (1953)

Bing Crosby and Bob Hope make cameos as skeletons. The film is a remake of *The Ghost Breakers* (1940), which starred Hope and was directed by this film's director, George Marshall.

Scarface (1983)

A sign reading "The World Is Yours" can be seen on a blimp in the film. An identical sign appeared on top of a building in the film *Scarface* (1932).

Scavenger Hunt (1980)

Board game mogul Milton Parker (Vincent Price) is named after two of the biggest game companies, Milton Bradley and Parker Brothers.

Scent of a Woman (1992)

Another unintentional in-joke: Toward the end of the film, the score from Charlie Chaplin's film *City Lights* (1931) can be heard. David J. Wally, the film's associate producer, told film critic Roger Ebert that, although director Martin Brest is such a lover of Chaplin that he called his company City Lights Films, and both films deal with blindness, the use of the song was coincidental. The song is "La Violetera," written by Jose Padilla, not Chaplin. When Brest was researching music for the film, he found several recordings by the group the Tango Project which he later used in the film, one of which was "La Violetera."

Der Schattenmann (1995 TV)

People on the street can be seen using bags from the Bellheim warehouse. The owner of this fictitious warehouse was the main character in director Dieter Wedel's previous project, *Der Grosse Bellheim* (1992 TV).

Schindler's List (1993)

Coproducer Branko Lustig plays the nightclub maître d' in Schindler's first scene. Lustig is an Auschwitz survivor who has produced other films about the Holocaust, including *Shoah* (1985) and *Sophie's Choice* (1986).

Schlock (1971)

A list of classic films is presented in the film's prologue, ending with the great motion picture, *See You Next Wednesday*. Two different *See You Next Wednesday* movies are also promoted during the newscasts for the "movie on 6 at 6," and a third version is seen on a poster in the theater lobby, playing on a double bill with *The Blob* (1958). The poster art for this *See You Next Wednesday* was actually from *King Kong vs. Godzilla* (1963). *See You Next Wednesday* is the title of a script that director John Landis wrote at the age of 15. It was apparently not very good overall, but Landis uses bits and pieces of it in many of his films, and includes the phrase, either spoken or on a poster, into almost all of his films. Some have noted that the line "See you next Wednesday" was spoken in the film *2001: A Space Odyssey* (1968) by Frank Poole's dad at the end of Frank's birthday transmission, but Landis denies that this was its origin. He says it was simply coincidental.

Some of the films mentioned in the opening credits are referred to in the film as well. Dr. Shlibovitz explains to reporter Joe Putzman that his peculiar headgear was designed by Dr. Heywood Floyd Jerome. Dr. Heywood Floyd was the name of the lead character, played by William Sylvester, in *2001: A Space Odyssey*.

When Schlock sees the picture of the large banana, "Also Sprach Zarathustra," the music from *2001: A Space Odyssey*, begins to play. There is then a parody of the scene at the start of *2001* where the ape discovers the use of a bone as a weapon and throws the bone skyward.

The scene where Schlock meets the little girl at the edge of the pond is a reference to a similar scene in *Frankenstein* (1931).

Forrest J Ackerman appears uncredited as the movie patron that Schlock sits beside in the theater. Schlock steals his popcorn. Ackerman was the creator of the first successful sci-fi/horror magazine, *Famous Monsters of Filmland*.

After Schlock is killed at the end, Mindy's boyfriend says "I'm sorry," to which she replies, "Love means never having to say you're sorry," the famous line from *Love Story* (1970).

Then, as the cops look at the dead Schlock, the dumb cop says, "'Twas beauty killed the beast," the final line from *King Kong* (1933).

The Scoundrel (1935)

Writer-producer-director Ben Hecht won an Academy Award for his script for this film, and he also has a cameo in the flop-house.

Scream (1996)

There are many references to director Wes Craven and his films, and to Craven's friend John Carpenter and *his* films.

The caller at the beginning of the film asks Drew Barrymore if she thought the *Nightmare on Elm Street* series of films was good. She answers, "The first one was, but the rest sucked." Craven directed *A Nightmare on Elm Street* (1984), but was replaced as director on all the film's sequels.

One character says that their story is "starting to sound like some Wes Carpenter flick."

There is a discussion about Carpenter's habit of casting Jamie Lee Curtis (his ex-girlfriend) in many of his movies, and someone suggests that if the cops watched Curtis's *Prom Night* (1980), they would have no trouble solving the case.

A reporter at the high school asks, "So how does it feel to be almost brutally butchered?" She is played by the star of *The Exorcist* (1973), Linda Blair.

Mr. Himbry, the kid-hating high school principal, is played, uncredited, by Henry Winkler, who was most famous for playing perennial teenager Arthur "Fonz" Fonzarelli on *Happy Days*.

Just before he is killed, Mr. Himbry sees the high school's janitor. He is dressed like Freddy Krueger in the *Nightmare* films, in a striped shirt and fedora. In those films, Krueger was originally a high school janitor.

The Screaming Skull (1958)

Director Alex Nicol plays the servant in the film.

Scrooged (1988)

In the middle of the closing song, "Put a Little Love in Your Heart," Bill Murray ad-libs a bunch of dialogue, including "Feed me, Seymour!" which is a line from the film *Little Shop of Horrors* (1986), in which Murray appeared.

The two bums with Michael J. Pollard who think that Frank Cross (Murray) is Richard Burton are played by siblings Logan and Anne Ramsey.

Search and Destroy (1995)

Producer Martin Scorsese has a cameo as an accountant.

Second Sight (1989)

Using Bobby (Bronson Pinchot) to flip through channels, Wills (John Larroquette) happens upon Pinchot's show, *Perfect Strangers*. Pinchot is not seen, but Mark Linn-Baker can be heard yelling, "Balki!" Pinchot's character's name.

Semi-Tough (1977)

Burt Reynolds's character wears jersey number 22, the number Reynolds wore as a football player at West Palm Beach High School and Florida State University (see also *The Longest Yard*, 1974).

Sgt. Bilko (1996)

Bilko is investigated by two Army number-crunchers, one male, one female. The woman, Lt. Monday, is played by Catherine Silvers, the daughter of Phil Silvers, who starred as Sgt. Ernie Bilko in the series that originated the character, *You'll Never Get Rich*.

Sgt. Pepper's Lonely Hearts Club Band (1978)

When the golden Sgt. Pepper vane comes to life at the end, it becomes Billy Preston, who sings "Get Back." Preston actually played with the Beatles on the original recording of "Get Back" in 1969.

Serial Mom (1994)

A portrait of director John Waters is carried past the camera in the school "bring-and-buy" scene.

Seven (1995)

The man who is pointing the gun in Brad Pitt's face in the alleyway (you can only see his arm clearly) is director David Fincher. Fincher was unhappy with the way the actor was holding the gun so he opted to do it himself and do it right.

The guy scraping Somerset's name off of the door is *Hollywood Reporter* writer George Christie, a well-respected columnist.

The Sex Symbol (1974 TV)

Horror film director-producer William Castle (*The Tingler*, 1959; *The House on Haunted Hill*, 1958) plays Jack P. Harper in the film.

The Shadow (1994)

When Lamont and Margo kiss at the end of the film, the camera spins around them, and when it stops, a truck can be seen to the left in the background with the last name of director Russell Mulcahy on it.

Shadow of a Doubt (1943)

Director Alfred Hitchcock can be seen on the train to Santa Rosa, playing cards. He has the entire suit of spades in his hand, including the symbolic ace.

Shakes the Clown (1991)

Robin Williams appears in this Bob Goldthwait film as a mime teacher, but the role is credited to "Marty Fromage" (see *Tapeheads*, 1988).

Shampoo (1975)

Longtime horror film director-producer William Castle (*The Tingler*, 1959; *House on Haunted Hill*, 1958) plays Sid Roth.

Shane (1953)

When Jack Palance was cast as the creepy bad guy, he promised director George Stevens that he could ride a horse ... but he couldn't. Although he took lessons during filming, his memorable entrance in the film, shot early on, featured Palance leading his horse into town, because he still could not ride one.

Shanghai Surprise (1986)

Coexecutive producer George Harrison, who also wrote the songs for the film, has a cameo as a nightclub singer.

Shattered Spirits (1986 TV)

Star Martin Sheen's daughter, Renee Estevez, plays a teenager talking on a telephone.

She's Having a Baby (1988)

The BMW's licence plate is "SHAB," which is an acronym of the film's title.

There is a credit which reads: "Inspiration: Nancy Hughes." This was director John Hughes's way of acknowledging that the film is a semiautobiographical account of the early years of his own marriage.

The Shining (1980)

Danny can be seen wearing a sweater with a crude drawing of a rocket and the text *2001* on it, referring to director Stanley Kubrick's *2001: A Space Odyssey* (1968).

A Shock to the System (1990)

Graham (Michael Caine) says that his father was a London bus driver. Caine's father was also a London bus driver.

Shocker (1989)

The first victim of Horace Pinker shown onscreen is a girl with a bloody arm carried away on a stretcher (seen on television). The girl is "played" by director Wes Craven's star in his earlier film *A Nightmare on Elm Street* (1984), Heather Langenkamp.

When he is in the body of Pastori, the cop, Horace Pinker shoots and then jumps into the body of a jogger. The jogger is played by Craven's son, Jonathan Christian Craven.

Doreen, the girl behind the lunch counter watching television at the start of the film, is played by Craven's daughter, Jessica Craven.

At the film's end, Jonathan (Peter Berg) walks out of his house and his next-door neighbor asks him, "Was that real?" The neighbor is played by director Wes Craven.

Shoot the Moon (1982)

The child actors sing the theme from director Alan Parker's *Fame* (1980).

A poster can be seen on a wall for Parker's film *Pink Floyd—The Wall* (1982), which was actually released five months later.

The Shootist (1976)

Lauren Bacall's character has the first name "Bond," after John Wayne's friend and frequent costar Ward Bond.

The flashbacks are clips from old John Wayne movies. John Bernard Books's (John Wayne) old friend was Ricky Nelson (as Colorado in scenes from *Rio Bravo*, 1954). Books's victims were Christopher George and Johnny Crawford (both in scenes from *El Dorado*, 1967), and Leo Gordon (as Ed Lowe in a scene from *Hondo*, 1953). Scenes from *Red River* (1948) were also used.

Short Circuit (1986)

The robots are designed very similar to the large fighting machines in *The Terminator* (1984). In fact, at the beginning of the movie, there is a closeup of flowers on a green field, and then the robots roll over them. This was a common theme of scenes in the *Terminator* films.

The Silence of the Hams (1994)

This Italian-American co-production is mainly a spoof of two films: *The Silence of the Lambs* (1991) and *Psycho* (1960).

The Silence of the Lambs references: Billy Zane plays an FBI agent named Jo Dee Fostar (Jodie Foster starred in *The Silence of the Lambs* as an FBI agent). Dom DeLuise plays Dr. Animal Cannibal Pizza, a parody of Dr. Hannibal "Cannibal" Lecter. DeLuise's name may also have been inspired by another comedic villain he played: Pizza the Hutt in *Spaceballs* (1987).

As for *Psycho*, Jane (Charlene Tilton) runs away from the real estate office where she works with a large sum of money. A detective named "Martin Balsam" (played by Martin Balsam, who also played the detective in

Psycho) is hired to look for her. She ends up at the Cemetary Motel, a replica of the Bates Motel, complete with spooky house and domineering mother. The owner, Antonio Motel (Ezio Greggio), spies on her through a hole in the wall and knifes her in the shower. Balsam investigates at the motel, goes into the house, says, "I feel I've done this before!" and falls down the stairs, filmed just as in *Psycho*. At the end, the spirit of Alfred Hitchcock kills Greggio "for fucking up his movie."

Among the other film and TV references:

There's a parody of the interrogation scene with Sharon Stone in *Basic Instinct* (1992) involving a blonde woman named "Sharon Bone."

In the Unbelievably Bad Maniacs Wing, Zane sees an inmate parodying Kathy Bates's character in *Misery* (1990).

Charlene Tilton throws money on herself in her underwear as a parody of *Indecent Proposal* (1993).

The second time Fostar goes to see Dr. Cannibal, he rises up, dressed like Gary Oldman in *Bram Stoker's Dracula* (1992).

Zane walks out of the explosion of an oil truck á la Arnold Schwarzenegger. The tanker driver yells, "Where ya going?" and he answers with Schwarzenegger's signature line: "I'll be back."

When the Ranger (John Astin) comes down his stairs, he says, "Welcome to my humble abode," a favorite line of Gomez Addams (Astin's character on *The Addams Family*). *The Addams Family* theme music is played, and there is a disembodied foot named "Smelly Thing."

Among the pages heard in the hospital ("Dr. Godot to the waiting

room..."), there's a page for "Dr. Butcher." *Dr. Butcher, M.D.* (1979) was a big Italian zombie movie.

The dead come to life and dance in a parody of Michael Jackson's "Thriller" video.

When all the main characters take off their masks at the end, the motorcycle cop reveals himself to be The Ranger. He takes off his disguise just like Schwarzenegger took off his fat lady disguise in *Total Recall* (1990).

There are a number of cameos as well:

Dom Deluise's son Peter plays the prison official who lets Malicious Mel (Rudy DeLuca) out. DeLuca has metal teeth, just like the ones he wore in Mel Brooks's Hitchcock spoof *High Anxiety* (1977).

Dom's other son, David DeLuise, has a cameo as the cop who calls Dr. Cannibal "Dr. Please" at his pizza parlor.

The guy who dies on the street at the beginning and says, "It was the gimp..." is played by director Joe Dante. The guy who limps away from him is played by director John Carpenter.

The FBI agent who arrests Hillary Clinton is played by director John Landis.

And the guy who checks out of the Jack the Ripper Motel is played, uncredited, by Mel Brooks, who spoofed Hitchcock himself in *High Anxiety*. Brooks later gave Greggio a cameo in his film *Dracula: Dead and Loving It* (1995).

The Silence of the Lambs (1991)

Noted low-budget filmmaker Roger Corman gave this film's director Jonathan Demme his first break in film, so Demme gave Corman a cameo as FBI director Hayden Burke in this film.

Demme's long-time producer, Kenneth Utt, has a cameo as Dr. Akin.

Silent Night, Bloody Night (1972)

The history of the asylum in the film is told using flashbacks, and all of the inmates of the asylum are played by New York City underground movie veterans. They include Ondine, Jack Smith, Tally Brown (*Night of the Juggler*, 1980) and female impersonator Candy Darling, who died two years after making this movie.

Silent Running (1971)

The spaceship is named the *Valley Forge*, after the location used for filming some of the movie's interior scenes: a decommissioned aircraft carrier named the USS *Valley Forge*.

Silver Bears (1978)

The film ends with Donald Luckman (Tommy Smothers) writing his book in jail. He types a few words, gets up, and lets fly a yo-yo for a few moments. Smothers is a well-known yo-yo enthusiast, and created the character of "Yo-Yo Man" on his television series.

Silverado (1985)

Lawrence Kasdan cast some family members in the film. His son Jon is the little boy at the outpost who points and shouts, "Look, ma!" just before Kevin Kline shoots the man who stole his horse. His son Jacob plays the stable boy who tells Sheriff John Cleese to come see the gallows burning, and Kasdan's wife Meg appears as the barmaid in the Turley Saloon who serves Danny Glover a shot of whiskey.

Singles (1992)

Some Seattle-based musicians have parts in the film. Eddie Vedder, Stone Gossard and Jeff Ament (of the group Pearl Jam) play Eddie, Stone and Jeff, the other members of Cliff Poncier's (Matt Dillon) band, Citizen Dick. In one scene, they are sitting around a table at a coffee shop. Gossard is sitting beside Dillon, Ament reads the band's review, and Vedder says, "A compliment for us is a compliment for you."

In the scene where Cliff shows off the new speaker system in his car, Chris Cornell of the Seattle-based group Soundgarden walks up with his head bobbing to the music. Soundgarden and the Seattle group Alice in Chains also perform on stage in the film.

Director Cameron Crowe appears as the man who interviews Cliff in the club at the start of the film.

Crowe's mother, Alice Marie Crowe, plays Dr. Jamison's (Bill Pullman) nurse.

Director Tim Burton (*Batman*, 1989; *Edward Scissorhands*, 1990) has a cameo as a video director named Brian. He is called "the next Martin Scorsese" (pronounced "skor-SEEZ").

The Sinister Urge (1959)

Director Edward D. Wood, Jr., has a cameo in the fight scene, and posters of his movies cover the walls of the porn director Johnny Ryde, who claims that he used to make "good films."

The Sky's the Limit (1943)

Fred Atwell (Fred Astaire) mentions Ginger Rogers and Rita Hayworth. Astaire and Hayworth had costarred in *You'll Never Get Rich* (1941) and *You Never Were Lovelier* (1942), and Astaire and Rogers were frequent costars in films such as *Top Hat* (1935) and *The Gay Divorcee* (1934).

Joan Manion (Joan Leslie) mentions

James Cagney. Leslie had just starred in *Yankee Doodle Dandy* (1942) with Cagney.

Atwell (Astaire) says he learned to dance at Arthur Murray. Astaire had previously been in a dispute with the dancing school chain over the unauthorized use of his likeness.

Sleeper (1973)

Douglas Rain provides the voice of the evil computer. Rain was also the voice of HAL 2000 in *2001: A Space Odyssey* (1968) and *2010* (1984).

The Sleeping Car (1990)

The evil ghost of the sleeping car compartments, known as The Mister, is played by makeup effects expert John Carl Buechler.

Sleepwalkers (1992)

Director Mick Garris included a number of directors in cameos in the film:

John Landis plays the lab technician who shows the photos to the sheriff, and Joe Dante plays his assistant. Landis is munching on a sandwich, and Dante points out that the background and clothes are in focus. Landis was the one who got Garris his first big break, that of directing *Psycho IV: The Beginning* (1990 TV). Garris gave Landis a cameo in that film as well.

Screenwriter Stephen King appears as the cemetery caretaker who complains that the cop's death is not his fault.

Clive Barker and Tobe Hooper play a couple of forensic technicians at the cemetery crime scene. Hooper is the first one that King complains to (he is bagging some evidence) and Barker is the second one (he swats away a fly and takes off his gloves).

Garris's wife, Cynthia Garris, plays Laurie, the police dispatcher.

Mark Hamill also has an uncredited cameo as the sheriff who appears early on in the film.

As the sheriff (Jim Haynie) rushes out to his deputy's aid, he tells Laurie to get reinforcements from Castle Rock. Castle Rock is the fictional town that is the most frequent locale of Stephen King's stories. It is also the name of the monthly newspaper devoted to King and his activities.

Sleuth (1972)

Laurence Olivier's wife, who is often referred to but never seen, is named Margot Channing. This was the name of Bette Davis's character in director Joseph L. Mankiewicz' earlier film, *All About Eve* (1950) (see also *Connecting Rooms*, 1971).

Smokey and the Bandit II (1980)

Test pilot Chuck Yeager has a cameo as a party guest.

Smokey and the Bandit 3 (1983)

Director Dick Lowry also appears in the film as the Sand Dumper.

Sneakers (1992)

Mother (Dan Aykroyd) wears a Tragically Hip T-shirt during the party. Aykroyd introduced the Canadian band to the United States when they were all guests on *Saturday Night Live*. In the scene where they search through Werner Brandes's trash, he's wearing a T-shirt with "Aleka's Attic" on it. This was a band that costar River Phoenix had formed.

After he's searched Werner Brandes's garbage, Mother holds up half of a neatly folded box of Cap'n Crunch cereal and says, "Nicest garbage I've ever seen." In the '70s, Cap'n Crunch came with a small whistle in the box. A famous hacker named "Captain

Crunch" (John Draper) discovered that this whistle could be used to get free phone calls (this procedure was nick-named "phreaking").

The prefix "555" is usually used in films because no real numbers begin with these three digits. However, director Phil Alden Robinson hired a real number for this film. The female NSA agent gives Carl (River Phoenix) her home phone number at the end: 273-9164, area code 415. Upon calling the number, a fake answering machine message could be heard, but the message has since been discontinued.

Soapdish (1991)

Stephen Nichols plays the presenter at the Daytime Emmy Awards at the beginning and end of the film. Nichols is best known for his portrayal of Steve "Patch" Johnson on the soap opera *Days of Our Lives.*

Society (1989)

Horror film reviewer Chas. Balun has a cameo as a "slimesucker"—com-plete with close-up—that Balun is incredibly proud of.

Some Kind of Wonderful (1987)

The three main characters have names that correspond to the Rolling Stones: Amanda Jones (John Paul Jones and the Stones song "Amanda," which is heard in the film), a drummer named (Charlie) Watts and a character named Keith (Richards).

Some Like It Hot (1959)

Tony Curtis has to impersonate a millionaire and, as part of his dis-guise, does an impression of Cary Grant's voice. However, Jack Lemmon scathingly tells him that "Nobody talks like that!" Curtis was a huge fan of

Grant's and says that he learned how to woo women by watching Grant in films.

Something Evil (1972 TV)

Jeff Corey met budding director Steven Spielberg on the series *The Psychiatrist,* and Speilberg was so impressed with Corey that he went to Corey's acting workshop. Spielberg did not participate, said Corey, but "he just watched, watched, watched." Spielberg would later thank Corey by casting him in this horror film as Gehrmann.

Something Wild (1986)

The two old ladies in the re-sale shop are the mothers of the Talking Heads' David Byrne, who wrote the film's music, and director Jonathan Demme.

The band at the high school reunion is the Feelies, a favorite of Demme's. He filmed the video for their song "Away."

Melanie Griffith's dad is played by Demme's longtime producer, Kenneth Utt. He also served as production manager on the film.

Sommersby (1993)

The cow is named Clarice, which was also the name of star Jodie Foster's character in *The Silence of the Lambs* (1991).

Son-in-Law (1993)

Brendan Fraser appears as his char-acter from star Pauly Shore's *Encino Man* (1992).

Song of the Thin Man (1947)

Nick Charles (William Powell) finds a razor blade and remarks, "Somerset Maugham has been here," referring to the author's then-best-seller *The Razor's Edge.*

The Sons of Katie Elder (1965)

John Wayne wears his *Red River* "D" belt buckle in this film (see *Rio Bravo*, 1959).

Sorceress (1994)

Producer Fred Olen Ray appears in the film as Bill Carson.

Soup to Nuts (1930)

Otto Schmidt (Charles Winninger) is the owner of a costume store which is bankrupt because he spends his time making Rube Goldberg–style inventions. Goldberg was a cartoonist whose work appeared in many American newspapers in the early 1900s. He drew one-panel cartoons of outlandish contraptions that were designed to accomplish simple tasks. Rube Goldberg himself appears in this film as a nonpaying customer in Gus Klein's (George Bickel) restaurant.

South Central (1992)

This film is based on the book *Crips*, by Donald Bakeer, and Bakeer himself appears in the film as Dr. King. Bakeer's son, Musa, also plays a small part in the film.

Spaceballs (1987)

There are many direct parodies of the *Star Wars* trilogy. Dark Helmet is Darth Vader, Lone Starr is Han Solo, Barf is Chewbacca, Princess Vespa is Princess Leia (complete with headphones that look like Leia's hair buns), Dot Matrix is C-3PO, the Schwartz is the Force, the Dinks are the Jawas, Yoghurt is Yoda, and Pizza the Hutt is Jabba the Hutt.

There are also some relatively obscure *Star Wars* references. For instance, the Spaceballs' ship changes into a maid, and, as the heroes watch, Barf (John Candy) says, "It's not just a spaceship ... it's a Transformer!" This line is a take-off of Obi-Wan Kenobi's line in *Star Wars*: "That's not a moon ... it's a space station!"

The heroes barely escaping from the exploding ship is straight out of *The Empire Strikes Back* (1980).

Among all the space RVs parked at the diner is the Millenium Falcon from the *Star Wars* trilogy. It is just to the right of the runway.

The ridiculously long opening shot of the spaceship is a parody of the fly-by shot of the spaceship at the beginning of *Star Wars*.

When President Skroob (Mel Brooks) meets the twins, he tells them to "chew their gum," referring to the Doublemint gum commercial.

Dark Helmet (Rick Moranis) says to go to Ludicrous Speed, but Col. Sanders (George Wyner) says that they cannot. Dark Helmet snaps back, "Whattsa matter, Colonel Sanders? Chicken?" Col. Sanders was the name of the spokesman for Kentucky Fried Chicken.

When the Dinks first appear, they are singing the theme song from *The Bridge on the River Kwai* (1957).

The four leads meet Yoghurt in a scene reminiscent of the "meeting the Wizard" scene in *The Wizard of Oz* (1939). Also, as the image of Yoghurt fades away at the end, he chants, "What a world ... what a world...," the final words of the Wicked Witch of the West in *The Wizard of Oz*.

The Spaceballs' ship breaks into pieces, two of which land on the beach of a planet. They look like pieces of the Statue of Liberty, and two apes ride up on horseback, referring to the final shot of the film *Planet of the Apes* (1968).

Lone Starr asks the King where the Princess is, and he is told that "she was just passing Jupiter 2." Jupiter 2 was the name of the space ship on the series *Lost in Space*.

After Dark Helmet captures Princess Vespa's ship, his Troop Leader starts toward the ship, but Dark Helmet says that he will handle it. The Troop Leader answers, "Jawohl, Lord Helmet!" He is played by Tommy Swerdlow, the son of the film's co-producer, Ezra Swerdlow.

The VCR operator who fetches the *Spaceballs: The Movie* videocassette is played by the film's second assistant director, Mitchell Bock.

John Hurt is besieged once more by the chestburster alien that sprang from his chest in *Alien* (1979) and groans, "Not again!" The astronauts with him also look identical to Hurt's costars in *Alien*. The black man sitting beside him has a blue bandanna on his head like Yaphet Kotto; the woman looks a little like Sigourney Weaver; and there is a man with a baseball cap behind Hurt who resembles Tom Skerritt.

After bursting out of Hurt, the alien then proceeds to break into the song sung by the frog in the classic Warner Bros. cartoon *One Froggy Evening* (1955).

Just before the spaceship changes into a maid, President Skroob says to prepare the ship for metamorphosis, and Dark Helmet replies, "Ready, Kafka!" This is a reference to Franz Kafka's novel *Metamorphosis*, which is about a man who transforms into a cockroach.

Spellbound (1945)

Director Alfred Hitchcock comes out of an elevator at the Empire Hotel, carrying a violin case and smoking a cigarette.

Spies Like Us (1985)

Director John Landis has a habit of casting his fellow directors in cameos in his films. Directors in this film include:

Michael Apted (*Gorillas in the Mist*, 1988; *Thunderheart*, 1992) as an "Ace Tomato Company" agent who meets the car at the drive-in. He is the one who says, "Mr. Ruby?"

Martin Brest (*Beverly Hills Cop*, 1984; *Scent of a Woman*, 1992) as the security guard at the drive-in who radios down and orders "Two Pepsis to go."

Joel Coen (*Raising Arizona*, 1987; *Miller's Crossing*, 1990) as the security guard at the drive-in who says, "The drive-in is closed."

Larry Cohen (*It's Alive!* 1974; *The Stuff*, 1985) as an "Ace Tomato Company" agent who meets the car at the drive-in. He is the one who says, "Mr. Keyes?"

Costa-Gavras (*Missing*, 1982; *Music Box*, 1989) as a Tadzhik highway patrolman who arrests and interrogates Chevy Chase and who has his grenade returned to him.

Terry Gilliam (*Brazil*, 1985; *Twelve Monkeys*, 1995) as Dr. Imhaus of the Zurich Relief Fund (the first doctor on the left in the tent).

Frank Oz (*Dirty Rotten Scoundrels*, 1988; *What About Bob?* 1991) as the GL-G20 test monitor who catches Chase and Dan Aykroyd cheating.

Sam Raimi (*The Evil Dead*, 1983; *Darkman*, 1990) as the security guard at the gate of the drive-in on the passenger side of the car.

Bob Swaim (*Half Moon Street*, 1986; *Masquerade*, 1988) as the special forces commander who late in the film bursts in through the wall.

Cinematographer Robert Paynter appears as Dr. Gill of the Northampton Trauma Institute. He is the last one introduced.

Famed special effects pioneer-producer Ray Harryhausen (*Jason and the Argonauts*, 1963; *Clash of the Titans*, 1981) appears as Dr. Marston of the Northampton Trauma Institute. He answers a question about penicillin.

Special effects artist Derek Meddings (*Batman*, 1989; many James Bond films) appears as Dr. Stinson of the Northampton Trauma Institute. He is between Harryhausen and Donna Dixon.

The "Ace Tomato Company" agent who says, "Won't you gentlemen have a Pepsi?" is played by blues guitarist B.B. King. King performed a couple of songs, including the title tune, in Landis's previous film, *Into the Night* (1985). Landis even directed the video for King's song from his film.

See You Next Wednesday is on the recruitment poster behind the desk of the commander of the army training post (see *Schlock*, 1971).

The film is similar in tone and style to the Bob Hope and Bing Crosby *Road* movies, and, in one desert scene, Hope makes a cameo.

The Spirit of '76 (1990)

Director Lucas Reiner has a cameo as the fireworks barker.

Reiner gave his dad, Carl, a cameo as Dr. Von Mobil and his brother, Rob, as Dr. Cash.

Spitfire (1942)

There is a throwaway bit of conversation in a pub where someone is trying to guess the name of Niven's newest girlfriend. They ask, "Is it Elsie Trubshaw?" "No," replies Niven, "it is not Elsie Trubshaw" (see *Four Men and a Prayer*, 1938).

Splash (1984)

Screenwriters Lowell Ganz and Babaloo Mandel have cameos in the film. Ganz plays Stan, the tour guide, and Mandel plays Rudy.

The script was based on producer Brian Grazer's book, and his wife, Corki Corman-Grazer, appears in the film as a married woman.

The Spoilers (1942)

William Farnum has a bit part, playing Wheaton in this film. There had been three previous versions of this film, all called *The Spoilers*—in 1914, 1923, and 1930—and another was filmed after this one: *The Spoilers* (1955). William Farnum made his film debut playing Roy Glennister in the 1914 version. John Wayne plays Glennister in the 1942 film.

Spy Hard (1996)

Leslie Nielsen plays special agent Dick Steele, modeled after James Bond. Bond at the time was being played by Pierce Brosnan, who had previously played detective Remington Steele on television.

This is a take-off of James Bond spy films, and some direct references have been included. As Steele (Nielsen) comes into the spy headquarters, he does a send-up of Sean Connery's hat-toss in the Bond films. Also, when Steele is fighting a nun at the convent, he throws urine samples in her face, which is what Bond (Connery) did to the villain in *Never Say Never Again* (1983).

Many other films and television series are spoofed, including:

Pulp Fiction (1994)—Nielsen and Nicolette Sheridan do the dance that John Travolta and Uma Thurman did in the film.

True Lies (1994)—The "horse in

an elevator" scene and when Nielsen rises up in the jet fighter to face the villain.

Cliffhanger (1993)—Nielsen hanging on to his girlfriend's hand, with bulging biceps, then dropping her.

Mission: Impossible (1996)—The tape self-destructing at the beginning.

Butch Cassidy and the Sundance Kid (1969)—The bicycle sequence set to the tune of "Raindrops Keep Falling on My Head."

Speed (1994)—The entire bus sequence, including the line "Pop quiz … what do you do?"

Home Alone (1990)—The Macaulay Culkin lookalike named "McLucky" and his entire sequence. The villains beat him up, saying, "This is for *Getting Even with Dad!*" "And this is for *My Girl!*" both of which were Culkin films.

When McLucky faces off against the two thugs, Tchaikovsky's "The Nutcracker Suite" plays in the background. Culkin was the Nutcracker Prince in *The Nutcracker* (1993).

Terminator 2: Judgement Day (1991)—Nielsen is about to destroy the microchip with a sledgehammer when he is stopped by the scientist, who says it could be used for world peace. This is a parody of the scene in the Special Edition version of *Terminator 2* that was released on videotape and laserdisc with scenes originally cut out of the film. In one excised scene, Sarah Connor is about to destroy the Terminator's CPU chip with a hammer when she is stopped by her son, John.

Sister Act (1992)—The nun choir sequences.

Apollo 13 (1995)—The rocket knocking the pod off course at the end, and the line, "Houston … we have a problem."

As seen from the helicopter, the word "adios" is written out in white stones, just as the word "goodbye" was written out at the end of the final episode of *M*A*S*H*.

Barry Bostwick (who has a Ted Kennedy-esque accent throughout the film) says, "Remember the last time Steele was placed in the line of fire?" And then there is a spoof of the film *In the Line of Fire* (1993). Steele even has a picture of himself with JFK on the wall of his house. The line "If you want to see me again, turn around now" is also from *In the Line of Fire*.

Steele and Nicolette Sheridan put on their gear to break into Rancor's stronghold in a parody of Arnold Schwarzenegger's similar scene in *Commando* (1985).

As the bus jumps the gap, it is silhouetted against the moon, just as the bikes were in the film *E.T., the Extra-Terrestrial* (1982).

The two girls in bikinis popping their gum is a reference to the Doublemint Gum commercials.

Robert Culp, who had starred in the series *I Spy*, makes a cameo appearance as an unruly airplane passenger.

Stage Fright (1950)

At one point, director Alfred Hitchcock turns to look at Jane Wyman in her disguise as Marlene Dietrich's maid.

Hitchcock's daughter, Patricia, also appears as Chubby Banister.

Stairway to Heaven (1946)

Peter Carter's (David Niven) friend, played by Robert Coote, is named Bob Trubshawe (see *Four Men and a Prayer*, 1938).

Stakeout (1987)

As police detectives Emilio Estevez and Richard Dreyfuss try to kill time, they throw movie quotes at each other, trying to stump one another. Dreyfuss gets the line "They're dustin' off the hot seat for me!" which he correctly identifies as being said by Lee J. Cobb in *On the Waterfront* (1954). He seems unbeatable until Estevez gives him the line, "This was not a boating accident!" And Dreyfuss, who went on to international fame uttering that line in *Jaws* (1975) while examining the body of the first shark victim, is totally stumped. This scene was included in the film because Estevez and Dreyfuss were playing the game on the set in real life ... and Dreyfuss couldn't get the line either! Incidentally, Dreyfuss's actual line in *Jaws* was "This was not a boat accident!"

The Stand (1994 TV)

Texas State Patrol Officer Joe Bob Brentwick is played by famous low-budget drive-in movie critic Joe Bob Briggs. Briggs is a big fan of "Big Steve King," as he calls him, and jumped at the chance to make a cameo in one of the adaptations of King's novels.

Director Tom Holland (*Fright Night*, 1985; *Thinner*, 1996), who would later go on to direct Stephen King's *The Langoliers* (1995 TV), has a cameo as Carl Hough.

Teddy Weizak, the man who drives Nadine (Laura San Giacomo) to Mother Abigail's in Boulder, is played by Stephen King himself.

Stand by Me (1986)

The names of all the towns in the movie (set in Oregon) are real places in Maine, where author Stephen King grew up.

The Star Chamber (1983)

Robert Costanzo plays Sgt. Spota. Director-screenwriter Peter Hyams has

included a character named "Spota" in many of his films since *The Hunter* (1980), which he wrote.

Caroline Stout is played by Hyams's daughter, Danna.

Star 80 (1983)

Cliff Robertson plays Hugh Hefner in this biopic, and Keith Hefner, son of the real Hugh, plays a photographer in the film.

A Star Is Born (1954)

A drunk requests that Judy Garland sing the song "Melancholy Baby." The drunk is played by an extra, but the voice is that of Humphrey Bogart.

Star Spangled Rhythm (1942)

The harassed and excitable producer played by Walter Abel is named G.B. de Soto, in an imitation of B.G. de Sylva, then a Paramount producer.

Star Trek: First Contact (1996)

The host of the nightclub on the holodeck is played by Ethan Phillips, who starred as Neelix in the series *Star Trek: Voyager*.

Robert Picardo, who plays the Doctor in *Star Trek: Voyager*, also appears in a cameo.

In the fight on the deflector dish, the Maglock system display includes the line "Subsystem: AE35." This is a reference to the system which directed the communications dish towards the Earth in *2001: A Space Odyssey* (1968). It was called the AE-35 Unit.

Star Trek: Generations (1994)

Whoopi Goldberg, who repeats her role of Guinan from the series, is not listed in the credits. She wanted to appear in the film, but her contract stipulates that she gets top billing and a sizeable salary, which would have been impossible for this film. So she talked her manager into accepting a part at bargain-basement prices. The caveat on this appearance was that Paramount could not use Whoopi's name in any advertising associated with marketing the film—not even a mention in the credits.

Star Trek—The Motion Picture (1979)

Pictures of the NASA space shuttle USS *Enterprise* are seen. The shuttle was named after the starship from the original *Star Trek* series.

Star Trek II: The Wrath of Khan (1982)

After Saavik fails the Kobiyashi Maru test, in which the entire bridge crew dies, Kirk (William Shatner) sees Spock (Leonard Nimoy) and says, "Aren't you dead?" At the end of the film, Spock does die. During production, this secret was leaked, and Kirk's line to Spock was included to try to belay the then-rampant rumors that Spock died in the film.

There is a conversation between Kirk and Scotty where Scotty says "I had a wee bout, but Dr. McCoy pulled me through." James Doohan, who plays Scotty, had actually experienced a heart attack in real life in between *Star Trek* films.

Star Trek III: The Search for Spock (1984)

The voice on the flight recorder was provided by *Trek* producer Harve Bennett.

Star Trek IV: The Voyage Home (1986)

The punk on the bus is played by executive producer Kirk Thatcher. Thatcher also wrote and performed "I Hate You," the song which is playing

on his stereo, with his band, Edge of Etiquette.

Star Trek V: The Final Frontier (1989)

Producer Harve Bennett, who was the main force behind the filming of *Star Trek V*, appears as the Starfleet officer who orders Kirk and the Enterprise back into action.

William Shatner's daughter, Melanie, plays the blond ensign on the bridge of the *Enterprise*.

Star Trek VI: The Undiscovered Country (1991)

The crewman who awakens Captain Sulu (George Takei) is played by Christian Slater, who only gets minor credit during the closing titles. He took this bit part because, ever since he was a kid, he always wanted to be in a *Star Trek* movie. According to Takei, Slater "pulled some strings, twisted some arms and did whatever he could to get a part in *Star Trek VI*." Actually, Slater's mother, Mary Jo Slater, was the casting director of the film.

Star Wars (1977)

R2D2 is named after a film term for a certain section of dialogue: Reel 2, Dialog 2. Ditto for R5D4: Reel 5, Dialog 4. Director George Lucas and a coworker were editing *American Graffiti* (1973), when the coworker asked for "R2, D2" and it apparently stuck in Lucas's mind.

"Darth Vader" means "dark father" in Dutch, foreshadowing the revelation that Vader is Luke's father. George Lucas has said that the name was indeed inspired by the phrase "dark father" as a hint to the identity of Vader, who turns out in the sequels to be Luke's father.

Han and Luke "transfer" Chewie

from cell block 1138. Also, "THX 1138" was going to be the serial number of the guard with the faulty transmitter on the Death Star, but this was changed (see *American Graffiti*, 1973).

Princess Leia's cell number is "21-87," which was the name of a 1964 abstract Canadian short film that Lucas loved. The eight-minute film, directed by Arthur Lipsett, is about a machine-dominated society, and centers around a man who waits for his number to be chosen.

The Tatooine scenes were filmed in Tunisia, which has a town called "Tatahouine."

Lucas has acknowledged, that, among other movies, *Star Wars* was chiefly influenced by Akira Kurosawa's *The Hidden Fortress* (1958). The Imperial general that Vader chokes mentions "the Rebels' hidden fortress" just as Vader cuts him off.

James Earl Jones receives no credit for providing the voice of Darth Vader. He did not feel he had done enough to deserve credit, and he did not want to take anything away from David Prowse's portrayal of Vader. Previously, there was a similar controversy concerning the role of the possessed Regan Mac-Neil in *The Exorcist* (1973). Linda Blair was nominated for an Academy Award for the role, but her "devil-voice" in the film was provided by Mercedes McCambridge. McCambridge claimed that director William Friedkin promised her a special credit, then reneged on his promise. Eventually, Friedkin did give McCambridge credit onscreen, but the Academy Award nomination contributed to the controversy. Jones did not want a similar fate to happen with Prowse and his character in *Star Wars*, so he went uncredited. Jones was credited, however, in *Star Wars: Special Edition* (1997).

The State of Things (1982)

The film centers on what happens when a film crew attempts to complete a remake of Roger Corman's *The Day the World Ended* (1956) on location in Portugal. The film is really a homage to Corman, who also has a cameo as "the lawyer."

Stay Tuned (1992)

Jeffrey Jones puts John Ritter through all different kinds of television-related hell, finally culminating in the worst hell of all—Ritter finds himself back in the sitcom in which he starred in the late '70s and early '80s, *Three's Company*.

Staying Alive (1983)

Tony (John Travolta) decides to go to acting agencies with his pictures and resumés. On his way to the first one, he walks along a crowded sidewalk and bumps into a tough-looking guy wearing sunglasses. The guy is played by the film's director, Sylvester Stallone.

Stealing Home (1988)

In the final baseball game, the announcer says, "Now pinch-hitting for Costner ... number nine, Billy Wyatt." *Stealing Home* came out just after Kevin Costner's *Bull Durham* (1988).

Steamboat Bill Jr. (1928)

Buster Keaton plays a prissy college boy who comes back to visit his steamboat-owner father. Upon seeing the beret on his son's head, Bill's father takes him to get a real hat. For a few minutes, Keaton tries on hats characteristic of other silent film stars. Finally, while everyone in the shop is conveniently looking the other way, Keaton ends up with his own trademark porkpie hat on his head. He then rips it off before anyone can see it.

The Story of Mankind (1957)

Alexander Graham Bell is played by Jim Ameche, son of Don Ameche. Don had played Bell in the film *The Story of Alexander Graham Bell* (1939), and was so popular that the telephone was known for years afterward as "the Ameche."

Straight Talk (1992)

The television director of Dolly Parton's show is played by the film's director, Barnet Kellman.

Strange Boarders (1938)

Tom Walls sees a picture of Disraeli and says, "Good old George, what a make-up," a reference to George Arliss's 1929 Academy Award–winning role.

Strange Invaders (1983)

Just after her landlord gets zapped, Nancy Allen flips on her television, and sees the "aliens land on Earth" film *The Day the Earth Stood Still* (1951).

Allen's skeptical coworker is played by director Joel Coen (*Raising Arizona*, 1987; *Fargo*, 1996). At the time, Coen was an assistant film editor on films such as *Fear No Evil* (1981) and *The Evil Dead* (1982), which was made by his buddies, Sam and Ted Raimi.

Strangers on a Train (1951)

Director Alfred Hitchcock boards a train early in the film with a double bass fiddle as Farley Granger gets off.

Hitchcock's daughter, Patricia, also appears as Barbara Morton, the sister of Ann Morton, Ruth Roman's character.

Street Justice (1989)

Director Richard C. Sarafian has a cameo as a taxi driver.

Street Trash (1987)

The melting bum on the fire escape burns off a businessman's face. The businessman is played by screenwriter Roy Frumkes.

The Strongest Man in the World (1975)

The school in the film is Medfield College, the same school as in the Disney films *The Absent-Minded Professor* (1961) and *Son of Flubber* (1963).

The Stupids (1996)

Director John Landis has a habit of casting his fellow directors in cameos in his films. This film was shot in Toronto, Canada, and Landis gave some Canadian directors cameos:

David Cronenberg (*Dead Ringers*, 1988; *The Fly*, 1986) plays Stanley Stupid's supervisor at the post office.

Atom Egoyan (*The Adjuster*, 1991) plays the studio security guard who lets Mrs. Stupid backstage.

Norman Jewison (*In the Heat of the Night*, 1967; *Moonstruck*, 1987) plays the director of the television talk show.

Some non–Canadian directors also have cameos:

Robert Wise (*The Day the Earth Stood Still*, 1951; *The Sound of Music*, 1965) plays Stanley's neighbor.

Costa-Gavras (*Missing*, 1982; *Music Box*, 1989) plays the gas station attendant who fixes the hole in Stanley's gas tank.

Mick Garris (*Sleepwalkers*, 1992) plays Jerry, the reporter who thinks up the "Two Alien Pilots..." headline. Landis was the one who got Garris his first big break, that of directing *Psycho IV: The Beginning* (1990 TV). In return, Garris gave Landis a cameo in the film.

Landis also cast his son, Max Landis, as the graffiti artist who is sprayed with white paint.

In many of Landis's films, when police or government agents appear, they can be heard shouting "Hut! Hut! Hut!" Here, the soldiers in the army base are heard shouting it.

The song playing in the car of the woman who is lighting her cigarette in front of the television studio is "The Girl from Ipanema." Landis enjoyed inserting this song into his films.

Submarine Command (1951)

Sam Carlson (Arthur Franz) has the line, "Anyone seeing a psychiatrist should have his head examined." This is a saying credited to movie producer Samuel Goldwyn, known as a Goldwynism.

Sudden Death (1995)

The head of security at Pittsburgh's Civic Arena is named Spota (played by Bill Dalzell III). He is the bald man going over security at the start of the film with Hallmark (Dorian Harewood). Director Peter Hyams has included a character named "Spota" in many of his films since The Hunter (1980), which he wrote.

Summer Heat (1987)

Director Michie Gleason's dad, Charles H. Gleason, appears as the judge.

Summer School (1987)

Director Carl Reiner has a cameo as lottery-obsessed Mr. Dearadorian, Mark Harmon's predecessor.

Sunset Boulevard (1950)

Max, the butler played by Erich von Stroheim, is supposed to be the former celebrated director of the Gloria Swanson character, Norma Desmond (Gloria Swanson). In fact, at one point, Norma invites or forces her houseguest to watch one of their former collaborations on her posh personal home movie screen. Swanson and von Stroheim actually did work together in their respective heydays, and it was their final collaboration, where von Stroheim asked Swanson to portray a prostitute, that ended his Hollywood directorial career. After minimal shooting of the movie, Swanson, whose squeaky clean image would not allow her to continue to portray such a sinful character, marched off the set, leaving von Stroheim without his leading lady, and consequently the film was shelved. Von Stroheim, his reputation as a director sullied, marched back to Europe and continued a very celebrated career, but never saw the same success or fame that Hollywood brought him. His first return to Hollywood was to shoot the nearly autobiographical part in Sunset Boulevard, accepting the wholly self-deprecating role only because he needed the money badly. And the prostitute film that Swanson and von Stroheim worked on? The scant footage which remained after the production was killed was edited and used in Sunset Boulevard as the film that Norma and Max produced, and that Norma later inflicts on her guest.

The "bridge table" scene features four old-timers of the Hollywood scene as themselves. In the film, they are referred to as "The Waxworks." They are actors Anna Q. Nilsson, Buster Keaton, H.B. Warner and columnist Hedda Hopper.

The Super Cops (1974)

David Selby and Ron Leibman star

as "super cops" Robert Hantz and David Greenberg. The real Hantz and Greenberg also have cameos in the film.

Super Mario Bros. (1993)

In the other dimension, ruled by King Koopa (Dennis Hopper), the legend goes that the previous King had been deevolved to primordial slime and now covered the entire city. In essence, he is "everywhere." This gave Toad (Mojo Nixon) the chance to proclaim, "The King is everywhere!" on his way to being deevolved. This is a reference to the song recorded by Mojo Nixon and his partner Skid Roper, titled "Elvis Is Everywhere."

Superman (1978)

In the film serials of *Superman* in the '50s, Superman was played by Kirk Alyn and Lois Lane by Noel Neill. In this film, Alyn and Neill play the parents of young Lois Lane on the train.

When Clark Kent needs to change into Superman, he runs toward a phone booth (the stereotypical Superman-changing-place) and looks at the half-length open-air phone booth that he finds in exasperation. He hurries off to find a more private place to change.

The Sure Thing (1985)

College student John Cusack has a poster in his room for director Rob Reiner's *This Is Spinal Tap* (1984).

Suspicion (1941)

Director Alfred Hitchcock can be seen mailing a letter at the village postbox about 45 minutes into the film.

Suspira (1977)

A glass feather is plucked from an ornament. Director Dario Argento's first film was *The Bird with the Crystal Plumage* (1969).

The Swarm (1978)

There are posters in this film for producer-director Irwin Allen's previous disaster film *The Towering Inferno* (1974).

Swing Shift (1984)

Director Jonathan Demme's mentor, B-movie producer Roger Corman, has a small part as Mr. MacBride.

Swingers (1996)

The licence plate of Trent's (Vince Vaughn) car is THX 1138, after the groundbreaking George Lucas sci-fi film *THX-1138* (1970).

Take Me Out to the Ball Game (1949)

The song "O'Brien to Ryan to Goldberg" is a parody of a popular poem by Franklin Pierce Adams called "Tinker to Evers to Chance." Tinker, Evers and Chance were a famous double-play trio (shortstop, second baseman, first baseman) for the Chicago Cubs from 1903 to 1910.

Tales from the Darkside: The Movie (1990)

The mummy in the "Lot 249" segment is played by the film's makeup artist, Mike Deak.

Talk Radio (1988)

A radio station employee can be seen reading an issue of *Playboy* in which director Oliver Stone was interviewed.

The Tall Guy (1989)

The name "Ron Anderson" is very similar to the name of the actor who plays him: Rowan Atkinson.

One of the other contenders for the award Anderson wins is Griff

Rhys-Jones, half of the comedy duo "Alas Smith and Jones." The other half was Mel Smith, the director of this film.

Smith himself appears as a drunk at the "Elephant!" opening night party who congratulates Jeff Goldblum, then falls down.

Anderson refers to his sidekick (Goldblum) as "Perkins." When performing live, Atkinson frequently uses Angus Deayton as his sidekick, who is always named Perkins. Deayton appears in the film as an actor offered lots of excellent roles in Goldblum's agent's office.

The car that Goldblum races to the hospital in at the end of the film (a blue Aston Martin, licence plate "COMIC") belongs to Atkinson. Goldblum is pulled over by the police for speeding just as Atkinson was in real life in the very same car. Atkinson lost his license as a result of the incident.

Tango and Cash (1989)

Gung-ho cop Ray Tango (Sylvester Stallone) is asked by one cop, "What's with you?" Another cop answers, "He thinks he's Rambo." Well, he was. Tango responds, "Rambo is a pussy."

Tapeheads (1988)

The last line in the film is uttered by an FBI agent. He warns Josh and Ivan, "Remember what we did to Jello Biafra?" Biafra, lead singer of the rock group the Dead Kennedys, got into some real trouble with the FBI. The actor who plays this agent is Jello Biafra.

As Josh (Tim Robbins) sets up his equipment in the new apartment, Ivan (John Cusack) is watching a man named Don Druzel sell his book, *Prosperity Through Exploitation* on televi-

sion. The actor credited for playing Druzel is named "Jack Cheese," but in reality, Druzel is played by a short-haired, soft-spoken actor named Bobcat Goldthwait. Goldthwait and Robin Williams once formed a comedy team, calling themselves "Jack Cheese and Marty Fromage."

Targets (1968)

Writer-director-screenwriter Peter Bogdanovich appears in the film, playing Sammy Michaels, the writer-director of Boris Karloff's film within the film.

The old film footage featuring Karloff is from two of his previous films, *The Terror* (1963) and *The Criminal Code* (1931).

Tarzan's Magic Fountain (1949)

The original Tarzan, Elmo Lincoln of *Tarzan of the Apes* (1918), has a bit part.

Tarzan's New York Adventure (1942)

Elmo Lincoln, who first played Tarzan in film, on *Tarzan of the Apes* (1918), appears as a roustabout.

Taxi Driver (1976)

Martin Scorsese dedicated this film to Bernard Herrmann. The longtime Hollywood composer died one day after completing this film's score.

Scorsese has two cameos in the film. He plays the passenger in Travis Bickle's (Robert De Niro) cab who spies on his wife in a window, and later he is seen sitting on the steps of the campaign headquarters as Bickle goes in.

Teenage Mutant Ninja Turtles (1990)

Michelan Sisti, the actor inside Michaelangelo, has a cameo as the Domino's Pizza deliveryman.

After Rafael and Casey Jones (Elias

Koteas) fight in the park, Raphael gets hit by a taxicab. The passenger in the cab is played by Josh Pais, the actor inside of Raphael.

Tempest (1982)

Director Paul Mazursky and his wife, Betsy, play theatrical producer Terry Bloomfield and wife Betsy.

The Ten Commandments (1956)

Charlton Heston plays Moses, and Heston's son Fraser plays Moses as an infant. Fraser Clarke Heston went on to write the screenplays for *The Mountain Men* (1980) and *Mother Lode* (1982), both of which starred his father.

The Terminator (1984)

The Terminator of the future who breaks into the humans' safehold is played by Franco Columbu. Columbu is a friend of Arnold Schwarzenegger's and was his main bodybuilding rival when they were competing.

Terminator 2: Judgment Day (1991)

When the Terminator first meets Sarah Connor, he repeats the line that Kyle Reese used to get her to come with him in *The Terminator* (1984)— "Come with me if you want to live."

The badge on the T-1000's uniform reads "Austin," after producer Stephanie Austin.

The Terminator (Arnold Schwarzenegger) carries a gun in a box of roses through a mall. This scene was used in a video by Guns n' Roses, who were included on the film's soundtrack.

The Terminator says, "I need a vacation" at the end of the film. Schwarzenegger ad-libbed this line, which he had used in his earlier film, *Kindergarten Cop* (1990).

T2 coscripter William Wisher plays the guy who takes pictures of the Terminator as he crashes through the window of the clothing shop in the shopping mall.

Edward Furlong's acting coach, Mike Muscat, plays Moshier, the security guard in Cyberdyne's front lobby.

When the Terminator walks into the tear-gas-filled lobby of the cybernetics lab, he turns back and says to John and Sarah Connor, "Stay here. I'll be back." (see *Commando*, 1985)

In the scene where we see both the real Sarah and the T-1000 disguised as Sarah behind her, the "other" Sarah is played by Linda Hamilton's twin sister, Leslie Hamilton Gearren.

The Benthic Petroleum gas station takes its name from the company who employed the divers in *The Abyss* (1989). Benthic would also show up on a tanker truck in *Twister* (1996). Production designer Joseph Nemec, who was responsible for the appearances of Benthic, worked on all three films.

Terror from the Year 5,000 (1958)

This film was made by the legendary American International Pictures (AIP), producers of many horror and exploitation films. The movie that the couple goes to see on the mainland is AIP's *I Was a Teenage Frankenstein* (1957).

Terror House (1972)

The film's producer, Michael Macready, son of actor George Macready, has a cameo.

Tex (1982)

The film's screenwriter, Charlie Haas, appears as Lee, and Mrs. Barnes is played by S.E. Hinton, whose novel Haas's screenplay was based on.

The Texas Chainsaw Massacre 2 (1986)

As Ranger Enright (Dennis Hopper) goes into his hotel room, a man walks by and is pelted by popcorn. The man is this film's director (and director of the original *The Texas Chainsaw Massacre*, 1974), Tobe Hooper. Presumably, the popcorn is supposed to have been thrown by his fans, unhappy with his current work.

That Thing You Do (1996)

The slow-motion running shot of the band chasing a race horse is a take-off of the film *Chariots of Fire* (1981).

This film was Tom Hanks's directoral debut (he wrote it as well), and he cast many of his friends and former co-workers in it in cameos. For example:

Peter Scolari appears as Troy Chesterfield, the television music show host in the film. Scolari and Hanks have been good friends ever since starring in the sitcom *Bosom Buddies*.

In the *Beach* film, the heroine dances with a character named "Goofball" to make her boyfriend jealous. "Goofball" is played by Hanks's stand-up comedy coach and costar in *Punchline* (1988), Barry Sobel.

Coproducer Jonathan Demme, who directed Hanks in his Academy Award–winning role in *Philadelphia* (1993), plays the director of the "major motion picture."

The Play-Tone photographer who takes pictures of the band when they meet the company president is played by Gedde Watanabe, Hanks's costar in *Volunteers* (1985).

Ron Howard is a good friend of Hanks (he directed Hanks in *Apollo 13*, 1995) and Ron's brother Clint (also in *Apollo 13*) has a cameo as the Los Angeles disk jockey at KJZZ.

Hanks's wife, Rita Wilson, appears as Margueritte, the oversexed waitress at The Blue Spot jazz club.

They All Laughed (1981)

The credits have a dedication to Dorothy Stratten. Stratten, who stars in the film, was a former *Playboy* Playmate who was murdered by her boyfriend soon after the film was made. There was a documentary made about her and her story was also filmed as *Star 80* (1983).

They Live (1988)

The two alien movie critics on TV at the end (meant to be parodies of Gene Siskel and Roger Ebert) discuss sex and violence in the movies and one has the line, "Filmmakers like George Romero and John Carpenter have to show some restraint." Carpenter directed the film.

They Were Sisters (1945)

Screenwriter Roland Pertwee has a bit part as Sir Hamish Nair.

They Won't Forget (1937)

There is a famous Hollywood story that Lana Turner was discovered at Schwab's Drug Store, sipping a soda. In reality, it was in Currie's Ice Cream Parlor that she was first noticed by talent scout Billy Wilkerson, who confirms that she was sipping a soda at the time. He took her to the Zeppo Marx Agency, who secured Turner her first role—a bit part in this film in which she is sipping a soda in a drugstore.

The 39 Steps (1935)

Director Alfred Hitchcock can be seen tossing some litter while Robert Donat and Lucie Mannheim run from the music hall.

Throw Momma from the Train (1987)

The first name in Owen Lift's (Danny DeVito) story "Twenty Girls I'd Like to Pork" is that of DeVito's pal from the two *Romancing the Stone* films, Kathleen Turner.

Screenwriter Stu Silver appears as Ramon.

THX-1138 (1971)

THX stands for "Tomlinson Holman's eXperiment." Holman was a friend of director George Lucas, and inventor of the THX sound system used extensively by Lucas. The number, though, has no special meaning. Lucas once told an interviewer he just likes the sound of it.

Tight Little Island (1949)

Compton MacKenzie, who wrote both the screenplay for this film and the book it was based on, appears as Captain Buncher.

Tightrope (1984)

Executive producer Fritz Manes, who produced many of Clint Eastwood's films, appears as Valdes.

A Time to Love and a Time to Die (1958)

This film was based on a novel by Erich Maria Remarque, who also plays the schoolmaster, Pohlmann.

The Time Travellers (1964)

Forrest J Ackerman appears as a technician. Ackerman was the creator of the first successful sci-fi/horror magazine, *Famous Monsters of Filmland*.

Timecop (1994)

When Jean-Claude Van Damme prepares to go into the past with his new partner, he takes out a stick of Black Black chewing gum, a Japanese brand. During 1994, Van Damme appeared in commercials in Japan for Black Black chewing gum.

The guy who proposes the TEC program to the senators at the start of the film is named George Spota (Scott Lawrence). Director Peter Hyams has included a character named "Spota" in many of his films since *The Hunter* (1980), which he wrote.

As Atwood (Jason Schombing) gets out of his car in 1929, a newsboy runs up to him and offers him a paper. The newsboy is played by Peter Hyams's son, Nick.

Timerider (1983)

Director William Dear plays one of the technicians.

Tin Cup (1996)

Through the film, Don Johnson is described as so cruel that he is mean to children, old people and dogs. After his television interview at the open, two golf fans with their grandson and a dog ask for his autograph and he sloughs them off. The fans are played by Kevin Costner's mother and father, and the kid is Costner's son, Joe.

To Be or Not to Be (1983)

Frederick and Anna Bronski (Mel Brooks and Anne Bancroft) move in with Sasha (James Haake) at 52 Kubelski Street. The name can be seen on the street sign outside the building when Tim Matheson finds it. The original *To Be or Not to Be* (1942) starred Jack Benny, whose real name was Benjamin Kubelski.

To Catch a Thief (1955)

Director Alfred Hitchcock can be seen sitting beside Cary Grant on the bus.

To Grandmother's House We Go (1992 TV)

This television movie stars the Olsen twins, Mary-Kate and Ashley. Bob Saget, their costar on the popular series *Full House*, has an uncredited cameo as a game show host.

Tombstone (1993)

Val Kilmer flips a poker chip over his knuckles. This was his "signature" move, which he did for the first time in *Real Genius* (1985) with two quarters.

The real Wyatt Earp's fifth cousin, Wyatt Earp, has a cameo as Billy Claiborne.

Tommy (1975)

Director Ken Russell has a cameo as one of the cripples in the "Eyesight to the Blind/ Marilyn Monroe" sequence.

Tootsie (1982)

Director Sydney Pollak plays Michael Dorsey's (Dustin Hoffman) harried agent, George Fields.

The guest at Michael's birthday party who toasts him is played by the film's co-scripter, Murray Schisgal.

Top Gun (1986)

Val Kilmer flips a pen over his knuckles. This was his "signature" move, which he did for the first time in *Real Genius* (1985) with two quarters.

Top Secret! (1984)

During Nick's (Val Kilmer) rendition of "Tutti Frutti" in the posh restaurant, there is a shot of the kitchen staff bopping along to the song. The chef, who is holding a cleaver and a chicken, is played by Burton Zucker, the father of two of the film's directors, Jerry and David Zucker.

At one point during "Tutti Frutti," Nick hangs from a chandelier. He drops down behind two women and takes the hand of one of them as he sings. This woman is Charlotte Zucker, Jerry and David's mom.

The shot with a Nazi falling from a high wall and shattering was undoubtedly a spoof of the fate of many movie bad guys, but the specific fall looked exactly like a similar scene in the film *Escape from Athena* (1979).

Topaz (1969)

In the airport, director Alfred Hitchcock can be seen being pushed in a wheelchair. Hitchcock gets up from the chair, shakes hands with a man, and walks off to the right.

Torch Song (1953)

Joan Crawford's clumsy dance partner in the opening number is played by the film's director, Charles Waters, himself a well-known choreographer.

Torch Song Trilogy (1988)

Torch Song (1953) director Charles Walters auditions as one of the dancing partners.

Tormented (1960)

Producer-director Bert I. Gordon's daughter, Susan, has a cameo.

Torn Curtain (1966)

Director Alfred Hitchcock can be seen sitting in the lobby of the Hotel d'Angleterre with a blond baby on his lap.

Total Recall (1990)

Johnnycab whistles the Norwegian national anthem.

Michael Ironside's sidekick from *V: The Final Battle* (1984 TV), Mickey

Jones, became a good friend of Ironside's and was the best man at his wedding. He also has a cameo in this film as the burly ex-miner who talks to Doug Quaid (Arnold Schwarzenegger) on the train on Mars.

Director Paul Verhoeven so enjoyed Ironside's portrayal of Ham Tyler in *V: The Final Battle* that he had Ironside wear Tyler's actual outfit in this film.

The name on the passport used by Quaid in his disguise as the large, red-haired woman is "Priscilla Allen." Priscilla Allen is the real name of the actress who plays Quaid's disguise.

The Town That Dreaded Sundown (1977)

Producer-director Charles B. Pierce has a cameo as a cop.

Toy Story (1995)

The desk lamp and yellow ball with a blue stripe and a red star are references to the previous Pixar film *Luxo Jr.* (1986).

Mr. Potato Head insults another toy by saying, "What are you looking at, you hockey puck?" This is a popular put-down by comedian Don Rickles, who provides the voice of Mr. Potato Head. The toy he says it to is a hockey puck.

When Woody calls the meeting of the toys, he is standing in front of the bookshelf, on which there are several books. Three of the books are titled *Tin Toy*, *Red's Dream*, and *Knickknack*. These were the names of three computer-animated short films made by Pixar, the company who also made *Toy Story*, and directed by this film's director, John Lasseter.

The license plate of the family's car is A-113, a number that frequently appears in episodes of *The Simpsons* (see *The Simpsons*).

All the car licence plates seen in the film have some special meaning to members of the crew. One car's license plate is "HTT1195," which apparently means "Hits the Theaters 11/95," referring to the film's U.S. release date.

Under the tanker truck, Buzz Lightyear tells Woody about Emperor Zurg's new weapon which can destroy an entire planet, and that only he has the information that reveals the weapon's sole weakness, which he must deliver to Star Command. This is a reference to Princess Leia's delivering the Death Star's specifications to the rebels in the film *Star Wars* (1977).

The store which sells Buzz Lightyear dolls is called Al's Toy Barn. (Tim Allen's television sidekick [Richard Karn] on *Home Improvement* is named Al.)

Syd's sister serves Buzz tea from a Utah Teapot, a famous data model seen in countless computer animations.

The name of the moving company, Eggman Movers, is in honor of Ralph Eggleston, who was the film's art director.

The toolbox that Buzz Lightyear (voice of Tim Allen) pushes out of the way to rescue Woody (voice of Tom Hanks) is from Binford, which is the name of the fictional tool company that sponsors the program on Tim Allen's show, *Home Improvement*.

As Buzz and Woody try to get into the moving van, Molly is listening to "Hakuna Matata," from another Disney film, *The Lion King* (1994), on the car radio.

Toys (1992)

The words used by the General in an attempt to stop the rampaging sea creature are "Klaatu Barada Nikto," the same words used to stop the robot

Gort in *The Day the Earth Stood Still* (1951).

Traces of Red (1992)
Mr. Marlyn is played by the film's screenwriter, Jim Piddock.

Trading Places (1983)
The film *See You Next Wednesday* is on a poster in Jamie Lee Curtis's apartment (see *Schlock*, 1971).

When Dan Aykroyd is arrested, he is given the prison number 7474-505B. This was Jake Blues's prison number in Aykroyd's *The Blues Brothers* (1980).

Director John Landis cast Muppeteer and budding film director Frank Oz as the cop who finds angel dust on Aykroyd.

To get some money, Aykroyd has to pawn his watch. The pawnbroker is played by reknowned blues guitarist Bo Diddley.

The Train Robbers (1973)
John Wayne's and Ann-Margret's characters' names, "Lane" and "Mrs. Lowe," are the same as Wayne's and Geraldine Page's characters' names in *Hondo* (1953).

Trainspotting (1995)
There are many references to the Beatles:

While watching the train, the four friends arrange themselves in the same manner as The Beatles did on the back of the album *Sgt. Pepper's Lonely Hearts Club Band*.

The scene where the four friends cross the road and enter the hotel is reminiscent of the cover of the album *Abbey Road*.

The writing on the wall of the Volcano Nightclub is the same as that in the Moloko bar in *A Clockwork Orange* (1971).

Transylvania 6-5000 (1985)
Director Rudy DeLuca appears in the film as suspected werewolf Lawrence Malbot. Malbot turns out to only be cheating on his wife. Lon Chaney, Jr.'s, name in *The Wolf Man* (1941) was Lawrence Talbot.

The Treasure of the Sierra Madre (1948)
The American in the white suit at the beginning of the film that Fred C. Dobbs (Humphrey Bogart) begs money from is played by director John Huston.

Trent's Last Case (1952)
Orson Welles remarks, "I saw *Othello* in London last year, but the fellow was not very good." The year before, Welles had appeared in a London production of Othello as the title character.

Trespass (1992)
James Picken, Jr., plays Officer Reese and L. Warren Young plays Officer Foley in Bob Gale and Robert Zemeckis's script (see *1941*, 1979).

Trick or Treat (1986)
Director Charles Martin Smith has a cameo as the high school teacher.

Troll (1986)
Witch Eunice St. Clair (June Lockhart) casts a spell on herself that takes several decades off of her age, and from then on she is played by Anne Lockhart, June's daughter.

Phil Fondacaro, the actor who plays the troll, has a second role in the film. He is the college professor neighbor of the Potters who happens to be a dwarf.

There is a sci-fi film on television in the movie in which a young man discovers that his dog is actually a man from Mars. The man is played by low-budget sci-fi director Charles Band (*Metalstorm: The Destruction of Jared-Syn*, 1983; *Trancers*, 1985).

Tron (1982)

Flynn's program is named "Clu." CLU is an old programming language.

The Trouble with Harry (1955)

Director Alfred Hitchcock walks past the parked limousine of an old man who is looking at the exhibition of paintings.

True Lies (1994)

When Arnold Schwarzenegger learns that his daughter is being held hostage by the terrorists, he "borrows" a Citation fighter plane. The pilot, who tells him he will have to sign for it, is played by Mike Cameron, the son of director James Cameron.

Tucker: The Man and His Dream (1988)

When the car is unveiled to the public for the first time, under the sheet covering the car, the licence plate reads "GIO." This was the name of director Francis Ford Coppola's son. Gio Coppola inspired Francis to make the film, but died at 22 in a boating accident before it was completed. The film is also dedicated to Gio, " ...Who Loved Cars."

Turtle Diary (1985)

Playwright Harold Pinter, who wrote this film's screenplay, appears in a cameo as a bookstore customer.

Twelve Monkeys (1995)

A radio announcer is named Roger Pratt. Roger Pratt was the name of the film's director of photography.

There are many references to Alfred Hitchcock films, and *Vertigo* (1958) in particular:

They have similar title sequences.

Cole (Bruce Willis) and Dr. Railly (Madeline Stowe) go to see a Hitchcock film festival, and they watch a scene from *Vertigo*.

Like Kim Novak in *Vertigo*, Dr. Railly disguises herself using a blonde wig.

29th Street (1991)

29th Street is based on the life of Frank Pesce, and the real Frank Pesce plays his own brother, Vito.

The film is dedicated to the late actor James Franciscus, who was involved with a dispute over who was going to produce it. Franciscus eventually relented and accepted a relatively small sum for his share of the picture.

Twilight Zone—The Movie (1983)

Bill (Billy) Mumy played the lead in "It's a Good Life," the original *Twilight Zone* episode on which the third segment (directed by Joe Dante) is based. He appears in the third segment as Tim, the man at the roadside restaurant seated closest to the camera who says Anthony (Jeremy Licht) is "screwing up the football game."

Dick Miller also appears in this segment as sandwich and seafood diner owner Walter Paisley (see *Hollywood Boulevard*, 1976).

The teacher who takes the omnipotent youngster under her wing is named Helen Foley (Kathleen Quinlan). This was the name of one of Rod Serling's favorite teachers. It was also used in the original series (see *The Twilight Zone*).

In John Landis's segment, when Vic Morrow is in the swamp in Vietnam, a troop of GIs fire on him, and then one says, "I told you guys we shouldn't have shot Lt. Niedermeyer!" referring to their commanding officer. In the end credits of Landis's *National Lampoon's Animal House* (1978), the character of Niedermeyer (Mark Metcalf) is listed as being "killed by his own troops in Vietnam."

There is a rumor that the phrase "See you next Wednesday" is spoken in German when Bill (Vic Morrow) is being shot at on the building (see *Schlock*, 1971). However, this is not true. The German officers are pretty much saying what one would expect them to be saying—conversational chitchat about "the American."

Stephen Bishop plays "Charming G.I." (a pun on "Guy") (see *Kentucky Fried Movie*, 1977).

Twin Dragons (1992)

Director Hark Tsui has a cameo as a card player.

His contemporary, director John Woo (*Hard-Boiled*, 1992; *Broken Arrow*, 1996), also has a cameo. He is the priest at the wedding.

Twins (1988)

Sylvester Stallone is seen on a poster advertising *Rambo III* (1988), which was in theaters against *Twins*. Julius (Arnold Schwarzenegger) compares his biceps to Sly's ... and laughs. Good-natured kidding between the two continued in their films.

Schwarzenegger warns the doctor who delivered him, "If you're lying, I'll be back" (see *Commando*, 1985).

When Julius visits Vincent (Danny DeVito) in prison, Vincent calls him "Mr. Universe," a bodybuilding title that Schwarzenegger actually held for several years.

Director Ivan Reitman's son Jason plays Granger's (Hugh O'Brian) grandson, and Reitman's daughter Catherine plays Granger's granddaughter.

Twister (1996)

The tornado-chasing team led by Helen Hunt and Bill Paxton see what they think is only a small tornado. However, when they realize the enormous size of it, one of the team says, "That's no moon, it's a *space station!*" This is a reference to the scene in *Star Wars* (1977) when the heroes first see the death star, passing it off as a moon because of its size. Obi-Wan (Alec Guinness) then gets an odd look on his face and says, "That's no moon ... it's a space station!"

The tanker truck has the company name "Benthic Petroleum" on the side. Benthic Petroleum was the company that the divers worked for in *The Abyss* (1989), and it also appeared on the gas station in *Terminator 2: Judgment Day* (1991). Production designer Joseph Nemec, who was responsible for the appearances of Benthic, worked on all three films.

The Two Jakes (1990)

Van Dyke Parks has a bit part as Francis Hannah. Parks also provided the music for the movie.

2001: A Space Odyssey (1968)

Director Stanley Kubrick's daughter Vivienne Kubrick appears as Dr. Heywood Floyd's daughter.

HAL sings the song "Daisy" as he is shut down. This was the first song ever played by a nonmechanical computer.

The *Jupiter* explorer's serial number is CRM 114. This is a number that Kubrick enjoyed putting in his films. The CRM-114 was the name of the message decoder on the ill-fated bomber in Kubrick's *Dr. Strangelove, or How I Learned to Stop Worrying and Love the Bomb* (1964).

An unintentional in-joke: the

letters in the computer's name, "HAL," preceed "IBM" in the alphabet. However, writer Arthur C. Clarke has said that he was not aware of this, and if he had noticed, he would have changed them. HAL, according to Clarke, stands for Heuristic ALgorithmic.

2010 (1984)

2010 (and *2001*) author Arthur C. Clarke shows up not once but twice. He is seen feeding pigeons on a park bench outside of the White House (not visible on the video version), and then, in the hospital, on the cover of *Time* magazine as the president of the United States opposite *2001: A Space Odyssey* (1968) director-producer Stanley Kubrick as the Russian premier!

The commander of the Leonov is named Kirbuk, a palindrome of "Kubri(c)k."

The Twonky (1953)

William Phipps appears in an uncredited cameo as one of the men in white coats who take Hans Conreid away to the nuthouse at the end of the film. Phipps had starred in writer-director Arch Oboler's previous film, *Five* (1951), and Oboler asked Phipps if he would play the part as a "good luck" thing.

UHF (1989)

Director Jay Levey plays Gandhi in the "Gandhi II" and "Gandhi on Ice" scenes.

Under Capricorn (1949)

Director Alfred Hitchcock appears in the town square during the parade, wearing a blue coat and brown hat. Ten minutes later, he is one of three men on the steps of Government House.

Under Siege (1992)

Jordan Tate (Erika Eleniak) was *Playboy* Playmate for July 1989; so was Eleniak.

Under the Boardwalk (1989)

Roxana Zal plays a character named "Gitch": half-girl, half-bitch. This is a reference to Gidget, the beach-loving California teenager played by numerous actresses, including Sandra Dee in the film *Gidget* (1959) and Sally Field in the series *Gidget*. Her name stood for "half-girl, half-midget." The two old-timers (Sonny Bono and famed real-life surfer Corky Carroll) even watch an episode of *The New Gidget* on the beach.

The Underneath (1995)

There is a line about there being no such person as "Jeanette Scott." She was the set decorator for the film.

One of the screenwriters is named "Sam Lowry," but it is actually director Stephen Soderbergh. Sam Lowry was the name of Jonathan Pryce's character in *Brazil* (1985). The Writer's Guild insisted that *The Underneath*'s writing credit be shared by Soderbergh with Daniel Fuchs, who had done the 1949 screen adaptation of Don Tracy's novel for *Criss Cross*, which *The Underneath* was very loosely based on. For some reason, the "based upon" credit would not satisfy the guild. So Soderbergh resigned from the guild and chose the Lowry pseudonym for its connotation of bureaucracy run amok.

An Unmarried Woman (1978)

Hal, the obnoxious dim sum diner, is played by director Paul Mazursky.

Until the End of the World (1991)

Director Wim Wenders was a big fan of the film *2001: A Space Odyssey*

(1968), and included what he called a "very obvious" reference to the film at the end of this one. Claire is wished happy birthday while in space, just as Dr. Floyd was in *2001*.

The Untouchables (1987)

The shootout sequence on the steps in the train station is a homage to Sergei Eisenstein's *Battleship Potemkin* (1925), which involved a sequence of soldiers marching down the staircase at Odessa. In both films, a baby carriage bounces down the stairs in the middle of the action.

The Usual Suspects (1995)

Redfoot (Peter Greene), the intermediary who meets the thieves in Los Angeles, has the line, "Feed it to the gimp." Greene appeared as Zed in the film *Pulp Fiction* (1994), along with a character known as "The Gimp."

The true identity of the Turkish villain Keyser Söze has been greatly debated, but it is generally assumed to be Verbal Kint (Kevin Spacey). The fact that "söze" is Turkish for "verbal" does help support this. He is named after Keyser Sume, a lawyer whom screenwriter Christopher McQuarrie met. McQuarrie liked the sound of the name and used it in early drafts of the script. It was changed to Söze later on when the lawyer asked to read the script just to ensure that the character with his name was presented in a fashion that would not dissuade clients from hiring him. McQuarrie said, "I was confident that we'd get his permission. We'd all fallen in love with the name. Anyway, I opened the script to the page where he kills his family. And I closed it and said 'We've got to change the name.'"

Söze's enemies were said to be Hungarians, and "kint" is Hungarian for "outside."

The V.I.P.s (1963)

Asked for her phone number, Elizabeth Taylor gives "Grosvenor 7060," which was the number of MGM's London office.

Valentino (1977)

Director Ken Russell plays director Rex Ingram.

Valley of the Dolls (1967)

Jacqueline Susann, who wrote the novel that the film was based on, appears in a bit part as a reporter.

Vampire in Brooklyn (1995)

Mitch Pileggi, who had starred in director Wes Craven's *Shocker* (1989) and went on to greater fame as F.B.I. Assistant Director Skinner on *The X-Files*, appears in a cameo in this film as a favor to director Craven. He plays Tony, one of two Italian hitmen who chase Julius into an alley and are killed by Max (Eddie Murphy). Tony's heart is ripped out.

Vertigo (1958)

About 11 minutes into the film, director Alfred Hitchcock walks past "Elster's" shipbuilding facility, just before James Stewart arrives from the opposite direction. Hitchcock is carrying a musical instrument case, most likely a trumpet case, according to *The Art of Hitchcock* author Donald Spoto.

A Very Brady Sequel (1996)

Like the first film, this sequel has numerous references back to the original television series, starting with the title (a reference to the television movie *A Very Brady Christmas*, 1988 TV) and the final sequence in Hawaii. The cast of the original series also had a very popular "Hawaiian episode." Jan's imaginary boyfriend, George Glass, was also in the series.

Greg and Marcia have libidinous feelings for each other once they realize they are not really related. This is a reference to the affair that Barry Williams and Maureen McCormick, the original Greg and Marcia Brady, had while on the television show.

The soiled horse statue is sent to an antique store on Sherwood Avenue, after Sherwood Schwartz, the creator of the original series.

At the wedding at the end, the Bradys' dog, Tiger, runs out onto the street, followed by cousin Oliver. The relevance of Tiger is explained in *The Brady Bunch Movie* (1995). Cousin Oliver (Robbie Rist) was a character who joined the series in the fifth and final season when the producers decided they needed a cute, younger character on the show. However, Oliver was not well received and was written out. (A similar character named "Seven" appeared in some episodes of *Married with Children*, but, again, the character was not popular, and he disappeared without explanation [see *Married with Children*].)

The opening of the film parodies the opening of *Raiders of the Lost Ark* (1981), right down to the logo of the Paramount mountain dissolving into an actual peak, just as it does in all of the Indiana Jones films.

Mike Brady goes to the police station and speaks with a detective played by Richard Belzer, who plays Detective Munch on the show *Homicide*. Munch is filmed in the unsteady handheld style of modern crime dramas, including *Homicide*, but Mike is shot in a steady, serene style.

John Hillerman plays Whitehead,

the Hawaiian-based entrepreneur, a reference to the role he played on *Magnum, P.I.*

Carol's first husband and Whitehead's son become the Professor and Gilligan on *Gilligan's Island. The Brady Bunch*'s producer, Sherwood Schwartz, also produced *Gilligan's Island.*

The woman who shows up at the end claiming to be Mike's wife is the genie Jeannie (Barbara Eden) of the '70s sitcom *I Dream of Jeannie*.

Viva Max! (1969)

The film refers indirectly to the John Wayne film *The Alamo* (1960) by showing a painting of Wayne as Davy Crockett defending the Alamo. Normally there is a disclaimer which states "all characters depicted in this motion picture are fictitious and any similarity to actual persons...," and so on. In this film, the disclaimer reads "all characters depicted in this motion picture except John Wayne are fictitious and any similarity to actual persons..."

Volunteers (1985)

Tom Hanks's character is named Lawrence Bourne III. Hanks saves the village, and, as the film fades to black for the credits, a large group of "volunteers" gather around Hanks, chanting "Lawrence, Lawrence, Lawrence ..." This is a reference to the scene in *Lawrence of Arabia* (1962) in which T.E. Lawrence (Peter O'Toole) marches across a traintop to the chants of "Lawrence, Lawrence, Lawrence ..."

Walker (1988)

Screenwriter Rudy Wurlitzer plays Morgan, stuntman Rick Barker appears as Breckenridge, the Clash's Joe Strummer (who provided the music for the film) plays Faucet, and

Miguel Sandoval, who cast the film, appears as Parker French.

Wall Street (1987)

Gordon Gekko's son, Rudy, is played by director Oliver Stone's son, Sean.

Stone himself appears in a montage of scenes as a trader placing a phone order.

The credits contain the line, "Dedicated to Louis Stone, Stockbroker, 1910–1985." Stone was the father of director Oliver Stone. "His spirit influenced the film," Stone has said. "There were good stockbrokers portrayed. My father represented older values, as opposed to the newer values on Wall Street."

The War of the Roses (1989)

Oliver Rose (Michael Douglas) cuts the heels off of his wife's (Kathleen Turner) shoes. Jack Colton (Douglas) did the same to Joan Wilder's (Turner) in *Romancing the Stone* (1984).

The War of the Worlds (1953)

Producer George Pal and associate producer Y. Frank Freeman, Jr., have cameos as a pair of bums who listen to a radio in front of a store.

The War Wagon (1967)

John Wayne wears his *Red River* "D" belt buckle in this film (see *Rio Bravo*, 1959).

Warlock: The Armageddon (1993)

Director Anthony Hickox has a cameo as the Dark Leader.

Waxwork (1988)

The English prince who eagerly watches the Marquis de Sade whip his victims is played by the film's director, Anthony Hickox.

This film was dedicated to a slew of horror film directors and horror writ-

ers. "Dedicated to Hammer [films], [Dario] Argento, [George] Romero, [Joe] Dante, [John] Landis, [Steven] Spielberg, [H.G.] Wells, [John] Carpenter, Mom and Dad and many more …"

Waxwork II: Lost in Time (1992)

Writer-director Anthony Hickox has a cameo as the King's officer.

Wayne's World (1992)

The police officer in Stan Mikita's Donuts is named Officer Koharski (Frederick Coffin), after NHL referee Don Koharski. Koharski was once told by New Jersey Devils coach Jim Schoenfeld to "have another donut, you fat pig!"

Frankie Sharp, a.k.a. "Mr. Big," the record executive who signs Wayne and Garth at the end, is played by Michael Jackson's manager, Frank DiLeo.

The motorcycle cop that pulls Wayne over and shows him a photograph is played by Robert Patrick, parodying his character from the film *Terminator 2: Judgment Day* (1991). Patrick even asks him, "Have you seen this boy?"—a question he asked in the previous film.

The "Do you have any Grey Poupon?" bit in the car is a parody of a popular commercial for Grey Poupon Mustard.

The sequence in Milwaukee after Wayne and Garth see Shotz Brewery on the way to the Alice Cooper show is a parody of the opening credits of the Milwaukee-based show, *Laverne and Shirley*.

Landmarks in the film are based on similar places in Mike Myers's hometown of Toronto. There is a real club called the Gasworks in Toronto, and the Stan Mikita Donuts is based on the real-life Tim Horton Donut chain across Canada, which was founded by hockey player Tim Horton.

Wayne's World 2 (1993)

Mr. Big and Stan Mikita's Donuts are back (see *Wayne's World*, 1992).

The opening sequence with a bust of William Shakespeare and fire pole is a parody of the television series *Batman*.

The Jim Morrison sequence, the roadie saying that he "had the same dream," and the line "If you book them, they will come" are a spoof of *Field of Dreams* (1989).

The sequence in which Wayne, Garth and their buds spy on Cassandra and Bobby (Christopher Walken) is done in the style (and to the tune) of *Mission: Impossible*.

Wayne and Garth get lost while looking through the park, then feel tremors and see the water in their plastic cup vibrate. They then look out the window and see a dinosaur, in a parody of *Jurassic Park* (1993).

The noise heard when Wayne sees the naked Indian in his bedroom is the introduction to the Aerosmith song "Janie's Got a Gun."

The sequence of Wayne saving Cassandra from marrying someone else is a parody of *The Graduate* (1967), and is even set to the tune of Simon and Garfunkel's "Mrs. Robinson."

Garth's "there is some bad red rope licorice..." speech is a take-off of the speech from Woodstock regarding "bad pot."

The Indian looking at the garbage left after Waynestock and crying is a nod to the famous Public Service Announcements with Iron Eyes Cody.

Weekend at Bernie's (1989)

Jack Parker, the inebriated man who is the first to arrive at Bernie's party and who is also the last to leave, is played by the film's director, Ted Kotcheff.

Weekend at the Waldorf (1945)

Walter Pidgeon imitates John Barrymore and Ginger Rogers says, "Why, that's right out of *Grand Hotel*!" *Weekend at the Waldorf* was adapted from *Grand Hotel* (1932).

Welcome Home, Roxy Carmichael (1990)

Director Jim Abrahams's family—his wife Nancy, and two kids, Joseph and Jamie—appear in the film as the fishing family.

We're Back! A Dinosaur's Story (1993)

As the dinosaurs dance around Times Square, it is possible to see a theater marquee advertising *Jurassic Park* (1993), which was directed by executive producer Steven Spielberg.

Westworld (1973)

The costume that the robot (Yul Brynner) is wearing is the same one Brynner wore in *The Magnificent Seven* (1960), 13 years earlier.

Whatever Happened to Baby Jane? (1962)

Jane Hudson's (Bette Davis) old film being shown on television is actually an old Bette Davis film, *Parachute Jumper* (1933).

What's New, Pussycat? (1965)

A stranger who bumps into Peter O'Toole in a nightclub turns out to be Richard Burton, who says, "Excuse me, haven't you seen me somewhere before?" O'Toole answers, "I know the name, but I can't remember the face." O'Toole then says goodbye and, "give my regards to ... what's her name" (i.e., Elizabeth Taylor).

O'Toole approaches Woody Allen,

who is playing chess at an outdoor cafe, and he passes by a table of look-alikes of famous artists, including Henri Toulouse-Lautrec and Vincent Van Gogh, complete with bandaged ear.

What's Up, Doc? (1972)

In the film *Love Story* (1970), Jenny (Ali MacGraw) says the famous line to Oliver (Ryan O'Neal): "Love means never having to say you're sorry." The line was said again in this film to Howard (Ryan O'Neal) by Judy (Barbra Streisand). He answers with, "That's the dumbest thing I've ever heard."

At the end of this film, which was made by Warner Bros., Ryan O'Neal unwinds on the jet back to Iowa from the madcap farce he has been through, thinking he has left Barbra Streisand behind (though she is in the next seat, unbeknownst to him). A Warner Bros. Bugs Bunny cartoon (from which this film took its name) is playing on the in-flight movie. Actually, it is a pastiche of the Bugs title, the Porky sign-off, and another bit in between.

When Harry Met Sally... (1989)

Harry (Billy Crystal) can be seen reading Stephen King's *Misery*. *Misery* (1990) would be director Rob Reiner's next film.

The woman who says, "I'll have what she's having" after Sally (Meg Ryan) fakes her orgasm is Rob's mother, Estelle Reiner.

The Whereabouts of Jenny (1991 TV)

Coexecutive producer Tony Danza has a cameo as a drunk, rowdy patron.

Where's Poppa? (1970)

The film was directed by Carl Reiner, who cast his son, Rob, as a fervent draft resister.

White Dog (1982)

Director Sam Fuller has a cameo as Charlie Felton, Kristy McNichol's agent.

Fuller's daughter, Samantha Fuller, also appears as Helen.

White Nights (1985)

Colonel Chaiko, the KGB agent who hounds Mikhail Baryshnikov, is played by Polish director Jerzy Skolimowski (*Moonlighting*, 1982; *The Lightship*, 1985).

White Palace (1990)

The White Palace customer is played by Glenn Savan. Savan wrote the book *White Palace*, upon which this film was based.

Who Framed Roger Rabbit (1988)

The eminent Toon director Raoul J. Raoul, who is directing Roger's cartoon at the start of the film, is played by megaproducer Joel Silver.

Toontown's countryside and streets are populated with pre–1947 cartoon characters. Apparently, it was not uncommon for animators of the era to "reuse" old characters and backgrounds from old cartoons, but this film makes use of as much old-time animation as the animators could find. There are bits from *Water Babies*, *The Tortoise and the Hare* and *Snow White and the Seven Dwarfs* mixed in with the Three Little Pigs and Mickey's nephews. Other examples:

The penguin waiters at the Ink and Paint Club are from *Mary Poppins* (1964).

The crow musicians who back up Jessica Rabbit are from *Dumbo* (1941).

R.K. Maroon tells Eddie that he got Dumbo and half the cast of *Fantasia* (1940) on loan. This would explain the appearance of the hippo in a tutu and the brooms that Eddie sees sweeping up by themselves outside of Maroon's office. They are from *Fantasia*.

Judge Doom's henchmen, the weasels, are from *The Wind in the Willows*, which was released as the first half of the animated film *The Adventures of Ichabod and Mr. Toad* (1949).

Disney's Reluctant Dragon of *The Reluctant Dragon* (1941) appears in the group of Toontown residents in the final scene.

The password to get into the Ink and Paint Club: "Walt sent me" (as in Walt Disney).

There are many little tidbits in the background as well. For example, the Toontown Hotel men's room has the graffiti "For a good time, call Allyson Wonderland" scrawled on the wall. There are storefronts labelled "Big Bad Wolf Wrecking Company" and "Three Little Pigs Construction Company," and a Disney memo lying in the middle of the road. The "Hotternhell" stove in Roger and Baby Herman's opening sequence is a tribute to the "Coldern-hell" refrigerator in the Tex Avery cartoon *King Size Canary* (1947).

When Eddie (Bob Hoskins) brings Roger to Dolores's (Joanna Cassidy) bar, she says, "Is that a rabbit in your pocket or are you just happy to see me?" This is taken from an innuendo by Mae West, "Is that a gun in your pocket...."

The Judge comes to the bar looking for Roger, and one of the barflies says, "I seen a rabbit," then introduces his invisible friend Harvey. Harvey was the name of the invisible six-foot rabbit in the film *Harvey* (1950).

The Whoopee Boys (1986)

The man who yells at Barney and Jack for being in the pool is played by composer Jack Nitzsche.

Whore (1991)

Theater marquees for two other Ken Russell films, *Crimes of Passion* (1984) and *The Lair of the White Worm* (1988), are seen in the film.

The Wild Life (1984)

Tom's (Christopher Penn) father is played by director Leo Penn, who is Christopher's real-life father.

Willow (1988)

Although the name was never mentioned onscreen, during production the two-headed moat monster was called the Ebersisk, after film critics Roger Ebert and Gene Siskel.

The evil, skull-faced General Kael (Patrick Roach) was named after the *New Yorker*'s film critic, Pauline Kael.

Willow utters the same spell as Merlin did in *Excalibur* (1981).

The Wings of Eagles (1957)

The film director, John Dodge, is played by Ward Bond as an imitation of *Wings of Eagles* director John Ford, complete with sunglasses, pipe and fedora. During a film screening, he points to the screen and asks, "How'd you like that kid with Beery?" The film being screened is *Hell Divers* (1932), starring Wallace Beery and a young "kid," Clark Gable.

Wired (1989)

As the actor who plays John Landis is seen walking across the *Blues Brothers* set, the sound of helicopters can clearly be heard in the background, a reference to the tragedy on the set of *Twilight Zone—The Movie* (1983).

Wisdom (1986)

John Wisdom (Emilio Estevez) can be seen on a bus adorned with the graffiti "Plate O' Shrimp," a reference to *Repo Man* (1984), which also starred Estevez (see *Repo Man*, 1984).

Wise Guys (1986)

Two of the birthday party guests are played by Charles and Catherine Scorsese, parents of director Martin Scorsese (*Raging Bull*, 1980; *Casino*, 1995).

The Witches of Eastwick (1987)

Keith Jochim's character, Walter Neff, has the name of the insurance salesman in Billy Wilder's *Double Indemnity* (1944).

The musical pieces that Carel Struycken performs on the piano in this film were actually composed by Struycken. He is listed in the credits as providing "incidental music."

Witness (1985)

Amish patriarch Jan Rubes asks John Book (Harrison Ford) if he could help with the construction of a new barn. Book smiles and says that he spent some time as a carpenter. Ford actually did—in fact, he had been installing a door in Francis Ford Coppola's office when George Lucas asked him to audition for the part of Han Solo.

Woman on Pier 13 (1950)

The title of the film really has nothing to do with the picture. The patriotic, flag-waving film's original title was *I Married a Communist*, but it was released just when Senator Joseph McCarthy was making the word "Communist" a dirty word, so the title was changed in midrelease.

Word of Honor (1981 TV)

While Karl Malden is talking to someone on the sidewalk, a passerby bumps into him. Malden snaps, "Watch it, Sekulovich!" Malden's real name was Mladen Sekulovich, and he enjoyed sneaking his given name into many of his film and television appearances.

Working Girl (1988)

Sigourney Weaver emerges from a helicopter, returning from a lengthy absence with a souvenir of her hospital stay—a stuffed gorilla. Director Mike Nichols picked it out without knowing about Weaver's 1988 film, *Gorillas in the Mist*; and, although Weaver thought it might come off as a joke, it was still used. It was simply coincidence.

The World According to Garp (1982)

When an airplane crashes into Garp's new house, the pilot who emerges from the wreckage is played by director George Roy Hill, who is himself a private pilot.

The referee at the wrestling match is played by *The World According to Garp* author John Irving.

The Wrong Man (1956)

Director Alfred Hitchcock narrates the film's prologue.

Wyatt Earp (1994)

Director Lawrence Kasdan's son, Jon, has a small role in the bar.

Xanadu (1980)

Gene Kelly adopts the name Danny McGuire, which was the name of the character he played in *Cover Girl* (1944).

Yellow Submarine (1968)

Besides the obvious references to Beatles songs and the songs themselves, a few less obvious references have been sneaked in. For example, when Fred first asks for Ringo's assistance, he cries, "Help! Won't you please please help me?" This is a line from the Beatles song "Help!"

Yellowbeard (1983)

Coscripter Bernard McKenna plays Askey.

You'll Never Get Rich (1941)

In reference to the Cole Porter song "Night and Day" sung by Fred Astaire in *The Gay Divorcee* (1934), Porter ended "The Wedding Cake Walk," sung in this film, with the phrase "night and day." He asked permission from RKO to quote the line.

There is a bugle call before a Fred Asatire–Ginger Rogers dance (see *The Gay Divorcee*, 1934).

Young and Innocent (1938)

Director Alfred Hitchcock appears as a photographer outside of the courthouse.

Young Doctors in Love (1982)

Many soap opera stars of the time have cameos as their soap characters. They include:

John Beradino and Emily McLaughlin (Dr. Steve Hardy and Nurse Jessie Brewster on *General Hospital*) can be seen preparing for surgery. He asks her if Elizabeth Taylor has called, and she snaps his rubber glove.

Michael Damian (Danny Romalotti on *The Young and the Restless*) has laryngitis, and gets to kiss a candy striper. His pal, Steven Ford (Andy Richards on *Y&R*) tries the same trick but ends up kissing a tray.

Chris Robinson (Dr. Rick Webber on *General Hospital*) is seen at his desk, treating a man whose shoe flies off whenever he sneezes.

Stuart Damon (Alan Quartermaine on *General Hospital*) appears as a doctor with a broken wristwatch.

Tom Ligon (Lucas Prentiss on *The Young and the Restless*) says to Jamie

Lyn Bauer (Lauralee Brooks on *Y&R*), "Mrs. Bauer ... I don't like the way your husband looks."

Kin Shriner (Scotty Baldwin on *General Hospital*) thoroughly examines Janine Turner (Laura Templeton on *GH*), then tells her he is a lawyer. Shriner's character, Baldwin, actually was a lawyer on the series.

Jackie Zeman (Bobbi Spencer on *General Hospital*) plays the nurse who announces that the strike is over and hands out scrubs to the new interns at the end of the film.

Also, three soap stars, two of whom went on to later fame, make uncredited cameos. Richard Dean Anderson (Dr. Jeff Webber on *General Hospital*), who later played *MacGyver* on television, appears as Phil's (Taylor Negron) drug connection, password "vanilla." Demi Moore, then reporter Jackie Templeton on *General Hospital* (the sister of Janine Turner's character), has a bit part as the arriving doctor who Simon (Michael McKean) mistakes for Stephanie at the end of the film. Longtime *All My Children* star Susan Lucci (Erica Kane) appears in a gold lamé jumpsuit at Dr. Prang's party, asking all the men if they are rich doctors.

Near the start of the film, Ted McGinley "fixes a duck." The duck is a reference to Lucy Coe's duck, Sigmund, on the soap *General Hospital*.

Director Garry Marshall has a cameo in this, his first film, as well. He breaks a stalk of marijuana off of a plant and sneakily puts it in his pocket.

The sound that accompanies the opening and closing of the doors leading into the operating room is the same sound that was used when doors opened on the starship *Enterprise* on the series *Star Trek*.

The first time Simon asks about

Stephanie's heart during the climactic operation, the cardiac monitor plays the opening theme of the Pac Man video game. Later, when a doctor says, "Blood pressure falling," the sound effect used for R2D2 in the *Star Wars* movies is heard. After Dr. Ludwig reduces the body part by 2 millimeters, the five tones from the alien ship in *Close Encounters of the Third Kind* (1977) ring out. At the end of the operation, the theme from *Jaws* (1975) is played, followed by the closing notes from the Pac Man video game.

When the ambulances pull up to the hospital at the start, an announcement is heard: "The white zone is for the immediate loading and unloading of patients only." This is a reference to a similar line in the similar spoof film, *Airplane!* (1980).

Among the joke pages heard over the P.A. system is the call for "Dr. Howard, Dr. Fine, Dr. Howard." This page, which has been heard in countless hospital-based films and television series, is from the Academy Award-nominated Three Stooges short, *Men in Black*, a parody of the popular Clark Gable movie, *Men in White* (1934). In it, Moe (Howard), Larry (Fine) and Curly (Howard) play doctors, and all through the episode, the page comes over the hospital speakers. At the end of the short, the Stooges get ticked off at being paged all the time, and demolish the automated board giving the pages.

Young Frankenstein (1974)

Frau Blucher, Cloris Leachman's character, is named after Gebhard Leberecht von Blücher, the Prussian marshal whose arrival with reinforcements helped the British defeat Napoleon's army at the Battle of Waterloo.

Young Guns (1988)

Tom Cruise, disguised with a beard and moustache, appears as a bad guy who walks out of a door and is shot. He was put in the film because he was visiting the set and he said that he had never been in a film gunfight.

Young Guns II (1990)

Jon Bon Jovi, who wrote the song "Blaze of Glory" for this film, appears as the scruffy guy who gets shot in the chest and blown backwards after Doc (Kiefer Sutherland) and Chavez (Lou Diamond Phillips) get out of the pit jail.

Megaproducer Don Simpson has a cameo as the Pinkerton Man.

Executive producer John Fusco also plays the branded man.

Young Sherlock Holmes (1985)

The "cycling across the moon" shot is a reference to *E.T., the Extra-Terrestrial* (1982), directed by producer Steven Spielberg.

After the end credits, Rathe (Anthony Higgins), the villain, signs a hotel register under the name "Moriarty." This was the name of the true Sherlock Holmes's greatest nemesis.

You're a Big Boy Now (1966)

The nightclub has scenes from director Francis Ford Coppola's *Dementia 13* (1963) projected onto the wall.

A Zed & Two Noughts (1985)

A newspaper reports the death of the American architect Stourley Kracklite. This was the name director Peter Greenaway used for his lead character in *The Belly of an Architect* (1987) two years later.

In-Jokes
in Television

The A-Team

In the episode "Steel," the team visit Universal Studios. Face (Dirk Benedict) watches a Cylon (from the film and television series *Battlestar: Galactica*) walk by and starts to say something. Benedict had previously played Starbuck, one of Galactica's original pilots.

Absolutely Fabulous

Lady Penelope Creighton-Ward, a puppet from the Gerry Anderson series *Thunderbirds Are Go*, appears in a dream sequence on the show. Sylvia Anderson (Gerry's wife, who was the voice of the original Lady Penelope) again provides the voice for the puppet, as a favor to old friend Jennifer Saunders, one of the show's creators and stars.

The Addams Family

Thing, the disembodied hand-in-a-box on the show, was always credited as being played by "himself." Thing was actually acted on the set by Ted Cassidy, who played Lurch, the towering butler. When Cassidy, as Lurch, appeared in the same shot with Thing, or when Cassidy wasn't available, Thing was played by assistant director Jack Voglin, who, at 6'3" was almost as big as Cassidy himself.

The voice of Cousin Itt was that of writer-producer Nat Perrin, who spoke gibberish on tape, then ran it back at high speed.

The Adventures of Brisco County, Jr.

In the episode "No Man's Land," Brisco is treated for his wounds by a female doctor, who introduces herself as "Dr. Quintano, medicine woman," a reference to the show *Dr. Quinn, Medicine Woman*.

In "Stagecoach," Timothy Leary parodies himself, playing a character named Dr. Milo. At one point he gives a eulogy of selected Beatles lyrics: "When I find myself in times of trouble ["Let It Be"], I say 'boy, you gotta carry that weight.'["Carry That Weight"] I am he, you are he, you are

153

me, we are all together, ["I Am the Walrus"] speaking words of wisdom ["Let It Be"]. Come together, right now ["Come Together"]. Amen." During the eulogy, an organ playing "Let It Be"–like music is heard in the background.

There were many offhand lines that were, essentially, puns. One is from "High Treason Part 2," where Wickwire says, "If I sell just one airship, it'll be a good year" (Goodyear Blimp). Brisco says "A lead Zeppelin. That'll be your stairway to heaven!" (rock group Led Zeppelin's "Stairway to Heaven"). Bowler is given a doughnut by a little kid, and says, "Thanks for the doughnut, Duncan" (Dunkin' Donuts). Brisco sends his hometown girlfriend home to get a firearm by saying, "Annie, get your gun" (the Irving Berlin musical *Annie, Get Your Gun*).

In one episode, Bowler says, "You hit the sheriff!" and Brisco responds, "But I didn't hit the deputy." The Bob Marley song "I Shot the Sheriff" also contains the line "But I didn't shoot the deputy."

The female spy in "Stagecoach" was named Emma Steed, a reference to the characters of Emma Peel and John Steed from *The Avengers*.

The U.S. Attorney Ginger Breakstone is a parody of the government agent James West from *The Wild Wild West*. The music that plays when he appears is even similar to the theme of *Wild Wild West*. He appears in "Socrates' Sister," "Showdown," "Deep in the Heart of Dixie," and "A.K.A. Kansas."

Airwolf

In the pilot episode, Stringfellow Hawke (Jan-Michael Vincent) and Dominic Santini (Ernest Borgnine) try to find a place suitable for hiding Airwolf. This location is later called "The Lair." Hawke winks at Dominic, saying that they need to scout locations, "you know, for Bellisario's film?" Donald Bellisario is the creator, writer and producer of *Airwolf*.

Alfred Hitchcock Presents (original series)

Although director Alfred Hitchcock appeared in cameo roles in many of his films, he only made one appearance on his television series. It was in the episode "Dip in the Pool," starring Keenan Wynn and Fay Wray. His picture can be seen on the cover of a magazine that a passenger is reading.

Alfred Hitchcock Presents (1980s)

George Lazenby appears in an episode titled "Diamonds Aren't Forever," as "James ..." Lazenby seems to have gotten a lot of mileage out of the one time he played Bond in *On Her Majesty's Secret Service* (1969) (see also *The Return of the Man from U.N.C.L.E.*, 1983 TV, and the series *The Master*).

In the original series, Billy Mumy starred in an episode called "Bang! You're Dead." When the episode was rewritten and filmed for this series in 1985, it included Mumy in a cameo as a clerk.

Alias Smith and Jones

This lighthearted 1970s western was about two outlaws who try to earn amnesty by going straight and assuming the names "Smith" and "Jones." The title for the series comes from the movie *Butch Cassidy and the Sundance Kid* (1969). Butch and Sundance use the aliases "Smith" and "Jones" while trying to go straight in Bolivia.

Alien Nation

Newcomers (aliens) in the series were allowed to choose their names, and many decided upon famous actors' names (John Barrymore, Buster Keaton), names from works of literature (Silas Marner, Dorian Gray), or names from the history books (Betsy Ross, Paul Revere, Johnny Appleseed, Jean Paul Sartre). In the episode "Chains of Love," Newcomer Clara Bow (who took her name from an actress of the 1930s) is thought to be a "black widow" killer, but the real killer turns out to be a Newcomer named Ted Healy. A subplot of the episode concerns the Three Stooges. The real Healy originally hired the Stooges as part of his act, and catapulted them to fame.

All My Children

The show is Carol Burnett's favorite soap opera, and she has made guest appearances on it. In the episode broadcast March 16, 1976, the first time that Burnett appeared on the show, she showed up in a hospital as Mrs. Johnson, the cleaning woman character from her series. When she later appeared as a regular on the show as Verla Grubbs, Langley's daughter, Elizabeth Taylor decided to make a guest appearance, chatting with Verla in a restaurant scene, because she knew Burnett was there.

When Marcy Walker returned to *All My Children* as Liza Colby, a character that she had played in the 1980s, she was introduced to someone as "Liza Colby, our station manager, leader and guiding light," to which she replied, "Well, I don't know about guiding light." Marcy Walker's most recent acting stint before returning to this show was on *Guiding Light.*

For years, a story about the show's early days has circulated regarding Joe Martin's son, Bobby. According to legend, Bobby went upstairs to polish his skis and was never heard from or referred to again. While there once was a Bobby Martin on the show who faded into oblivion, he did so at summer camp, not in his attic. The writers of the show decided to have a little fun with the legend in an episode where Opal Gardner (Jill Larson) is accidentally locked in the attic of the Martin house. While rummaging around for something she could use to get out, she stumbles upon a skeleton beside a pair of skis. Hanging above the skeleton's skull is a baseball cap with the name "Bobby" stencilled on the front of it. The soap *Days of Our Lives* had a similar character, Dr. Tommy Horton, who the show's writer, Margaret DePriest, described as the "legendary character who went upstairs and never came down."

While in Budapest, Erica Kane (Susan Lucci) is kidnapped by Edmund Grey, who wanted revenge on his half-brother, who was Erica's lover. When Erica finds out that her lover is two-timing her, she decides to help Edmund. She gets on the phone and plays the part of a tortured kidnap victim to the hilt. Edmund compliments her performance, saying "You deserve an Oscar," to which Erica responds, "I'd settle for an Emmy." This was a stab at Lucci's famed losing streak at the Daytime Emmys.

The Alvin Show

In his book *Rock On*, Norm Nite notes that the Chipmunks' creator Ross Bagdasarian named Alvin, Simon and Theodore after Liberty Records executives Al Bennett and Si Warnoker and recording engineer Ted Keep.

American Gothic

In the episode "Resurrector," there is a scene where Sheriff Buck (Gary Cole) goes to a radio station and says a few words into the microphone. This is a reference to Cole's former series, *Midnight Caller*, in which he portrayed a talk-radio show host.

Animaniacs

In an episode which featured a sketch called "The Please, Please, Please Get a Life Foundation," they show a fan of the show who rattles off dozens of bizarre and very overly specific facts about *Animaniacs*. The character is practically reading from the Cultural References Guide for Animaniacs (CRGA), which was compiled on the Animaniacs newsgroup on the Internet. It lists every in-joke, reference and spoof ever shown on the show.

The "$25,000 in-joke" as voice actor Maurice LaMarche put it, was the cartoon "Yes, Always," which parodies a recording session made many years ago with a very cranky Orson Welles. Outside of the industry, the cartoon makes very little sense. The jokes are slightly altered lines to ones Welles spoke in the commercial recording. For instance, "Show me a way to say that and I'll go down on you" appears in the cartoon, spoken by the Brain, as "Show me a way to say that and I'll ... make cheese for you." The Brain's voice is patterned after that of Welles.

In the sketch "Super Strong Warner Siblings," a parody of the Mighty Morphin Power Rangers, a giant bug falls onto a building which just happens to be the Saban building (makers of *Mighty Morphin Power Rangers*). There is no visual reference that would identify the building as belonging to Saban, but it is an exact replica of the real one.

As the World Turns

In an airport scene in which actress Eileen Fulton (who played Lisa Hughes) returned to the show, a woman walks up to her and asks if her name is "Eileen" (the actress' name). Lisa snaps at the woman, saying, "The name is Margaret Elizabeth McLarty." This is Fulton's real name.

The Avengers

Diana Rigg's character's name, Emma Peel, comes from "m-appeal," shortened from the term "man appeal."

Babylon 5

An Earth Alliance Omega–class destroyer in the series is named the Schwartzkopf, after General Norman Schwartzkopf, who gained recognition for Operation Desert Storm.

In one episode, pictures of Earth Alliance President Luis Santiago and the woman running against him in the election are shown. The pictures are actually of *Babylon 5*'s executive producer, Doug Netter, and wardrobe designer Ann Bruice.

In another episode a human is talking to an ombudsman on board *Babylon 5* seeking damages from an alien for the alien's ancestors having kidnapped his ancestors from Earth. The alien is a grey-skinned, big-headed, bug-eyed *X-Files*/*Close Encounters*/*Communion*–style alien ... in other words, flying saucer men were *real* in the *Babylon 5* universe.

In one episode, the female political officer bares her breasts to Captain Sheridan in an attempt to seduce him, and First Officer Ivanova holographically "beams" in on them. As an aside to Sheridan, she says "You're about to go where everyone has gone before," putting a spin on *Star Trek*'s famous credo.

The denizens of "Downbelow" are called "lurkers," a term for those on the Internet newsgroups, including those related to *Babylon 5*, who read messages but never leave any.

Garibaldi has a "Zen Motorbike," a reference to the book *Zen and the Art of Motorcycle Maintenance.*

When fictional names submitted for a megacorporation and a mineral on the show were rejected for legal reasons, the show's creators went to the Internet *Babylon 5* community and asked for suggestions. The resulting names used were Quantium-40 for the mineral and Universal Terraform for the company. Q-40 is mentioned in both "The Parliament of Dreams" and "Mind War" and Universal Terraform in "Mind War." The waiter mentioned in "Parliament" is named for David Strauss, who submitted Q-40.

The location of Babylon 5 is at Grid Epsilon 470,18,22, which corresponds to the original location of the Babylon 5 Internet topic newsgroup on GEnie (Page 470, CAT 18, Topic 22). The first mention of a planet's coordinates in "Mind War" were Grid Epsilon 471,18,25, which corresponds to a topic in the Babylon 5 Category on GEnie.

The voice for the main computer on the station is provided by Haley McLane, script supervisor on the *Babylon 5* production staff.

The remaining in-jokes are listed by episode.

"The Soul Hunter": The arrival of the space liner *Asimov* is announced. Isaac Asimov is an accomplished sci-fi writer. It reappears in "The Believers" and "A Late Delivery from Avalon," in which it brings Michael York to Babylon 5.

"Born to the Purple": Screenwriter Robert Ditillio appears as Norg. He would reappear as an ambassador in "Deathwalker."

"Infection": Vance Hendricks says to Dr. Franklin, "Stephen? Stephen, there's a Martian war machine parked outside. They'd like to have a word with you about the common cold." This is a reference to the film *War of the Worlds* (1953), based on the classic H.G. Wells sci-fi novel. In the film, the invading Martians are destroyed by common cold germs (the novel does not contain this ending, nor does Orson Welles's famous radio play).

"The Parliament of Dreams": At one point, Sinclair says, "See you next Wednesday." Although this is sort of an in-joke, it had nothing to do with John Landis. It was an offhand line, slightly based on the fact that in most markets, *Babylon 5* airs on Wednesdays. Creator J. Michael Straczynski has said that if they would have known about the John Landis connection, it never would have been used (see *Schlock*, 1971, for the John Landis reference).

"Mind War": As Psi Cop Bester (Walter Koenig) leaves the station, he gives Sinclair an odd salute—a circle of thumb and forefinger at the forehead—and says, "Be seeing you, Commander." This is a tribute to one of creator J. Michael Straczynski's favorite series, *The Prisoner*, in which the salute was given with an identical comment, but the hand motion framed the eye instead—an appropriate twist for a telepath's salute (see *The Prisoner* for the origin of the salute).

Bester, by the way, is named after sci-fi writer Alfred Bester, who wrote *The Demolished Man* and *The Stars My Destination*, a couple of books about beings with psionic power.

"And the Sky Full of Stars": The names of Knight 1 and Knight 2, never spoken onscreen but listed in the credits, are reminiscent of *The Prisoner*, as is the whole interrogation process.

"Deathwalker": Screenwriter Robert Ditillio appears as an ambassador. He had also appeared in "Born to the Purple" as Norg.

"Believers": Garibaldi and Sinclair discuss a request by the Shakespeare Corporation to transport a load of pfingle eggs to Babylon 5. Pfingle eggs and the Shakespeare Corporation are references to *Under the Eye of God* and *A Covenant of Justice*, two books in the Tracker series by David Gerrold, who also wrote this episode.

"Survivors": Rod Perry plays a character named General Netter, after *Babylon 5* producer Douglas Netter.

"By Any Means Necessary": The Rush Act, the Earth law enabling the senate to empower someone to end an illegal strike using any means necessary, usually by force, was named after ultraconservative television and radio commentator Rush Limbaugh.

Nearly all of the show's production crew appear in this episode. The man yelling "I say we *strike*!" is the episode's director, Jim Johnston. In this episode and the episode "Grail," John Flinn, the series' director of photography, plays a character named ... John Flinn. He appeared in the episode "Convictions" as well, as "Obnoxious Man."

"Signs and Portents": The raider on the station says, "Six to One" (i.e., "Number Six calling Number One") when contacting his ship. This is yet another reference to *The Prisoner*, in which Patrick McGoohan was Number Six and the head of The Colony was Number One.

"TKO": Ivanova is seen reading *Working Without a Net* by Harlan Ellison. Ellison is a well-known science fiction author and editor and also serves as creative consultant for the show. The book is to be his autobiography, which he plans to write around the year 2000. Ellison borrowed the prop when filming was completed and casually carried it with him to a few places, just to drive his friends and fans crazy, making them think that there was a book of his out there that they had missed.

Garibaldi's old friend in this episode is named Walker Smith (Greg McKinney). Walker Smith was the real name of boxer Sugar Ray Robinson.

"Grail": The transport *Marie Celeste*, which Thomas boards at the end of the episode, is a reference to a sailing ship found adrift in 1872 by the crew of the ship *Dei Gratia*. The *Celeste's* crew was missing, as was her single lifeboat, but there were half-eaten meals in the mess hall and other evidence the crew had left suddenly. Investigators found that Captain Morehouse of the *Dei Gratia* had dined with Captain Briggs of the *Celeste* the night before departure, and Morehouse and his crew were tried for murder. There was no hard evidence, and they were acquitted. The missing crewmen were never found.

"Eyes": Lennier's (Bill Mumy) chant, "Za ba ga bee," is the title of an album by the group Barnes and Barnes, of which Mumy is a member. When it came time for the chant, nothing had been scripted; it was supposed to be a soft, under-one's-breath kind of chant. Mumy asked the producers if they had anything in mind, and they said no, so he ended up chanting his album cover. The producers didn't find out what the chant meant until after the episode aired.

"A Voice in the Wilderness": The phrase "Eye Am Knot a Number Aye Ama Free Man" appears on a computer screen when the shuttlecraft initially sent to explore Epsilon III is damaged. This is a reference to *The Prisoner*, where this line is spoken during the opening sequence by Patrick McGoohan.

Executive production assistant Kelly Coyle appears as the Earthforce liaison in this episode.

"A Voice in the Wilderness, Part II": The list of words being down-loaded from the station's language files by the aliens appears briefly on screen. It seems to contain words with no apparent connection:

ORAK
SKYNET
NOMAD
FORBIN

Orak was the box of flashing lights that was the most powerful computer within the Federation on the series *Blake's Seven*. Skynet was the defense computer that became self-aware and tried to wipe out humanity in the film *Terminator 2: Judgment Day* (1991). Nomad was the eponymous probe which wanted to wipe out biological life in the *Star Trek* episode "The Changeling." Dr. Charles Forbin (Eric Braeden) was the name of the creator of a U.S. defense computer that tried to take over the world in the film *Colossus: The Forbin Project* (1970).

When Captain Pierce is going to launch fighters to land on the planet and Sinclair threatens to destroy them, Pierce argues for a moment and then backs down. He turns briefly to the screen and a computer graphic is dis-played showing him calling down the ships. One of the ships in the top left corner of the screen has the flight number THX-1138, after the ground-

breaking George Lucas sci-fi film *THX-1138* (1970).

The heavy cruiser EAS *Hyperion* was named after the *Babylon 5* Internet archive at Hyperion.COM.

"Babylon Squared": Major Krantz, Babylon 4's commander, says that "Babylon 4 has come unstuck in time." This is how Billy Pilgrim's condition is described in the first line of Kurt Von-negut's classic novel *Slaughterhouse-Five*. The phrase is used again, by Zathras, in the episode "War Without End."

"The Quality of Mercy": Londo takes Lennier to the Club Dark Star, which is named after the sci-fi cult spoof *Dark Star* (1974).

"Chrysalis": G'Kar, in a message to Na'Toth, says, "Expect me when you see me." This is the same phrase used by Gandalf to Frodo in *The Lord of the Rings* by J.R.R. Tolkien.

"Points of Departure": The Jupiter 2 is listed as being docked at the sta-tion. Jupiter 2 was the name of the ship in the series *Lost in Space*.

"Revelations": Jack, Garibaldi's aide, uses the "Be seeing you" farewell from *The Prisoner*, this time with fingers circling the eye (see the *Baby-lon 5* episode "Mind War").

"The Geometry of Shadows": Elric's (Michael Ansara) warning to Vir, "Do not try the patience of wiz-ards, for they are subtle and quick to anger," is almost verbatim from Tolkien's *The Lord of the Rings*, in which Gildor, an elf, tells Frodo, "But it is said: Do not meddle in the affairs of wizards, for they are subtle and quick to anger." Incidentally, the name "Elric" is from Michael Moorcock's series of fantasy novels.

"A Distant Star": The "fixer" (sup-ply officer) who gets Garibaldi the ingredients of bagma caude is named

Orwell, after *1984* author George Orwell. Incidentally, a "fixer" is a character class from a popular role-playing game, *Cyberpunk 2020*. In the game, a fixer's specialty is smuggling goods, which was what Orwell was hired for as well.

"The Long Dark": The Soldier of Darkness, an invisible killer, is made visible by white outlines when shot with an energy weapon. This is a tip of the hat to the Monster from the Id in the film *Forbidden Planet* (1956).

As Amis (Dwight Schultz) leaves his cell, he wraps a towel around his neck and claims, "I've got everything a man needs." This is a reference to Douglas Adams's *The Hitchhiker's Guide to the Galaxy*, in which he claims that regardless of everything else, as long as a space traveler knows where his towel is, he is safe.

"A Spider in the Web": The Earth Alliance's Omega-class destroyer *Pournelle* is the ship that destroyed Abel's ship. It is named after sci-fi author Jerry Pournelle.

Ms. Amanda Carter (Adrienne Barbeau), who is from Mars, has an ancestor named John. Edgar Rice Burroughs, author of the Tarzan books, also wrote a series of sci-fi novels about John Carter from Mars.

"Soul Mates": The name of Timov's father, "Alghul," means "The Demon" in Arabic. It may also be connected to the character Ras Al-Ghul ("Head of the Demon") from the DC Comics *Batman* series. Ras's daughter, Talia, has been the Batman's lover, and is the mother of his child. Talia is also the name of one of Londo's exwives in this episode.

"The Coming of Shadows": The Centauri Emperor who died in 2259 while visiting Babylon 5 was named Turhan, after the actor who played

him, Turhan Bey. And the Centauri Prime Minister who was believed assassinated on Centuri Prime when Emperor Turhan died was named Malachi, after the actor who played him, Malachi Throne. They appeared in this episode, but were not named until the episode "Knives."

"All Alone in the Night": The aliens that abduct members of other races and torture them are called Streibs. This is a reference to sci-fi author Whitley Streiber, who has written about such aliens and even claims to have been an abductee himself.

"Acts of Sacrifice": Glenn Morshower appears as Franke, named after the show's scorer, Christopher Franke.

"There All the Honor Lies": Ivanova says "This isn't some kind of Deep Space franchise, this place is *about* something." This was a jab at *Babylon 5*'s competition, *Star Trek: Deep Space Nine*.

"And Now for a Word": The ship Heyerdahl (which has a pine-tree air freshener on its bridge—seen in the opening teaser) is named after Norse adventurer Thor Heyerdahl, whose Kon-Tiki expedition attempted to prove that South American natives could have populated some South Pacific islands.

"In the Shadow of Z'ha'dum": The name Ministry of Peace and its abbreviation Minipax are from the novel *1984* by George Orwell.

"Confessions and Lamentations": This episode features a previously unseen alien (or at least, a humanoid who is presumably alien) wearing a suit with an elaborate helmet. The helmet bears a striking resemblance to the mask of Morpheus, the King of Dreams, from Neil Gaiman's *Sandman* comic book. As *Sandman* is one of

Straczynski's favorite comics, this is likely an intentional homage.

"Comes the Inquisitor": One of the Narn in the meeting with G'Kar is played by Dennis Michael, a CNN reporter who was doing a story on *Babylon 5*'s make-up group, Optic Nerve. He was made up as a Narn for part of his news story.

"The Fall of Night": The semi-regular character Lt. David Corwin (Joshua Cox), who is a lieutenant in the Command and Control area, is named after Norman Corwin, J. Michael Straczynski's friend and mentor.

After President Santiago is killed, President Clark is hurriedly sworn in. The image of this ceremony is patterned to look like the famous photo of Lyndon Johnson's inauguration aboard Air Force One soon after the assassination of John F. Kennedy. Everything is in the same place: the judge holding the bible, the former president's wife, and so forth.

"Convictions": Lennier puts off a boring seatmate in the docking bay waiting room by telling him he has "Netter's Syndrome," a contagious disease, and has seven days to live. Douglas Netter is one of the producers on the series. This comment also had fans guessing that Lennier would be killed off in the next episode, which was aired seven days later.

"Voices of Authority": Julie Musante (Shari Shattuck) is named after two *Babylon 5* fans, Julie Helmer and Mark Musante.

"Dust to Dust": The dust vendor's two aliases, Lindstrom and Morgenstern, are the surnames of two regular characters from *The Mary Tyler Moore Show* who each later had their own series. They are Phyllis Lindstrom (*Phyllis*) and Rhoda Morgenstern (*Rhoda*).

"Exogenesis": Duncan has a line, "I don't like being poked by doctors," that was originated by Alex (Malcolm McDowell) in *A Clockwork Orange* (1971).

The ship carrying the Vindrizi is called the Dyson, most likely named for physicist Freeman Dyson.

Marcus quotes from Dickens's *A Christmas Carol* to Garibaldi, and from Shakespeare's *Macbeth* when he wakes Duncan up. Note that Marcus never names the play, instead calling it "the Scottish play," and replaces "Macbeth" with "Marcus" in his quote. The reason for this is that there is a superstition among actors that referring to Macbeth by name is bad luck.

Marcus (Jason Carter) refers to his fighting staff as a Copeland J5000 while trying to convince the Vindrizi it is a medical instrument. This is a reference to producer John Copeland.

"Point of No Return": Many of the Nightwatch members in this episode are production staff members, including the production secretary and an assistant director.

"Ceremonies of Light and Dark": The voice of Sparky the Computer, the artificial intelligence, is creative consultant Harlan Ellison. Sparky's name is visible both in the end credits and, very briefly, as the last line item in the computer's status messages when it reboots.

The song "Dem Bones" was also sung in the final episode of *The Prisoner*.

"Interludes and Examinations": The masked alien is a Gaim, whose name is a reference to comic artist Neil Gaiman. The title character of Gaiman's *Sandman*—one of creator J. Michael Straczynski's favorite works—wears a similar-looking mask.

Batman

The show's producer, William Dozier, provides the voice of the narrator.

James Brolin has small parts in numerous episodes; for example, he plays driver Ralph Staphylococcus in "The Cat and the Fiddle." At the time, Brolin was the roommate of the show's casting director, Michael McLean, which explains his frequent appearances.

Kathy Kersh, Burt Ward's (Robin) second wife, plays the Joker's moll, Cornelia, in the episode "The Impractical Joker."

After many requests to executive producer Bill Dozier for an acting role in the series, frequent writer Stanley Ralph Ross finally managed to capture the highly coveted nonspeaking role of Ballpoint Baxter in "The Penguin's Nest." He wore thick bottle glasses for his role.

TV host Steve Allen has a cameo in "The Batman's Kow Tow" as television host Allan Stevens.

William Dyer, Adam West's lighting stand-in, gets screen credit as a policeman in "The Sandman Cometh," and often played cops on the show with no credit.

The series' dialogue coach, Milton Stark, plays several roles in the series, including an art browser in "Flop Goes the Joker," a zoologist in "The Joker's Hard Times," Mr. Tamber in "Penguin Is a Girl's Best Friend" and Irving Bracken in "Black Widow Strikes Again."

The Neosaurus in "How to Hatch a Dinosaur" was taken directly from an episode of Lost in Space.

In the episode "The Funny Feline Felonies," Pierre Salinger plays underworld lawyer Lucky Pierre. Salinger previously worked as John F.

Kennedy's press secretary, and was, at the time of the show, a senator from California. He got the role as a result of meeting producer Bill Dozier at a cocktail party.

John Beradino plays a doctor in the episode "Penguin's Clean Sweep"; he had portrayed Dr. Steve Hardy on the soap General Hospital for five years. Incidentally, Beradino continued on General Hospital until his death in 1996.

Cliff Robertson appears as the villain Shame (a takeoff on Alan Ladd's western hero, Shane, 1953), and his wife, Dina Merrill, plays Shame's moll, Calamity Jan, in the episodes "The Great Escape" and "The Great Train Robbery." Jerry Mathers, who had played "Beaver" Cleaver for years on Leave It to Beaver, also has a cameo as Pup, the doorman in "The Great Escape."

In "The Entrancing Dr. Cassandra," Dr. Cassandra (Ida Lupino) uses her "Alvino-ray gun" to flatten the Dynamic Duo paper thin. Scripter Stanley Ralph Ross wanted to call the weapon a Ronald ray-gun. "This was the only time they really censored me," Ross has said. "The weapon took the third dimension out of them and made them into cardboard cut-outs. At the time, Ronald Reagan was our [California's] governor. Alvino Rey was an old-time bandleader from the forties."

Producers Bill Dozier and Howie Horowitz appear as themselves at the beginning of the final episode, "Minerva, Mayhem and Millionaires." On the show, Dozier keeps his securities in a grandfather clock while "millionaire producer" Horowitz keeps his cash in a television set.

Occasionally, Batman and Robin appear in a shot, scaling the side of a building while hanging on to their Batropes. These bits, called "bat-climbs," would often include a cameo by a celebrity who would open a window of the building that the Dynamic Duo were climbing. Stars did the Batclimb cameos for just $100 daily scale, and they included Jerry Lewis (in the first one), Dick Clark, Don Ho, Milton Berle, Sammy Davis, Jr., Howard Duff, Andy Devine as Santa Claus, Art Linkletter, and Edward G. Robinson. Van Williams and Bruce Lee once appeared in a batclimb as the Green Hornet and Kato from the show *The Green Hornet*, as did Bill Dana as his character of Jose Jiminez, Werner Klemperer as Colonel Klink from *Hogan's Heroes*, Ted Cassidy as Lurch from *The Addams Family*, and, in the final Batclimb, local entrepreneur Carpet King, a role earned supposedly because he sold producer Bill Dozier some Persian rugs.

Batman: The Animated Series

The clock tower battles at the end of the episode "The Clock King" are director Kevin Altieri's homage to *Castle Cagliostro*, a Japanese feature animated by Miyazaki. It was this movie that got Altieri, who had been doing special effects in film, interested in animation.

In the episode "Beware the Grey Ghost," someone is bombing Gotham's municipal buildings using the M.O. of a villain from the old (fictional) *Grey Ghost* television show. Batman goes to Simon Trent, the actor who played Grey Ghost, his childhood hero, and, after initial hesitation, Trent agrees to help Batman. Simon Trent is on hard times, and the only character that he is remembered for is the Grey Ghost. The aging hero's voice is provided by Adam West, who was in a similar situation, and had played Batman in the original television series.

"Beware the Grey Ghost" was full of in-jokes: producer Bruce Timm provided the voice of the Mad Bomber, and he described some more: "The Grey Ghost is Batman's hero, and The Shadow [a pulp hero of the 1930s whom the Grey Ghost resembles] was Bob Kane's inspiration for Batman. That's doubled by the fact that Adam West was my childhood hero and my inspiration for getting into *Batman*." The Batcave shrine to the Grey Ghost even has a poster on the wall with the Ghost in the same pose as Batman is in the series' logo.

Charlie Collins, the average, everyday guy who outwits the Joker in "Joker's Favor," was styled after series producer Alan Burnett.

Twitch, the snitch at the beginning of the episode "Off Balance," was drawn as a caricature of *Batman* (1989) director Tim Burton.

In the episode "Deep Freeze," the robot inventor is named Rossum. The name comes from the Czechoslovakian play which introduced the term "robot," Karel Capek's *R.U.R.* In the play, the man who invents the robots is named Rossum.

Beverly Hills 90210

Series creator Aaron Spelling's son, Randy Spelling (Tori's brother), has appeared as one of Steve's younger brothers.

Blake's Seven

In the final episode, Janet Lees Price, the wife of the lead actor, Paul Darrow, decided she wanted to take a role, just for the fun of it. He agreed, as long as he got to kill her! The episode, and the series, ends with all of the focal characters except the villain appearing to be massacred, so one more killing wasn't really all that big a deal. Price was cast as a communications officer who is shot dead by Avon, the character her husband played, just before the final cataclysm.

The Bold and the Beautiful

Given Sally Spectra's (Darlene Conley) background as a knockoff designer from New York, it makes perfect sense that her daughter Macy Alexander's (Bobbie Eakes) name would be borrowed from two department stores back east: the world-famous Macy's and the lesser-known (and now bankrupt) Alexander's.

Bosom Buddies

In the episode "Other Than That She's a Wonderful Person," a girl mentions to Henry (Peter Scolari) that she is from California. He says, "Do you know Leonard Ripps?" She says, "No." Henry says, "He lives there." Leonard Ripps was one of the writers of the show. This segment is cut out of the syndicated version of the show, but was in the originally broadcast episode.

In "Cablevision," Penny Marshall appears as herself and Kip (Tom Hanks) interviews her and asks, "Do you and Shirley really hate each other?" She goes on to say something like, "It's hard being part of a comedy team working together every week ... but you wouldn't know anything about that."

The show was produced by the same team that did *Laverne & Shirley* and in "The Rewrite," Hildy & Buffy sing "5-6-7-8 Schlmiel, Schlamozel, Hops & Rev Incorporated" exactly like Laverne & Shirley do at the beginning of their show's theme song. Also in "Cablevision," the whole cast sings part of the theme song: "And we'll do

it our way, yes our way, make all our dreams come true..."

Kip and Henry occasionally mentioned the Cleveland Browns, which was Tom Hanks's favorite football team.

The Brady Bunch

In "You Can't Win Them All," the episode where Cindy appears on a game show, Carol (Florence Henderson) casually tells Mike that she is inviting the Bernsteins and some other people to dinner. At the time, that was Henderson's last name; she was married to Ira Bernstein.

The emcee of the game show is played by the real-life father of Christopher Knight (Peter Brady).

In the episode "The Teeter-Totter Caper," two college boys named Ralph Nelson and Alan Rudolph set the world's record for staying on a teeter-totter. Ralph Nelson was the show's unit production manager, and Alan Rudolph was the assistant director.

In "Juliet Is the Sun," Greg tries to cheer Marcia up by telling her that a classmate named Lloyd Leeds likes her. The name is a combination of production assistant (and later producer) Lloyd Schwartz and producer Howard Leeds.

Florence Henderson's real-life daughter, Barbara Bernstein, appears in a handful of episodes. She is Suzanne, a girl in a beauty parlor in "The Hair-Brained Scheme," Marcia's friend Ruthie in "The Slumber Caper," and her friend Peggy in "Everyone Can't Be George Washington."

Creator Sherwood Schwartz cast his daughter, Hope Sherwood, in a number of episodes, usually as Rachel, an occasional friend of Greg's.

Robert Reed's daughter Carolyn plays Marcia's friend Karen in "The Slumber Caper."

When Alice wins the stereo, they pick it up from a television and appliance shop named "Lloyd's." This is a reference to writer-producer Lloyd Schwartz.

At the very end of the episode where Peter breaks the vase, Mike Brady yells out the front door, "Hi, Doug! Peter will be out in a second!" Then, as Peter walks up to the door with his camping gear, Carol says to him, "Be good, and do everything Mr. Kramer tells you." Douglas Kramer was the executive in charge of production for the show.

In the episode "Miss Popularity," Jan wants to go to the dance with a boy named Billy Garst. Bill E. Garst was the film editor for the show.

In "Mail Order Hero," the Joe Namath episode, Marcia calls Mike Connors a "far out" guy because he went out of his way to visit a sick child. Robert Reed had a recurring role on Connors's series *Mannix* during the same time that *The Brady Bunch* aired.

In "The Hair-Brained Scheme," Carol tries to impress Bobby with the names of famous people who never quit, like Thomas Edison. She finally mentions the name Carl Mahakian, and Bobby says he never heard of him. Carol explains why: "He quit." Mahakian was the show's postproduction coordinator.

Buck Rogers in the 25th Century

In the episode "Planet of the Slave Girls," originally aired on September 27, 1979, Buster Crabbe, the original Buck Rogers in serials of the thirties, makes a cameo appearance as Brigadier Gordon. He is named after Flash Gordon, who Crabbe also played in the thirties. Brigadier Gordon flies a ship in combat and tells Buck, "I've been doing this sort of thing since before you were born."

The public address system in the series often had joke pages, as do many medical shows (see *St. Elsewhere*). Some pages were for fictional sci-fi characters. Once, the P.A. system paged Captain Christopher Pike to come to the Veterans' Affairs Office. Pike was the first captain of the USS *Enterprise* on the series *Star Trek*. Pike's ultimate fate was revealed in the *Star Trek* episode "The Menagerie." He had aged at an accelerated rate and had become an immobile old man.

Buck walks through a spaceport in one episode, and Adam Strange is paged. Adam Strange was a DC Comics character, a human archaeologist who was transported to the planet Rann in the comic series *Mystery in Space*.

The mother ship on the series is named the *Constitution*, and her commander, played by Jay Gardner, is named Admiral Asimov, after sci-fi writer Isaac Asimov.

Crichton, the haughty robot worn around Twiki's neck, was named after sci-fi author Michael Crichton.

Cagney and Lacey

Desk Sergeant Coleman (Harvey Atkin) kept his first name—Ronald—secret for many years. Ronald Colman was a Hollywood leading man of the 1930s and 1940s.

Executive producer Barney Rosenzweig appears in one episode as a Broadway producer.

Rosenzweig's mother-in-law, Jo Corday, was also seen frequently as Josie the Bag Lady.

Captain Power

Series creator J. Michael Straczynski also created the series *Babylon 5*, and in the episode "Final Stand," Tank mentions that he is from the Babylon 5 Genetic Engineering Colony.

In the episode "A Summoning of Thunder Part 2," when Hawk activates the first power suit Mentor says, "And so it begins." This has been confirmed by Straczynski as a "Koshism," or a statement commonly used by the *Babylon 5* character Kosh.

Car 54, Where Are You?

Joe E. Ross plays Officer Gunther Toody, and his wife is played by Beatrice Pons. Pons had previously played Ross's wife on the series *The Phil Silvers Show*.

Caroline in the City

In one episode, Caroline's boyfriend Del asks her to hold his ATM card so he won't spend too much at a casino. Caroline (Lea Thompson) points out that he has handed her his video rental card and says, "What, do you think you'll have an uncontrollable urge to rent *Howard the Duck*?" Del hands over the ATM card and says, "I'll have you know that *Howard the Duck* was a very underrated picture." Thompson was the costar of the well-known bomb *Howard the Duck* (1986) and wife of its director, Howard Deutsch.

Cheers

In the episode "Old Flames," the film *Gandhi* (1982) is mentioned in the bar, and Cliff (John Ratzenberger) raves about it. Ratzenberger played Jacqueline Bisset's driver in *Gandhi*.

The evil foosball table subplot of "Achilles Hill" is an inside joke: the *Cheers* actors are real foosball addicts. Woody Harrelson liked to shoot spitballs at George Wendt during breaks in filming. A spitball can sometimes be seen just above Wendt's eyebrow.

This series apparently takes place in the same universe as *St. Elsewhere*. In the episode "Little Sister, Don't Cha," Carla goes to St. Eligius to have her kids (see also *St. Elsewhere*).

Chicago Hope

There have been many jabs at *ER* in the series. In one episode, Kronk (Peter Berg) tells a kid that his brother is going to be transferred to County Hospital (the hospital in *ER*). The kid says he didn't want his brother being sent to that "dump."

In the episode "Songs of the Cuckoo Birds," Geiger (Mandy Patinkin) desperately asks Shutt (Adam Arkin) to be present at a dinner with his soon to be ex-wife. Even though Shutt has Chicago Bulls tickets, he agrees, and asks his wife Camille to come along. She says, "Tonight? Now?" "It's important to him," Shutt insists. "*ER*'s on tonight!" Camille protests. "If I can give up Michael Jordan, you can give up Anthony Hopkins," Shutt says. "Edwards," Camille corrects him. "Whatever," he says.

Birch (Peter MacNichol) and Watters (Hector Elizondo) attend a court hearing at 10 A.M. on a Monday. The judge asks them, "I thought you were scheduled for Thursday at 10?" Birch says, "Yes, your Thursday at 10 was not good for us so we were moved to Monday at 10." This was a reference to the show being scheduled against *ER* Thursdays at 10 P.M., the low ratings it received, and its subsequent move to Mondays at 10 P.M.

In "Transplanted Affections," the episode where Geiger (Patinkin) returns for an operation, Shutt (Arkin) says that people tell him that his new haircut makes him look like George Clooney. He asks Kronk (Berg) to confirm this, but Kronk says, "I don't know who that is." Clooney starred in *Chicago Hope*'s competition, *ER*.

In this episode, Geiger (Patinkin) is back to perform a heart transplant. During the operation, he hands the heart to Camille. Suddenly, he thinks twice, grabs the heart from Camille and says, "No offense, I'll take this." The season before, there had been an episode where she dropped a heart in the operating room and someone kicked it.

Noah Wyle (Carter on *ER*) sneaked onto the *Chicago Hope* set one day and, as a practical joke on the crew, he appeared in a shot. Kronk, Nyland, and Birch come out of the men's locker room, and Wyle casually breezes past them. Kronk (Berg) says, "Hey! hey, you! Who are you?" Wyle comes back and asks if this is Cook County Hospital (the hospital on *ER*), and Kronk says, "No, it's Chicago Hope." Wyle is not only a good friend of Peter Berg's, he is also Kathryn Grody's godson. Grody is Mandy Patinkin's wife.

In the episode "Right to Life," Shutt (Arkin) tells Watters he should take a trip to Fiji. Adam Arkin ad libbed this line. Peter Berg had been vacationing in Fiji during the Christmas hiatus, and was stuck there for a few days, messing up the shooting schedule.

In a May 1996 episode, "Ex Marks the Spot," a medical practitioner who administered acupuncture to a patient who could not be put under anesthesia flirts with Dr. Aaron Shutt (Arkin) and suggests he should ask her out sometime. The actress who played this character, Phyllis Lyons, was at the time dating Arkin in real life.

In the episode "Parent Rap," Kate Austin (Christine Lahti) is mad that her father won't undergo surgery. He believes that prayer alone will heal him. She says, sarcastically, "God is going to clear your arteries. And I'm going to win an Academy Award." This was a reference to the fact that Lahti was in the running at the time for an Academy Award for Best Live-Action Short for the film *Lieberman in Love* (1995). As it turns out, she won.

When Austin runs into Geiger in "Parent Rap," they discuss her father needing an operation, and Austin comments that "he wants God." Geiger replies, "I said I was available." This refers to an earlier episode in the season where Shutt had commented to Austin, "It's rumored that God has a Geiger complex."

Shutt and Geiger talk in a cemetery at the end of this episode. Shutt tells Geiger what he and his father did Thursday nights while his mother played bridge: "We'd make crappy spaghetti and watch crappy TV." This could be taken as a direct swipe at NBC's Thursday night viewing schedule.

Geiger (Patinkin) and Birch (MacNichol) share a love for model trains. This is because both Patinkin and MacNichol are also big fans of model trains. The set of trains on the bookshelf in Geiger's office is actually Patinkin's childhood set.

At the start of one episode (aired February 5, 1996), a woman claims to have been abducted and impregnated by aliens. She has some strange burns on her hand and, at one point, her bed sheets glow. As she is being brought in at the beginning, the music that is heard in the background is the theme of the sci-fi television show *The X-Files*.

In the episode "Full Moon," Geiger (Patinkin) sings "Rockabye Your Baby" at Russo's, the little dive where he sometimes performs. The piano player is Patinkin's longtime concert accompanist, Paul Ford.

In the episode aired Monday, April 1, 1996, Dr. Michael Dinner is paged to go to Neurology. The page is heard when Nyland and Kronk walk into the restaurateur's room after unsuccessful surgery to place a catheter in a vein. This was one of the last episodes coexecutive producer Michael Dinner worked on before leaving *Chicago Hope* and moving on to other projects. Bill D'Elia took over as coexecutive producer.

The names on the surgical schedule on the wipe board behind the nurse's station in this episode are actually names of the show's crew members. They include:

Hart—Producer James C. Hart

Klein—Medical technical advisor and frequent nurse extra, Linda Klein, R.N.

Fraser—Camera operator Walt Fraser

Werner—Production coordinator Sarah Werner

Skelton—Script supervisor Robin Skelton

Roysden—Set decorator Thomas L. Roysden

Jacobs—Lead person in the Art Department, Ron Jacobs

A group of nuns can be seen in the background in some episodes. This is a reference to *St. Elsewhere*, which also had scenes with nuns milling around in the background. Executive producer John Tinker was also involved with *St. Elsewhere*.

In one episode, Shutt (Arkin) is conspicuously absent, except for one very brief scene at the end where he just sort of appears before Watters (Elizondo), and tells him, "I really don't envy you your job ... having to be in charge of everyone, everyone

looking up to you all the time." Watters looks at him and says, "Where have you been, Aaron?" Shutt replies, "I've just been trying to keep out of sight." He gives him an enigmatic little smile and walks past him. Watters watches him go, perplexed. The joke is that Adam Arkin directed this episode of *Chicago Hope*.

In the second season episode "From Soup to Nuts," a mental patient who thinks that he is Eva Peron takes a look at Geiger (Patinkin) and says, "I know you..." It later occurs to the patient where he "knows" Geiger from (Mandy Patinkin played Che Guevera in *Evita* on Broadway). When he tells Geiger he won't tell anybody who he is (he never calls Geiger [or Patinkin, or "Che"] by name), he adds in a whisper, "Not much to ask for...," which is a line from *Evita*'s "Don't Cry for Me Argentina." The song was also sung as a sort of hymn for Geiger's ex-wife's wedding in this episode. Patinkin even gets to sing one line solo. "Eva Peron" was the reverend at the wedding.

There was once a page for Dr. Fleischman, the name of the doctor played by Rob Morrow on *Northern Exposure*.

The first time that Kronk (Berg) tries to sing in the operating room, the song he sings is the opening credits theme from the movie *Aspen Extreme* (1993), in which Peter Berg costarred.

CHiPs

After he eats lunch at Lucy's in the fifth season episode "In the Best of Families," the episode with the mother and son thieves, Officer Baricza (Brodie Greer) finds his cruiser doors and lights missing. In the background of this scene, the Partridge Family bus can be seen.

Adam Rich guest starred in the sixth-season episode "Fallout" as Louis, an abused child. He wore a shirt with the number "8" on it. Rich had previously starred in the series *Eight Is Enough*.

Broderick Crawford (as himself, uncredited) gets pulled over by Jon. He says, "You know, I was making those *Highway Patrol* shows long before you guys were born." Crawford starred in the 1950s series *Highway Patrol*. Jon replies, "Yeah, they don't make TV shows like that anymore," taking a dig at *CHiPs*.

Cimarron City

Star George Montgomery's wife, Dinah Shore, guest starred in the episode aired December 20, 1958, "Cimarron Holiday."

City

This CBS show was originally (and intentionally) scheduled on Monday, directly opposite *The Hogan Family*, which this show's star, Valerie Harper, was fired from.

Clueless

The ending scene and music of the episode originally broadcast October 11, 1996, came directly from the film *The Apartment* (1960).

The Cosby Show

Bill Cosby occasionally pulls some Jell-O Pudding Pops out of the freezer. Cosby did commercials for Jell-O Pudding Pops.

The Critic

In the ninth episode, "L.A. Jay," Jeremy is seen reading three issues of *Variety*. The headlines on the three: "NBC Sinks to 5th," "Conan Replaced by Dancing Chicken" and "Watching FOX Linked to Brain Damage." For a long time, FOX, the network on which the show airs, was considered "the

fourth network," and the NBC line is a dig at how bad NBC was then doing. The second headline is a reference to the talk show host Conan O'Brien, and the last is FOX's self-deprecating humor.

By the way, in this episode, film critic Jay Sherman goes on sabbatical to Hollywood to write a movie sequel. Roger Ebert did the same when he cowrote the script for *Beyond the Valley of the Dolls* (1970).

In the seventh episode, "Every Doris Has Her Day," Jay says, "At last! I think I know who my real mother is! Oh, that psychological scar is healed forever! Now, if I can only get past my failed marriage, my blood curdling senior prom and my ill-conceived canoe trip in hillbilly country. " The last two are references to *Carrie* (1976) and *Deliverance* (1972).

Cybill

Cybill (Cybill Shepherd) asks a foreign cab driver, who is a fan of hers, "Do you know who Candice Bergen is?" The driver replies, "Who?" and Cybill says, "I love you!" Shepherd and Bergen, who starred in the show *Murphy Brown*, built up a friendly rivalry over the years that they were both on the air.

In the 1996 season opener, Cybill twice mentions a hair color commercial that she had done, followed by the statement, "but I'm worth it." This is a reference to Shepherd's L'Oreal commercials which use that ad line.

In the first season, Cybill admits to appearing nude in films in the past, but just once on a diving board in an art film years ago. Shepherd actually did do a nude scene on a diving board in the Peter Bogdanovich film *The Last Picture Show* (1971).

Dallas

In the 1990 season, Barbara Eden began appearing as oil baroness LeeAnn de le Vega, who had been impregnated by J.R. Ewing (Larry Hagman) many years earlier and now schemed to gain control of Ewing Oil. Eden had previously costarred with Hagman in *I Dream of Jeannie*.

Days of Our Lives

A quirky character called Logan Michaels has appeared in the series. He spoke only in rhyme and talked to a stuffed parrot most of the time. This was a jab at Michael Logan, who is the soap opera columnist for *TV Guide*.

One storyline had most of the cast relocate to the fictional town of Aremid. One of the soap's classic villains had the last name DiMera, a palindrome of Aremid.

Supposedly when Drake Hogestyn is doing a scene he hates, he scratches his chest to let his fans know.

Hogestyn formerly played minor league baseball in the New York Yankees organization, and his character has made numerous references back to his playing days. He has coached little league teams and even made references back to the Yankees.

Kimberly and Shane's favorite song was "Friends and Lovers" by Gloria Loring. Loring was once a regular on the show, playing Liz Chandler DiMera.

When Jack and Jennifer Devereaux (Matthew Ashford and Melissa Reeves) visit Los Angeles, they come upon Macdonald Carey's star on the Hollywood Walk of Fame. Carey played Dr. Tom Horton on the show.

Bill Hayes played Doug Williams in the series and he also appeared as Williams's twin brother. However, when he played Williams's twin, Hayes was credited as "George Spelvin." This pseudonym comes from the theater: what "Alan Smithee" is to film, "George Spelvin" is to theater (see appendix).

Dinosaurs

There is a purple character named Blarney, referring to Barney the dinosaur, the popular children's show character.

Dr. Who

In the episode "Silver Nemesis," the crowd on the guided tour of Windsor Castle consists of the show's crew members. Nicholas Courtney, who played the Brigadier on the show, also appears in the tour group.

The episode "Remembrance of the Daleks" was set in England, around the time that *Dr. Who*, the series, began being broadcast on the BBC. In one scene, an announcer on a television in the background can be heard: "And now it's time for the first episode in our brand new science fiction series, D...," and he is cut off as the scene changes.

At the end of "The Five Doctors," each of the Doctors comment on each other as they part company. Jon Pertwee and Patrick Troughton's obvious animosity for each other is evident, and Troughton calls Pertwee a "scarecrow." Just before appearing in this episode, Pertwee had played the scarecrow in the British television version of *Wurzel Gummidge*.

Doogie Howser

In the hospital, Doogie (Neil Patrick Harris) walks up to a bed, looks at his clipboard, and says, "Mr. Boombotz?" He pulls the curtain aside, revealing the fictional Mr. Boombotz to be his friend Vinny.

Vinnie Boombotz is the name of the doctor that Rodney Dangerfield refers to in his comedy routines.

Dream On

John Landis cocreated the series, and the phrase "See you next Wednesday" appeared twice (see *Schlock*, 1971).

In the 1990 episode "The Trojan War," it is written on a chalkboard in a delicatessen.

In the 1991 episode "Futile Attraction," Landis plays Judith's therapist, Herb. At the end of their session he tells her, "See you next Wednesday."

The Drew Carey Show

The cartoonist who draws the strip "Dilbert," Scott Adams, has a newsletter on the Internet, and he jokingly includes lists like "Friends of Dogbert" and "Enemies of Dogbert." In one newsletter, Adams added Drew Carey to the Enemies List because of his eerie physical resemblance to Dilbert. Carey contacted Adams by e-mail and asked if he would take him off the list if some Dilbert merchandise was placed around the set of his sitcom. Adams agreed, and on January 17th, Dilbert and Dogbert dolls were clearly visible in Carey's cubicle on the show. Carey was then removed from the enemies list and promoted to Sainthood.

The Duck Factory

Voice man Wally Wooster is played by longtime cartoon voice man Don Messick (Boo Boo Bear, Scooby Doo, many others).

Duckman

Bernice meets a man named Arnoud through a computer dating service in the episode "Sperms of Endearment." He is named after Arnoud Morsink, the keeper of the "Frequently Asked Questions" page on *Duckman* on the Internet.

Due South

Many characters in the series are named after famous Canadians and Canadian landmarks. For example, Fraser's deaf wolf, Diefenbaker, is named after former Prime Minister John Diefenbaker. Other examples:

In the episode "Diefenbaker's Day Off," Madolyn Smyth-Osborne (wife of former Toronto Maple Leaf Mark Osborne) plays an investigative reporter named MacKenzie King, after the former prime minister of Canada, William Lyon MacKenzie King.

In "Manhunt," Leslie Nielsen plays legendary mountie Sgt. Duncan "Buck" Frobisher, named after Frobisher Bay, which was, in turn, named after explorer Sir Martin Frobisher. Incidentally, Fraser was to originally have been named Frobisher, but they changed it during shooting. Furthermore, Nielsen had great qualifications to play the role—his father was a mounted policeman.

In "Hawk and a Handsaw" and "Victoria's Secret," Deborah Rennard plays Dr. Esther Pearson, named after former Canadian Prime Minister Lester Pearson. Also in "Victoria's Secret," Lee Purcell plays State's Attorney Louise St. Laurent, named after former Canadian Prime Minister Louis St. Laurent.

In "The Man Who Knew Too Little," the three killers are named after Canadian universities: Laurier (Sir Wilfrid Laurier), Brock, and McGill.

Incidentally, the pathological liar in this episode, Ian MacDonald, is named after a member of the *Due South* staff. The real Ian MacDonald is producer Paul Haggis's assistant.

In "The Blue Line," with Fraser's

hockey-playing buddy, the supporting characters are named after hockey players. Miguel Fernandes plays Broda (Turk Broda), Wayne Best plays Hall (Glenn Hall), and Kevin Hicks plays Paul Henderson. Also, Tracey Cook's character is named Dawn Charest, a combination of Canadian politician Jean Charest and former hockey coach and current broadcaster Don Cherry.

Fraser's boss, the tough-as-nails Maggie (Margaret) Thatcher, is named, appropriately, after the former British prime minister, a lady who ruled with an iron fist.

The episode titled "The Mask" ran a week before the 1996 Gemini Awards, the Canadian awards for the arts, were announced. In this episode, a car rental place called Gemini Car Rentals figured into the plot line. This same car rental place had been featured in an episode one year earlier.

In "Hawk and a Handsaw," Benton tries to explain to the admitting people at the psych ward why a Mountie is stationed in Chicago. He says, "It's a long story … it takes exactly two hours to tell." The pilot for the series was exactly two hours long.

In the U.S. season premiere, "The Vault," Ray tells Fraser that he has endangered his life 24 times, which, by coincidence, was the 24th episode of *Due South* filmed (including the pilot movie). Additionally, in this episode, the bank officer is named Cooper, after Scott Cooper, who is the story department coordinator for *Due South* and the unofficial liaison to the fans of *Due South* on the Internet.

Fraser has given "Pinsent" as his mother's maiden name. Actually, his father is played by veteran Canadian actor Gordon Pinsent.

In the episode titled "The Edge," Fraser and Ray have to work with

three Secret Service agents as the security detail for a NAFTA summit. The three agents are named Bush, Casey and Helms, all of which were names of former heads of the CIA.

In once scene set in an airport, Tara O'Shea is paged over the PA system. Tara O'Shea started the DSOUTH-L listserve, the Internet group that worked to get *Due South* renewed in the summer of 1995.

In the episode "Some Like It Red," Fraser goes undercover as a woman in a Catholic girls school, and in one scene, Ray and Fraser dance like John Travolta and Uma Thurman in *Pulp Fiction* (1994).

In the episode "Starman," there is a UFO sightseeing tour to Roswell, Illinois, referring to Roswell, New Mexico, site of a famous UFO incident in the 1940s.

In the 1996 season finale, three television reporters are seen on covering the action. Two of them are named Tracy Wightman and Heather Park, which are the names of two fans of the show who frequent the Internet, one Canadian and one American.

Since the show was set in Chicago but filmed in Toronto, there were only so many prop Illinois license plates to use on cars in the show. Late in the first season, many fans noticed a plate reading "RCW 139" had a habit of appearing very frequently. For example, it is the villain's van plate in *The Promise*, FBI Agent Ford's car plate in *Chinatown*, and has over a dozen other appearances. This was much discussed on the Internet mailing list, so much so that the show's fans decided to name the first *Due South* convention after the plate: "RCW 139." The producers threw the list a few nods with unneccessary closeups of the plate on some episodes of the show and even made the plate number the key clue in the final episode, titled "Flashback."

Dynasty

In 1986, Kate O'Mara played Caress, an author who was the sister of Alexis Carrington (Joan Collins). In real life, Collins's sister Judy is a best-selling author.

Eerie, Indiana

In the third episode of the series, "The ATM Machine," Simon (Justin Shenkarow) celebrates his ninth birthday. His birthday cake is a wedding cake inscribed, "Good Luck, Julia and Kiefer." This episode was aired just about the time that Julia Roberts and Kiefer Sutherland's relationship was ending.

The fourth episode, "The Losers," centered around the fact that objects in Eerie tend to disappear without a trace. In the Bureau of Lost can be seen, among other things, a life buoy marked "Titanic," a wooden sled with "Rosebud" on it (a reference to Citizen Kane, 1941) and an alien pod from the film Invasion of the Body Snatchers (1956).

The EERIE magazine Simon is holding in the laundromat in "The Losers" is an actual black and white magazine put out by Warren Publishing from 1965–1983. It was famous for its bizarre stories and quality artists. The magazine can also be seen in following episodes.

The seventh episode, "Heart on a Chain," where Simon kisses Melanie in the graveyard, has a reference to the film The Fly (1958). As the camera pans past a spider web, the faint cries of "Help me!" from the film can be heard.

Simon's goldfish, who died while Simon was in the second grade, was named Nosferatu, after the vampire in the film Nosferatu (1922).

The fourteenth episode, "Mr. Chaney," is about the mysterious "Eerie Wolf." The title character is named after Lon Chaney, Jr., the star of The Wolf Man (1941).

Also in this episode, series creator Joe Dante's The Howling (1981), itself brimming with in-jokes, is being shown on cable.

In the eighteenth episode, "Reality Takes a Holiday," Marshall (Omri Katz) finds a television script in his mailbox, then finds himself in Hollywood, his family out of character and his name "Omri"—who is destined to die in the script. The television director is played by (who else?) Joe Dante.

Emergency!

The names "Rampart" (the station's name), "Gage" (John Gage, one of the paramedics, played by Randolph Mantooth) and "DeSoto" (Roy DeSoto, the other paramedic, played by Kevin Tighe) were taken from street names in the city of Los Angeles.

E/R

In the 1984-85 comedy series, Nurse Julie Williams (played by Lynne Moody) was the niece of George Jefferson of The Jeffersons.

ER

One of the make-up artists on the show is named "Gandhi Bob." He was first called this by Anthony Edwards when they worked together on the film Summer Heat (1987). It was a difficult shoot, but when Bob showed up part way through the production, things got strangely peaceful and Edwards started calling him Gandhi. The name stuck, and they continued to work together for many years until Edwards recommended him for *ER*.

Eric Laneuville, who played orderly Luther Hawkins on *St. Elsewhere*, and went on to direct several of that show's episodes, has directed one episode of *ER* as well, "Summer Run." He also appeared in a brief cameo as an unnamed character in "Do One, Teach One, Kill One," the episode shot after "Summer Run."

Falcon Crest

Richard Channing always referred to the homicidal Erin Jones (Jill Jacobsen) as "Miss Jones." When asked why he never used her first name, he replied, "I could never call you Erin. Sounds like one of the Waltons." *Falcon Crest* creator Earl Hamner, Jr., also created *The Waltons*.

The Fall Guy

The theme song "The Unknown Stuntman," sung by Lee Majors, opens with the line, "Well, I'm not the kind to kiss and tell, but I've been seen with Farrah..." Farrah Fawcett and Lee Majors had once been married. They divorced some years before this show.

Family Affair

Executive producer Don Fedderson's son Gregg appeared occasionally as Cissy's boyfriend, Gregg Bartlett.

Family Matters

The character of Steve Urkel (Jaleel White) was named after a real person. The real Steven Erkel is a middle-aged white man who is an independent producer of educational films. *Family Matters* cocreator Michael Warren befriended Erkel when they both attended UCLA, where Warren was a basketball star. According to a *Los Angeles Times* article a few years ago,

being one vowel away from America's Favorite Nerd has had a subtle effect on the real Steve Erkel's life. Once, a sales clerk in a furniture store tore up Erkel's sales order in disgust after reading the name on Erkel's credit card, believing that he was dealing with a prankster.

The Flash

Streets and buildings were often named after DC Comics artists and characters. Garrick Avenue and the Garrick Gallery both appeared on the show. Jay Garrick was the name of the Golden Age Flash in the comics. Doctor Carter Hall was also mentioned once. Carter Hall was the secret identity of the character Hawkman.

In one episode, there is a reference to and a shot of the Hotel Infantino, on the corner of Fox and Broome. These were named after Carmine Infantino, Gardner Fox and John Broome, three comic-artists who drew the Flash.

Forever Knight

In one episode, a dead prostitute was given the name of one of the show's fans on the Internet.

In another episode, the name Janet Dornhoff, who is another on-line fan of the show, is on a list of recent appointments of a murder victim.

The Four Seasons

This series was created by Alan Alda as a continuation of his film *The Four Seasons* (1981). Alda's daughters, Beatrice and Elizabeth, who had also appeared in the film, here played Ted Callan's (Tony Roberts) daughter, Lisa, and Beth Burroughs, who headed west with Lisa hoping to find a job as a writer. Alan himself also appeared occasionally as lawyer Jack Burroughs.

Fraggle Rock

The only fraggle to have successfully made it into the "outside world" is Gobo's uncle Traveling Matt. A traveling matte is a process used in computer animation and graphics.

Frasier

The end "tag" scene (seen during the end credits) of one episode features the characters sitting on the couch and looking at something through magnifying glasses. According to series creator David Lee, they are trying to read the credits, which had then just recently begun to be "squeezed" into the far right third of the screen in order to get more advertisement on the screen for the network. There have been many complaints that the credits are hard to read.

In a 1995 episode of *Frasier*, the show begins with Frasier, Niles, and Martin stuck in a cab in heavy traffic. The pregnant cabbie goes into labor, and so the Cranes have to use the radio to try to get help. Martin identifies their vehicle as "Cab 804." This is a reference to a well-known two-part episode of *Taxi* called "Cab 804." The same people who created *Taxi* also created *Frasier*. Furthermore, the pregnant cabbie was played by Charlayne Woodard, who once played a cabbie on *Taxi*.

Through the series, all of the voices of the callers to Frasier's call-in show have been provided by famous celebrities, and during the closing credits of episode #48, "Dark Victory," which concerned Martin's birthday party, there are numerous "Thanks for calling" photos of some who have called. These photos were of Kevin Bacon, Macaulay Culkin, Sandra Dee, Shelley Duvall, Art Garfunkel, John Lithgow, Amy Madigan, Rosie Perez, Sydney Pollack, Carly Simon, Gary Sinise, James Spader, Mary Steenbergen, Lily Tomlin and Alfre Woodard. Other callers have included Billy Barty, Mel Brooks, Jeff Daniels, Eydie Gorme, Linda Hamilton, Patty Hearst, Eric Idle, Steve Lawrence, Timothy Leary, Jay Leno, Malcolm McDowell, Reba McEntire, Mary Tyler Moore, Jane Pauley, Christopher Reeve, Ben Stiller, Garry Trudeau, Katarina Witt and Steve Young.

Furthermore, in the episode in which Bulldog is dumped by a woman that he loves, he goes on the air and takes a call from a caller asking whether he thinks the Seahawks would be leaving Seattle. The caller was sportscaster Marv Albert.

Friends

In one episode, Rachel's (Jennifer Aniston) mom talks about how she wants to be more like Rachel (discussing a possible divorce with Rachel's dad), and Rachel says, "If you wanted to be more like me why didn't you just copy my haircut?" This is a reference to fans of the show getting "Rachel" cuts.

Joey has a role on *Days of Our Lives*, on which Jennifer Aniston's real-life father, John Aniston, costars as crime boss Victor Kiriakis.

At the beginning of the episode "The One with the Dozen Lasagnes," the songs that the characters are humming are the themes of *The Odd Couple* and *I Dream of Jeannie*.

General Hospital

There was once a page for Dr. Fleischman, the name of the doctor played by Rob Morrow on *Northern Exposure*.

Rock singer Rick Springfield, who was a regular on the show, refused to sing onscreen, so producers included songs of his in the background instead, like "Jessie's Girl," which was heard in disco scenes. Further, characters occasionally commented on how much they hated his songs when one started playing in the background.

June Lockhart occasionally appears as the grandmother of Felicia, a regular character. Once, Foster, a dog belonging to Lucky, a neighbor boy, appeared at Felicia's door. June Lockhart opened the door, looked at Foster, and asked "What is it, girl?" This was a line used quite often by Lockhart on the old television series *Lassie*, where she played Timmy's mother. Foster is not a collie (he is a French Mastiff masquerading as a mutt), but he is a boy dog (as was the real Lassie).

The George Gobel Show

George's wife on the show (played by Jeff Donnell, and later Phyllis Avery) was named Alice, after Gobel's real wife.

Get Christie Love!

The show starred Teresa Graves, who was previously a regular on *Laugh-In*. In the episode broadcast February 5, 1975, six members of the *Laugh-In* crew guest starred. They were Arte Johnson, Henry Gibson, Jo Anne Worley, Judy Carne, Johnny Brown and Gary Owens.

Get Smart!

The writers of the show had a habit of naming KAOS villains after people involved with the show. Producer Daniel Melnick, who later became a motion picture studio head and is currently an independent producer, gave his name to "Melnick—the Smiling Killer" and "Put a Red in Your Bed" Melnick, who was the villainous furniture salesman who kidnapped 99 and

put a double in her place to poison Max.

In one episode, when Max Smart is at the airport, an announcement asks Mr. Buck Henry (who was the cocreator of the show) to collect his poodle from the baggage counter.

The Girl from U.N.C.L.E.

Noel Harrison plays Mark Slate, and in one episode with guest star David McCallum as Illya Kuryakin (from *The Man from U.N.C.L.E.*) , Mark takes a bronx showgirl and tries to make a lady of her to impersonate a THRUSH agent. This was a parody of the role of Professor Higgins made famous by Noel's father, Rex Harrison, in *My Fair Lady* (1964).

In one episode, Mark Slate is chased through a movie set. The film company is MGM (the makers of the show) and it turns out Slate is running through a lot of sets from this show and *The Man from U.N.C.L.E.*

Good Grief!

Joel Brooks's room is an exact replica of the set of *The Honeymooners*. It is even shot in black and white.

Guiding Light

When Buzz and Nadine Cooper (Justin Deas and Jean Carol) appear on the fictional game show *Soulmates*, they become local celebrities. Nadine loves all the attention, but Buzz does whatever he can to avoid it, saying, "I don't like publicity." Deas himself rarely grants interviews and has even been known not to pick up the Emmy awards he has won.

Gunsmoke

John Wayne was initially asked to play the part of Matt Dillon, but when he turned it down, he suggested a colleague of his, James Arness, for the part. Wayne did agree to narrate the pilot episode, though.

Hardcastle and McCormick

At the end of the episode originally broadcast March 11, 1984, a character named Beaver walks through the scene, greeting Hardcastle and McCormick. The character is played by Jerry Mathers of *Leave It to Beaver* fame.

The Hardy Boys (1990s)

In the episode where the Hardys hide a bird from the police, they steal one of the villains' wallets, look inside and see a picture of him. One says to the other, "Well, he's no Parker Stevenson." Parker Stevenson starred with David Cassidy as the Hardy Boys in the original *Hardy Boys* series in the 1970s.

Hart to Hart

Robert Wagner's wife, Natalie Wood, has a cameo in the series pilot. She is billed in the closing credits as "Natasha Gurdin," which was Wood's real name.

Hawaii Five-0

Wo Fat, McGarrett's chief nemesis, was named after a prominent Honolulu restaurant, Wo Fat Chop Sui, which is now owned by the People's Republic of China, according to the newsletter of the Iolani Palace Irregulars (the Hawaii Five-O Fan Club) and has been renamed. There is even a shot of the original restaurant in the episode "Termination with Extreme Prejudice."

The balcony that McGarrett stands on during the opening credits was part of a building owned by the wealthiest Chinese American resident in Hawaii,

Chinn Ho. Kam Fong's character in the series was named for him.

Two reporters who appeared in the series were played by actual members of Hawaii's news media. Bob Sevey was the news anchor for KGMB (*Hawaii 5-0*'s affiliate station), and Hal Lewis (AKA "Akuhead Pupuli") hosted a morning radio talk show on KGMB-AM.

At the airport in the episode "Murder Is a Taxing Affair," there is a page for Ken Pettus. Pettus was the story editor at the time and wrote several scripts.

There was more than one episode in which the scene is a hospital, and "Dr. Freeman" is paged. Usually all dialogue and action would stop while the announcement was made. Leonard Freeman created *Hawaii Five-O*.

In "Face of the Dragon," an Army colonel receives a telephone call from "General Freeman," another reference to the series creator.

In "The Sleeper," Andrew Duggan gives an alibi that he was home watching an old movie, *God's Little Acre* (1958), on television. Jack Lord was in *God's Little Acre*.

In "The Two-Faced Corpse," Steve tells one of the crew to check with a "Professor Lafferty" at the university about something. Perry Lafferty was CBS's West Coast vice president in charge of production. He was the one who made the original decision to let Leonard Freeman make the *Hawaii Five-O* pilot and offer it to the network.

Also in "The Two-Faced Corpse," Steve is golfing with a couple of guys when an idea occurs to him. One of the guys he is golfing with is played by Frank Fasi, who was, at the time, mayor of Honolulu.

Early in the series, in a couple of

episodes, there were mentions of "Chief Dann" of HPD. This was a reference to CBS Network Vice President Mike Dann.

In later episodes, "Judge Ariyoshi" is mentioned. George Ariyoshi was, at the time, governor of Hawaii.

In the episode "Computer Killer," McGarrett has a list of possible suspects on his blackboard. One name on the list is Marc Baxley. Baxley had several minor roles on the series, and had a behind-the-scenes role with the series, as staff or stuntman.

In "How to Steal a Masterpiece," much of the story takes place in the art gallery of a millionaire's mansion. The paintings around the top row of the gallery are Jack Lord's work.

Highlander

The episode "Revenge of the Sword," guest starring Dustin Nguyen as a martial arts movie star, has numerous references to James Bond. Duncan MacLeod introduces himself as "Bond ... James Bond," the villain strokes a cat, á la Blofeld, and the bit with Jimmy (Nguyen) being almost burned to death in a coffin in the crematory is right out of *Diamonds Are Forever* (1971). Also, Johnny Leong (Robert Ito) is the head of The Tong Society, the organization that Dr. No was the head of in *Dr. No* (1962).

In the episode "Legacy," a line from *Monty Python and the Holy Grail* (1975) is heard: "Bring out your dead!"

In "Counterfeit Part I," the voice coach who prompts Lisa (Meilani Paul) is actually the *Highlander* staff voice coach. Incidentally, Meilani is the wife of *Highlander* star Adrian Paul.

The hooded figure who haunts MacLeod in the episode "Shadows" is played by F. Braun McAsh, the fightmaster for the series.

Highway to Heaven

In a Halloween episode, Mark (Victor French) is seen watching *I Was a Teen-age Werewolf* (1957) on television. The film starred Michael Landon, and Mark sees the actor and says to Jonathan (Michael Landon), "This actor reminds me of you." Jonathan says, "I can tell you how it turns out."

The Highwayman

In one episode, a genetically designed perfect soldier named McClone goes AWOL and is pursued by evil clones and government scientists. The character, a take-off of the character of *McCloud*, was intended to continue in his own series (see *McClone*, 1989 TV).

Hogan's Heroes

The show's co-creator, Bernie Fein, had an actor friend named Robert Hogan. In an early script, the lead character of the show had another name. Fein decided to rename the character after his friend, and even suggested Robert Hogan for the role of Robert Hogan, but Bob Crane was cast. Hogan did appear in an episode as a guest star. Hogan says this caused him much confusion throughout his career, with people confusing him for the famous character. He has said, "I can't tell you how many people, on hearing my name, say, 'one of Hogan's Heroes, huh?' You can't tell everyone and they don't really care so I smile weakly and nod."

In the episode "The Return of Major Bonacelli," Bonacelli (Vito Scotti) enters and Hogan says, "Major Bonacelli!" Bonacelli answers, "You have a wonderful memory for faces,

Colonel!" However, in the earlier episode featuring Major Bonacelli, "The Pizza Parlor," the part was played by a different actor, Hans Conreid.

Home Improvement

Tim (Tim Allen) hires his brother in one episode, and they have an argument, yelling "Can too!" and "Can not!" back and forth. Tim ends the argument with, "Can too … to infinity and beyond!" This was a line of Buzz Lightyear's (voice of Tim Allen) in the film *Toy Story* (1995).

Homeboys in Outer Space

There are many *Star Trek* in-jokes in the series. For example, one main character is named Tyberius (played by Flex). Tiberius was James T. Kirk's middle name. James Doohan (Scotty from *Star Trek*) has made guest appearances as an inept ship's engineer named Pippen. Scottie Pippen is a very popular player in the National Basketball Association.

Homicide: Life on the Street

In the episode "I've Got a Secret," Pembleton and Bayliss are investigating possible negligence on the part of a doctor who may have caused the death of a patient. They have a conversation about how doctors get all the credit, but homicide detectives do just as good a job, and Pembleton says, "You want glory? Go work in ER. Homicide is fine by me." This is a dig at another ensemble drama show, *ER*, which many considered to be on a par with *Homicide*, but which got much better ratings and much more attention ("glory") than *Homicide*.

In the episode "Doll Eyes," Bayliss mentions that he is going to see a Dr. Ehrlich about his back problems. Dr. Ehrlich was the name of the character played by Ed Begley, Jr., on *St. Elsewhere*.

A boy is shot in one episode, and his parents agonize over pulling the plug on their brain-dead son. Once he is officially pronounced dead, his organs are placed into containers, and the container for the heart is marked "Chicago Hope." A messenger runs down a hospital hall with it and gives it to *Chicago Hope*'s Dr. Geiger (Mandy Patinkin), who is eating a sandwich at the nurse's station. Geiger drops the sandwich and runs off with the heart.

The Honeymooners

In the episode first broadcast January 26, 1956, "The Baby Sitter," Alice gets a telephone that has the number BEnsonhurst 3-7741. However, between the original airing and the time the show went into syndication, it must have been discovered that it was someone's real number. It was dubbed over as "BEnsonhurst 3-5555," but in one scene, Jackie Gleason still clearly mouths the original.

Howdy Doody Time

There were always exactly 48 freckles on Howdy's face, representing the 48 states in the Union in the 1950s.

The Incredible Hulk

The lead character was originally named Bruce Banner in the Marvel comic, but the name was changed to David Bruce Banner for the series because the network did not want a hero named Bruce. Apparently, they found the name "Bruce" to be effeminate and they didn't want any homosexual inference.

Bill Bixby's old costar on *My Favorite Martian*, Ray Walston, appears in the episode named "My Favorite Magician" as an aging magician who uses Bruce Banner (Bixby) as his assistant.

Bixby's old costar on *The Courtship of Eddie's Father*, Brandon Cruz, appears in the episode "747" as a kid who helps Banner land an airplane.

Inspector Gadget

Gadget's (voice of Don Adams) nemesis was named the Claw, which was also the name of a villain on Adams's previous series, *Get Smart!*

J.J. Starbuck

In February 1988, Ben Vereen joined the cast as Starbuck's sidekick, E.L. "Tenspeed" Turner. Vereen had played the same character in another Stephen J. Cannell–produced series, *Tenspeed and Brown Shoe.*

The John Larroquette Show

Catherine (Alison LaPlaca) mentions that she has been on five failed sitcoms. LaPlaca had indeed been on *Duet, Open House, Stat, The Jackie Thomas Show* and *Tom.*

The Kids in the Hall

The hair stylist for *SCTV* later worked on the shows *CODCO* and *The Kids in the Hall* and she reused many of the wigs from *SCTV* on the two subsequent series. For example, the hair of the cab driver who delivers a baby on *The Kids in the Hall* (Dave Foley) was actually the hair of the *SCTV* character Sammy Maudlin (Joe Flaherty).

The Kindred

Stacy Haiduk's character is named Lillie Langtry, after the famous British stage actress of the 1890s.

Knots Landing

Laura's (Constance McCashin) two younger children, Daniel and Meg, are named after McCashin's own children, and Daniel Weisman, McCashin's son, even plays her son, Daniel Avery.

Mac and Anne Matheson's song from their younger days was the Mamas and the Papas' "Dedicated to the One I Love." Anne would play it whenever she felt nostalgic and she sang it to Mac on a March 1987 episode. Anne was played by Michelle Phillips, a member of the Mamas and the Papas.

Kukla, Fran and Ollie

The witch on this childrens' puppet series is named Beaulah, after the show's producer, Beaulah Zachary.

Kung Fu (original series)

Kwai Chang Caine (David Carradine) is played as a boy in flashbacks by David's brother, Keith Carradine.

Kung Fu (second series)

The "damn hot dog joke" surfaces a number of times in the series. The joke goes: "What did the Zen Master/Buddhist Monk say to the Hot Dog Vendor? Make me one with everything." The first time it occurs, Peter takes Kwai to a hot dog cart, Kwai orders "one with everything" and Peter cannot stop laughing. Another time, their friend from the mental hospital is the hot dog vendor, and once more the "Emperor of China" and a student demonstration hero are with them at the hot dog stand.

In the episode "May I Walk with You," there is a Jon Cassar Day Care Center. Cassar directed the episode.

In "Dragonswing I," guest star Ian Ogilvy said, "I'm no saint." Ogilvy played the Saint in the syndicated series *Return of the Saint*, 1979–80.

In one episode, mug shots appear on

a computer screen. They are actually pictures of the show's crew members.

Peter is looking through files in one episode, and he sees a Penn/Teller file. Penn and Teller are a magic-comedy duo.

In the first season, there was a villain named David Chow. David Chow was one of David Carradine's trainers for the original series.

L.A. Law

In a Martinez's first scene, Stuart (Michael Tucker) shows him around the office and asks where he had come from. Martinez answers, "Santa Barbara." Martinez had just left the soap *Santa Barbara* for his role on this show.

Legend

When John DeLancie starts up his experimental vehicle in the pilot for this Richard Dean Anderson series, he says, "Engage!" imitating Jean-Luc Picard on *Star Trek: The Next Generation*. De Lancie had previously tormented Picard on that show as the omnipotent alien Q.

Lois and Clark: The Adventures of Superman

When Tempus the time-traveler (Lane Davies) appears, he keeps throwing in comments drawn from the voice-over lead to the 1950s George Reeves *Superman* show, describing Clark Kent as the "mild-mannered reporter for a great metropolitan newspaper," for instance. The joke was even carried into the headline of a newspaper: "Not Bird, Not Plane, Superman."

The old Superman credo shows up in various ways on the show, even as titles to episodes such as "Strange Visitor (From Another Planet)," "Neverending Battle" and "Man of Steel Bars." In "All Shook Up" there is a

billboard with an ad that reads, "The Metroliner: Faster Than a Speeding Bullet." Clark says, "Not bad for a mild-mannered reporter" in "Requiem for a Superhero." In "Tempus Anyone" when Lois is in an alternate reality, she finds a Clark Kent who has never become Superman, and so when she gets him aside privately, she lets him know she knows a lot about him. "How many people know you come from another planet? That you can bend steel in your bare hands, leap tall buildings in a single bound?" In the first-season episode in which Lex is testing Superman's powers, Lex asks if Superman is "more powerful than a locomotive? Is he faster than a speeding bullet?" All of these phrases were taken from the introduction to the George Reeves series of the 1950s.

In the episode "The Phoenix," Besselo Street is mentioned. It is where Sheldon Bender's office (Lex Luthor's attorney) is located. Besselo was the real surname of George Reeves, who played the original Superman.

The Coates orphanage, seen in the episode "Season's Greedings," is named after Phyllis Coates, who played the first Lois Lane on television. Coates also plays Lois Lane's mom in "The House of Luthor." However, in later episodes, Mrs. Lane is played by Beverly Garland.

Cat (Tracy Scoggins) manages to lure Clark to her apartment in one episode, then smiles and says she would like to slip into something a little more comfortable. "To everyone's surprise," Scoggins said, "I came out in a baggy, grey sweatshirt. At my request, because I'm a runner, the shirt read Metropolis U. Women's Track and Field."

References to the Jim Croce song

"You Don't Mess Around with Jim" appear in a couple of episodes. The song contains the line "Don't tug on Superman's cape," which was even the title of one episode of *Lois and Clark*. In "Man of Steel Bars," Superman temporarily ends up in jail and a cellmate grabs his cape and says, "Look, I'm tuggin' on Superman's cape" and a prisoner in an adjoining cell says, "What are you gonna do next? Spit into the wind?"

In "When Irish Eyes Are Killing," the name Dennis O'Neal ends up on a bank deposit box card. O'Neal is a comic book artist who has drawn Superman comics in the past, though he is more famous for doing Batman.

Screenwriter Bryce Zabel wrote the episode "Strange Visitor," and in that episode it is revealed that Clark's spaceship came to Earth on May 17, 1966. May 17 is Zabel's birthday, and 1966 is the year of Dean Cain's birth.

Zabel also makes a cameo appearance in his episode "All Shook Up" as a priest listening to Cat Grant's confession.

Jimmy Simons, line producer for *Lois and Clark*, is seen in the background of the episode "Whine Whine Whine" robbing a liquor store.

The producers of the show posted the letters "FOLC +3 ⁷⁄₈" on the newsroom announcement ticker in the *Daily Planet* newsroom at the very beginning of the episode "Oedipus Wrecks" to show that they are aware of, and responsive to, the fans of the show. FOLC is an acronym which originated on the Internet. It stands for "Fans Of Lois & Clark." Some have suggested that the numbers "3 ⁷⁄₈" refer to how many episodes were left in the season at the time. There were three to follow this episode, and the stock

ticker appeared about one eighth of the way through this one.

After the Nazi group takes over the television transmissions in one episode, their leader walks up to make a speech in front of a huge American flag. This is a reference to the opening shot of *Patton* (1970), in which Patton (George C. Scott) made a similar inspirational speech in front of a huge replica of the Stars and Stripes.

When Herkimer Johnson rides his bike in the episode "Oedipus Wrecks," music plays in the background. It is the music which accompanied Miss Gulch (Margaret Hamilton, who also played the Wicked Witch of the West) when she rode her bicycle in *The Wizard of Oz* (1939).

In the episode "Contact," where Lois is abducted by aliens, Star hypnotizes them and says, "You are in a Warm and Fuzzy place…" One of the phrases coined by fans of the show on the Internet is commonly abbreviated to "WAFF." It stands for "Warm And Fuzzy Feeling." This describes those scenes that are overly sentimental or emotional.

The evil villain and software mogul in this episode is named Bob Fences, in a parody of real software mogul Bill Gates, head of Microsoft ("fences," "gates"). Also, his company is named Nanoware, after Microsoft, with "nano" being smaller than "micro."

Early on in "Contact," when Superman is talking to the evil psychiatrist, the psychiatrist says, "You're looking at me as if I were Lex Luthor!" There were a great many questions raised about the doctor on the Internet newsgroup concerned with *Lois and Clark*, regarding his physical resemblance to John Shea (who plays Luthor) and Luthor's nasty behavior, and the producers probably inserted this line at the last minute for the fans.

In the episode "Witness," Superman goes to a school on Career Day and a little kid suggests that maybe, when they need to contact Superman, they should just beam a search light into the sky with a big "S" symbol on it, just as they did in the *Batman* films. The kid behind him says that it is a dumb idea.

In one episode, Superman (Dean Cain) talks to an ex–football player who raises orchids. The football player explains that he used to play for the Buffalo Bills, but he blew his knee out and that ended his career, and now he raises orchids ... something he says is "much more relaxing, and definitely less painful." Superman smiles and says, "I know what you mean." At one time, Cain held the NCAA record for interceptions and was a free safety with the Buffalo Bills, but he had a career-ending knee injury and took up acting.

In the episode "Top Copy," television personality Diana Stride claims on her show that Clark is Superman, and Jimmy comments that he always thought they looked a bit alike. Perry White (Lane Smith) then says that he has been told he looks like Richard Nixon, "but I've never been in the White House!" Smith had previously played Nixon in the television movie *The Final Days* (1989TV).

Cain's then-girlfriend, pro volleyball player Gabrielle Reece, had her name immortalized on Gabby's Deli, a restaurant where Lois and Clark have lunch in the episode "Virtually Destroyed."

In the episode "House of Luthor," the owner of the *Daily Planet*— Franklin Stern, played by James Earl Jones—is introduced. The character, which was originated in the comics,

was named after Superman comics writer Roger Stern.

The clone president signs Lex Luthor's pardon in "I Now Pronounce You." If you freeze-frame the close-up of the pardon, you can see the message, "if you can read this, we held the shot too long."

The show's executive producer, Robert Singer, and his real life girlfriend Eugenie Ross-Leming (coexecutive producer and writer for *Lois and Clark*) have cameo appearances in the episode "I Now Pronounce You." They play two motorists arguing over a fender-bender.

Dean Cain's mom, actress Sharon Thomas, appears in the first season episode "Green Green Glow of Home" as a Smallville denizen named Maisy. She serves Lois and Clark soft drinks at the Corn Festival and says "with Clark, what you see is what you get" to Lois. In the second season, Thomas is seen in "Season's Greedings" (which was written by her son) as a woman fighting Lois Lane for an Atomic Space Rat toy, which caused greediness. In the third season, she plays a nun who kisses Superman's cheek when he rescues the toys for the mission in an episode titled "Just Say Noah."

Tribute has been paid to both of the creators of Superman. In "Season's Greedings," screenwriter Dean Cain gives Clark Kent the middle name Jerome after Superman cocreator Jerome (Jerry) Siegel. And in the episode "Tempus Fugitive," the field where Superman's spaceship is discovered is called Shuster's Field, after Joe Shuster.

Teri Hatcher's (Lois Lane) dad, a retired physicist, has a nonspeaking cameo as a policeman in "Never on Sunday."

Hatcher has described herself as a female nerd in high school because she belonged to the chess and math clubs. This bit of information was incorporated into Lois's character, who admits in "Pheromone, My Lovely" that she belonged to the math and chess clubs in high school.

The theme music for the show has been whistled on the show: Superman whistles a few notes in "That Old Gang of Mine," Clark whistles a few notes in "Bolt from the Blue," and the villain whistles a few notes in "And the Answer Is."

The theme song is also heard in the second season episode "Wall of Sound." Lois goes undercover in a night club, and uses a special listening device to spy on the owner. By mistake, she tunes it into AM radio, and one of the snippets of music that is heard is the theme song.

In "Tempus Anyone," the villain (Tempus) has Lois blindfolded on a crumbling building ledge. He is watching on a television monitor while eating popcorn and says, "The only thing that would ruin this would be a commercial," and sure enough, the program breaks for a commercial.

In this episode, Majordomo, Tempus's helper, is named after the Internet address used to retrieve the Lois and Clark discussion mailing list: majordomo@vger.rutgers.edu. It has since been discontinued.

Tempus says that if he just wanted Lois dead, he would beat her to death with a frozen lamb chop and serve it with a nice merlot (a type of wine). Besides the obvious *Silence of the Lambs* (1991) reference (Hannibal Lecter spoke of eating somone's liver "with a nice Chianti"), this is also a reference to the episode "Lamb to the Slaughter" from the original *Alfred*

Hitchcock Presents television series. It was written by Roald Dahl and directed by Hitchcock himself. It first aired in 1958, and featured Barbara Bel Geddes as a woman who kills her husband with a frozen leg of lamb. When the cops show up, she cooks the lamb and serves it to them.

Dan Patterson and Craig Byrne, the copresidents of the Krypton Club, have their names on a plaque on a wishing well in the episode "Ultrawoman." The Krypton Club is an electronic fan club of the show and the comic.

Lois and Clark's address after they marry is 348 Hyperion Drive. Hyperion is the Internet location that has scans of the *Lois and Clark* promos. There was another mention of Hyperion in an episode of *Babylon 5*.

Near the end of the second season finale, "And the Answer Is…," there is a scene between Perry White and Jimmy Olsen. The dialogue goes as follows: Jimmy: "Maybe instead of standing around all day watching Lois and Clark, we should get lives of our own that are just a little bit more interesting." Perry: "I think you hit the nail on the head. It's like we're just supporting characters in some TV show that's only about them." Jimmy: "Yeah! It's like all we do is advance their plots." Perry: "I'll tell you the truth, I'm sick of it!" Jimmy: "Man, me too!"

In the episode "UltraWoman," Shelley Long proclaims to Dean Cain, "I'm going to knock you into next Thursday!" The following Thursday, Cain appeared on an episode of *Living Single*.

The Lone Ranger

The expression "Kemo Sabe," meaning "trusty scout," appeared for the first time in this series. The show's producer, James Jewell, coined the term. It was the name of his father's boys' camp: Kee-Mo-Sah-Bee.

Looney Tunes

The character of Foghorn Leghorn is based on the character of Senator Beauregard Claghorn (Kenny Delmar) on the old radio show *Allen's Alley*, right down to the voice and catch-phrase, "That's a joke, son…"

The line "I'll give you such a *pinch*!" is said by an elephant in one short. This was one of the catchphrases of Stinky, Joe Besser's bratty, juvenile character on *The Abbott and Costello Show*.

Lost in Space

The show was created and produced by Irwin Allen. The registration number on the space pod is "277-2210 IA." This was actually the phone number of 20th Century Studios, where *Lost in Space* was filmed, and the "IA" at the end stands for "Irwin Allen."

In the original pilot of the show, the *Jupiter 2* was originally called the *Gemini 12*. Gemini is the astrological sign for June and Irwin Allen's birthday was June 12.

The Love Boat

Florence Henderson meets Robert Reed (both of *The Brady Bunch*) and says, "Don't I know you from some place?"

Loving

In an episode featuring a crossover between this show and *All My Children*, the character Trevor Dillon from *All My Children* (played by James Kiberd, who used to be a regular on *Loving* as well) chases a criminal from Pine Valley (where *All My Children* takes place) to Corinth (where this show takes place). He gets into a

fender-bender with *Loving*'s Shana Alden (Susan Keith). During the course of the ensuing argument, Trevor expresses his sympathy for the jerk who is married to Shana, to which Shana replies, "and I feel sorry for the idiot who's married to you." Kibert and Keith were married to each other in real life.

Mad About You

In one episode, Carl Reiner appears as television host Alan Brady, the character he had played on *The Dick Van Dyke Show*.

When the show was getting moved to a new time slot for the umpteenth time in its first two seasons, a promo showed Paul Reiser and Helen Hunt sitting in their apartment talking to one another about moving to another apartment. Paul says, "I just don't understand why we have to move again…," to which Helen responds, "Because we were getting our *butt* kicked on Wednesday night!"

In one episode, Reiser and Hunt are playing Monopoly, and all of a sudden he opens a community chest card and says, "Look at this, you got the movie of the week!" Hunt appeared that week in a television movie.

During the episode aired January 5, 1995, Reiser and Hunt are being filmed, by Paul, for a documentary about artists' lives at home. At one point, a frustrated Jamie (Hunt) starts examining publicity photos and resumes of actresses. She tells Paul, "I'm hiring someone to play your wife. [This actress] did *Our Town* and three Breck commercials." In 1989, Helen Hunt appeared on Broadway in *Our Town*.

In one episode, Paul is asked if he has seen the *Alien* films. He replies, "Only the first one." Reiser appeared in the second one, *Aliens* (1986), as Carter Burke.

Around the time that Helen Hunt's film *Twister* (1996) was in theaters, there was an episode in which Jamie (Hunt) walks in on two of her friends playing the game Twister.

Magnum, P.I.

The islands' physician, played by Glen Cannon, is named Doc Ibold, after the series' production designer, Douglas Ibold.

Jonathan Higgins (John Hillerman) effortlessly adopts a Texan accent in one episode. Hillerman was born in Denison, Texas. Luther Gillis asks how he did it. Higgins says, "let's just say it's an old family trade." He also adopted this accent to play Higgins's long-lost and now dead half-brother Elmo Ziller from Texas.

At the beginning of the episode "Tigers Fan," which centered around a man who turns out to be a CIA agent, two men discuss an episode of *The Rockford Files* and "that annoying guy Lance White" who was in the story. Lance White was a character in the series played by Tom Selleck.

In the episode "The Taking of Dick McWilliams," TC and Rick run down some license plate numbers. TC says he has checked one out, but it probably is not their man because he is a cop from 5-0. Rick says, "What's his name?" TC replies, "McGarrett." Steve McGarrett was the name of Jack Lord's character on *Hawaii Five-O*.

In the episode "The Last Page," there is a store sign that says "Wo Fat." This was a real restaurant in Hawaii that Steve McGarrett's arch-nemesis on *Hawaii Five-O* was named after (see *Hawaii Five-O*).

José Ferrer and June Lockhart play the leads, a judge and his long lost love, in the first season episode "Lest We Forget." In the flashbacks to 1941, Ferrer's character is played by his son, Miguel Ferrer, and Lockhart's by her daughter, Anne Lockhart.

Magnum's address (prior to Robin's Nest), as seen on his driver's license in the second season episode "Memories Are Forever," was 11435 18th Avenue, Honolulu, Hawaii. In reality, this address was just a few doors down from MCA's *Magnum, P.I.* production offices.

In the second season episode "Try to Remember," Magnum's birthday is established as August 8, 1944. This is also creator Donald Bellisario's birthday.

Bellisario appears in a cameo in the 1986 season opener, "Death and Taxes." In the episode, Magnum saves an obnoxious reporter from being killed by a maniac at a swimming pool. Bellisario plays a sleazy desk clerk.

In the third season finale, "Faith and Begorrah," where Magnum searches for the ex-wife of his softball teammate, he wears not only his Detroit Tigers baseball cap, but, in some scenes, a cap from the University of Southern California, where Selleck played junior varsity baseball in college.

One episode is named "The Black Orchid." After the series suspended production in the late 1980s, Selleck, Larry Manetti, and two other entrepreneurs opened a restaurant in Honolulu's prestigious "restaurant row" called the Black Orchid.

Magnum reads a copy of *The National Review* in the episode "Pleasure Principle." This magazine is one of the few products that Tom Selleck has endorsed on television. Also, in the episode "L.A." a woman tries to give Magnum her ex-husband's shirt, which has the monogram "W.F.B." She even refers to her ex as "Bill." These are references to *National Review* editor William F. Buckley.

In the episode that began the fifth season, "Echoes of the Mind," Higgins mentions to Agatha that a soldier he once knew, Lt. Freebairn-Smith, was eaten by a tiger. This is a reference to Ian Freebairn-Smith, the series' original music composer, who was replaced by Mike Post and Pete Carpenter.

Magnum refers to having a cousin named Reni in the seventh season episode "The People vs. Orville Wright." The restaurant-club in Honolulu owned by Roger E. Mosley (T.C.) is called Reni's.

In the fourth season episode "On Face Value," where a woman is scarred in a car accident, Magnum says that the estate's tidal pool was originally built as a place to raise sea turtles. This is true in reality as well. The Eve Anderson Ranch, where the Robin's Nest scenes were filmed, is also known as "Pahonu," which means "turtle" in Hawaiian. It was at one time a turtle farm.

Robin Masters (Orson Welles, on Magnum's answering machine) tells Magnum to go undercover on a case and says that his password will be "Rosebud." "Rosebud" was Welles's dying word in his classic film *Citizen Kane* (1941).

In the third season episode "...By Its Cover," a parole officer remarks to Selleck that he looks like the "bunco type." Selleck appeared in the television film *Bunco* (1976TV).

In the seventh season episode "A.A.P.I.," Detectives Columbo (from *Columbo*), Theo Kojak (from *Kojak*) and Mike Stone (from *The Streets of San Francisco*) can be seen in the audience at the AAPI convention. They were played by lookalikes of Peter Falk, Telly Savalas and Karl Malden. Stephen J. Cannell also makes a guest appearance in this episode.

In the final season's opener, "Infinity and Jelly Doughnuts," Selleck's father Robert, mother Martha and son Kevin make guest appearances. Robert Selleck plays Magnum's maternal grandfather, Everett Wendel Currier. Martha Selleck plays Magnum's mom, Martha Katherine Peterson. Kevin Selleck is also in the scene that shows Robert and Martha.

Tom Selleck was originally going to star in *Raiders of the Lost Ark* (1981), but instead was contractually bound to *Magnum*, and in the episode entitled "Legend of the Lost Art," Magnum (Selleck) takes part in an adventure very similar to *Raiders*. Wearing a brown Stetson hat, gloves and leather jacket, and carrying a bullwhip (which he even uses a couple of times), Magnum sets out in search of the "lost art." Incidentally, the "lost art" is repeatedly mispronounced "lost ark." Examples include Magnum, in a fit of pique, saying "...lost ark... lost *art*"; the villain's henchman (Kabir Bedi) saying "lost ark" and Higgins correcting him, saying "a common mistake"; the main villain, Peter Riddley-Smyth (Anthony Newley), who is dressed in a white hat and suit reminiscent of *Raiders'* Belloq, saying "lost ark" twice; and, once it is found, even Higgins says, "The lost ark!" Magnum counters with "Art. Don't you mean art, Higgins?" Higgins replies, "Of course I do. The art is in the ark."

Riddley-Smyth is an eccentric who delights in recreating scenes from his favorite movies, and all through this adventure, guesses are made as to which movie this is based on. *The Maltese Falcon, The Treasure of the Sierra Madre, North by Northwest, Bad*

Day at Black Rock and *King Solomon's Mines* (1950) are suggested. Magnum finally thinks he has it figured out when he remembers the serial *Nyoka and the Lost Secrets of Hippocrates,* which is seen on television at the end of the episode ("Connie jumped out of the chariot before it went over the cliff!").

In the story, Magnum retrieves an artifact from a booby-trap-ridden cave, but it is taken from him by Riddley-Smyth. Then an old girlfriend of Magnum's named Connie (Margaret Colin), to whom he was "engaged to be engaged" seven years ago, is introduced. She outlasts all comers in a dancing (instead of drinking) contest and immediately punches Magnum when she sees him again. He leaves, and Riddley-Smyth's henchman, Bedi, threatens her with fire to get an artifact that will lead him to the lost art. Magnum appears out of nowhere, whips the fire out of his hand, and a bar fight ensues. During the fight, Magnum beans a bad guy with a bottle of whiskey that Connie hands him, is pushed along the top of the bar, and escapes being shot when Connie shoots another bad guy.

Later, when they go off together to find the art, he sees the vehicle on which she has been taken explode, then finds her tied up in the villain's tent. Then, when Magnum is driving a covered truck, a bad guy appears outside the door, and Magnum punches him off the truck and shakes his hand in pain.

Finally, Magnum and Connie, after using the artifact to channel sunlight and show the location of the lost ark (art), go down into a crypt-like room, find the art, and throw it up through the hole in the ceiling to the bad guys, who seal them in. At this point, Magnum finally figures out what movie this

is based on, and he tells Connie to use her clothing for torches. When she asks, "Why don't we use your clothes?" he replies, "'Cause I saw the movie." He uses her skirt as a torch, and she leaps onto his back, one leg over his shoulder, when they find out what the hissing sound is. "It can't be snakes ... there's no snakes in Hawaii."

They get out by breaking through the wall that the snakes are coming in through, and, when he confronts Riddley-Smyth, he is not shot by his henchmen because he tells Riddley-Smyth, "If they shoot me, I shoot you."

At the end of the episode, Magnum hangs up his hat and jacket in disgust, refusing to wear them again.

The Man from U.N.C.L.E.

Napoleon Solo was named after a character in Ian Fleming's James Bond novel *Goldfinger.* Solo was played in the 1964 film by Martin Benson.

In the pilot episode, a mailbox on a lonely Virginia country road at night can be seen. The address on the mailbox is actually the address of first season producer and pilot script writer Sam Rolfe when he lived in Virginia.

In "The Thor Affair," Solo (Robert Vaughn) and Illya (David McCallum) visit a school teacher in her classroom. On the blackboard are lots of chalk scribblings, but the letters "RFK" can clearly be made out, a subtle reference to Vaughn's friend Robert Kennedy, who was running for president at the time.

In the first season episode "The Brain Killer Affair," guest star Elsa Lanchester appears with her hair standing straight back with a silver streak in it on each side. This was the look she made famous as the *Bride of Frankenstein* (1932).

In "The Deadly Smorgasbord

Affair," there is a Dr. A.C. Nillson, a reference to the A.C. Nielsen television ratings system.

In the episode "The Cap and Gown Affair," the dorm is called "Felton Hall" after the series creator, Norman Felton.

In the "Pop Art Affair," Solo says he represents the "Felton Foundation."

In "The Monks of St. Thomas Affair," Solo and Illya go to a house to find a man, and the address is on Felton Avenue. This was used again in "The Hula Doll Affair."

In the first season episode "The Giuoco Piano Affair" a number of the guests at the party at Marian Raven's (Jill Ireland) house are played by creator Norman Felton, producer Sam Rolfe, writer-producer Richard Donner and writer-director Joe Cavelli. They are seen in two scenes and were fined by the Actors' Guild for appearing.

In "Off-Broadway," Solo says his name is L.B. Sternmacher, after film mogul Louis B. Mayer.

Married: with Children

In the first episode of the seventh season, a new character was added, named Seven. He was about 7 years old and was briefly part of the Bundy family, but viewer response to the character was bad, so he just disappeared from the show with no explanation. Later in the series, after he was gone, the camera zoomed in on a milk carton featuring a "Have you seen me?" picture of Seven. In another episode, thought balloons appear over Kelly's head, and in one of them, there is a picture of Seven with a big question mark next to him. Actually, Seven's disappearance was later explained, with a jab at the show *Dallas*. Kelly wakes up, having discovered that the whole season was

a dream, including the existence of Seven. *Dallas* used the "season was a dream" ploy to resurrect a character who had died in the series' past season.

Al wants to make shoes for God in one episode, and his family tries to change their last name. Kelly suggests "Berkowitz." This is a reference to serial killer Daniel Berkowitz, and a hint that they are related to Ted Bundy, another serial killer.

The "FOX viewing position," where the family holds various pieces of metal and tin foil around the living room, refers to the fact that in the early days, and in some cases still today, FOX affiliates were lower-powered obscure UHF stations.

Brandi Brandt appears in an episode late in 1987 playing a *Playboy* Playmate who was in that month's issue, which Al goes out to find. In reality, Brandt was the *Playboy* centerfold for October 1987.

In the episode, "Heels on Wheels," Kelly says, "Damn vegetarians! They find *one* cat's claw in the salad..." Christina Applegate is both a vegetarian and a cat owner.

The six rock stars that the Bundys hobnob with in first class in the episode "Rock of Ages" are Spencer Davis (of the Spencer Davis Group), Richie Havens, Robbie Krieger (of the Doors), Mark Lindsay (of Paul Revere and the Raiders), Peter Noone (of Herman's Hermits) and John Sebastian (of The Lovin' Spoonful).

David Garrison (Steve Rhodes) quit the series to go back to a Broadway career. When he came back to the series in the pirate episode, he tortured all the others by singing show tunes.

The Bundys go gold prospecting and Al buys a claim from an old grizzled prospector who Al says "looks like John Byner." Byner, a regular on *The*

Ed Sullivan Show and host of *Bizarre*, actually played the prospector.

At the end of the seventh season episode "Movie Show," when Kelly and Bud go to the movies, they sit in the theater during the end credits, and comment on the names of all the behind-the-scenes members of the crew as they go by: art director Richard Improta, associate director Sam W. Orender, and so on.

Series creators Ron Leavitt and Michael G. Moye appear as passengers in an elevator in the fifth season episode where Kelly moves out.

In the sixth season episode "Kelly Does Hollywood Part II," the fictitious show posters seen in the studio hall, *Black Cop, White Girl, The Homeless Detective, Amos and Andrew* and *Me and the Shiksa*, all feature Leavitt and Moye and staff writers, including Larry Jacobsen, in their credits.

Leavitt also appears in the sixth season episode "Al Bundy, Shoe Dick" as Jack Dallas.

In the episode where the Bundys go to the UK, story editors Jacobsen and Stacie Lipp do a walk-on together. Jacobsen says, "Shoe salesman." The voices of the two "nearby dogs" in this episode are provided by Leavitt and Moye.

In the seventh season episode where the Bundys vote, Leavitt and Jacobsen have cameo appearances during the closing news report. Cynthia Allison, who plays the news anchor, is really a reporter for KNBC in Los Angeles.

Buck the Dog's voice was provided by staff writer Kevin Curran (except for special episodes, when it was done by Richard "Cheech" Marin). This was not revealed until halfway through the sixth season.

Former child stars Gary Coleman (*Diff'rent Strokes*) and Danny Bona-

duce (*The Partridge Family*) appear in the episode "How Green Was My Apple," where Al and Jefferson fight over an apple.

Christina Applegate's (Kelly) mother, Nancy Priddy, appears as Mrs. Writeman in the fourth season episode where Al buys a used car.

Kelly gets a television job in one episode, and Jefferson (Ted McGinley) and Marcy visit her. A kid comes up to Jefferson and asks him, "Hey, aren't you that guy from *Happy Days*?" Jefferson replies, "No, kid, I don't know what you're talking about. My name is D'arcy, Jefferson D'arcy." Then another kid asks, "So was that your name on *Love Boat* too?" McGinley was a regular on both *Happy Days* and *The Love Boat*.

The eighth season episode "Assault and Batteries" was part of a FOX 3-D "FOX-o-rama" special. The end credits feature Al and Peg wearing 3-D glasses and looking at the names scrolling by on a screen. Peg says, "I don't get it."

In "Dial B for Virgin," in which Bud joins Virgin Hotline, Al and Peg go to a video store, and a cardboard stand-up of *Dutch* (1991), starring Ed O'Neill (who plays Al), appears in the store. O'Neill's eyes are blacked out on the stand-up, and there's a bin of copies of the film that the store is trying to give away. Peggy picks one up, then sighs and drops it, disgusted.

In "The England Show, Part 1," when the Bundys fly to England, the pilot of the plane announces, "Can the man in seat 37b please put on your shoes? I'm choking." Al shoots back, "What? They show the movie *Dutch* and they think *I* stink?"

Leavitt and Moye named the family after their favorite wrestler, King Kong Bundy, and late in the series, Bundy even appeared on the show, denying that he was related to them.

M*A*S*H

A picture of Harry Morgan's wife can be seen on Sherman Potter's desk as Potter's wife, Mildred.

In Charles's (David Ogden Stiers) portion of the "Dreams" episode, he envisions himself as a magician. Stiers's first major role was in the 1978 film *Magic.*

One episode's storyline concerns Father Mulcahy (William Christopher) possibly having hepatitis, which is a reference to the fact that Christopher had himself just gone through a bout of the illness.

One of the films shown in the mess tent is the fictional *Bonzo Runs for President.* This was a dig at then–California governor Ronald Reagan running for president. Reagan appeared with the chimpanzee Bonzo in *Bedtime for Bonzo* (1951).

The Master

In this series starring Lee Van Cleef, an episode titled "The Hostage" has George Lazenby and David McCallum as guest stars. Both of them are supposed to be their famous spy characters (Lazenby as James Bond from *On Her Majesty's Secret Service* (1969), McCallum as Illya Kuryakin from *The Man from U.N.C.L.E.*), but McCallum is the villain, as though Kuryakin had become cynical in his later years.

Maverick

Bret Maverick's (James Garner) birthday is April 7, 1847. Garner's is also April 7.

Both Beau and Bart, in separate episodes, can be heard whistling the theme to the television series.

After James Garner staged his famous walkout from the series, the studio attempted to freeze him from working elsewhere. In one episode, two con men, discussing what to do with $10,000, suggest to Bart that he "should send it to [his] brother Bret ... he must need the money by now."

Melrose Place

Billy's (Andrew Shue) secretary, whom he dated, was named Elisabeth after his sister, actress Elisabeth Shue.

When Alison (Courtney Thorne-Smith) runs off to Palm Springs, Billy says, "You know, this isn't summer school," referring to the movie *Summer School* (1987) that Thorne-Smith was in.

In a 1995 episode, Michael and Kimberly are reprimanded by the chief of staff. His name, prominently shown on his door, is Calvin Hobbes, after the comic strip *Calvin & Hobbes.*

Millennium

Frank Black's address (as seen on the envelope at the end of the pilot) is Ezekiel Drive. Ezekiel is the name of a biblical prophet.

The episode "Gehenna" gets its name from a biblical term. It is a contraction for the Hebrew phrase "Ge-Ben-Hinnom" or "Valley of the Son of Hinnom," a place where trash was burned outside of Jerusalem and where, apparently, child sacrifice by immolation took place. It is also an allusion to hell—since the fires in the valley were never extinguished, the Hebrews reckoned it to what hell must be like.

The Millionaire

Tido Fedderson, wife of the show's producer, Don Fedderson, appeared in every episode of the series, usually in a cameo.

Mr. Smith

The voice of Mr. Smith, the talking orangutan who starred in this series, was provided by longtime television writer-producer Ed Weinberger.

Moonlighting

In one episode, someone makes a reference that the show had only won one out of the sixteen Emmy awards that it had been nominated for.

The Mothers-in-Law

Desi Arnaz, who was the show's executive producer, appeared occasionally as bullfighter Raphael del Gado.

Murder, She Wrote

The episode broadcast May 3, 1987, appropriately titled "Strangest of Bargains," reunited three of the stars of the film *Strange Bargain* (1949): Harry Morgan, Jeffrey Lynn and Martha Scott. They even played their characters from the film: Lt. Richard Webb, Sam Wilson and Georgia Wilson.

The puppet-show episode "Something Foul in Flappieville" included a foster child named Stevie who is adopted at the end of the episode. Stevie was played by Ian Shaw, grandson of Angela Lansbury. The opening credits even read "And Introducing Ian Shaw as Stevie." David Shaw, who is Lansbury's stepson (via husband Peter Shaw) and Ian's father, is also the head of Lansbury's production company.

Murphy Brown

Murphy (Candice Bergen) comes into her house, expecting a call from the doctor. She asks Eldin (Robert Pastorelli), "Have they called?" He answers, "Yes, but I thought you'd already chosen your long distance phone company." In another episode, Murphy herself answers the phone at work and says, "No, I don't want to change long distance carriers." Bergen does commercials for the long-distance phone company Sprint.

In another episode, Jim Dial complains about broadcast personalities who prostitute themselves by doing commercials, and while naming products that are hawked, he mentions "long-distance carriers" while looking directly at Murphy. He also complains about celebrities doing commercials for antacids (Charles Kimbrough [Jim Dial] has done ads for Mylanta) and satellite dishes (Joe Regalbuto [Frank] has done ads for Direct TV satellite dishes).

My Two Dads

After getting drunk, Paul Reiser and former Monkee Davey Jones (as a guest) sing first the *My Two Dads* theme song, then the Monkees' theme, ending with, "Hey, hey, we're the ... I never could remember how that goes."

Guest Tony Danza (as himself) is told that the series family has two dads, and says, "What a great idea for a TV show!"

Ned and Stacey

At one point in the first season's finale, Ned (Thomas Haden Church) watches television with Stacey's sister and her husband. He laughs at something and says, "That *Wings* is one zany show." Church had previously played Lowell the handyman on *Wings*.

The New Lassie

Jon Provost, who had played Timmy in the old *Lassie* series, appears as Uncle Steve.

Newhart

The final episode of this series contains the ultimate in-joke. The characters are seen a few years into the future, and at the end, Dick Loudon (Bob Newhart) gets hit by a golf ball and loses consciousness. Newhart wakes up in bed and tells his wife about the crazy dream he just had ... which was the entire *Newhart* series. His wife turns over ... and it is Suzanne Pleshette. Pleshette had played Emily Hartley, Newhart's wife on *The Bob Newhart Show*. In effect, *Newhart* was all a nightmare in the mind of psychiatrist Robert Hartley (Newhart's character on *The Bob Newhart Show*).

Newsradio

There are occasional references to Dave Foley's previous series, *The Kids in the Hall*. In one episode, Dave goes out and gets Bill the patch. He says, "I don't think he's a very good doctor." This is a reference to the "Bad Doctor" character, played by Foley, that appeared repeatedly on *The Kids in The Hall*. He had a long, "I'm a bad doctor" monologue in the original. In another *Newsradio* episode, Dave has a fantasy about space alien women. *The Kids in the Hall* once did a long sketch, known to fans as "the mini movie," about space women who go around making the world sexier. The sketch is called "Sex Girl Patrol."

In the episode originally broadcast October 23, 1996, Beth the secretary comes into Dave's office and tells him to sign some sort of order form. Afterwards, Dave says, "Hey, I didn't just sign for a stolen jeep, did I, Radar?" Beth, somewhat puzzled, replies, "I'm sorry, Dave. I don't watch *Star Trek*." Dave's line was actually word-for-word from an episode of *M*A*S*H*.

Night Court

Dan Fielding (John Larroquette) is being held at gunpoint by a woman with multiple personalities and he turns on the television to try to find a kind, gentle character for her to assume. However, he tunes into *The Texas Chainsaw Massacre* (1974) and says, "Seen that already." Larroquette's first job in showbiz was narrating the opening of his friend Tobe Hooper's *Texas Chainsaw Massacre*.

When Dan's mother visits, we find out his dirty little secret ... his first name is really "Reinhold." This is also the first name of the show's creator, Reinhold Weege.

9 to 5

Executive producer Jane Fonda (who also starred in the original film, *9 to 5*, 1980) appeared in one episode as a night watchperson.

Northern Exposure

In the final episode with Joel (Rob Morrow), Adam (Adam Arkin) refers to Joel as "Quiz Show Boy" when he directs his questions to him. This is a reference to Morrow's appearance in the film *Quiz Show* (1994).

Maggie's mother appeared three times during the series. In the first two appearances, she was played by Bibi Besch, who was even nominated for an Emmy for the role. However, the last time Maggie's mother appeared, in the final-season episode "The Mommy's Curse," she was played by a different actress, Debra Mooney. During the episode, she says, "Things change, Maggie. Take me, for instance."

Nowhere Man

There have been many references to the television show *The Prisoner*. In "Heart of Darkness," where Tom Veil tries to infiltrate a conspiracy training camp, the trainees are all assigned numbers ... and Tom is assigned "Number Six," the designation of the main character in *The Prisoner*.

N.Y.P.D. Blue

A character named Buck Naked has appeared twice on the show. He is an elderly man who flashes people and screams, "I'm Buck Naked!" He was a recurring character on creator Steven Bochco's previous series, *Hill Street Blues*.

The two main characters on the show, Andy (Sipowicz) and Bobby (Simone) have the same first name as two of *Hill Street Blues'* uniformed cops, Andy Renko and Bobby Hill.

In the episode "Girl Talk," when Martinez and Russell leave the bar after interviewing the bartender, they are walking along and, in the background, not really in focus, is a New York City Transit bus with a billboard on the side advertising this show's sister show, *Murder One*. The two shows even had a couple of crossover episodes.

One Life to Live

Shortly after going blind, Nora Gannon (Hillary B. Smith) is tracked by an escaped rapist to her beach house. Her boyfriend Bo (Robert S. Woods) arrives, but the rapist makes her get rid of him. However, Nora tips Bo off about what is happening by saying, "Don't wait until dark," in their brief conversation. The film *Wait Until Dark* (1967) had a similar storyline, that of a rapist stalking a blind woman.

Walter Slezak makes a guest appearance as Laszlo Braedeker, godfather of Vicki Lord. Lord was played by Erika Slezak, Walter's real-life daughter.

John Beradino has appeared in the series as his character from *General Hospital*, Steve Hardy, and William Mooney has appeared as his *All My Children* character, lawyer Paul Martin.

One Step Beyond

John Newland was the creator, host, and occasional director of this science fiction anthology series, also known as *Alcoa Presents*, and he even appeared in one episode, "The Sacred Mushroom." This would be the equivalent of Rod Serling making an acting cameo in an episode of *The Twilight Zone*.

The Outer Limits (1990s)

In the episode "Second Soul," Dr. Alders calls up a list of recent casualties on his computer. The last name in the list is "Yoshida, Ron." Ron Yoshida was the editor of the episode.

In the episode "Resurrection," a sign indicates that all the robots are property of the Innobotics Corporation. Innobotics is the name of the company that built Valerie 23 in a first season episode.

Paradise

Hugh O'Brian, who played Wyatt Earp in the classic western series *The Legend of Wyatt Earp*, and Gene Barry, who played Bat Masterson in *Bat Masterson*, appear in the two-part second season opener as their old characters. Barry again played Masterson in *The Gambler Returns: The Luck of the Draw* (1991 TV).

Chuck Connors and Johnny Crawford, who played Lucas McCain and Mark in the series *The Rifleman*, were reunited on one 1990 show, but as different characters.

Parker Lewis Can't Lose

Parker's sister, Shelley (Maia Brewton), doesn't want to let the new principal, Dr. Pankow (Gerrit Graham), know that she is related to Parker, so she tells him her last name is Nemec. Parker (Corey Nemec) looks at the camera and responds, "Nemec?"

In the same episode, Parker is seen "reading" a book on television acting and refers the school review board to (ratings competitors) *Hull High*, a show that seems to be having "choreography problems."

In the episode where Frank Lemmer dates Mrs. Musso's neice, David Faustino (Bud Bundy of *Married: with Children*) shows up in detention with "Polk High" on his shirt, put there by Lemmer, regardless of the fact "I don't even go to this school!"

Above the word "English" on the English office door is scrawled the word "Diane." Diane English is a television executive.

Parker's school holds a rally in one episode and standing in the crowd are some students holding a banner saying "Thank you for not watching *Eerie, Indiana*." *Eerie, Indiana* was the show's ratings competition.

Principal Grace Musso and her lackey Frank Lemmer, also known as "Musso and Frank," were named after The Musso and Frank Grill, which is a famous old restaurant located on Hollywood Boulevard.

Party of Five

The picture that Julia supposedly takes of herself in the season finale was a picture that had previously been widely distributed on the Internet for quite a while.

Perry Mason

In the series' final show, Police Lieutenant Drum (Richard Anderson) interrogates witnesses to a murder in a television studio. The witnesses were played by the crew of the series.

Anderson also remembers the judge in the episode: "The last day of that last episode we had a courtroom scene. Every week, they needed a different judge, and they brought in some day player. The fellow playing the judge this last week approached me and said, 'Mr. Anderson, I've enjoyed watching you play this role the last year.' I didn't know who this guy was, but I could feel that he was something beyond a day player—I knew something was coming. We talked back and forth a little, he started to walk away, and then he said, 'Oh, by the way, my name is Erle Stanley Gardner.' They had put Gardner [novelist-creator of the character of Perry Mason] on the last day as the judge!"

The Phil Silvers Show (a.k.a. *You'll Never Get Rich*)

Early in 1959, CBS cancelled the show while it was at the height of its popularity and without consulting Silvers beforehand. This puts a new light on the last scene of the series final episode, titled "Weekend Colonel." Colonel Hall says to Captain Barker, "Wait a minute, Barker, it's 10 o'clock … time for my favorite television program." He switches on a small television set, which is connected to the closed circuit cameras that had just been installed on the base. The picture reveals Bilko and his henchmen locked behind bars. Hall says, "Wonderful show, isn't it? And the best part is … as long as I'm the sponsor, it'll never be cancelled." Bilko ends with, "Tha-tha-tha that's all folks."

An episode from the second season was entitled "Bilko's Television Idea." The plot revolved around the efforts of a television network to develop a new

sitcom vehicle for one of its star comedians. Having considered a number of
scenarios, they finally come up with
the idea of a show set on an army base.
This mirrored the real life situation
when Phil Silvers and Nat Hiken
spent several months trying to come
up with a suitable idea for what was to
be Silvers's first television show.

According to Silvers's autobiography,
boxer Rocky Graziano effectively acted
as a casting director for the show,
bringing in many former colleagues for
minor roles in the platoon. One of
them was named Cpl. Barbella, which
was Graziano's real name. And in the
episode "The Mess Hall Mess," Bilko
organizes a special dinner in honor of
the little-known President Graziano.

When Schick became a sponsor of
the show, the platoon members ceased
shaving by razors and lather and
switched to Schick electric shavers.
Likewise, the men no longer lit their
cigarettes with matches, using Schick
lighters instead.

Picket Fences

On the November 11, 1994 episode,
called "Rebels with Causes," in which
Waumbaugh has a seizure, Jill flies him
to Chicago Hope (of the series *Chicago
Hope*) for tests. Geiger is very rude to
her, and she complains to Watters.
"What is it with you people?" she asks
incredulously. "You think you're so special. You just may not be the best hospital in Chicago, much less the rest of
the country. More people go to that
other—what's its name—," referring to
Chicago Hope's competitor medical
series, *ER*. At the time, they were
scheduled opposite each other, and *ER*
was beating *Chicago Hope* so badly that
Watters shows his irritation and snaps
back, "We don't talk about that other
hospital!"

The X-Files episode "Red Museum"
was about teenagers in a small town
named Delta Glen, Wisconsin, being
abducted and returned with the words
"He" or "She Is One" written on their
backs. A couple of subplots in the
episode concerned bio-engineered
cows and a vegetarian sect in red
turbans. In the *Picket Fences* episode
"Away in the Manger," which aired
same week as "Red Museum," Carter
Pike mentions Delta Glen, which is in
a different part of the state (*Picket
Fences* is set in the fictitious town of
Rome, Wisconsin). Pike says, "The
FBI was crawling all over that town
last week," looking into a possible
connection involving the DNA of cows.
He even names Dr. Larson, who was
killed in a helicopter crash in the
X-Files episode. Originally, there was
to be an unprecedented internetwork
crossover on this particular episode
between *The X-Files*, which airs on
FOX, and CBS's *Picket Fences*, but it
never came to be. Both shows are
produced through 20th Century–Fox
Television, and the CBS drama aired in
the hour after *The X-Files*. Mulder and
Scully were going to appear in *Picket
Fences*, and the episode "Red Museum"
was also going to tie in with the *Picket
Fences* episode, but this line was all
that remained. Mulder's role was
rewritten for the character Agent
Morell, who appeared in the *Picket
Fences* episode.

In "Freezer Burn," creator-
producer David Kelley's wife, Michelle
Pfeiffer, has a cameo. The sheriff
interviews all the clients of George,
the dead masseuse, and she is one
of them. She is dressed frumpily,
with 1950s-style glasses and a floppy
hat.

The first season features a mayor
named Bill Pugin. Bill Pugin was the

name of the actor who played Marlee Matlin's sign language interpreter on the show *Reasonable Doubts*. At the time, Matlin was romantically involved with David Kelley.

Pinky and the Brain

In the opening sequence, Brain is writing equations on the chalkboard. One of the equations he writes is "THX=1138." This is a reference to the groundbreaking George Lucas sci-fi film *THX-1138* (1970).

In the episode set in the Middle Ages, Pinky and Brain attempt to cast a magic spell to take over the world. Among the standard ingredients on the shelf is a jar labeled "Ishtar Box Office Receipts." *Ishtar* (1987) was a film that lost an enormous amount of money. Needless to say, the jar is empty.

Police Squad!

This police-show spoof series is based closely on the very straight Lee Marvin cop series, *M Squad*. Creators Jerry Zucker, David Zucker and Jim Abrahams usually kept a video tape of a key *M Squad* episode on the set and referred to it repeatedly during filming. They continued the *M Squad* influence into the first film, *The Naked Gun: From the Files of Police Squad* (1988).

The Prisoner

Much speculation has been raised by fans of the show that Number Six is actually John Drake, the character that Patrick McGoohan played in his previous series, *Secret Agent*. McGoohan adamantly denies this. However, the similarities between the two series, some obviously intentional, tend to contradict him. There are a few reasons why McGoohan would prefer that John Drake not be associated with *The Prisoner*. One is financial: if Number Six actually was John Drake, then the creators of *Secret Agent* would definitely feel entitled to some kind of royalty. Besides that, McGoohan may have believed that any connection between this series and *Secret Agent* would serve to weaken the complex philosophical undertones of the series. McGoohan was probably hoping not to be typecast as John Drake, secret agent, as well.

Some instances in *The Prisoner* where parallels to *Secret Agent* appeared: in the episode "Dance of the Dead," Number Six appears at a carnival dressed in a tuxedo and looking very much like John Drake. Furthermore, the episode "The Girl Who Was Death" was originally written for *Secret Agent*, but rewritten for this series. Not only does actor Christopher Benjamin reprise his role of Potter from *Secret Agent* in this episode, but there is a minor character in this episode, a bowler, played by an actor named John Drake.

The episode "Free for All," where Number Six (Patrick McGoohan) runs for the office of Number Two, was written by McGoohan under the pseudonym of Paddy Fitz, which he derived from his mother's maiden name, Fitzpatrick.

George Markstein, a former reporter on British Intelligence matters during World War II, was the script editor for the show. He appears in the opening credits of each episode except "Fall Out," the final one. He is the man behind the desk when Number Six turns in his resignation. He also appears in the episode "Many Happy Returns," where Number Six escapes and makes his way back to London to tell his superiors of the Village. After leaving Mrs. Butterworth's, Number

Six sees Markstein, again sitting at his desk. Markstein and McGoohan had a falling out over the themes of the series, and, after 13 episodes, Markstein quit the program.

In several episodes, characters in the Village sign off with a salute of a circle made by the thumb and forefinger of the right hand and say, "Be seeing you." According to Norma West, who played the observer in the episode "Dance of the Dead," McGoohan explained the meaning of the salute to her during production of the show. It is the same salute that was used by ancient Christians: the sign of the fish.

A real estate sign is seen in front of Number Six's London house in the final episode, "Fall Out." The name of the real estate company is Lageu & Son, Estate Agents. John Lageu was the set dresser for this episode.

In the episode "Do Not Forsake Me, Oh My Darling," where Number Six switches bodies with the Colonel (Nigel Stock), he proves his identity by comparing his handwriting with a letter that he had addressed over a year ago. The address on the letter is Portmeirion Road, after the name of the real-life resort in South Wales where the series was filmed. During the filming of the series, the actual location of the Village was kept a secret (except for subtle hints like this) until the final episode, which contained the credit, "In the grounds of the Hotel Portmeirion, Penrhyndeudraeth, North Wales, by courtesy of Mr. Clough Williams-Ellis." Williams-Ellis was the architect of the resort, and was happy to make it available for filming, under the stipulation that the location was not revealed until after all filming was completed.

In the episode "Many Happy Returns," Number Six's birthday is established to be March 19, which is also McGoohan's birthday.

Punky Brewster

The name "Punky Brewster" was provided by NBC Entertainment executive Brandon Tartikoff, who had known a girl named Punky Brewster when he attended Lawrenceville School in New Jersey. The real Punky Brewster was tracked down and received a royalty for the use of her name. Incidentally, Brewster's dog on the show is named Brandon, after Tartikoff.

Quantum Leap

In the episode "Portrait for Troian," screenwriter Deborah Pratt appears as Troian Giovanni Claridge, writer-director Paul Brown as Julian Claridge, and creator Donald P. Bellisario as Timothy Mintz, who is seen in the mirror. Pratt was also married to Bellisario at the time and Bellisario and Pratt's daughter Troian (the episode "A Portrait for Troian" was named after her) appeared in another episode. She played Teresa, the daughter of the woman Sam leaps into, in the episode "Another Mother."

Ziggy the computer's voice is provided by Pratt as well. She is also the one who narrates the opening of each show.

During the basketball game in the second season's opener, entitled "The Leap Home," Al (Dean Stockwell) remarks that he feels "like Dennis Hopper in *Hoosiers*!" Stockwell and Hopper are good friends.

Roddy McDowall appeared as St. John, who assumed Al's position in "A Leap for Lisa." McDowall and Stockwell are also good friends. Hopper and McDowall both attended Stockwell's ceremony when he got his star on the Hollywood Walk of Fame.

At the end of "M.I.A." Roddy McDowall is given screen credit for providing the photo of young Al that is seen in Beth's living room. ("Dean Stockwell photograph courtesy of Roddy McDowell.") Roddy McDowell is a photographer and has long been known for taking pictures of other celebrities, especially close friends of his.

In "Thou Shalt Not," Bert is played by Stockwell's buddy Russ Tamblyn. In one scene, Bert dances with a woman and steps on her toes. He apologizes to her and says, "I haven't danced in a long time." Tamblyn is an exceptional dancer, and was one of the leads of the film *West Side Story* (1961). He also danced with Dean Stockwell in the last scene of *Human Highway* (1982).

Stockwell mentioned another friend of his on the series: Bob Dylan. In the episode "One Strobe Over the Line," he mentions catching a Bob Dylan concert "down in the Village."

In the episode "Roberto!," a video from the previous *Quantum Leap* episode "Glitter Rock" can be seen on a television behind Janie when she and Sam have their first argument.

During the filming of the episode "Runway," Bakula dislocated his foot. He still had to film three more episodes with his bad foot, so the writers wrote injuries into the stories. In "Future Boy," Sam trips and "sprains his ankle" when first leaving the time capsule. When Sam becomes the "Piano Man," he gets shot in the leg early on in the episode. During "Private Dancer" they apparently just shot Bakula full of painkillers.

Sam tells Al that he cannot possibly go out on stage and sing in *Man of La Mancha* in the episode "Catch a Falling Star." Al reassures him, and tells him that it is just the boondocks, "not Broadway." Bakula was a Tony-nominated Broadway musical and comedy leading man prior to landing the part on *Quantum Leap*. He had even performed *Man of La Mancha* in regional theater.

Dean's brother Guy Stockwell plays a bookie named Mr. Edwards in the episode "The Right Hand of God." He wanted the boxer that Sam leaped into to throw a fight.

Bellisario himself has appeared as a man in a bar in the episode "Mirror Image."

Screenwriter-director Chris Ruppenthal appeared as Joshua Raye (in the mirror) in "The B**gieman."

The white-haired man who is pushing Sam along in the gurney in "8½ Weeks" is played by Harold Frizzell, Scott Bakula's stand-in.

Director James Whitmore, Jr., has appeared as Clayton Fuller (seen in the mirror) in "Trilogy Part I," as the police captain in "Mirror Image," and as Bob Crockett in "8½ Months."

Costume designer Jean-Pierre Dorleac plays the guy who says "Butcher, baker…" in "Shock Theatre." Also, the nasty husband in "Southern Comforts" is named Jake Dorleac.

Producer Harker Wade appeared as Dylan Powell (seen in the mirror) in "Temptation Eyes."

Gooshie (Dennis Wolfberg) is named after a character in Bellisario's earlier series, *Tales of the Gold Monkey*. He was played by wheelchair-bound actor Les Jankey.

Sam's birthday (mentioned in "Starlight, Starbright" and "Mirror Image") is the same as Bellisario's— August 8. Also, Bellisario was born in

Cokeburg, Pennsylvania, the town in the episode "Mirror Image."

Bellisario's son Michael plays Martin Elroy, Jr., the son of the man Sam leaps into in "A Tale of Two Sweeties." He is also one of several kids sitting at the children's table at a wedding rehearsal dinner in "Camikazi Kid" and he and another boy are fixing a bicycle outside the bar when Sam runs out in "Mirror Image."

There are many historical references through the series. Examples include:

In "How the Tess Was Won," Sam hears a bespectacled young boy named Buddy singing his song "Piggy Soo-ee" and suggests he change it to "Peggy Sue," the name of Buddy Holly's first hit.

In "Camikazi Kid," Sam runs into a black kid named Michael in a hotel men's room. Sam teaches him to moonwalk, a move popularized by Michael Jackson.

In "Thou Shalt Not...," Sam performs the Heimlich Maneuver on Dr. Heimlich at a bake sale.

In "The B**gieman," the neighbor's kid is named Stevie, and his mother is named Mrs. King. His dog is named Cujo and his girlfriend is named Carrie, references to Stephen King novels.

In "It's a Wonderful Leap," Sam, as a taxi driver, tells a young boy that one day there will be skyscrapers all over Manhattan, and there will be a tall, glass tower (the Trump Tower) where he drops him off. The doorman opens the door for the boy's father and says, "Good evening, Mr. Trump," and the boy's father says, "Come along, Donald."

In the episode "Dr. Ruth," Sam encounters Anita Hill, the woman from the Clarence Thomas Supreme Court confirmation hearings.

In the episode "Lee Harvey Oswald," where Sam leaps into Oswald, there is a scene where Oswald, as a private in the Marines in 1959, is stationed at MACS-9, in Tustin, California. He has a duty roster, and a Marine sergeant who has just been transferred there comes up to him and asks Oswald if he can help him locate some of his buddies that are also stationed there. The sergeant has a name over his pocket: "Bellisario." Scott Bakula mentioned this scene while hosting the *Quantum Leap* marathon on the Sci-Fi Channel, and apparently this incident actually took place between Donald Bellisario (the series creator) and Lee Harvey Oswald.

Quincy, M.E.

In an episode that guest stars Michael Durrell as an incompetent emergency doctor, an overweight man has a heart attack while bowling. The paramedics are told to take him to Durrell's clinic, but one paramedic says, "I think we should take him to Rampart." Rampart was the fictional hospital in the series *Emergency!*

Ray Bradbury Theater

The episode "Banshee" is based on an experience in creator Ray Bradbury's early career: the assignment from director John Huston to write the screenplay for *Moby Dick* (1956) and the subsequent voyage to Ireland to work with Huston on the project. In the episode, a young screenwriter named Douglas Rogers (Bradbury's middle name is Douglas) journeys to the manor house of maverick film director John Hampton (Peter O'Toole) to work with Hampton on the script for his next film, *The Beast.*

The Real World

In an episode in which Eric and a few others horse around in a shopping mall, Eric mentions John Musacha. "John Musacha" is an alias used by the comedy team known as the Jerky Boys. This episode was filmed before the Jerky Boys came out with their own album, while their material was only found on underground tapes.

ReBoot

The penguin that appears in the episodes "Identity Crisis," "Trust No 1," and "Web World Wars" is a tribute to animator Nick Park's award-winning Claymation short, *The Wrong Trousers*.

In "Talent Night," when Megabyte is playing the guitar, Bob commands Glitch for a B.F.G. This is a reference to the DOOM PC game. There, BFG stands for Big Ferocious Gun. Here it stands for Big Fancy (or Fucking) Guitar.

In the episode "The Tear," Alpha Wing proceeds on heading 1138. This is a reference to George Lucas's futuristic film, *THX-1138* (1970).

The Guardian of Mainframe, Bob, takes his name from a file format used on the old Bosch FGS animation system that was popular in the 1980s: the files were referred to as .bob files.

The real name of Captain Capacitor, the Crimson Binome, is "Gavin." He is named after *ReBoot* creator and head animator Gavin Blair.

The wise man in the series is named Phong and his favorite game is Pong. Both of these became big names in computer graphics in the early 1970s. Pong, created by Atari, was the first successful coin-operated video game. Phong Bui-Tuong described a better method for shading polygons in June 1975. His method produces more realistic images than Gourand shading.

The Trias Effect is revealed to be the only thing capable of stopping Megabyte's Medusa Virus. Jenny Trias was the ABC head of children's programming.

In order to go through the stained-glass window to the castle in "Quick and the Fed," Bob says "B.S.'n P." to Glitch. Also, the writing on the life raft that comes out of Enzo's big gun in "The Belly of the Beast" reads "B.S.'n P. Approved." And in "Talent Night," the Small Town Binomes sing "BS&P" to the tune of "YMCA." B.S.'n' P. stands for the ABC Broadcast Standards & Practices (BS&P) department. Broadcast Standards and Practices is the network self-censorship department that decides what can and cannot be seen and heard. *ReBoot* episodes have often been changed based on demands made by the ABC network BS&P department. Sometimes it is as small a change as removing a sound effect. BS&P demanded that *ReBoot* not show acts of violence that were easily imitated (such as throwing a rock through a window), so the animators started putting digs at them into the storyline. Enzo's big gun had to be made nonviolent, hence the life raft. Note that Miss Emma Fee in the episode "Talent Night" is a "Prog Censor."

Many characters, places, objects and terms take their names (or variations thereof) from computer terms. For instance, the football-shaped familiar belonging to Hexadecimal is named Scuzzy, after SCSI, or "Small Computer System Interface," which is used for disks and tape drives and pronounced "scuzzy." Wizzywig is a production company in Mainframe, used by Enzo to convince Dot and Bob that

Megabyte kidnapped him in "The TIff." It is named after WYSIWYG, or "What You See Is What You Get" (pronounced "whizzywig"), which describes a word processor that shows what the finished page looks like. Insulting terms in the show include calling someone "basic" (after BASIC, Beginners All-purpose Symbolic Instruction Code, a simple computer language) and "low density" (which describes a floppy disk with only 720 K bytes instead of 1440 K). The unseen mayor of Mainframe is named command.com, after the program on MS-DOS personal computers that listens for commands to be typed on the keyboard. There is an ad for the establishment DeeCee's Power Bar on the billboard outside Dot's Diner. A D.C. power bar is a thick wire carrying several amperes of direct current. Enzo's red and yellow dog with the incredibly strong jaws is named Frisket, which is a stencil used by airbrush artists to cover certain parts of a painting while they work on other parts. At one point, Dot says, "that's creepy, it gives me the jaggies." "Jaggies" is the stair-step effect when a diagonal line is drawn on a bitmap. The band in "Talent Night" named The Primitives consist of a cone, a sphere and a cube. In 3-D solids modeling, intricate shapes are formed by using variations of the "primitive shapes": sphere, cube, cone and cylinder.

The episode "Trust No 1" takes its name from the motto of Fox Mulder (David Duchovny) of *The X-Files*, and the opening title is even in the typeface of *The X-Files* opening titles, green glow and all. Two characters appear that are parodies of the *X-Files* characters of Mulder and Dana Scully (Gillian Anderson): Fax Modem and Data Nully. Anderson even provides the voice for Agent Nully, and Nully is wearing the same sort of cross necklace that Scully wears. Anderson's ex-husband, production designer Clyde Klotz, worked for a time on *ReBoot*.

In this episode, when Mainframe Security turn their spotlights on, they go green, green, green, yellow, red, the order of the lights at an NHRA drag race. And the garbage man in the opening says, "Garbage In, Garbage Out ..." This is a programmers' mantra which means that feeding unreliable data to a computer program produces unreliable results.

Red Dwarf

The words "Level Nivelo" are on the walls of the ship's corridors. "Nivelo" is Esperanto for "level." The ship and its crew are all supposed to be bilingual, knowing both English and Esperanto.

In the episode "Stasis Leak," Rimmer complains, "Everything always goes wrong for me. I'm probably the only person in the world to buy a Topic Bar without a single hazelnut in it." Topic Bars are candy bars sold in the U.K. One ad campaign for them used the slogan "A hazelnut in every bite."

"Gordon Bennett" is a name used by the characters, most notably Holly, as an expletive ("Gordon Bennett! What was that?"). James Gordon Bennett was an American newspaper tycoon and multimillionaire who is listed in the *Guinness Book of World Records* for "Greatest Engagement Faux Pas." Bennett's engagement to Caroline May was broken in 1877 when he arrived late and drunk at the May family's New York mansion and urinated in the fireplace in front of his hosts. Today, Bennett's name is used in England as a euphemism for an expression of disbelief.

Most of the reversed dialogue in the episode "Backwards" is pretty much what the subtitles say it is, or what you'd expect from the context. There are, however, two notable exceptions:

When Lister and the Cat steal a bicycle, its owner yells after them, "You scoundrels! Return my bike immediately!"...at least, according to the subtitles. What he actually says, however, is, "Oi! Hey! Oi! You robbing bastards, that's our tandem!"

Later, when the stage manager comes in to yell at Rimmer and Kryten, he appears to be blaming them for starting the "fight." Here is what he is actually saying: "Frankly, your act's crap! Anyway, anybody could have done it. I hate the lot of you. Bollocks to you! ... You are a stupid, square-headed bald git, aren't you? I ain't pointing at you, I'm pointing at you. But I'm not actually addressing you, I'm addressing the one prat in the country who's bothered to get hold of this recording, turn it round, and actually work out the rubbish that I'm saying! What a poor, sad life he's got!"

In the episode "Camille," Lister is watching *Tales of the Riverbank: The Next Generation*. *Tales of the Riverbank* was a Canadian series from the 1970s using live animals who talked and lived in a little riverbank community. It is perhaps better known as *Hammy the Hamster*.

Remington Steele

Stephanie Zimbalist's (Laura) father, Efrem Zimbalist, Jr., has appeared as Steele's mentor, Daniel Chalmers. Chalmers was eventually discovered to be Steele's dad.

Renegade

Executive producer Stephen J. Cannell appeared as a regular on this series

as crooked cop Lt. "Dutch" Dixon. He is the one who frames Reno (Lorenzo Lamas) for murder.

Rhoda

The show's producer, Lorenzo Music, provides the voice of Rhoda's unseen doorman, Carlton.

RoboCop

The two newscasters are named Rocky and Bull, after the cartoon moose and squirrel, *Rocky and Bullwinkle*.

Rocky and Bullwinkle

The "J."s in Rocket J. Squirrel and Bullwinkle J. Moose are in honor of their creator, Jay Ward (also see *The Simpsons*).

Roger Ramjet

In one episode, Doodle, one of the cadets, says to Roger, "That's as funny as a Gary Owens joke." Owens, a professional announcer and voice-over man, provided the voice for Roger Ramjet.

Roseanne

Lecy Goransen, who plays Becky, left for three years of college and was replaced by Sarah Chalke, who played the same character. At the end of Chalke's first episode, the family sits around watching *Bewitched* and Rosanne comments on how they simply changed the actor who played Darrin Stephens on that show (Dick York was replaced by Dick Sargent). Rosanne says that she couldn't believe that a television show could do something like that and the whole family agrees with her that they preferred the original Darrin.

When Goransen returns, everyone asks Becky questions like, "where were you … it seems like you've been gone three years!" Then, in the closing shot, they sing a song reminiscent of *The Patty Duke Show*'s "Identical Cousins" with both Beckys (Chalke and Goransen) "mirroring" each other even though they look nothing like each other.

Llanford, the setting for the show, is named after Llanview, the town in Roseanne Arnold's favorite soap, *One Life to Live*.

Three *One Life to Live* regulars have even appeared on the show as their soap characters. They are Clint Ritchie (as Clyde Buchanan), Bob Woods (as Bo Buchanan) and John Loprieno (as Cord Roberts).

Ryan's Hope
Young heroine Mary Ryan Fenelli was named after a writer on the show, Mary Ryan Muniestieri.

St. Elsewhere
On *St. Elsewhere*, almost all of the pages over the loudspeaker were inside jokes. Friends of the writers were always listening to see if they got paged each week. Other pages were of fictional characters from other shows. One example was a page for "Dr. Morton Chegley," who was played by Lloyd Nolan on the series *Julia*. Dr. Auschlander (Norman Lloyd) refers to Dr. Morton Chegley as his personal physician in at least one episode, as well. Another time, Dr. John Robinson was paged. This was the name of the character played by Guy Williams on *Lost in Space*. The classic "Dr. Howard, Dr. Fine, Dr. Howard…" has also been used (see *Young Doctors in Love*, 1982).

The name of an NBC executive was once given to a cadaver.

Jack Riley, who played the troubled Mr. Carlin on *The Bob Newhart Show*,

appeared in one episode as Mr. Carlin, a patient in the psychiatric ward. He is watching television with John Doe #6 (Oliver Clark), an amnesiac who appeared a number of times on *St. Elsewhere*. Incidentally, Clark also played a patient of Dr. Hartley on *The Bob Newhart Show*. While channel surfing, they come upon *The White Shadow*, and Mr. Carlin comments, "Hey, *The White Shadow*. The guy who came up with this show sure had his act together." That guy was Bruce Paltrow, *St. Elsewhere*'s executive producer. Then they switch to *The Mary Tyler Moore Show*. John Doe #6 begins to believe he is Mary Richards and that various staff members are other *MTM* show characters. One of the guest stars in this *St. Elsewhere* episode was Betty White, a regular on *Mary Tyler Moore*, and when "Mary" sees Betty White's character, he exclaims, "Sue Ann! Sue Ann Niven, the Happy Homemaker! It's me, Mary!" *The Mary Tyler Moore Show*, *The Bob Newhart Show*, *The White Shadow* and *St. Elsewhere* were all MTM productions.

In an episode appropriately titled "Cheers" and originally broadcast on March 27, 1985, Westphal, Craig and Auschlander stop by the bar on *Cheers* for drinks. The "Cheers" sign is also visible during one of Jack's strolls through Boston (see *Cheers*).

Ehrlich (Ed Begley, Jr.) and Axelrod (Stephen Furst) try to cheer up Fiscus (Howie Mandel) by putting surgical gloves over their heads and blowing them up. When this fails to do the trick, one of them notes that it wasn't that funny even when they saw some comic do it on television, either. Mandel's inflated-rubber-glove-on-the-head was a trademark from his stand-up routine.

Mandel's stand-up career received a

number of ribs during the series. In a third season episode, Mark and Ellen Craig have their first lovemaking session after several months. Afterwards, Ellen turns on the television to see who is on *Merv Griffin*. Mark says, "Probably some stupid comic." She turns on the television (not seen by the viewer), and we can clearly hear Howie Mandel doing his stand-up routine. Mark says, "What's he wearing ... a hand? Turn it off."

Warren Coolidge, one of the orderlies, was played by Byron Stewart, who played the same character on *The White Shadow* (which was produced by the same company). He even explained that he played basketball at Boston College on the recommendation of his coach, but he blew out his knee and that is why he was working at St. Eligius. In one episode, Timothy van Patten, who had played Salami on *The White Shadow*, appears on *St. Elsewhere* as another character, and Coolidge spots him and says, "Hey Salami ... it's me, Coolidge!" Van Patten replies, "I don't know what you're talking about ... you got the wrong guy."

Mark Craig convalesces at home, recovering from his hand injury and playing with toy trains. He remarks, "This is the most fun I've had since closing the Kim-Chi Palace with B.J. Hunnicutt." Presumably, Craig knows the surgeon from the series *M*A*S*H* from their days in Korea.

Two police officers are introduced as "Mike Stone" and "Pete Malloy." Stone was a character on *The Streets of San Francisco* and Malloy was one of the leads on *Adam-12*.

The name of the hospital's anesthesiology resident, Dr. Stephen Kiley, was taken from the show *Marcus Welby, M.D.* James Brolin played Kiley

on that show. He was Welby's young associate who made house calls on motorcycle.

Westphall refers to "Paul Lochner, my colleague at Boston General" in one episode. Dr. Paul Lochner was the name of James Daly's character on the show *Medical Center*.

In one episode, a patient named "Cindy Cation" is mentioned. She apparently has had over a hundred episodes, but Dr. Fiscus feels she will last forever. This is a reference to *St. Elsewhere* passing the 100 episode milestone number to go into syndication.

During their trip to Philadelphia, Mark Craig (William Daniels) says to his wife, "I don't know what it is about this place—it makes me feel like singing and dancing." This is an allusion to Daniels's role as John Adams in the movie musical *1776* (1972). Craig even sings the song "It's Hot as Hell in Philadelphia," from the film *1776*, and in the same episode he reminisces that when he was in medical school (in Philadelphia), he was "obnoxious and disliked," a direct quote from *1776*.

The episode in which Ehrlich has cold feet about his wedding to Lucy contains several references to the movie *The Graduate* (1967). There is even a scene where Mark Craig (William Daniels), berating Ehrlich for his immaturity, says to him, "When are you going to graduate?" Daniels played the father of Dustin Hoffman's character in *The Graduate*.

Early in season six, there is a scene with Jack Morrison (David Morse) and his wife Joanne as Jack prepares to leave for work. Joanne is not actually seen, and there is a big deal made about the fact that she is in bed hiding under the sheet. Jack, in reference to a party they are planning, says, "I've invited thirty-something guests." The reason Joanne is not shown is because Patricia Wettig, who played Joanne, had left the show at the end of season five to take the role of Nancy Weston on the show *thirtysomething*.

As Birch (Jamie Rose) picks up her severance check in a fifth season episode, Griffin (Bruce Greenwood) gives her a bouquet of flowers, saying "Red roses for a blue lady." *Lady Blue* was a short-lived police drama that aired in the 1985-86 season starring Jamie Rose in the title role. It had just been cancelled prior to Rose getting her role on *St. Elsewhere*.

A fourth season episode features a patient who thinks he is a vampire. Axelrod explains that his symptoms are actually caused by a rare genetic disease. He replies to Axelrod, "After all these years as a misfit of science, it's going to be hard to live as a manimal like you." *Misfits of Science* and *Manimal* were two short-lived NBC series.

In a fall 1986 episode, after the rival medical series *Kay O'Brien* debuted opposite *St. Elsewhere*, one physician mentions to another that "O'Brien" had gone to New York. The other doctor slyly retorts, "I'll bet she won't last thirteen weeks." He was right.

The series' final episode was packed with in-jokes.

The episode opens with Dr. Fiscus examining a well-dressed older man with white hair and glasses. Fiscus says, "So you see, General Sarnoff, it's quite a network and optic nerves need their rest. So do your eyes a favor and cut down on the time you spend in front of the television." General Sarnoff was a broadcasting pioneer and former head of RCA.

A patient named Mr. Pearson is having his hair cut before starting chemotherapy. Dr. Griffin calls the barber "Floyd," a reference to Floyd the Barber (Howard McNear) on *The Andy Griffith Show*. The barber on this show is even dressed like *Andy Griffith*'s Floyd.

Mr. Pearson's heart stops beating while the doctors are saying goodbye to each other. There is an announcement over the intercom: "Code Blue ... Room 222 ... Code Blue...," a reference to *Room 222*, the old high school series which also starred Eric Laneuville, who plays Luther Hawkins on *St. Elsewhere*.

One of the doctors does an autopsy on a Henry Blake, patient #4-0-7-7, whose cause of death is thought to be injuries sustained in a helicopter crash, referring to Maclean Stevenson's character from *M*A*S*H* and his fate.

Also in the final episode, Coolidge runs around the hospital looking for a one-armed patient named Mr. Mirkin. When he spots him, he says, "Dr. Kimble's looking for you!" Nurse Rosenthal refers to him as "Mr. Mirkin, Dr. Kimble's patient. He's a fugitive." Eventually, we are told that Coolidge captures the man on top of a water tower on the hospital roof. All this is a reference to the television series *The Fugitive*.

During Coolidge's chase, he is blocked by a hospital gurney, and cries out, "C'mon, move that gurney, Hal!" This is a reference to the director of *Late Night with David Letterman*, Hal Gurnee.

Another couple of *Mary Tyler Moore* references were seen in the final episode. Several characters gather for a group hug. When someone needs a tissue, they all walk over to get it, still embracing each other. This is a copy of a scene from the final episode of *The Mary Tyler Moore Show*. Ehrlich also asks about the song "It's a Long Way to Tipperary," which was sung by the *Mary Tyler Moore* cast in the series' finale.

Near the end of the episode, we meet one of the new first year residents who introduces himself as "Brandon Falsey ... Dr. Falsey. I arrived today." Mr. Pearson says to him, "I hate hospitals," and Falsey responds, "Yeah, this one's a dump ... but I'll turn it around." Brand and Falsey (Joshua Brand and John Falsey) were the names of the creators of the show. By the end of the first season, they had departed on less-than-amicable terms. This conversation is probably intended as a dig at them.

Sanford and Son

Redd Foxx plays a character named Fred Sanford. Foxx's real name was John Elroy Sanford, and his brother and father were both named Fred.

Santa Barbara

Marcy Walker decided to leave this show to star in the new Stephen J. Cannell series *Palace Guard*. In her last scene, Walker is shown getting into a limousine and being driven away from Santa Barbara. For the role of the chauffeur, the producers cast Stephen J. Cannell himself, the joke being that he was literally taking her away from *Santa Barbara*.

In one scene, magician Rafael Castillo (Henry Darrow) opens his suitcase and starts removing props. Among the objects he pulls out is the Daytime Emmy that Darrow had recently won for his portrayal of Castillo. He examines it for a moment, wonders aloud how it had gotten in there, and then sets it aside.

Saturday Night Live

In an episode with the original cast, John Belushi, playing Samurai Tailor,

made a suit for Buck Henry. Belushi nicked Henry for real with his sword and Henry had to have a band-aid put on his forehead before he could continue. By the end of the show, as a joke, everyone was wearing band-aids.

Saved by the Bell

In the wedding special, the name of the diamond is the "Considine Diamond." Gary Considine was the executive in charge of production for the show's Grade 12 season.

Scarecrow and Mrs. King

As the series opened, Mrs. King (Kate Jackson) had just recently divorced, and in one 1985 episode, Mr. King finally shows up. He was played by Sam Melville, who had played Kate Jackson's husband in the series *The Rookies*.

SCTV

Dave Thomas doubled as the show's voice-over announcer for the first two years, and he ad-libbed. One example: almost all of the promos for shows on SCTV had the tag line "Thursday night at 9," even though they couldn't possibly all be scheduled at the same time. At the end of the opening credits, Thomas originally introduced himself as "And Dave Thomas as The Beaver," again, just because he thought it was funny.

Red Rooster, who goes up to fix the SCTV satellite in the "Russian Show," is loosely based on Red Adair, the oil well fire fighter, but his voice, manner, dress, and beard are based on SCTV writer-producer Alan Rucker.

In "Six Gun Justice," a parody of the old-time cowboy serials, Eugene Levy plays a character modeled after Tom Mix. The character's name is Don Mills, and was named after a street

(Don Mills Road) and community in Toronto.

In the sketch "Shakespeare's Greatest Jokes," Joe Flaherty identifies himself as Sheldon Patinkin (an SCTV producer) and Dave Thomas identifies himself as Bernard Sahlins (an SCTV producer who goes back to Second City's earliest days). The sketch was originally written for Sir John Gielgud and Sir Ralph Richardson to do. They backed out after reading the script, however, because they said it "profaned the bard." The two producers' names were last minute back-ups when Thomas and Flaherty had to do the sketch themselves.

In the sketch "Pre-Natal Exercises," Andrea Martin identifies herself as "Betty Thomas-Neishauser." Betty Thomas played Officer Lucy Bates on *Hill Street Blues*, and her roots were on the Second City stage. Joe Flaherty later made fun of her on one episode, and she finally showed up as a semi-regular on the final NBC season of SCTV.

The saxophone-playing detective played by Joe Flaherty, Vic Arpeggio, takes his name as a play on words of the name of the late 1950s television detective show named *Johnny Staccato*. "Arpeggio" and "staccato" are both musical terms.

The two newscasters played by Levy and Flaherty, Earl Camembert and Floyd Robertson, are named after real-life Canadian newscasters Earl Cameron and Lloyd Robertson.

The celebrity interviewer played by Martin Short, Brock Linehan, is modeled after real-life Canadian interviewer Brian Linehan.

Rick Moranis appears in a "Do you know me?"–type commercial for a credit card as sculptor Henry Moore. He turns sideways, and there is a hole

through the side of his head. Moore's artwork (including his famous statue "Two Large Forms," outside of Toronto's Art Gallery of Ontario) is known for having large holes in it.

The character of Libby Wolfson's husband, who was played by Rick Moranis, was based on SCTV Producer Barry Sand.

There was a running joke on SCTV for quite a while in which Johnny LaRue (John Candy) was producing low-budget movies for Guy Caballero (Flaherty). LaRue, of course, fancied himself an artiste and tried to "art" up his pictures, but Guy always turned LaRue down when he requested a crane shot (a camera mounted on a crane) because it would be "too expensive." The in-joke here is that the actual SCTV budget was usually too small for a real crane shot, and it wasn't until their first NBC episode that they got to use a really impressive crane shot at the end of "Polynesiantown." It was at the end of the second NBC Christmas episode that Santa Claus finally granted Johnny LaRue his wish and said, "You finally got your crane shot" (see also *Canadian Bacon*, 1995).

Bobby Bittman (Eugene Levy) wrote the quote "A filmmaker makes films. A *complete* filmmaker does more," in the opening of his autobiography as a filmmaker. He read it to Dick Cavett (Rick Moranis). This is a reference to the Jerry Lewis book entitled *The Complete Filmmaker*.

Moe Green (Harold Ramis), who is kidnapped and eventually joins his abductors, is named after Alex Rocco's character, Don Corleone's Las Vegas connection, in *The Godfather* (1972).

The "Zontar" sequence, where Conrad Bain's twin brother Hank aids aliens in the takeover of SCTV, is a parody of the paranoia-alien takeover science fiction films of the 1950s and 1960s. However, it is a direct take-off of the low-budget sci-fi film *Zontar, The Thing from Venus* (1968). In the film, characters end up with alien mind-control devices on the back of their necks. In the SCTV spoof, the crew members who are taken over have lettuce leaves on the backs of their necks.

SeaQuest D.S.V.

In the episode "Hide and Seek," the helicopter from the series *Airwolf* makes an appearance.

The late Carol Bridger (seen as a hologram in the episodes "To Be or Not to Be," "Knight of Shadows" and "Ocean on Fire" and in pictures in "Treasures of the Mind" and "Vapors"), wife of Nathan Hale Bridger (Roy Scheider), is played by Scheider's wife, Brenda King. Executive producer Clifton Campbell also asked Roy if he wanted his son, Christian, to play the part of Bridger's grandson, Michael (who appeared in *Brave New World*), but Roy did not want an acting life for his son.

In the first season's opener, "To Be or Not to Be," Lucas wears a Florida Marlins jersey that says "World Champions 2010"—a reference to Scheider's film *2010* (1985).

In the episode "Sympathy of the Deep," Bridger is sitting at a cafe and behind him is a store sign that reads: "Quint's Nautical Treasures." Quint was the name of Robert Shaw's seafaring character in the Scheider film *Jaws* (1975). Quint's is an actual store at Universal Studios in Florida. This scene was filmed in front of the store.

In the first season episode "Hide And Seek," guest starring William Shatner, his transmission to seaQuest contains the call number "UNDW-JTK-NCC1701" at the bottom of the screen. This is meant to stand for "UNDerWater—JTK—Naval Construction Contract 1701," but in reality, NCC1701 was the call number of the USS *Enterprise* in the original *Star Trek* series, and the "JTK" would also refer to Shatner's character in the series, James T. Kirk.

Nametags of officers on the show have referred to series of the past. There were "J. Webb" (Jack Webb, who starred in the series *Dragnet*), "F. Nitti" (gangster Frank Nitti, an adversary of *The Untouchables*), "J. Barnes" (Peggy Lipton's character on *The Mod Squad* was named Julie Barnes) and "Baretta" (a reference to Robert Blake's detective series of the same name).

In the first season's finale, Royce Applegate's wife played Crocker's (Applegate) wife on the video letter.

There is a character in the second season of the series named Brody, which was Scheider's character in *Jaws*.

The Secret Service

This *Thunderbirds*-style marionette show, created by Gerry Anderson, contained a character named Father Stanley Unwin. His voice is provided by British comedian Stanley Unwin, whose comedic gimmick was a nonsensical way of speaking that came to be known as "Unwinese." Anderson was a great fan of his. When *The Secret Service* was still in its planning stages, the part of the offbeat pastor-spy was created and written specifically for Unwin, who also provided the full-body double in the live-action shots.

Seinfeld

Kramer reports to Jerry and his friends once that he had been horribly insulted by a woman he had broken up with: "She called me a hipster doofus!" The term "hipster doofus" had been applied to the Kramer character a couple of months earlier in a review of *Seinfeld* in *The Atlantic Monthly*, and the writers could not resist using the line—it was even repeated in a couple of other episodes.

The scene in the episode "Bro / Manzere" where Kramer is pursued by a group of German tourists is a take-off of a similar scene in the film *Marathon Man* (1976), where former Jewish concentration camp survivors recognize the "White Angel," a death camp dentist-torturer played by Sir Laurence Olivier. The scene flips back and forth from comic to serious as Kramer shows the Germans the Manzere.

In one episode, George (Jason Alexander) dances through the street in joy, swinging around a lamp post. This *Singin' in the Rain* (1952) dance is the same as the one Alexander did when he appeared in commercials for McDonald's McDLTs.

The "switch" dialogue in the episode "The Switch" ("It cannot be done," "Are you in or are you out," "I couldn't do it without you" and so on) is a reference to the film *The Sting* (1973).

Jerry and Kramer take a bus to Parsiphone, New Jersey, to find Jerry's parents, and Kramer's nose starts to bleed. He says, "Look at me … I'm fallin' apart here!" and, as Jerry puts his arm around him, the music swells in a parody of the film *Midnight Cowboy* (1969). The song that plays in the background is "Everybody's Talking" by Harry Nilsson, from the film.

The green Klein bicycle hanging in the background of Jerry's apartment was placed there because Michael Richards (Kramer) is into cycling.

In the episode "The Wigmaster," Elaine (Julia Louis-Dreyfus) is told that she has fabulous hair. Louis-Dreyfus does commercials for Nice and Easy hair color. In the commercials, everyone marvels at how beautiful her hair is.

In one episode, George and his girlfriend Susan cuddle in bed while watching the show *Mad About You*. In an earlier episode of *Mad About You*, Kramer (Michael Richards) made a guest appearance. Apparently, his apartment across the hall from Jerry used to be Paul's (Paul Reiser) bachelor pad.

Sesame Street

Ernie and Bert are named after characters (played, respectively, by Frank Faylen and Ward Bond) in *It's a Wonderful Life* (1946).

In the *Elmo Saves Christmas* special, Elmo wishes every day was Christmas, but he learns that maybe it's not so good an idea. During the episode, Ernie and Bert walk past a pile of television sets playing *It's a Wonderful Life*. George Bailey (James Stewart) is heard yelling, "Bert! Ernie! What's with you two?" Bert and Ernie (the Muppets) look at the set and do a double take when they hear their names.

In one episode, Kermit directs a scene from *Oklahoma* starring Forgetful Jones & the Cows, and has to shoot many retakes. Each time the slate is raised, the name of the cameraman is visible on it. It was the name of *Sesame Street*'s actual cameraman.

Big Bird's teddy bear is named Radar, which is a reference to Radar O'Reilly (Gary Burghoff) on *M*A*S*H*, who also had a teddy bear.

There was once a silly British Muppet dressed in a suit and bowler hat who taught us that one should never answer the telephone by saying, "Watermelons and cheese!" This muppet was a parody of Monty Python's John Cleese, and was even named "Monty."

Once, Bob was offered a job as a piano player but turned it down at the end because he did not want to leave his friends. He then offered to call a dog he knows who plays the piano ... named Rowlf. Rowlf was the name of the piano-playing dog on Jim Henson's *The Muppet Show*.

Sidekicks

Ernie Reyes, Jr.'s (Ernie Lee), younger brother, Lee Reyes, appears in flashbacks as a younger version of Ernie.

Silk Stalkings

Executive producer Stephen J. Cannell occasionally appears in the series as D.A. Roy Conroy.

The Simpsons

In "The Last Temptation of Homer," Department of Labor workers slide down on wires in a parody of the scene in Terry Gilliam's *Brazil* (1985) in which Tuttle (Robert De Niro) saves Lowry (Jonathan Pryce) from the torture chamber.

Later in the same episode, Lisa steps out of a clam shell, imitating Uma Thurman's emergence in another Terry Gilliam film, *The Adventures of Baron Munchausen* (1989).

The titles of the two films at the local adult movie theater are *Terms of Endowment* and *I'll Do Anyone*, parodies of the films *Terms of Endearment* (1983) and *I'll Do Anything* (1994), both directed by *Simpsons* executive producer James L. Brooks.

Wealthy, stingy Mr. Burns lives at the corner of Croesus and Mammon. Croesus was a king of Lydia in the 6th century BC and was well-known for his vast wealth. Mammon was the Aramaic personification of riches, avarice and worldly gain.

Sideshow Bob, Bart's archnemesis, has the last name Terwilliger. This name is taken from the film *The 5,000 Fingers of Dr. T* (1953), which was written by acclaimed kids' author Dr. Seuss. This camp classic is about a piano teacher who kidnaps 500 children and chains them to a giant piano. The hero is a little boy named Bart, and the T in Dr. T. stands for Terwilliger. In fact, the character of Bart Simpson is probably also partly based on the kid in this film.

Creator Matt Groening set the show in Springfield, but intentionally did not indicate what state it is in. He wanted it to give the impression of "Anytown, U.S.A." Springfield is the most popular name in the United States, and was also the name of the city in the series *Father Knows Best*, a show that featured a "perfect" television family, the complete antithesis of *The Simpsons*. This ambiguity has led to much speculation by fans of the show, bordering on obsession, about which state the Simpsons' home of Springfield is in. Many fans have sought out obscure facts mentioned in the show to try to determine Springfield's exact location. To aggravate these fans, in the episode where Apu becomes an American citizen, during his studies with the Simpsons, Homer says that "they may ask you to locate your town on a map of the U.S." Homer examines a map, looking for Springfield ... and points at Chicago. Lisa interrupts, "Dad! You're not pointing anywhere *near* Springfield! It's over here, Apu," and just as she points to it ... Bart steps in front of them, completely blocking the map from view.

In "Mr. Lisa Goes to Washington," Lisa enters an essay contest and the camera scans the hometowns and home states of each of the entrants. When it shows Lisa's home, Springfield, it begins to fade out, but her home state's initials can still be seen. However, they are the letters "NT," which don't correspond to any of the states. This abbreviation also appeared on Homer's driving license in one episode. According to the series producers, the fictional state referred to by NT is "North Takoma."

In the episode featuring the Springfield cat burglar, Homer has a flashback about dropping a bomb on some beatniks. The bomb gets stuck and Homer gets on and rides it down to the ground in a parody of the scene in *Dr. Strangelove, or How I Learned to Stop Worrying and Love the Bomb* (1963). When he comes out of the flashback, Homer yells "Take that, Maynard G. Krebs!" Maynard G. Krebs was the name of the beatnik character played by Bob Denver on the show *The Many Loves of Dobie Gillis*.

When Springfield finds out that the cat burglar has buried millions of dollars under a large "T," they all dash off madly to find it. This sequence is a reference to the film *It's a Mad Mad Mad Mad World* (1963), in which a horde of people search for a cache of money under "a big W." A toon version of Phil Silvers even shows up drifting down the river in his car, just as Silvers did in the film. The "treasure" in this episode is found beneath a palm tree shaped like a "T," and the palm trees in the shape of a "W" from the film can be seen to the left in the back-

ground. In the crowd standing around the hole can be seen toon versions of Silvers, Milton Berle and Buddy Hackett, all from the film.

Sideshow Bob's prison number is 24601. At the school fair, in a booth run by the one-armed man who also runs the Army Surplus store, Principal Skinner finds the Iron Hood that he wore when he was a P.O.W. in Vietnam. His prison number was also 24601, as was Jean ValJean's in *Les Miserables*.

In the episode where Homer gets an illegal cable hookup, he watches a very Jerry Seinfeld–like comic say "Don't you just hate when there's no toilet paper?" and just before going to church, he is watching the "Davey and Goliath" Christian cartoon. One of the participants in "The Ultimate Fighting Championship," who "spent some time in prison for aggravated assault" sounds a lot like Mike Tyson.

After Lisa gets trashed on the "water" at Duff World, she comes into the security office and proclaims, "I am the lizard queen!" This is a reference to rock singer Jim Morrison's proclamation, "I am the lizard king!"

In the opening sequence, Marge accidentally puts Maggie through the supermarket scanner, and the "price" of Maggie shows up as $847.63. This is a reference to a magazine article that said $847.63 is the average monthly cost to raise a baby in the United States.

The number A-113 appears frequently. This is animator Brad Bird's signature line. It is the number of the room in which he learned how to animate.

Bart crosses Moe's name off of his list of substitute teachers that the class has gotten rid of, and the name just above Moe's is Gabe Kaplan, who played teacher Gabriel Kotter on *Welcome Back, Kotter.*

During the episode "Lisa's Wedding," Lisa sees into the future, and, in the future, Marge and Homer are seen watching television and Marge says something to the effect of "FOX degenerated into a soft-core porn network so gradually that I didn't notice it until recently." FOX is *The Simpsons'* network.

In the "Mr. Plow" episode, the Simpsons stay up until 3:30 AM to see Homer in a commercial. Lisa says, "Dad, your commercial is on!!" Homer replies with, "It may be on a crappy channel, but the Simpsons are on TV!", which is another dig at FOX.

In the episode "Fish Called Selma," there was yet another self-deprecating FOX reference, this time the movie studio rather than the television network. At the end, the television host says that 20th Century–Fox is backing Troy McClure's new movie, stupid title and all. And at the beginning of the scene where Troy took Selma to see his latest film, there is a closed, out-of-business FOX movie theater up the street.

The opening sequence of "Treehouse of Horror" includes a glimpse of a gravestone with the name "Paul McCartney" on it, referring to the "Paul is dead" mania.

In the episode where Homer takes all of the sugar from a wrecked truck and puts it in his backyard, Marge asks him to get rid of it and Homer breaks into a speech in an Italian accent: "First you get the sugar, then you get the power, then you get the women." This is a quote from the film *Scarface* (1983), where Al Pacino said it in the same accent with one change: "First you get the money..."

The episode "Homer's Barbershop Quartet" has many direct Beatles references and allusions, but some of the more obscure are:

The LP cover of *Meet the Be Sharps* is a parody of the cover of the *With the Beatles* album, and the Be Sharps's back cover parodies the back cover of *Sgt. Pepper's Lonely Hearts Club Band.*

The *Bigger Than Jesus* cover is based on the Beatles' *Abbey Road* album cover.

After recording "Baby on Board," Nigel says, "Gentlemen, you have just recorded your first number one." This is allegedly what producer George Martin said after the Beatles recorded "Please Please Me."

Nigel getting Homer to keep his marriage a secret echoes Brian Epstein's similar instructions to John Lennon.

The JFK airport and press conference scenes are directly lifted from the Beatles' arrival in the United States in February 1964 (even down to Barney/Ringo combing his hair!).

After Lisa goes to the jazz radio station to play Bleeding Gums Murphy's record as a tribute to his death, she comes outside and sees a cloud that sprouts Murphy's face. As he speaks to her, his face changes to that of Mufasa from *The Lion King* (1994), who calls for "Kimba, uh ... I mean Simba" to avenge him, then of Darth Vader, then of James Earl Jones saying "This is CNN." The voices of Bleeding Gums Murphy, Mufasa, Darth Vader and the CNN announcer were all provided by James Earl Jones.

In one episode, Bart is sitting on the couch, and on the television is heard, "Next, *The Jetsons Meet the Flintstones.*" Bart cracks, "Uh, oh. I smell another cheap cartoon cross over." All of a sudden, Jay Sherman, of the show *The Critic*, walks into the room with Homer. Homer says, "Bart, I'd like you to meet Jay Sherman," and Bart says, "I love your show! I think all kids should watch it!" Bart then turns away from Homer and Jay and whispers, "Uuugh. I feel so dirty."

Lisa tells Bart of a cartoon movie that she saw for which Dustin Hoffman and Michael Jackson provided voices. She says, "They didn't use their real names, but you could tell it was them." This is a reference to the fact that both Hoffman and Jackson have provided voices for *The Simpsons*, both uncredited.

In the episode "Bart Sells His Soul," there is a scene of a psycho Milhouse playing in the sandbox with his toy soldiers. This was a reference to a famous routine Michael Richards did on the show *Fridays* in the early 1980s.

Once, Bart went over to Milhouse's house, which was being fumigated. He was met at the door by a guy in an enclosed "space suit" who intoned, "Leave this place. You are in grave danger!" This is a line that the similar-looking Ambassador Kosh said, in exactly the same tone of voice, in an early episode of *Babylon 5*.

Dr. Hibert and his family are mod-eled after Dr. Huxtable and his family on *The Cosby Show*, which at one time was a ratings competitor of *The Simpsons*.

The "J." in Bart J., Homer J., and Abraham (Grampa) J. Simpson is a token of admiration for *Rocky and Bullwinkle* (Rocket J. Squirrel and Bullwinkle J. Moose) and their creator, Jay Ward (see *Rocky and Bullwinkle*).

Many of the opening credits sequences, which show Bart writing something over and over on a black-board, contain in-jokes. They include Bart writing:

It's potato, not potatoe. (A reference to Dan Quayle's gaffe.)

I am not a 32 year old woman. (But Nancy Cartwright, who does Bart's voice, is.)

I will not defame New Orleans. (New Orleans complained about the opening song in the episode "Oh Streetcar!")

I will never win an Emmy. (This was the first episode after the 1992-93 Emmy nominations were announced. It was the first time that the show was eligible for "Best Comedy Series," but it was not nominated. However, the show has won "Best Animated Show" Emmys in the past.)

My homework was not stolen by a one-armed man. (A reference to the recently released *The Fugitive*, 1993.)

I will not celebrate meaningless milestones. (This was used for the 100th episode of *The Simpsons*.)

In the "couch opening," when the Simpsons run out and sit on the couch in a few episodes, a huge foot comes down and squashes the couch and everybody on it, reminiscent of the opening of *Monty Python's Flying Circus*.

Homer awakens from a nightmare to see his family chanting, "We accept you ... One of us...," which was the refrain chanted by the army of freaks at the end of Tod Browning's classic horror film, *Freaks* (1932).

In the episode "One Fish, Two Fish, Blow Fish, Blue Fish," one of the char-acters at the Japanese Karaoke bar is named "Richie Sakki," which is the name of the show's line producer.

Newscaster Kent Brockman reports in one episode: "the following people are gay" and a list of names scrolls up the screen very quickly. Amongst the names are just about all of the produc-tion team.

There are numerous CFL (Canadian Football League) references in the series. In "When Flanders Failed," Homer watches the CFL draft instead of attending Flanders' BBQ, and they specifically mention the Saskatchewan RoughRiders and their inability to score more than five "rouges" in the previous season. In another episode, Lisa is at the library looking for books on football, and one of the subjects she reads out loud is "Football, Oddball Canadian Rules."

The episode with the Spinal Tap guest appearance features a mention of Highway 401, which is the main highway through Toronto and Ottawa in Canada.

Sideshow Bob's (Kelsey Grammer) brother Cecil hires him out of prison, then tries to frame him. Cecil's voice is provided by David Hyde-Pierce, who also plays Niles, the brother of Frasier Crane (Grammer) on *Frasier*. Bob and Cecil's rapport is very similar to that of Frasier and Niles, right down to their discussions on wine. Other *Frasier* references in this episode:

An information screen appears at one point, reading, "*Frasier* is a hit comedy series...," in the style of the title screens on *Frasier*.

When Bart jumps Cecil, he says, "Guess who?" Cecil answers, "Maris?" Maris is the name of Niles's wife on *Frasier*. She has never appeared on screen.

Cecil's apartment has a wine rack beside the kitchen sink and a baby grand piano in the living room, just as Frasier's apartment does.

The Single Guy

In one episode, Jonathan (Jonathan Silverman) goes to see a psychologist, but at the end he gets a new one. The new one is a big black man with glasses who grins and hugs Jonathan. He is played by NBC newscaster Al Roker.

Sledge Hammer!

Executive producer Bill Bixby appears in one episode as a convict.

Kurt Paul appeared occasionally in the second season as coroner Norman Blates, named after Anthony Perkins's creepy character in *Psycho* (1960), Norman Bates.

Sliders

Quinn has a cat on Earth Prime. Its name is Schroedinger, and is named after Erwin Schroedinger, an Austrian theoretical physicist who became known for his mathematical equation describing the wavelike behavior of electrons. One of his theories involved a cat in a box. He proposed that if you put a cat in a box with no way of actually seeing the cat and pumped poison gas into the box, can you say with absolute certainty that the cat will die? Author Umberto Eco even wrote a book on theoretical physics called *Schroedinger's Cat*.

Cleavant Derricks's (Rembrandt) twin brother, Clinton Derricks-Carroll, has appeared in a couple of episodes. He usually plays "that" world's Rembrandt, whenever the two are on screen together. He appeared in "The King Is Back," "Greatfellas" and "The Prince of Slides."

In-jokes are listed by episode.

"Into the Mystic": When Wade (Sabrina Lloyd) recognizes the alphabet of witchcraft on the chart in the doctor's office, she explains by saying that her friend Sabrina was into that kind of stuff. This is considered to be a two-way in-joke, Sabrina being the actress's real name and also the name of a witch comic book character ("Sabrina, the Teenaged Witch") that appeared in Archie Comics.

The whole sorcerer bit with the floating fake apparition, the spooky forest, the huge castle and the four main characters being sent on a task by the sorcerer is out of *The Wizard of Oz* (1939). The sorcerer's assistant, Mr. Gale (Hrothgar Matthews), also has the same surname as Dorothy in *The Wizard of Oz*.

Doctor Xang (Christopher Neame) says that he will keep Quinn's brain with that of the "beloved ex-president, Edward Wood, Jr." Edward Wood, Jr., was the famous low-budget filmmaker responsible for, among others, *Plan 9 from Outer Space* (1959).

"Gillian of the Spirits": Quinn is made invisible and unheard to everyone except one girl, Gillian (Deanna Milligan). Quinn and Gillian take a cab ride, and she talks to him in the back seat. Since the taxi driver cannot see Quinn, he asks her, "You talking to me? You talking to me? There's no one else here, so you must be talking to me…" These lines were used by Robert De Niro in the film *Taxi Driver* (1976)."

"The Good, the Bad and the Wealthy": In this episode with the gunslinging lawyers, a kid says that Quinn came out of the sky, "like the *Mighty Morphin Texas Rangers* on TV." This was a reaction to *TV Guide's* pan of *Sliders* last season when they compared it to *Mighty Morphin Power Rangers* rather sarcastically.

The hired gunslinger played by Lochlyn Munro in this episode is called (and listed in the credits as) only "Billy the Kid." However, both the script and a FOX press release referred to him only as Billy "The Kid" Gates, a reference to Microsoft CEO Bill Gates.

At the end of this episode, Quinn (Jerry O'Donnell) jumps through the portal and the kid calls after him, "Quinn? Come back!" This is a refer-

ence to the kid at the end of *Shane* (1953) who cries, "Come back, Shane!"

"El Sid": This episode is named for Sid (Jeffery Dean Morgan), the vicious, pathological boyfriend of a beautiful woman, who follows the sliders through the vortex. Besides being a play on words on the Spanish hero El Cid, "El Sid" is an anagram of "slide."

"Greatfellas": Singer Mel Torme appears as himself in this gangster-themed episode. Torme got the role through his family—his son is the series' executive producer, Tracy Torme.

"As Time Goes By": The first half of this episode, the second season's finale, is set in a world where caucasians are mostly illegal aliens from Canada, and there are many references to Canada. This is because the next season's episodes were to start shooting in Los Angeles, after filming in Vancouver, B.C., for all the first two seasons. There are many digs at Canada:

At the start of the episode, a street person comes up to the sliders and says, "Kinda nippy out here, eh? Reminds me of Vancouver." The episode was indeed shot in Vancouver.

The defense attorney asks her defendants, "Did you come here because of political prosecution from Canada? Will it be dangerous for you to go back?" Brown answers, "No, not really." As a result of the trial, they are sentenced to be deported to Vancouver.

On the way to being deported, Wade says, "I want to go home … I don't want to spend the rest of my life in Canada." Brown replies, "You think I do? It's wet, it's cold … All they listen to is Anne Murray and Gordon Lightfoot."

Kit Richards, Daelin's brother, helps Quinn save Remmy, Wade, and Arturo from deportment. Quinn (Jerry

O'Connell) knew the Daelin (Brooke Langton) on his world, and when Kit introduces himself to him, Quinn says, "I remember you!" Kit later calls him "Homey." Kit is played by Jerry O'Connell's brother, Charlie. Charlie appeared later in the episode "Dragon-Slide."

"Double Cross": The villain in this episode is Logan St. Clare (Zoe McLellan), Quinn's double. She was named after the production company for the show, St. Clare Entertainment.

"Electric Twister Acid Test": Reed Michener (Corey Feldman) and Quinn (Jerry O'Connell) say goodbye and slide their hands over each others' palms. This was a hand signal that Feldman and O'Connell used when they both starred in the film *Stand By Me* (1986).

"The Guardian": Arturo (John Rhys-Davies) finds out he is dying and decides to enjoy life. He goes to an opera and Wade asks him, "I thought you wanted to try new things?" Arturo replies, "Your generation thinks nothing of seeing *Indiana Jones* thirteen times." Rhys-Davies played Sallah, Indy's faithful servant, in the films *Raiders of the Lost Ark* (1981) and *Indiana Jones and the Last Crusade* (1989).

"Desert Storm": The end credits read: "In Memory of: Ken Steadman." Steadman, who plays Cutter in this episode, died when his dune buggy flipped over while performing a stunt on the show.

"DragonSlide": O'Hara, the cop who brings Melinda (Michelle Rene Thomas) back to the sorcerer, is played by Jerry O'Connell's brother, Charlie. Charlie had also appeared in "As Time Goes By." However, in this episode, he is billed as "Charlie O'Donnell."

Snoops

At the end of an episode involving the FBI and organized crime, Lt. Akers (John Karlen) is seen talking to Tim Reid and Daphne Maxwell. They are strolling by a river, and a policewoman walks up to Karlen, says, "Keep off the grass, please ... oh, sorry, lieutenant," and walks off. The policewoman was played, uncredited, by Tyne Daly, who was married to Karlen on their old show, *Cagney and Lacey*.

Space: Above and Beyond

During one of the many funerals, the name of an exgirlfriend of one of the behind-the-scenes workers was placed on the "casket" that was jettisoned into space. James Morrison (Col. McQueen on the show) mentioned this in an interview.

Scott Wheeler, one of the CGI animators on the show, also placed the name of his wife, Lana, onto the texture of every ship or set piece he built for the show.

Creators James Wong and Glen Morgan came to this series directly from their writing duties on *The X-Files*, and in the April 12, 1996, episode specially aired before the *X-Files* episode, "Jose Chung's 'From Outer Space,'" David Duchovny had an uncredited cameo as Alvin, an Artificially Intelligent pool player at the resort Bacchus.

In one scene of the above episode, characters watch old black and white Abbott and Costello films on television, directed by Clyde Bruckman. Glen Morgan's brother, Darin, used this name for the lead in an episode of *The X-Files*, "Clyde Bruckman's Final Repose."

Spenser: For Hire

In the episode "Sleepless Dreams," in which a brother and sister conspire to hide the fact that the brother killed their mother, all the characters are named after characters in *The Partridge Family*. One character is even named "Bob Claver," after the show's creator. Apparently, according to the show's producer, no one has ever caught this reference.

Star Trek

The access tubes that have been used as crawlspaces through the Enterprise were named Jeffries Tubes, after set designer Matt Jeffries, who designed the exterior of the U.S.S. *Enterprise* as well.

In-jokes are listed by episode.

"The Man Trap": This episode contains the first appearance of McCoy's medical instruments. Because of the Salt Vampire's craving for salt, various scenes were planned to include salt shakers. Futuristic-looking salt shakers were gathered, but at the last minute it was decided not to use them for fear that they might not be recognized as salt shakers, so they were all customized into the medical sensors in this episode instead.

"Charlie X": The color portraits of Yeoman Janice Rand (Grace Lee Whitney) which Charlie produces on the back of the playing cards are actually publicity photos of Whitney.

"What Are Little Girls Made Of?": Most of the overtones of horror in this episode can be attributed to author Robert Bloch's love of the work of H.P. Lovecraft. Lovecraft's classic horror stories describe "the Old Ones"—ancient, all-powerful entities that dominate the human race. In this episode, the android Ruk refers to his creators as "the Old Ones," and the pyramid-shaped doors in the caverns fit Lovecraft's descriptions of the dwellings of his creatures.

"Dagger of the Mind": Character names in *Star Trek* episodes are usually significant. In this episode, for instance, Suzanne Wasson plays an inmate named Lethe who has forgotten her past criminal life. In Greek and Roman mythology, Lethe is known as the "river of forgetfulness."

"Miri": Among the children (or "oldies") in this episode were Grace Lee Whitney's two sons (Whitney played Yeoman Janice Rand) and William Shatner's daughter Melanie, who is shown walking away with Captain Kirk (Shatner) at the end of the episode. Melanie would later play an ensign on the *Enterprise* bridge in the film *Star Trek V: The Final Frontier* (1989).

"The Squire of Gothos": Many of the sets and props were supplied by Paramount's extensive prop department, and several of them were from previous Paramount films, including Cecil B. DeMille's *The Buccaneer* (1938). In fact, the full body costume of the salt vampire from "The Man Trap" can be seen propped up in an alcove near the front door of Trelane's home.

Trelane's parents' voices are supplied by James Doohan (Scotty) and Barbara Babcock (who appeared in the *Trek* episode "A Taste of Armageddon").

"Arena": The voice of the Metrons—both the warning message and the entity itself—is supplied by actor Vic Perrin. His first line in this episode is very similar to the opening speech that he would give for each episode of the television series *The Outer Limits* ("we will control all that you see and hear").

"The City on the Edge of Forever": The historical "playbacks" of the Guardian's screen include scenes from many old motion pictures.

At the end of the opening teaser, Kirk looks up into the sky and the camera pans up, following his gaze to a starry background, in a style that is very similar to a *Twilight Zone*–style fade-out.

"Operation: Annihilate": The dead body of Kirk's brother, George Samuel Kirk, is played by William Shatner, complete with grey hair and fake moustache.

"The Trouble with Tribbles": The planet near the Klingon border which is claimed by both the Federation and the Klingon Empire is called Sherman's Planet. It is named after Holly Sherman, a friend of the episode's writer, David Gerrold.

"By Any Other Name": The purple galactic barrier that was created for the episode "Where No Man Has Gone Before" is also seen in this episode, but no attempt is made to hide the fact that it is actually stock footage. In fact, when Kirk is told about the barrier by Rojan, he says, "Yes, I know. We've been there before."

"Patterns of Force": The names in this episode all resemble their historical counterparts from Nazi Germany. The victimized planet is Zeon (for "Zion," both the town of Jerusalem and the Jewish faith), and the main characters of Zeon are Isak (Isaac), Davod (David), and Abrom (Abraham). Also, the party chairman in the episode is named Eneg, which is "Gene," as in Roddenberry, spelled backwards.

"The Ultimate Computer": The voice of the M-5 computer is provided by James Doohan.

Commodore Robert Wesley (Barry Russo) leads a squadron of starships in an exercise against the *Enterprise*. "Robert Wesley" was the pen name that Gene Roddenberry used while he was in the LAPD. Wesley is Roddenberry's middle name.

"Assignment: Earth": The voice on the radio at Cape Kennedy is that of James Doohan.

"And the Children Shall Lead": The evil entity, Gorgan, is played by famous defense attorney Melvin Belli. His son, Caesar Belli, also appears in the episode as Steve O'Connel, one of the children.

"Whom Gods Destroy": Steve Ihnat plays a villain named Garth, named after the villain he played in an episode of the Anne Francis private eye series, *Honey West*.

"Requiem for Methuselah": Rayna Kapec's (Louise Sorel) surname was taken from the Czechoslovakian writer Karel Capek, who first coined the term "robot" in his 1921 play, *R.U.R.*

"All Our Yesterdays": Ian Wolfe plays a librarian named Mr. Atoz. The name was formed from the phrase "A to Z," an appropriate name for a librarian.

Star Trek: Deep Space Nine

Quark's most dedicated customer is the often-seen but never-heard sad-faced alien, Morn. He is also never credited. The character's name is an anagram of that of another barfly in another Paramount series, Norm (George Wendt) on *Cheers*.

The station's doctor, Dr. Bashir, has an Arabic name. "Bashir" is Arabic for "Bringer of Glad-Tidings."

In-jokes are listed by episode.

"Past Prologue": Susan Bay, who plays Admiral Roman, is the wife of Leonard Nimoy. She appeared again as Roman in the episode "Whispers."

"A Man Alone": Odo checks a monitor for information regarding the Bajoran criminal, and one of the names that appears on the monitor is

Robert della Santina, the show's unit production manager.

"Babel": Kira calls up some medical records, and she finds the name "Surmak Ren," a combination of the name of Ron Surma, *Star Trek*'s casting director, and Ren the chihuahua of the cartoon show *Ren and Stimpy*. When a detailed biography is called up, the names "Surmak Hoek" and "Surmak Stimpson" (Ren [Hoek] and Stimpy) appear. Also, Surmak Ren was employed at "The Akira Advanced Genetics Research Facility, Bajor," named after *Akira*, the Japanese animation series.

"Q-Less": Q (John de Lancie) suggests that he and Vash visit Vadrus 3, whose inhabitants think they are the only intelligent life in the universe. This is an obscure reference to a god in the fantasy world of Glorantha, created by Greg Stafford for the game *Runequest*.

"The Nagus": Rom gets chewed out for putting the Hoeks next to another race. The Hoeks are named after Ren Hoek of *Ren and Stimpy*.

"Invasive Procedures": Verad Dax and Sisko have a conversation in which there is a mention of the cliffs of Bole. This is thanks to Cliff Bole, a frequent director of *The Next Generation* and *Deep Space Nine*, as well as several episodes of *MacGyver*.

"Cardassians": A long list of names is seen on a computer screen that Garak looks through. The list contains many in-jokes, including corrupted versions of the names of many members of the DC Comics superhero group, the Legion of Super Heroes.

"The Jem'Hadar": Alan Oppenheimer plays Captain Keogh. He is named after Captain Myles Walter Keogh, who was with General Custer at the Battle of Little Bighorn. He is

perhaps best known to Civil War buffs as the owner of Comanche, the surviving horse of the battle (see also *Homefront*, below).

"Past Tense": Many characters take their names from members of *The Magnificent Seven* (60). Jim Metzler plays San Francisco businessman Chris Brynner. In the film, Yul Brynner plays a character named Chris. Dick Miller and Al Rodrigo play security guards named Vin and Bernardo. In the film, Steve McQueen played Vin and Charles Bronson played Bernardo. Tina Lifford plays a computer operator named Lee, which was the name of Robert Vaughn's character in the movie. And Webb's son, Danny (Richard Lee Jackson), is named after the little boy in *The Magificent Seven*, played by Mario Navarro.

"The Way of the Warrior": Patricia Tallman, who plays the weapons officer aboard the *Defiant*, was a frequent stunt double on *Star Trek: The Next Generation* (e.g., Crusher's in "Suspicions"). She also appeared, credited, in an episode of *Star Trek: The Next Generation*.

"Little Green Men": The three Ferengi—Quark, Rom and Nog—land on Earth in 1947. They are detained and observed by the military. The general in charge says, "Did you take care of that idiot in Roswell who told the press we found a flying saucer?" He is told that the man has been convinced that it was a weather balloon. Roswell, New Mexico, was the supposed real-life landing site of an alien spaceship, which was followed by a huge government cover-up. It was explained that the "spaceship" was nothing but a weather balloon.

When he is scared, Rom cries out, "I want my Moogie!" We later meet Moogie (i.e., "Mommy") in the episode

"Family Business." "Moogie" is a corruption of a nickname used by one of the writers for a member of their family.

The four main human characters have names of three actors and a character from alien invasion and sci-fi movies of the 1950s. Charles Naper plays General Denning, named after Richard Denning of *The Day the World Ended* (1956). Megan Gallagher plays Nurse Garland, named after Beverly Garland, the star of *It Conquered the World* (1956). Conor O'Farrell plays Professor Carlson, named after Richard Carlson of *It Came from Outer Space* (1953). Captain Wainwright (James G. MacDonald) is named after Dr. Ed Wainwright (Peter Graves) in the film *The Beginning of the End* (1957).

"Our Man Bashir": Bashir's episode is a parody of the spy films and television series of the 1960s, most of all the James Bond series. The villain's name, Dr. Hippocrates Noah, takes his first name from the father of modern medicine (appropriate for Dr. Bashir) and his last name is a takeoff of *Dr. No* (1962) (coincidentally, the villain in the Bond film spoof *Casino Royale*, 1967, was also named Dr. Noah). The episode's title is from the title of another Bond spoof, *Our Man Flint* (1966), starring James Coburn.

"Homefront": Commander Benteen of the Lakota is named after Captain Frederick W. Benteen, one of General Custer's captains at Little Big Horn. Benteen's ship is named in honor of the victors of the Battle of Little Bighorn. Another of Custer's captains, Myles Walter Keogh, gave his name to a starship captain in the episode "The Jem'Hadar."

"Paradise Lost": Odo and Sisko break into classified Starfleet files and discover that Admiral Leighton had reassigned over 400 officers. Sisko recognizes the names Daneeka, McWatt, Snowden, Orr, and Moodus. These were all officers on the USS *Okinawa* when Leighton was the captain and Sisko his executive officer. These were also all names of minor characters in the Joseph Heller novel *Catch-22*.

The Cadet that tells Sisko all about the covert mission is named Riley Aldrin Shepard, after astronauts Edwin "Buzz" Aldrin and Alan Shepard.

"Looking for Par'Mach in All the Wrong Places": Quark speaks to Grilka about war, and says, "War ... what is it good for? Absolutely nothing." This is a line from the song "War," by Edwin Starr, and covered in 1985 by Bruce Springsteen. This is an episode which takes its title from a Johnny Lee song ("Lookin' for Love").

"Trials and Tribble-ations": When Bashir questions if O'Brien and Sisko are wearing the proper-colored tunics, O'Brien says, "Don't you know anything about this period in time?" Bashir answers, "I'm a doctor, not a historian!" slightly rewording one of Dr. McCoy's favorite lines from *Star Trek*.

"For the Uniform": Dax's crack about author Victor Hugo's heroines being "so two-dimensional" is a reference to Disney's cartoon of Hugo's *The Hunchback of Notre Dame* (1996), then in theaters.

Star Trek: The Next Generation

The blue-skinned race known as Bolians, to which Mott the barber belongs, is named after Cliff Bole, a frequent director of TNG and DSN.

The name of the Ferengi comes from the Hindu term "firangi" or "ferangi," which was originated in the nineteenth century and is still in use today. It is a derogatory term that the natives of India used to describe the "white-skinned" British settlers in India and Afghanistan. The Ferengi were originally intended to be a caricature of the white, straight, European male—greedy, sexist, etc.

The access tubes that have been used as crawlspaces through the *Enterprise* and other Starfleet ships were named Jeffries Tubes, after set designer Matt Jeffries, who designed the *Enterprise* from the original *Star Trek* series as well.

Some of the people who work in the set design department of Paramount Pictures are anime (Japanese animation) fans, and have been able to sneak anime references into Paramount's various *Star Trek* television series. According to set manager Rick Sternbach, there is at least one reference per episode in *Star Trek: The Next Generation*. Usually these references are in computer displays or in the sets themselves. Examples are listed below in the episodes "Conspiracy," "Loud as a Whisper," "The Measure of a Man," "Contagion," "The Icarus Factor," "Samaritan Snare" and "Menage a Troi." The alien race Nausicaans (which the young Picard fights with in "Tapestry"), are also named after an anime series (see "The Measure of a Man").

Wesley Crusher, who some have taken to represent a younger version of Gene Roddenberry, takes his first name from Gene's middle name: Wesley.

The episode "Legacy" was the 80th of the series. This was an important milestone, since the original *Star Trek* series only lasted 79 episodes. In that 79th and final episode of the original *Star Trek*, "Turnabout Intruder," the Enterprise finds itself at Camus II,

where Dr. Janice Lester is doing archaeological research. *Star Trek: The Next Generation* made note of this milestone in its 80th episode by including the line "bypassing an archaeological dig on Camus II," or, in effect, passing the record set by the previous series.

In-jokes are listed by episode.

"Encounter at Farpoint": The military uniform that Q wears is that of a Marine Corps lieutenant colonel. And his rank, ribbons and badges are all identical to those worn by Lt. Col. Oliver North when he testified at the Iran-Contra hearings in 1986-87, just before "Farpoint" went into production.

"The Naked Now": Data quotes a limerick that begins, "There was once a lady from Venus, whose body was shaped like a..." It was written by David Gerrold while he was still working on *The Next Generation* in its early days, and the complete limerick can be found in the third book of his *War Against the Chtorr* series: *A Rage for Revenge*. The limerick appears on a page opposite another dirty limerick which seems to be about Gene Roddenberry.

During the scan of records, a parrot wearing a Starfleet shirt, complete with insignia and nacelles, can be seen. This same screen also reappears in "Conspiracy." This is a reference to Gene Roddenberry, who had the nickname "The Great Bird of the Galaxy." The name comes from a line said by Sulu to Janice Rand in the original *Star Trek* episode "The Man Trap": "You're the great bird of the galaxy." The parrot comes from Roddenberry's ideology of Pantheism, the doctrine which identifies God with the universe, everything being considered as part of or a manifestation of Him.

"**Hide and Q**": The script for this episode was the first one to be credited to writer Maurice Hurley, who later became the show's coexecutive producer. However, after a rewrite by series creator Gene Roddenberry, Hurley substituted his pen name, C.J. Holland.

"**11001001**": 11001001 is binary, and is converted to 201 decimal, or hex C9. Under the Z-80 microprocessor series, "C9," in assembly language, is known as "Unconditional Return," which was the original, appropriate title for this episode.

"**When the Bough Breaks**": Three of the kidnapped *Enterprise* children are played by McKenzie Westmore, Amy Wheaton, and Jeremy Wheaton. Amy and Jeremy are Wil's sister and brother, and McKenzie is the daughter of makeup supervisor Michael Westmore.

"**Heart of Glory**": Kunivas of the Klingon Defense Corps is played by Robert Bauer. He had been a drummer in a band, the Watch, with bassist Michael Dorn, who plays Worf in the series.

"**Symbiosis**": This episode was filmed after "Skin of Evil," in which Tasha Yar (Denise Crosby) is killed, but it was aired before it, so the last scene filmed by Crosby was actually in this episode. What was her very last scene (before coming back in subsequent episodes)? Watch as Crusher and Picard exit the cargo bay at the end of the episode. Just as the doors begin to close, in the background, Tasha leans over from behind a console and waves goodbye to the camera.

"**Conspiracy**": The topographical map of the planetary surface is actually a very sketchy drawing of the Japanese cartoon characters Kei and Yuri. Yuri is on the right side, and Kei is upside

down. Kei and Yuri are the main characters in the Japanese animated series *Lovely Angels* (AKA *The Dirty Pair*). They are members of World's Welfare Work Foundation. Their job is to take care of problems that crop up. However, they usually leave the place in worse shape than when they arrived, although it is usually not their fault. *Lovely Angels* has contained *Star Trek* in-jokes in it as well.

"**The Neutral Zone**": On the family tree of Claire Raymond, which is recalled by Troi, there are references to various shows, including *Dr. Who*: W. Hartnell m. P. Troughton, J. Pertwee m. T. Baker, P. Davison m. C. Baker. William Hartnell, Patrick Troughton, Jon Pertwee, Tom Baker, Peter Davison and Colin Baker were the six actors who had played the Doctor at the time. There is also a listing for J-L. Picard m. W. Riker. Other references include *Gilligan's Island* and *M*A*S*H*. Also, the face pictured on the screen is Peter Lauritson, one of the producers of TNG.

In one shot, a female sciences officer walks off of a turbolift. She is played by Susan Sackett, who was a writer on the show as well as Gene Roddenberry's personal assistant. She got the walk-on after winning a bet over losing weight.

"**The Child**": In this episode, Doctor Pulaski refers to "Cyano Acrylates" as a possible source of the Ikner radiation that was causing the plague samples to grow. Cyano acrylates are the active ingredients for SuperGlue.

"**Loud as a Whisper**": The conference table, "made to resemble indigenous rock," had various markings on it. Most notable to *Lovely Angels–Dirty Pair* fans are the markings "Kei" and "Yuri" (see "Conspiracy").

"The Measure of a Man": When Riker is showing off Data's arm to the JAG representative, there is a pad on her desk which lists Data's parts, including "Nausican Valve" and "Totoro Interface." Also, it is noted that part of Data's construction is made out of something called "Yurium" (see "Conspiracy"). *Nausicaä of the Valley of Wind* (1984) is one of the most popular Japanese animes of all time. In it, Nausicaä, the princess of a small nation in a post-holocaust world, tries to stop other warring nations from destroying themselves. *My Neighbour Totoro* (1988) was also a very popular anime. In it, two young girls and their father move to the Japanese countryside in the early 1950s and discover the existence of Totoros, magical forest spirits which only children can see.

"The Dauphin": In this episode, a planet is named Daled 4. Daled is the fourth letter in the Hebrew alphabet, and has the numeric value of four.

"Contagion": The Iconian artifact has various markings on it, including "Kei and Yuri," "Dirty Pair" (see "Conspiracy"), "Totoro" (see "The Measure of a Man") and "Gundam." "Mobile Suit Gundam" is a Japanese anime series which began in 1979 and included two television series and a number of films.

The various views seen through the portal include one of Toronto's City Hall and Nathan Phillip's Square (depicting the arches over the reflecting pool–skating rink).

In this episode, the Romulan ship that attacks the *Enterprise* is named the *Harkonnen*, which was the name of the family that attacked the Atriedes family in author Frank Herbert's *Dune* series.

Another Galaxy Class starship is also mentioned: the USS *Yamato*. This starship was named after the flagship of the Japanese fleet that fought in World War II at both the Coral Sea and Midway before it was sunk by torpedo bombers from an American carrier. Many years later, a Japanese animation series was done in which a battleship is reconfigured to become a starship in order to recover something called the "Cosmo DNA." This series was called *Starship Yamato*, also after the Japanese ship. In the United States, this series was better known as *Star Blazers*.

"The Icarus Factor": The TNG art department had a field day putting in references to Japanese anime series. The mat has the chinese character of "sei" or "star" (as in "starry sky"). The two scrolls hanging on the walls say, in Japanese syllabic characters (hiragana), "urusei yatsura," after *Urusei Yatsura*, an anime series about three aliens which translates as "The Noisy Neighbours," or "Those Obnoxious Aliens." Also, while lunging at Riker, Riker's father says (in a terrible accent), "youroshiku onegaishimasu," which literally translates as "Please do me the favor of being kind to me," but in English it means "Pleased to meet you." Various other markings include "Kei," "Yuri" (see "Conundrum"), "Akira" (a Japanese animation company), "Tonari No Totoro" (see "The Measure of a Man"), and "Lum" (one of the three aliens in *Urusei Yatsura*, an electrically-charged princess, is named Lum).

John Tesh, host of *Entertainment Tonight*, was a huge *Star Trek* fan, and while filming a story on *Star Trek: The Next Generation*, he appeared as the final Klingon on the left side to administer the pain-stick to Worf.

"Q Who": The Borg baby seen on the Borg ship was played by Sam

Klatman. Klatman is the son of Carol Eisner, who is the secretary of unit production manager David Livingston.

"Samaritan Snare": Picard mentions "Nausicans" in a conversation with Wesley on the shuttlecraft.

"Up the Long Ladder": When Picard is looking at the list of ships trying to find the Mariposa, another ship listed is the *Buckaroo Banzai* captained by John Whorfin and built by Yoyodyne, the company that the red Lectroids ran in the film *The Adventures of Buckaroo Banzai* (1984). Whorfin (John Lithgow) was the red Lectroids' leader in the film. The same company name was seen on the USS *Hathaway*. In the film, Yoyodyne Propulsion Systems of Grover's Mill, New Jersey, was where Orson Welles's *War of the Worlds* scare actually happened.

The pregnant Bringloidi woman that Prime Minister Granger (Jon de Vries) is fascinated by is played by the wife of prop man Alan Sims. Sims and his wife also bred the miniature goats used in the episode.

"Peak Performance": A computer display shows the two ships *Kei* and *Yuri* (see "Conundrum").

"The Vengeance Factor": Mallon, the blond Gatherer that Brull places in command when he leaves, is played by Michael Lamper, who, at the time of shooting, was Marina Sirtis's boyfriend. They were married in June 1992.

"The Defector": Michael Williams, the holographic medieval swordsman who Data speaks with in his *Henry V* program, is played, uncredited, by revered Shakespearean actor Patrick Stewart.

"The High Ground": Brandi Sherwood, who was, at the time, Miss Teen USA, has an uncredited part as a bridge ensign.

"Deja Q": Corbin Bernsen appears uncredited as the second Q (commonly referred to as "Q2"). He had asked for a part because he enjoyed the series so much.

"Captain's Holiday": The name of the planet Raisa comes from the German word Reise, which translates as "trek."

"Hollow Pursuits": The antigrav units contain a flux capacitor. The flux capacitor was a essential part of the DeLorean time machine in *Back to the Future* (1985).

"Menage a Troi": The Ferengi security code begins with "Kei Yuri..." (see "Conspiracy"). The full code is "Kei Yuri Dirty Pair." Unfortunately, the commander gets cut off before he reaches the last word, and he uses the Japanese pronunciation (so people who have not seen the series in the original language are at a disadvantage).

"Transfigurations": In the sick bay, against the wall, there is an upside-down outline of the top portion of the TARDIS from *Doctor Who*.

"The Best of Both Worlds Part I" (also "Emissary," *DS9*'s premiere): The fatal stand of the Federation against the Borg and Locutus takes place at Wolf 359. "Wolf 359" was the title of an episode of *The Outer Limits*, starring Patrick O'Neal.

"Brothers": Brent Spiner (Data) also plays Data's creator, Dr. Noonian Soong, uncredited under heavy make-up. Spiner took on the triple role (he also plays Data's brother Lore) after Keye Luke became too ill to perform.

"Legacy": A label on a nuclear reactor in the episode reads, "Remember, you can never add *too much* water to a Nuclear Reactor." An issue of the sci-fi magazine *Starlog* includes a complete picture of the reactor, including some of the rules (some of which are apparently hysterical).

"**Identity Crisis**": Two of the Tarchannian aliens are played by Los Angeles radio personalities Mark Thompson and Brian Phelps ("Mark and Brian"), uncredited.

"**Qpid**": The scene where Worf smashes Geordi's lute, then says "Sorry," is a reference to a scene in *National Lampoon's Animal House* (1978) at the toga party.

The line of dialogue said by Picard during his sword fight, "There is something you should know ... I'm not from Nottingham," is from a sword fight in the film *The Princess Bride* (1987).

"**Half a Life**": One of the displays has the number "4077" in the corner, a reference to David Ogden Stiers's old series, *M*A*S*H*.

"**In Theory**": Picard's line "Now would be a good time" is a reference to Chekhov's line in *Star Trek IV: The Voyage Home* (1986), which in turn was used by Kirk during "The Doomsday Machine." Also, while it is not be visible in the actual show, someone on the production crew relabeled the shuttle pod "PONTIAC NCC-1701-D."

"**Darmok**": The writers were playing around with words in this episode. The word DARMOK becomes "KOMRAD" (comrade) when reversed. JILARD may also become JLpIcARD.

Gilgamesh is based upon Gilgamesh (from Sumerian lore), a character described as Solomon, Ulysses, and Hercules combined into one. One of the important factors after his friend's death is Gilgamesh's fear of death, which, although never playing a factor in battle, results in his constant search for immortality. In one manner or another, he comes very close, but always manages to miss.

"**The Outcast**": One of the technical phrases said in this episode is

"Reverse the polarity of the neutron flow." This was a phrase commonly used by the third doctor (Jon Pertwee) in the *Doctor Who* series.

"**The Next Phase**": One of the control panels on the Romulan Ship is modeled after Dr. Who's TARDIS control console.

"**The Inner Light**": Batai, son of Kamin (Patrick Stewart), is played by Stewart's real-life son, Daniel Stewart.

"**Relics**": With Scotty (James Doohan) on board, there are plenty of references to the old series. For instance, the "miracle worker" bit comes from *Star Trek III: The Search for Spock* (1984). The "It is green" bit comes from *Star Trek*'s "By Any Other Name," where Scotty tries to get an alien drunk. He exhausts his entire stock of alcohol, including a bottle of alien liquor that even Mr. Scott knows nothing about except that "It's green!"

"**Chain of Command, Part I**": During the transfer-of-command scene in Ten Forward, there is a blond woman standing in the foreground of the crowd. This woman is Jana Wallace, the show's script typist. Her name was used for a character in the episodes "Descent, Part I" and "Eye of the Beholder."

"**Aquiel**": The name of the Klingon battlecruiser that meets with the *Enterprise* is the *Qu'vatlh* (proper spelling, badly pronounced by Picard). This is listed in the *Klingon Dictionary* on page 58 as one of the Klingon curses.

"**Starship Mine**": The Arkarian waiter who turns out to be a terrorist is played by Arlee Reed, who is script coordinator Lolita Fatjo's husband.

Patricia Tallman, who plays the hijacker Kiros, was a frequent stunt double on *Star Trek: The Next Generation* (e.g., Crusher's in "Suspicions").

She also appeared in an episode of *Star Trek: Deep Space Nine*.

"**Second Chances**": Dr. Mae Jemison plays Ensign Palmer in this episode. Dr. Jemison is a NASA science mission specialist and was the first female African American astronaut in space. She is the first (and, as yet, only) real-life space traveler to appear in any *Trek* series or film.

"**Descent, Part I**": Guy Vardaman was a long-time extra, stunt performer and technician on the series who appeared in many uncredited, unnamed roles. His first named (albeit still uncredited) role was in this episode as Lt. (j.g.) Darien Wallace. He was named after Jana Wallace, the show's script supervisor. Vardaman played Wallace again (again, uncredited) in the episode "Eye of the Beholder." Jana herself also appeared uncredited in the episode "Chain of Command, Part I."

"**Descent, Part II**": Picard is stunned by a force field in his cell and Troi tells the Borg guard that he had better come in, or else Lore will be angry with him. This Borg was played by longtime *Trek* stuntman "Broadway Joe" Murphy. The crew nicknamed him "Joe the Borg" and his jerky motions after Picard pulls out his tube were dubbed the "Borgasm scene."

"**Eye of the Beholder**": The murdered Ensign, Marla E. Finn, was played by Nora Leonhardt, a longtime stand-in for Marina Sirtis.

"**Emergence**": The holographic man in the grey flannel suit on the train is played by Dennis Tracy, who was the longtime stand-in for Patrick Stewart as Picard.

Star Trek: Voyager

A possible unintentional in-joke: Roxanne Biggs-Dawson plays half–Klingon Lieutenant B'Elanna Torres. Biggs-Dawson played a character named Lt. Torres years earlier in the 1991 television movie *NYPD Mounted*.

The access tubes that have been used as crawlspaces through *Voyager* and other Starfleet ships were named Jeffries Tubes, after set designer Matt Jeffries, who designed the *Enterprise* from the original *Star Trek* series as well.

In the episode "Prototype," when Torres is working on the prototype, just before she gets it working, she makes a comment about the "flux capacitor," a reference to *Back to the Future* (1985). This could possibly be the same device as in *Star Trek: The Next Generation*'s "Hollow Pursuits."

The Doctor has often used the "I'm a doctor, not a…" line popularized in the original *Star Trek* series by Dr. McCoy. Although this is a blatant reference, it still does make sense in the show's context, because the holodoc is made up of a combination of many medical personalities, so why shouldn't McCoy be part of it?

In one episode, Neelix and Paris crash-land in a shuttle on a planet the crew of *Voyager* dub "Planet Hell" because of its poor climate and poisonous atmosphere. In real life, the actors call the sound stage where many planetside scenes are filmed (including, presumably, the ones in this episode), "Planet Hell" due to the heat of the lights.

In the episode "Threshold," when Tom Paris's transformation makes him look like David Bowman in his late-aging transformation stage in the film *2010* (1985), he says "It's all very clear to me now…," which is what Bowman said when he reached the same "state of awareness."

In "Deadlock," the references to

Kent State and experiments done there are because one of the writers attended Kent State.

The Doctor's creator, Dr. Louis Zimmerman, is named after longtime *Trek* set designer Herman Zimmerman.

MTV video jockey VJ Kennedy appears as a crewmember in the episode "Persistence of Vision."

In "Macrocosm," Janeway instructs the Doctor on how to get to Environmental Control. She describes a very roundabout route, to which the Doctor replies, "Who designed this ship, anyway?" This sounds very much like the writers making a joke at the set designer on the show.

"Future's End" contains a number of in-jokes. Neelix and Kes (Jennifer Lien) get addicted to watching twentieth century soap operas. Lien was a soap opera actress before joining *Star Trek: Voyager*.

As Janeway types on the computer in Starling's (Ed Begley, Jr.) office, she comments that it is like using "stone knives and bearskins." Spock used the same phrase to describe the radio tubes and twentieth century technology with which he used to build a tricorder in the *Star Trek* episode "City on the Edge of Forever."

Tom calls Rain's lab "groovy." As they leave the observatory, Tuvok asks him, "What does it mean, 'groovy'?" This is a reference to Spock's line when he and Kirk attempt to board a bus in *Star Trek IV: The Voyage Home* (1986): "What does it mean, 'exact change'?"

The Starlost

The name "Cordwainer Bird" in the credits was a pseudonym for writer Harlan Ellison. Ellison created the show, and he was so disappointed with

the result that he had his name removed. The name was partly a homage to Cordwainer Smith, another sci-fi author (actually another pen name) and partly Ellison's way of flipping the producers of the show "the bird"!

Starman

The episode "The System," which has Starman (Robert Hays) jailed and represented by a public defender, was directed by Bill Duke. Duke also had a cameo in the episode as Stephen Putnam.

Strange Luck

In the two-part episode "Brother's Grim," Chance Harper (D.B. Sweeney) finds his brother, who is in deep trouble and suspected of being a drug dealer. At the end of part two, Chance's brother has to disappear and he tells Chance that if he (Chance) is in any trouble to contact a man in the FBI, the only man he trusts: Fox Mulder. This was the name of David Duchovny's FBI agent character on the show *The X-Files*.

The Streets of San Francisco

For years, Karl Malden worked his own little in-jokes into whatever he was doing. In this series, when he would bawl out someone in his office, he would invariably take a moment to open the door and yell, "Get me a cup of coffee, Sekulovich!" to some unseen actor. Malden's real name was Mladen Sekulovich (see also *On the Waterfront*, 1954, and *Word of Honor*, 1981 TV).

Super Force

In this futuristic cop series' second season, a coroner character named Quincy Morris (Jack Swanson) is introduced. This was a reference to the series *Quincy, M.E.*, starring Jack Klugman as a coroner.

Tales from the Crypt

At the beginning of the episode where the four kids discover the mortician who is killing people and videotape him, they emerge from a movie theater. *Radio Flyer* is listed on the marquee, and there is a poster for *Lethal Weapon* (1987) outside the theater. Both films were directed by executive producer Richard Donner.

Tales of the Gold Monkey

Jake Cutter's (Stephen Collins) name was taken from the name of John Wayne's character in the 1961 film, *The Comancheros*. It was directed by Michael Curtiz, who also directed *Casablanca* (1942) (which was partly the basis of *Tales of the Gold Monkey*).

Sarah White's middle name in the series is "Stickney." It was added by Stephen Collins, who felt she needed a snooty-sounding middle name, and creator Don Bellisario agreed. Stickney is Collins's father's middle name.

In the series, Jake used to pitch for the Duluth Dukes minor league baseball team. The Dukes were a real Class "C" team (before the minor leagues were reduced to AAA, AA and A, there were also lower grades: B, C and D). The show's star, Stephen Collins, used to spend his summers on an island called Madeline Island in Wisconsin, about 90 miles from Duluth. It was the nearest "big" city, and he thought his island friends would get a kick out of seeing the Duluth uniform.

Tarzan

The 1990s Wolf Larson series had an episode which featured Ron Ely as a great white hunter who decides to hunt Tarzan. Ely played Tarzan in the 1960s series *Tarzan*.

TekWar

The DKB 9000 gun was named after the show's animators: Derek Grime ("D"), Kyle Menzies ("K") and Bob Munroe ("B").

The numbers B206 & B207 were occasionally used in the series. These were the suite numbers of the series' production offices.

Monitor shots often had photos of crew members standing in for villains.

Terrahawks

Terrahawks team member Kate Kestrel's civilian cover is as a pop singer for AnderBurr Records. This was a reference to Anderson-Burr Productions, creator Gerry Anderson's new production company.

Third Rock from the Sun

When John Lithgow and Jane Curtin get on a plane to fly to Chicago, Lithgow does his "There's something on the wing of this plane!" panic attack from *Twilight Zone—The Movie* (1983). Curtin tells him, "It's called an *engine*."

Thunderbirds

In the episode "Trapped in the Sky," the hero who tries to board a stricken FireFlash airliner in mid-flight is named Meddings, after the series' visual effects director, Derek Meddings.

Time Trax

The show's premise is that Darien (Dale Midkiff), the hero, travels back in time from the year 2193 to 1993, and it just so happens that the time machine dumps him in the ladies' room in the basement of the Smithsonian.

He even gets detained because of this. In an episode over a year later, he is in a nightclub and he is about to be surrounded and attacked. He is dancing with a woman at the time and he asks her if there is any other way out of the club, and she tells him there's a window in the ladies room. He whispers, "why do I always end up in the women's john?"

When the people in 2193 go through the museum to find appropriate clothing in which to dress Darien, they give him Elvis Presley's jeans. This is a reference to Midkiff's role as Elvis in the highly-rated television miniseries, *Elvis and Me* (1988 TV). When he puts on the jeans, he says, "Boy, Presley was thin back then."

T.J. Hooker

Leonard Nimoy, William Shatner's old shipmate, makes a guest appearance in one episode.

Toma

The series is based on the real-life exploits of Newark, New Jersey, detective David Toma, who relied on the art of disguise to apprehend his prey. Toma himself made cameo appearances in many episodes, usually in disguise.

Tracey Takes On

One sketch on this Tracey Ullman show takes place at a golf tournament. The name "McKeown" can be seen on the leader board. Ullman's husband, Allan McKeown, is an avid golf enthusiast.

Trials of O'Brien

David Burns plays The Great McGonigle, a legendary con man who was a crony of O'Brien's (Peter Falk) in this law series. The Great McGonigle

was the name of the con man played by W.C. Fields in the film *The Old-Fashioned Way* (1934).

The Trials of Rosie O'Neill

Each episode opens with Rosie in the office of her psychiatrist, who is played by series creator Barney Rosenzweig.

The Twilight Zone (old)

In the episode "Will the Real Martian Please Stand Up?" the bus parked outside the diner has the name "Cayuga Bus Lines" on the side. Rod Serling's production company was called Cayuga Productions.

In "Walking Distance," the local doctor's name is Dr. Bradbury, a homage to sci-fi writer Ray Bradbury.

As well, in "A Stop at Willoughby," the account being worked on is called the Bradbury Account.

In "The Hitch-Hiker," the protagonist is named Nan, the nickname of Serling's daughter Anne.

The teacher (Janice Rule) in "Nightmare as a Child" is named Helen Foley, after a beloved school teacher of Serling's. Joe Dante later used this name for another teacher in *The Twilight Zone—The Movie* (1983).

The Twilight Zone (new)

In the episode "A Matter of Minutes," concerned with time, Adam Arkin and Karen Austin hide in the ticket booth of a theater featuring the film *Time After Time* (1979).

Writer Rockne S. O'Bannon gave the writer in his 1986 episode "Personal Dreams" a familiar name: Rockne S. O'Bannon. O'Bannon was played by Martin Balsam.

Twin Peaks

In the first episode of the series, when the foreigners find out about Laura's death, they beat a hasty retreat back to Norway. One employee starts crying, "The Norwegians are leaving! The Norwegians are leaving!" bringing to mind Norman Jewison's 1966 film *The Russians Are Coming! The Russians Are Coming!* In the film, the Russian leader, Alan Arkin, says that they are not Russians, but in fact Norwegians.

Dale Bartholomew Cooper (Kyle MacLachlan) was named after D.B. Cooper, the man who hijacked an aircraft over the state of Washington, bailed out with a parachute, and disappeared without a trace. A film was even made about him, *The Pursuit of D.B. Cooper* (1981).

Laura Palmer was named after the title character in the film *Laura* (1944), in which the title character is found dead at the beginning of the film, just as Laura is in *Twin Peaks* (the movie character's full name is Laura Hunt). Waldo, the myna bird owned by Jacques Renault, and Bob Lydecker, his vet, were named after Clifton Webb's character Waldo Lydecker in *Laura*. Webb was nominated for an Academy Award for the role. Bob Lydecker is never seen but is called "the best damn veterinarian in these parts" by his best friend, Philip Michael Gerard.

In turn, Philip Michael Gerard, the one-armed man, is a tribute to *The Fugitive*'s one-armed man. In that series, the fugitive was pursued by a Lt. Philip Michael Gerard.

Twin Peaks' largest food freaks, Ben and Jerry, share their names with the all-natural ice cream merchants.

Laura Palmer's identical twin cousin, Madeleine Ferguson (Sheryl Lee), is a reference to the film *Vertigo* (1958), in which Judy (Kim Novak) posed as the "dead" Madeleine. As well, Jimmy Stewart's character in the movie was named Scottie Ferguson, giving this show's Madeleine her surname. In *Vertigo,* Scottie makes Judy dye her hair blond to look like Madeleine, à la James making Maddy up like Laura to catch the killer. One scene in this movie, in which Scottie is momentarily confused as to whether he is with Judy or Madeleine, shows this by having the room spin around them as they embrace, as with Leland-Bob's death hold on Madeleine.

FBI chief Gordon Cole (David Lynch) is named after a minor character in Billy Wilder's *Sunset Boulevard* (1950), one of Lynch's all-time favorite movies.

The tune that Cooper blows on his whistle is the flying saucer's tune in *Close Encounters of the Third Kind* (1977).

Catherine Martell's insurance salesman, Mr. Neff, is a reference to Walter Neff, an insurance salesman in Billy Wilder's *Double Indemnity* (1944).

When Windom Earle (Kenneth Welsh) poses as an old friend of Dr. Hayward, Donna's dad, he calls himself "Dr. Craig." Dr. Craig was the name of William Daniels's character on the series *St. Elsewhere.*

The reporter at the site of the burnt sawmill in a second season episode is series cocreator Mark Frost in an uncredited role. His father, Warren Frost, also appeared in the series as Dr. William Hayward, Donna Hayward's father.

Roger Hardy (Clarence Williams III) has a scene at the diner with his former costar on *The Mod Squad*, Peggy Lipton.

The Dickensian nature of the "Little

Nicky" plot (orphans, lost lineage, the revelation of hidden origins, misfortune and serendipity in general) naturally calls for a suitably Dickensian name for the orphanage. It is called the Dorrit Home For Boys. *Little Dorrit* was a novel by Dickens.

In the obligatory *Twin Peaks* sketch during the Kyle MacLachlan–hosted episode of *Saturday Night Live*, Cooper described to Truman a dream in which a hairless mouse sang a song about caves. In an episode of *Peaks* broadcast after this, Cooper said, "Harry, tonight we're going to do a little spelunking."

Wagon Train

In the episode originally aired November 23, 1960, which was directed by John Ford, John Wayne appears in a cameo role as General Sherman. Wayne is credited as "Michael Morrison," which was his real name.

The Waltons

The voice of the grown-up John-Boy who narrates the show is provided by Earl Hamner, Jr., the series' coexecutive producer. Hamner had based the show on his own recollections of growing up in rural Virginia.

War of the Worlds

This series is a continuation of the 1953 film. The story of the series is that the population of Earth has forgotten the original invasion. Ann Robinson, who starred in the original film as Sylvia van Buren and organized the film's 25th-year reunion, repeats her role in this series in the episodes "Thy Kingdom Come" and "The Meek Shall Inherit." She is committed to a mental institution for insisting that the aliens have returned, then freed by the main characters. The script for the first

season episode "Epiphany" was also written by a "Sylvia van Buren."

Weird TV

In one sequence, Francis, the creature in the trash heap, is chased by a huge shark-shaped car. Francis cries, "We're gonna need a bigger boat!" This was a reference to the line uttered by Brody (Roy Scheider) when he got his first good look at the shark while aboard the *Orca* in the film *Jaws* (1975) (actually, Brody said, "*You're* gonna need a bigger boat").

Welcome Back, Kotter

The show's producer, James Komack, provides the voice of principal John Lazarus.

Werewolf

Chuck Connors stars as 1,600-year-old fishing boat captain Janos Skorzeny, now a diabolical killer. Connors's character was named after a character in the television movie *The Night Stalker* (1971 TV), which led to the paranormal series of the same name. In the telefilm, Barry Atwater played a vampire named Janos Skorzeny.

The Whistling Wizard

In this 1951-52 childrens' puppet show, in order for the villainous Spider Lady to perform her black magic, she utters the words "Elia Kazan." Kazan was a Hollywood director who made, among other films, *A Streetcar Named Desire* (1951), *On the Waterfront* (1954) and *East of Eden* (1955).

The Wild Wild West

At the end of one episode, guest star Alan Hale, Jr., tells West that he (Hale) is going to an island for a long vacation. Hale had previously appeared as the Skipper on *Gilligan's Island*.

Hurd Hatfield appears as a guest star in the episode "The Night of the Man-Eating House." He plays a character who is aged at first, then regains his youth through supernatural means, and ages again at the episode's end. Hatfield is most famous for his first movie role, that of the ever-youthful Dorian Gray in the film *The Picture of Dorian Gray* (1945), in which the title character remains young until the very end, when he rapidly ages.

Wings

In the episode "The Big Wedding," Brian accidentally picks up tuxedos for the Hackel bar mitzvah instead of the Hackett wedding. The name is a reference to Dave Hackel, who is a writer and producer of the show.

Wiseguy

Lynchboro, the town in the Lynchboro arc (series of stories), was named after David Lynch, and referred to his town Twin Peaks. At the time these episodes were shown, *Twin Peaks* had not yet aired but did exist. Lynchboro even had a crying deputy, just like Twin Peaks.

When Vinnie calls him to come to Lynchboro, Roger Lococco (William Russ) has the line "You wouldn't believe how rusty I am." "Rusty" is actor William Russ's nickname.

The episode "Romp" reunites Ken Wahl with Tony Ganios and Jim Youngs from Wahl's first film, *The Wanderers* (1979). The episode shows the three of them chumming around with each other, just like in the movie.

In the Seattle storyline, the toxic-shock mad dog killer is named "John Kousakis." John Kousakis was the name of a well-known television director who had always wanted a homicidal maniac killer named after him.

WKRP in Cincinnati

The unintelligible lyrics sung over the show's closing credits are actually gibberish. Tom Chehak, a first season writer-producer who was present at the Atlanta recording session of the theme, recalls how Tom Welles, the opening theme's writer, suggested to Chehak and series creator Hugh Wilson a closing theme for the series. According to Chehak, the singer just started blurting out a bunch of nonsense words; if any of them were actual words, they're lost to history. Chehak remarked how great they all thought it would be to leave fans guessing forever—looks like they got their wish.

On the first day of filming the pilot episode, Richard Sanders (Les Nessman) got hit on the head with a studio light. He was rushed to the hospital and had to wear a gauze bandage throughout the episode. Figuring it added to the klutzy aspect of his character, Sanders took it upon himself to have a band-aid visible somewhere on him in every following episode, creating a kind of running joke. For a while, Hugh Wilson wanted to explain it, but he left it ambiguous. In the episode "Les' Groupie," it was revealed that Les owned a vicious dog named Phil, partly explaining his band-aids.

The character of Andy Travis (played by Gary Sandy) was based on Hugh Wilson's cousin, whose name is Andy Travis. The real Andy is a policeman, not a program director, but many of the traits of WKRP's Andy, including his love of cowboy hats, were taken from Wilson's cousin.

Jennifer's (Loni Anderson) doorbell plays the first few bars of the song "Fly Me to the Moon."

In the episode where Carlson runs for city council, he runs against a woman named Mitzi Monahan. Mitzi is played by Lillian Garrett-Bonner, wife of Frank Bonner (Herb Tarlek).

Les's reporting on the turkey drop in "Turkeys Away" is patterned after the famous report of the Hindenburg Zeppelin crash.

In the "Real Families" episode, there is a dig at *Little House on the Prairie*, which was *WKRP*'s chief competition during most of its run.

Series writer Bill Dial ("Preacher," "Turkeys Away") plays station engineer Bucky Dornster in two episodes: "Hold Up," in which Del's Stereo and Sound was held up, and "Baseball," where he plays third base for WKRP.

Also in "Hold Up," writer-creator Hugh Wilson, writer Tom Chehak and writer Blake Hunter play the three cops.

In the episode "I Do, I Do, For Now," the show's associate director (and former stage manager) Buzz Sapien plays the man in the elevator at the end who witnesses (and participates in) Jennifer and T.J.'s conversation.

Dog, the lead singer of the hoodlum rock group Scum of the Earth, is played by actor–rock singer Michael Des Barres. Des Barres was also the lead singer of the local group Detective, who performed Scum's music for the episode.

Clark Callahan, the blow-hard station manager at WPIG in the baseball episode, is played by Ross Bickell, who was Loni Anderson's husband at the time of the taping. Bickell was one of the hopefuls who had tried out for the part of Andy Travis, and he was the one who told Anderson of the auditions for the part of Jennifer.

Loni Anderson started out in theater in Minnesota, and once did a play with veteran actor Pat O'Brien, who convinced her to go to Hollywood. As thanks, Anderson got O'Brien a role in

this series as one of Jennifer's elderly wealthy dates.

Writer-producer Steve Marshall plays the second deliveryman in the episode "Jennifer's Home for Christmas."

Richard Sanders's writing partner, Michael Fairman, plays pilot and war veteran Buddy Barker in "The Airplane Show."

In the episode "Out to Lunch," where Herb discovers his drinking problem, Gordon Jump's (Arthur Carlson) daughter Cindy Jump appears as a girl in the bar.

In the episode "Changes," Venus (Tim Reid) is worried about being interviewed by a reporter from a black magazine. The reporter turns out to be Rick Jesperson, a white man. Jesperson is played by Tom Dreesen, who had previously been in a stand-up comedy team with Tim Reid named Tim and Tom.

Former WKRP receptionist Joyce Armor (Rosemary Forsyth), who Carlson thought was coming on to him in the two-part episode "An Explosive Affair," was named after series writer Joyce Armor ("Bailey's Show," "Ask Jennifer").

Mr. Armor (Parley Baer), the kindly old station manager who preceded Arthur Carlson (seen in "Bah, Humbug") was also named after Joyce Armor.

Major Hunter (Nicholas Worth), who presides over Gordon Sims's (Venus) military hearing in the episode "Who Is Gordon Sims?" was named after series writer Blake Hunter ("Goodbye Johnny," "Tornado").

Dr. Levin (Andy Romano), who delivers Carmen Carlson's baby in "The Baby," was named after series writer Lissa Levin ("The Doctor's Daughter," "Bah, Humbug").

Creator Hugh Wilson wrote the episode "Fish Story" under the pseudonym "Raoul Plager," because he thought it was the silliest episode he had ever written.

The X-Files

The inclusion of the mirror-imaged beans that germinate and sprout roots during the opening credits (they are on either side of the screen during the words "Paranormal Activity") could refer to a television special that was hosted by mentalist Uri Geller and paranormal debunker James "The Amazing" Randi. At one point in the show, Geller claimed that he could make seeds sprout by using his psychic powers. He put some seeds in the palm of his hand, made a tight fist and then concentrated his psychic powers on the seeds. After a couple of minutes Geller opened his fist and the seeds had begun to sprout. However, Randi noted that the "before" seeds were dry and small, but the "after" seeds were larger due to absorbed water. He said that simple substitution was a trick that any kid could master, and had a kid duplicate the trick. The germinating seeds could be an exaggerated reference to this.

Another intriguing image in the opening credits is the dark imprint of a hand with one bright red segment. This is a Kirlian photograph. Kirlian photos are supposed to show the aura of a living object. The color and composition of the aura are said to show general health, mental state, and so forth. For example, a stressed person would exhibit a spiky aura, whereas a relaxed person will have a much smoother line. All living things are said to produce a picture in Kirlian photography, but dead or inanimate objects will not produce anything. Creator Chris Carter

has said that he really only included the Kirlian photograph and the time-lapse of the germinating beans because "they looked cool." In fact, in the episode "Leonard Betts," Dr. Charles Burns, an expert in Kirlian photography, calls it "pretty cool."

The voice who says "I made this!" at the end of each show is not that of Chris Carter's son, as has been rumored—it is Nathan Couturier, son of supervising sound editor Thierry Couturier. Couturier said that when they were putting together the Ten Thirteen logo, Carter suggested using a child's voice and Thierry nominated his son, Nathan, who at the time was 9 years old. They got the sound they wanted in about ten takes.

Ten Thirteen Productions was named after Carter's own birthday, October 13, 1956 (10/13/56). Mulder's birthday has also been established as October 13, and this number appears in many episodes. Other appearances are listed below.

At the end of the opening credits, there is a line shown onscreen: "The Truth Is Out There." However, for the episode "Anasazi," the line was changed to "Ei 'Aaniigoo 'Ahoot'e," which is Navajo for "the truth is out there."

The number "11:21" that repeatedly appears on digital clocks in the series (e.g., at the end of the pilot; when Mulder calls Scully in "The Erlenmeyer Flask"; when Scully is woken up in the episode "Irresistible"; and when the faux Mulder wakes Scully in "Colony") is an affectionate nod by creator and executive producer Chris Carter to his wife, screenwriter Dori Pierson, whose birthday is November 21, 1948 (11/21/48). Other appearances of Pierson's birthdate in the series are listed below.

The names "Fox," "Mulder" and "Scully" all come from Carter's youth. His mother's maiden name is Mulder; he had a childhood friend with the given name "Fox" (a name he always liked); and when he was a kid he would listen to "the voice of doom" on radio: sportscaster Vin Scully.

Carter also uses his parents' names for Mulder, Scully and their relatives. Carter's father's name is William. Scully's father's name is William, Mulder's father's name is William, one of Scully's brothers is named William, and Mulder's middle name is William. Carter's mother's name is Catherine, and Scully's middle name is Katherine.

The production crew (and their names) have had many appearances in various episodes. Examples include:

First assistant director Tom Braidwood appears as Lone Gunman photographer Frohike in "E.B.E.," "Blood," "One Breath," "Fearful Symmetry," "Anasazi" and "The Blessing Way." Frohike is the short, dark, bespectacled one of the three. Braidwood's name is being written on Howard Graves's parking spot in "Shadows," and Mulder uses the alias "Tom Braidwood" to get into the secured government compound in Washington State in "E.B.E." Scully used the alias "Val Stefoff" in the same episode. Vladimir Stefoff is also a first assistant director on the series.

Stunt coordinator Ken Kirzinger appears as team captain John Richter, who speaks in the broadcast messages in "Ice."

Gillian Anderson's stand-in for scene blocking, Bonnie Hay, plays the part of a doctor in "Colony" and "End Game." She also appears as the night nurse in "D.P.O.," as a therapist in "Oubliette" and as a nurse, again, in "Talitha Cumi."

In the episode "Anasazi," Chris Carter appears as an FBI agent grilling Scully. He is the one who asks, "Weren't you originally assigned to Agent Mulder to debunk his work?" Producer R.H. Goodwin was also supposed to have a role in this episode as a gardener, but his scene was cut during filming.

Darin Morgan plays the part of the Flukeman in "The Host." Morgan is a screenwriter on the series and is the brother of coexecutive producer Glen Morgan.

Agent Pendrell (Brendan Beiser), the FBI scientific expert with a crush on Scully who appears in "Nisei," "731," "Apocrypha," "Avatar" and "Herrenvolk," is named after Pendrell Street, in the west end of Vancouver, where the series is filmed.

The remaining in-jokes are listed by episode.

"Pilot": The pilot takes place in Bellfleur, Oregon. Chris Carter was born in Bellflower, California.

The time of the autopsy is shown to be 10:56. These are Chris Carter's month and year of birth (October [13], 1956).

"Deep Throat": Mulder and Scully are stopped by two carfuls of government agents. Scully later phones to check the license of one of the cars. It is "CC1356." This stands for creator Chris Carter's initials and day and year of birth (the thirteenth [of October], 1956).

"Deep Throat" was file #DF101364, as noted in Scully's report at the end of the episode. Again, the number "1013" appears.

The article on Ellens Air Base that Scully reads from on microfiche was written by a "Chris Carter."

Colonel Budahas tells Mulder and Scully that his birthday is 11/21/48, the same birthdate as Carter's wife.

"Conduit": The address in Samantha Mulder's file is 2790 Vine Street. This was the former address of the *X-Files* production offices in Vancouver.

"Ghost in the Machine": The name of the fictional town, Crystal City, is an allusion to Silicon Valley.

"Ice": Writers (and San Diego Chargers fans) James Wong and Glen Morgan made Steve Hynter's character, Dr. Denny Murphy, a native of San Diego. As Mulder and Scully first approach him, he is listening to a tape of one of his all-time favorite plays, from an old Chargers-Raiders game. Chargers quarterback Dan Fouts throws a touchdown pass and Murphy jumps up and proclaims, "Fouts … is … God."

"Fallen Angel": UFO chaser Max Fenig appears in this episode, wearing a cap reading "NICAP." His cap can be seen hanging on Mulder's coat rack in his office in future episodes, one being "Beyond the Sea."

Deep Throat's warning to Mulder is a quote from *The Godfather* (1972): "Keep your friends close, but keep your enemies closer."

"Eve": The two little "Eve" girls are named Cindy and Teena, after the wives of writer-producers Glen Morgan and James Wong.

As Mulder and Scully question mother Ellen Reardon, Eve-girl Cindy Reardon is watching the cartoon *Eek the Cat* on television. This cartoon later featured Mulder and Scully parodies.

"Fire": There is a mention of a "three-pipe problem." This is a reference to Sherlock Holmes (whose relationship with Dr. Watson may have partly inspired the Mulder-Scully team). The harder that Holmes's cases were, the more he mulled over them while smoking his pipe. A "three-pipe problem" was especially tough.

The time of the autopsy Scully performs is 10:56 (Carter's birth month and year).

This is X-File #11214893, as reported by Scully. 11/21/48 appears again, as does the year this episode was filmed, 1993.

"Beyond the Sea": Max Fenig's NICAP cap (from "Fallen Angel") hangs on the hat rack in the X-Files office.

"Genderbender": The music used for the disco in the opening scene is from *X-Files* scorer Mark Snow's theme music for the television movie *In the Line of Duty: Street War* (1992 TV).

Steveston, Massachusetts, the town where the Kindred live, is named after Steveston, a small community south of Vancouver, beloved by the location manager for *The X-Files* because of its diversity of settings.

"Miracle Man": The autopsy time is 11:21, Chris Carter's wife's birthday.

"Tooms": Mulder mentions that he was listening to "four hours of ba-ba-booie" during an all-night stakeout. This is a reference to radio shock jock Howard Stern's radio show. "Ba-ba-booie" is Stern's nickname for his producer, Gary. The nickname started when Gary mispronounced the name "Ba-ba-Louie" as "BabaBooie." It sounded so goofy that they made a tape clip of it and tormented Gary with it. The term has also become popular as a catch phrase for prank calls to other radio stations.

The name on the door adjoining Tooms's cell is L. Robbie Maier. Rob Maier is the construction coordinator on the show.

"The Erlenmeyer Flask": The ending of this episode mirrors the ending of the pilot: Mulder calls Scully at

11:21 (Chris Carter's wife's birth date), and the Cancerman stores proof of alien existence deep within the Pentagon.

The room containing the people in tanks is behind door number 1056 — Chris Carter's birth month and year (October [13], 1956).

"Little Green Men": The X-Files Manifest is the list of those X-Philes (fans of the show) whose names appear on the airline passenger manifest that Scully examines in this episode. The list is as follows.

1. Alves, Paulette
2. Anglin, Donald
3. Bartle, Sylvia
4. Berreman, Xinh
5. Brice, Sarah
6. Brown, Kelly
7. Carstensen, Tere
8. Celio, Gail
9. Chen, Cliff
10. Dawson, Hayden
11. Dawson, Lori
12. Erickson, Harle
13. Ferguson, Garn
14. Giannini, Jodi
15. Gompf, Jan
16. Gonzalez, Pat
17. Gostin, Jeff
18. Grant, Charles
19. Grant, Betty
20. Hale, George E.
21. Harris, Andrew
22. Harris, Melissa
23. Hill, Linda Lee
24. Hill, Scott
25. Hofmann, Eliza

Cliff Chen (#9, above) is also the keeper of the Internet *X-Files* episode guide. Pat Gonzalez is the keeper of the "Frequently Asked Questions" page on *The X-Files* on the Internet. Charles Grant is an author of *X-Files* material. "George E. Hale" is a pseudonym that Mulder likes to travel under when he doesn't want to be found. In the episode "Sleepless" he calls Scully at the Academy using the name George Hale.

The senator in "Little Green Men" is named Senator Richard Matheson (Raymond J. Barry), after the sci-fi/horror author who wrote the two telemovies of the series *Kolchak: The Night Stalker*. Mulder would visit his office again in "Ascension."

The number 1013 (Chris Carter's birthday) appears over and over down a column of the "WOW Signal." It is under the heading "Galactic Longitude."

"The Host": The autopsy Scully performs is case number DP112148. These are Carter's wife's initials (Dori Pierson) and birthdate (November 21, 1948).

The autopsy is performed on John Doe number 101356, which is Carter's birthdate (October 13, 1956).

"Blood": The nurse buzzing on the door is buzzing the word "Kill" in morse code.

"Duane Barry": While filming this episode, Gillian Anderson was pregnant ... so when she goes to the store to "borrow" the barcode reader, she buys pickles and ice cream, the stereotypical food of pregnant women.

"Ascension": When Mulder plays Scully's frantic answering machine message, the time is 11:23. It can be assumed that she was abducted at 11:21.

"3": Club Tepes is named after Prince Vlad Tepes, or Vlad the Impaler, the inspiration for Dracula. In the first shot of Club Tepes, two bald clubbers walk by a picture of a man with a big black moustache on the wall. This is a picture of Vlad the Impaler.

In the garage, the Unholy Spirit (the

woman "vampire") says "I will live forever" in Transylvanian.

"One Breath": The Lone Gunmen invite Mulder to come over and jump on the Internet to "nitpick the scientific inaccuracies of *Earth 2*." This is a nod to the Internet *X-Files* community and quite possibly the *Netpicker's Guide to the X-Files*. Mulder's response? "I'm doing my laundry."

Writer Glen Morgan has said that he named Nurse Owens (Nicola Cavendish) after his grandmother.

The Thinker, who was mentioned in this episode and seen later in "Anasazi," is modeled after fan and America Online member Yung Jun Kim, also known as "DuhThinker."

"Red Museum": Gird Thomas, the peeping tom who writes "he/she is one" on the backs of the kids, shares his name with the famous Peeping Tom of Coventry—the original peeping tom.

"Aubrey": Mulder says, "I have this fascination with women named B.J." B.J. is the name of a character that Duchovny's then-girlfriend Perrey Reeves played on *Doogie Howser*. Reeves also appeared in the *X-Files* episode "3."

"Irresistible"—Creator Chris Carter has a namesake who plays in the NFL": Cris Carter, a wide receiver with the Minnesota Vikings. Cris appeared on television in Bock's (Bruce Weitz) office in this episode. He can be seen catching a pass for a touchdown, and then running, facing away from the television camera, so that his name is visible on his back. The Vikings were playing the Washington Redskins, who, incidentally, have a player named Carter on their roster as well: cornerback Tom Carter.

The name "Soames" appears on a headstone as Scully and Mulder walk through the cemetery. In the pilot, Scully and Mulder exhume the body of a boy named Ray Soames.

"Die Hand die Verletzt": This episode was the last one written by James Wong and Glen Morgan, who left the series to develop and produce the series *Space: Above and Beyond*. They said goodbye to the cast and crew by use of the cryptic line on the chalkboard at the end of this episode reading "Good-bye—It's been nice working with you." After *Space: Above and Beyond* was cancelled, however, Morgan and Wong returned to the show.

"Die Hand die Verletzt" was aired two days before Super Bowl XXIX, between the San Francisco 49ers and the San Diego Chargers, and writer-producers James Wong and Glen Morgan, who are big Chargers fans, made their loyalties evident. They were listed under the coexecutive producer credits as James "Chargers" Wong and Glen "Bolts, Baby" Morgan (see also "Ice").

Crowley High School was named after British ceremonialist Aleister Crowley, whose theories on "magick" greatly influenced the development of modern Wicca.

School psychologist Pete Calcagni (Shaun Johnston), the bespectacled member of the witchly quartet, is named after the husband of an *X-Files* fan.

The Ausbury family are named after Jill Ausbury, another fan of the show.

The other two teachers who make up the quartet, Paul Vitaris (Doug Abrahams) and Deborah Brown (P. Lynn Johnson) are named after Internet *X-Files* fans Paula Vitaris and Deborah Brown.

Jerry, the boy who is killed in the forest, is named after Jerry Jones, host of the America On-Line *X-Files* forum.

Susan Blommaert, who plays Mrs. Paddock, the substitute biology teacher, also played a biology teacher in a popular Butterfinger commercial.

"**Colony**": Ambrose Chapel, the CIA agent who speaks with Mulder and Scully, shares his name with a church in the Alfred Hitchcock movie *The Man Who Knew Too Much* (1956). In the movie, "Ambrose Chapel" was incorrectly assumed to be the name of a person.

"**End Game**": At the top of Mulder's e-mail to Scully, we see the line: "To: Dana Scully, 001013," another appearance of "1013."

"**Fearful Symmetry**": The title of this episode, in which a tiger escapes, is from the William Blake poem "The Tyger." The building where the tiger is captured is owned by Blake Towers.

"**Død Kälm**": The life raft that the crewmen jump into in the opening teaser has the number 925 on the side. September 25 (9/25) is the birthdate of Gillian Anderson's daughter, Piper.

"**Humbug**": The trailer park is named Gulf Breeze, after the location known as a hotbed for UFO sightings.

"**F. Emasculata**": The package mailed to the inmate is package number DPP112148, named after Chris Carter's wife, Dori P. Pierson, and her birthday.

The house number of the escaped prisoner's wife is 925, again the birthdate of Gillian Anderson's daughter, Piper (September 25).

Angelo Vacoo, who appears as Angelo Garza, is a production assistant in the offices of Ten Thirteen in Los Angeles. The part was written specifically for him.

"**Soft Light**": As Scully examines an air vent, the detective remarks that no one could fit through there, and Mulder jumps in with "You never know." This is a reference to Eugene Victor Tooms from the episodes "Squeeze" and "Tooms."

Mulder and Scully discover that the hotel victim worked for the "Morleys" cigarette manufacturer. This is the brand of cigarettes smoked by the *X-Files* character Cancerman.

"**Our Town**": Mr. Chaco and Chaco Chicken are named for Chaco Canyon, New Mexico, where the Anasazi tribe lived and where boiled bones such as those depicted in the episode were discovered.

"**Anasazi**": As Mulder is perusing the untranslated lines on his computer screen, the line "do-ray-me-fa-so-la-ti-do" (five lines under the Department of Defense heading) can be made out.

At the episode's beginning, the radio in Albert Hosteen's house reports that the New Mexico earthquake was felt as far south as Roswell and Corona. Roswell is the site of the famous alien spaceship crash, but according to some books concerned with "the Roswell crash," the UFO actually crashed at Corona, New Mexico; Roswell was just the largest town within 75 miles.

"**The Blessing Way**": The third season opener has a dedication at the end. It reads: "In Memoriam. Larry Wells. 1946–1995." Wells was the show's costume designer.

Krycek (Nicholas Lea) is an accomplice in the killing of Melissa Scully, who is played by Melinda McGraw, Lea's real-life girlfriend.

"**Paper Clip**": At the end of the episode, there is a line printed on the screen: "In Memoriam. Mario Mark Kennedy. 1966–1995." Kennedy was a major fan of the show who had organized on-line discussion sessions on the Internet. He died in a car crash.

Mulder's birthday is shown on his file as 10/13/60, which is also Chris Carter's birth month and day.

Samantha Mulder's birthday is shown on her file as 11/21/64, which is Chris Carter's wife's birth month and day.

One of Krychek's accomplices who beats Skinner up in the stairwell is played by stunt coordinator Tony Morelli.

"D.P.O.": When Darin is bothering his mother by changing the channels on the television, it ends up on a channel that is showing a music video. In the lower left corner of the screen we see the video's information: The Rosemarys, "Mary Beth Clarke, I Love You," JHartling Records, Director: Deb Brown. Mary Beth Clarke is an America On-Line X-Phile, JHartling is the screen name of another AOL X-Phile, and Deb Brown is yet another AOL X-Phile.

The Astadourian Lightning Observatory is named after Mary Astadourian, the chief researcher and office manager of the series' production offices, as well as Chris Carter's personal assistant.

Darin Peter Oswald is named for writer Darin Morgan.

The yearbook page from which Darin cuts Mrs. Kiveat's picture also contains yearbook pictures of director Kim Manners and prop master Ken Hawryliw.

Finding Sharon Kiveat's yearbook picture between the pages of an adult magazine could be a reference to the fact that the actress playing Sharon (Karen Witter) once modeled for *Playboy.*

Sheriff Teller was named for Teller, the mute half of the comedy-magic team of Penn & Teller. Both Penn and Teller have expressed a desire to appear in an episode of the show.

"Clyde Bruckman's Final Repose": The character of Clyde Bruckman (Peter Boyle) was named after a real-life one-time successful Hollywood writer-director. In 1955, Bruckman, driven to drink by professional failure and marital problems and armed with a pistol he had borrowed from Buster Keaton, shot himself to death in the restroom of a Hollywood restaurant after a meal for which he could not pay. Bruckman also directed several Laurel and Hardy comedies, and Scully watches a Laurel and Hardy film at the end of the episode, though that one was not directed by Bruckman.

The dead man under the wheels of Scully's car is named "Claude Dukenfield," which was the real name of W.C. Fields, who Bruckman directed in *The Fatal Glass of Beer* (1932), *The Man on the Flying Trapeze* (1935), and numerous short films in the silent era.

Detective Havez, the detective who is assigned to watch over Bruckman in the hotel room, is named after Jean C. Havez, who collaborated with the real Clyde Bruckman on numerous Buster Keaton film screenplays, including *Seven Chances* (1925), *The Navigator* (1924) and *Sherlock, Jr.* (1924).

The other police detective, Detective Cline, is named after Eddie Cline, a contemporary of Bruckman and Havez. He cowrote numerous Buster Keaton films with Keaton, including *The Haunted House* (1921), *The Boat* (1921) and *The Three Ages* (1923).

The hotel that the killer works for is named El Damfino, just like Buster Keaton's boat "Damfino" in his aforementioned movie *The Boat.* The man to whom Bruckman tries to sell life insurance "really wanted to buy a boat."

"Clyde Bruckman's Final Repose" refers back to an earlier *X-Files* episode cowritten by Darin Morgan's brother Glen. When Mulder gives Clyde all of the objects to see if he gets any "vibes" from them, Scully calls Mulder over to talk, and then Bruckman says, "I've got it, this is off of your New York Knicks T-shirt," to which Mulder replies, "Miss." In "Beyond the Sea," Mulder hands the blue scrap of cloth from the evidence bag to Luther Boggs (Brad Dourif), and Boggs does his little psychic spiel about where the killer had taken the kids. When he is done, Mulder takes the scrap and whispers to Boggs, "I tore this off of my New York Knicks T-shirt. It has nothing to do with the crime."

When the killer turns over the last tarot card, "Death," the camera immediately cuts to Bruckman, who is playing cards. He is holding aces and eights, also known as the "dead man's hand."

The actor who plays the Stupendous Yappi, Jaap Broeker, is actually David Duchovny's stand-in. He fills in for Duchovny when scenes are blocked or lighting is measured. Writer Darin Morgan saw Broekker on the set one day waggling his eyebrows and wrote the scene in this episode for him.

The bellhop is played by Stu Charno, husband of former *X-Files* staff writer Sara Charno, who wrote the episodes "Aubrey" and "The Calusari."

"The List": The chaplain is played by producer Joseph Patrick Finn.

The executioner, Perry Simon, was named after an NBC executive producer that Chris Carter knew while working for NBC.

"2Shy": When Mulder tells Scully about the test results of Incanto's skin sample, the time is 10:13 (Chris Carter's birthday).

"Nisei": Mulder has a strap-on gun

in the episode "Nisei" because so many people on the Internet newsgroup had mentioned the fact that Mulder is constantly losing his gun.

The boxcar that the doctors are killed in, before the opening credits, is car number 82594. 8/25/94 is the date that Chris Carter began working on his directorial debut, "Duane Barry."

After the MUFON woman opens the door and recognizes Scully, another woman comes to the door and says "She's one." The actress who says "She's one," Gillian Barber, is the same woman who played the mother in "Red Museum"—the episode in which kids disappeared and returned with the words "He/She is one" painted on their backs.

"731": The combination Scully gives Mulder to free him from the boxcar is #101331, another appearance of "1013."

The title of the episode refers to Camp 731, a germ warfare research station run in Manchuko (Japanese-occupied Manchuria) by General Shiro Ishii, who was known as the Japanese Dr. Mengele. Hideous experiments were conducted there on prisoners of war. After the war, Ishii and his crew were recruited into the American bio-war research establishment.

"War of the Coprophages": The name of the town, Miller's Grove, mirrors that of Grover's Mill, which was the supposed landing site of the Martians in the radio play and movie *War of the Worlds,* from which this episode takes its title. Both this episode and *War of the Worlds* involve mass hysteria, and there are other parallels between the two. For example, a sailor is seen buying chocolates and nylons, which were a popular gift of the 40's, when the radio play was broadcast.

Scully is seen reading *Breakfast at Tiffany's* by the fire. The title of this book was the answer to the question (or, rather, question for the answer) that David Duchovny had missed when he was on *Celebrity Jeopardy!* It ended up costing him the game.

The newscaster is named Skye Leikin, after a fan of the series who frequents the *X-Files* Internet newsgroup named Leikin Sky. She won an America On-Line trivia contest, the prize for which was to get her screen name in one of the episodes.

Dr. Bambi Berenbaum (Bobbie Phillips) is named after Dr. May R. Berenbaum, head of the Entomology Department at the University of Illinois, and author of such books on insects as *Ninety-Nine Gnats, Nits, and Nibblers; Ninety-Nine More Maggots, Mites, and Munchers;* and *Bugs in the System.*

At the end of the episode, Scully mentions that "Smart is sexy" in reference to the two scientists. "Smart is sexy" is also a phrase used by many magazines and news programs when talking about Mulder and Scully themselves.

The robotics researcher, A. Ivanov, has a name reminiscent of *I Robot* author I. (Isaac) Asimov.

"**Syzygy**": The two girls mention that they attend Grover Cleveland Alexander High School. This was another wrong answer by Duchovny on *Celebrity Jeopardy!* The answer was, "This president was named for the Reverend Stephen Grover of Caldwell, New Jersey." Duchovny said, "Who is Grover Cleveland Alexander?" when the correct question was, "Who is Grover Cleveland?" It was the only question he missed in regular play.

When Mulder brings the first girl into the police station, the time is 11:48 (Chris Carter's wife's birth month and year—November 1948).

This episode first aired on January 12, 1996. A syzygy of Mars, Mercury, and Uranus actually occurred on that date, just as it did in the episode.

The cross-dressing doctor, R. W. Godfrey, was named after the show's coexecutive producer, R. W. Goodwin.

"**Grotesque**": Agent Nemhauser shares his name with post production supervisor Lori Jo Nemhauser.

"**Piper Maru**": This episode, which is the name of a fictional sunken WWII submarine, was named after Gillian Anderson's daughter, Piper Maru. Piper made a cameo appearance on a bus in the episode "Avatar."

Chris Carter has acknowledged that the inscription "Drop Dead Red" on the submerged plane is a tribute to the show's "Intellectually Drop Dead Gorgeous Redhead," Gillian Anderson.

The flight Mulder and Krycek take back to Washington is flight number 1121 (Carter's wife's birthday).

The diver in this episode is named Gauthier, after Dave Gauthier, the *X-Files* effects supervisor.

The World War II pilot is played by Robert F. Maier, who is also the series' construction coordinator.

"**Apocrypha**": The number on the door of the silo where Krycek and the alien craft are being held is 1013 (Chris Carter's birthday).

"**Pusher**": The black and white film on TV when Mulder and Scully raid the Pusher's apartment is *Svengali* (1931), which was about a demonic artist named Svengali who uses hypnosis to control a young artist's model.

Dave Grohl of the rock group Foo Fighters (who appear on the *X-Files* soundtrack album) and his wife Jennifer Youngblood-Grohl appear uncredited in this episode. They can be seen walking in the background in the FBI headquarters just before Modell goes through the metal detector. Grohl is wearing a green down jacket.

The front page of the tabloid newspaper picked up by the Pusher in the grocery store line contains an "artist's impression" drawing of Flukeman from "The Host." Apparently, he washed up on Martha's Vineyard—Mulder's hometown.

The tabloid also contains a picture in the top corner which has a caption that reads "Depravity Rampant on Hit TV Show" and a picture of prop master Ken Hawryliw with a strip-o-gram on his birthday.

Holly, the secretary who beats Skinner up, is named after writer Vince Gilligan's wife.

When Skinner comes into the records office, Pusher tells him, "Take a walk, Mel Cooley!" Mel Cooley (Richard Deacon) was the immediate supervisor of Rob, Buddy and Sally on *The Dick Van Dyke Show*. A lot of jokes were made at his expense about his baldness and stuffiness, hence the connection with Skinner.

"Teso dos Bichos": The title is Portuguese for "burial ground of small animals."

Dr. Lewton was named after Val Lewton, producer of the movie *Cat People* (1942).

"Jose Chung's from Outer Space": The opening shot of what appears to be a *Star Wars* Star Destroyer–type ship turns out to be only the underside of a cherry picker. This is both a reference to *Star Wars* and a message to the fans, telling them that this is not just another stereotypical UFO alien abduction show.

The location on the screen is given as Klass County. Philip J. Klass is a well-known and very dedicated UFO debunker. His book *UFOs*

Explained is even paraphrased in this episode.

The red alien is an amalgam of the creature creations of stop-motion animation expert Ray Harryhausen, most notably his Ymir from the film *20 Million Miles to Earth* (1957), the Cyclops in Harryhausen's *The 7th Voyage of Sinbad* (1958), and various other creatures.

It has been suggested that the name "Jose Chung" refers to the name of noted psychiatrist Carl Gustav Jung. In his monograph *Flying Saucers: A Modern Myth of Things Seen in the Skies*, Jung notes that "just at the moment when the eyes of mankind are turned towards the heavens, partly on account of their fantasies about possible space-ships, and partly in a figurative sense because their earthly existence is threatened, unconscious contents have projected themselves on these inexplicable heavenly phenomenon and given them a significance they in no way deserve." This would certainly correspond to the theme of the episode. Actually, "Jose Chung" was the name that the show's writing staff used when making prank calls to the show's offices. "Jose Chung" would keep calling to find out the status of an unsolicited manuscript that he had sent to the show.

Scully says that Chung's *The Lonely Buddha* is one of her favorite books. This could be a possible reference to the novel *Siddhartha* by Herman Hesse. Hesse was an author of some stature and he was heavily influenced by Carl Jung (see above). *Siddhartha* is a book ostensibly about Buddha, but also a book about extremely altered perceptions.

Chung wants to create a new literary genre: nonfiction science fiction, which sounds a lot like the premise of *The X-Files*.

When Chrissy awakens, she imagines she sees a grey alien at the foot of her bed. It turns out only to be her stuffed cat. This may be a reference to the earlier episode in the season, "Teso Dos Bichos," which concerned hordes of killer pussycats. In fact, since Gillian Anderson is allergic to cats, the one that "attacked" her in that episode was actually a stuffed one.

Chung's thriller *The Caligarian Candidate* is mentioned. The title is an combination of two films which both dealt with mind-control. *The Manchurian Candidate* (1962) was about a brainwashed soldier who is led to believe in alternate versions of reality so that he may be fatally manipulated by political rogues. *The Cabinet of Dr. Caligari* (1919) is about a "magician" who hypnotizes a sleepwalker into committing a series of murders. At the end, however, Caligari is revealed to be a kindly doctor and no more than a figment of the insane narrator's imagination. Again, it is about perception.

Chung mentions the CIA's MK-Ultra mind control experiments. These are factual, as reported by a poster on the *X-Files* Internet newsgroup.

The hypnotist that puts Chrissy under is played by Alex Diakin, who also appeared in the episodes "Humbug," as the museum curator, and "Clyde Bruckman's Final Repose," as the last murdered psychic. Both these episodes were also written by Darin Morgan.

Detective Manners is named after the director of writer Darin Morgan's previous episode, "Humbug," Kim Manners. The production people on the show have also revealed that the "bleeps" refer to Kim Manners's propensity to constantly curse on the set. There is also the ironic play on words, showing, by swearing, that the character actually has no manners.

Roky Crikenson is named after psychedelic singer Roky Erickson, lead singer of the 1960s group The 13th Floor Elevators, who is credited as pioneering psychedelic rock. Later, in the early 1980s, he formed the group Roky Erickson and the Aliens, recording such songs as "I Walked with a Zombie" and "I Think of Demons." There was even a Roky Erickson tribute album, *Where the Pyramid Meets the Eye*. Erickson has suffered several bouts with mental illness, and, at one point, even claimed to be a Martian.

Roky's a lineman, just like Roy Neary (Richard Dreyfuss) was in *Close Encounters of the Third Kind* (1977).

The car of the men in black resembles the Batmobile not only in style, but in the way it takes corners and roars in and out of Roky's garage.

The first Man in Black's opening line is taken from UFO debunker Philip J. Klass's book, *UFOs Explained*. The line in the book reads, "No single object has been misinterpreted as a 'flying saucer' more often than the planet Venus."

Lord Kinbote is named after Charles Kinbote, a character in Vladimir Nabokov's novel *Pale Fire*. He is a professor of literature who may really be the deposed king (hence "Lord" Kinbote) of Zembla, Charles Botkin, or may simply be completely mad. The story has to do with perception and the subjectivity of narration. In *Pale Fire*, Kinbote is the narrator, but it turns out he is completely unreliable and anything he reveals cannot be trusted.

Roky's manifesto was written in screenplay format, which Chung was extremely annoyed at. A copy was sent to his publisher. The *X-Files* production offices are constantly deluged with unsolicited screenplays for the series, and this could refer to the producers' exasperation.

The arrangement of the three groups of individuals around Chrissy is identical in all three scenarios (the police station, the alien vessel, the Air Force office). That is to say, there is someone sitting directly in front of her, two off to the right, one off to the left, and so forth. This arrangement is also identical to the one used in the film *The Manchurian Candidate* during the hypnotizing scenes.

When Chrissy is under hypnosis, one of the Air Force men says to "ask her if the third alien [Kinbote] had a Russian accent!" The name Kinbote is from *Pale Fire*, a novel written by an Americanized Russian. Kinbote also appears in red (a Russian connotation) light.

Blaine, the man first seen sitting in his room being interviewed by Chung, is a jab at the incredibly obsessed fans of the show and science fiction in general. He has the line "I just want to be taken away to some place where I don't have to worry about finding a job."

Blaine is wearing a grey *Space: Above and Beyond* T-shirt. James Wong and Glen Morgan, who were writers on *The X-Files*, left to create the series *Space: Above and Beyond*. Glen's brother Darin wrote this episode. Also, the original airing of this episode was preceded by a special episode of *Space: Above and Beyond* which featured an uncredited cameo by David Duchovny.

On his wall, Blaine has a copy of the poster in Mulder's office which reads "I Want to Believe." However, on Blaine's wall, the words "Want To" are covered over.

Blaine's descriptions of Mulder and Scully echo the criticisms and observations of X-Philes on the Internet. He says Scully's hair was "red ... but it was a little ... too ... red, y'know?" Gillian Anderson dyes her hair for her role as Scully, and her hair color has been the topic of much discussion in the newsgroup.

A possible reference to *Twin Peaks*: Blaine says that Scully was actually a man dressed as a woman. Duchovny played a DEA agent named Dennis-Denise who dressed in drag on *Twin Peaks*.

Blaine describes Mulder by saying, "His face was so blank and expressionless." Some have criticized Duchovny for his unemotional and "bland" portrayal of Mulder.

Blaine also said that Mulder "didn't even seem human. I think he was a mandroid." In the episode of *Space: Above and Beyond* that preceded the episode, Duchovny did, in fact, play an Artificially Intelligent "mandroid."

Mulder's reaction to the dead alien has been referred to as his "girly scream." In Morgan's previous episode, "War of the Coprophages," Mulder refers to screaming at something, but justifying it by saying that it wasn't a girly scream. Scully replies, "Mulder ... are you sure it wasn't a girly scream?"

The alien autopsy is a reference to the FOX special *Alien Autopsy: Fact or Fiction?*, which was hosted by Jonathan Frakes and supposedly showed a real alien autopsy. The clock on the wall and the portable circular saw are identical to the ones seen in the FOX special. The cinematic style of both videos is remarkably similar in that it is jerky, ill-focused, and really doesn't linger on any one element long enough for a debunking analysis.

The Stupendous Yappi, played by Jaap Broekker, appeared in the previous Darin Morgan episode, "Clyde

Bruckman's Final Repose." Broekker is also David Duchovny's stand-in.

Yappi's video is named "Alien Body: Truth or Humbug?" This is a reference to the title of the FOX alien autopsy show, *Alien Autopsy: Fact or Fiction?* The word "humbug" also refers to Darin Morgan's other episode, "Humbug."

The two pilots are named Maj. Robert Vallee (who is autopsied) and Lt. Jacques Sheaffer. Jacques Vallee is a well-known writer on UFO phenomena. Some of his recent books propose that some UFO sightings have been staged by the military as disinformation campaigns or to test psychological warfare techniques, just like the storyline in this episode. Robert Sheaffer is a UFO skeptic and camera buff who faked a number of UFO photos. He used to send photos to skeptic Phil Klass while he (Sheaffer) was a student at Northwestern University. Several of his photos are shown in Klass's book *UFOs Explained.*

The Air Force representative who comes for Vallee and Sheaffer is named Sgt. Hynek. J. Allen Hynek was one of the principal investigators on Project Bluebook, which concerned UFOs. He also cowrote the 1975 book *From the Edge of Reality: A Progress Report on Unidentified Flying Objects* with Jacques Vallee. And he also served as a consultant for *Close Encounters of the Third Kind* and appeared in the film in a cameo as a scientist.

The Man in Black played by former professional wrestler Jesse "The Body" Ventura does a backbreaker, a popular wrestling move, on Blaine.

As Mulder and Lt. Sheaffer sit in the Ovaltine Diner, Sheaffer arranges his mashed potatoes into a replica of Devil's Tower, Wyoming, just like Dreyfuss did in *Close Encounters of the Third Kind.*

Mulder acting oddly and eating piece after piece of sweet potato pie is a reference to *Twin Peaks*, a quirky series that is often compared to *The X-Files* in style, tone and humor. The main character in *Twin Peaks* was an uncharacteristically odd FBI agent who loved cherry pie, and Duchovny appeared in the series as a transvestite DEA agent. A pie was also involved in the climax of Morgan's episode "Clyde Bruckman's Final Repose."

Alex Trebek's cameo as the second Man in Black is yet another jab at Duchovny's appearance on *Celebrity Jeopardy!* hosted by Trebek. Trebek would also be the perfect choice for the forces behind the conspiracy. They want every question answered by truth-seekers (e.g., Mulder) to leave them with more questions. And the phrase "all answers must be in the form of a question" would definitely apply.

Apparently, the role of the second Man in Black was originally to be played by Johnny Cash, but he was unable to appear. This would have produced a different in-joke, that of Cash being known as always dressing in black. Director Oliver Stone was also apparently considered for the role of the second Man in Black. Stone's film *JFK* (1991) suggested that President Kennedy's assassination was orchestrated by the Military Industrial Complex and was responsible for the biggest coverup of all.

Scully tells Chung that her story "probably doesn't have the sense of closure that you want, but it has more than some of our cases." This is true of many of the cases on the show, and this topic has also been discussed thoroughly on the newsgroup.

Mulder says Chung's publishing house is owned by Warden White Incorporated, a subsidiary of

McDougall-Kessler. McDougall-Kessler may be a reference to McDonnell-Douglas, an aircraft manufacturer and major U.S. defense contractor.

McDougall-Kessler may also be a reference to Bruce Kessler and Don McDougall, who both directed television in the 1970s, including episodes of *Kolchak: The Night Stalker*. The creators of *The X-Files* are great fans of *Kolchak*, which resembled this show in terms of creepiness, humor and general tone.

Mulder suspects that there is a covert agenda on the part of the Military Industrial Entertainment Complex. This refers to President Dwight D. Eisenhower's farewell speech to the nation in 1960, when he told the country to "beware the military-industrial complex." His theory was that the "Masters of War" (a phrase coined by Bob Dylan) were CEOs of multinational corporations who, in league with career military strategists, kept wars going and created new wars in order to keep demand for high-ticket, destructible manufactured goods (like planes and bombs and bullets) constant. In the years since Eisenhower made that speech, the United States has seen the consolidation of the media (entertainment and infotainment) with the military (e.g., in the Gulf War), so the word "entertainment" was added to Eisenhower's term.

At the end of the episode, we see that Roky has relocated to El Cajon, California. El Cajon, California, is where Darin Morgan and his brother Glen, also an *X-Files* writer, were born and raised.

The diagram of Roky's "inner world" at the end resembled the cover of a Roky Erickson and the 13th Floor Elevators album.

Blaine becomes the new lineman ...

possibly hoping, like Roy Neary and Roky Crikenson before him, to encounter aliens.

The cover of the book of Jose Chung's *From Outer Space* shows a picture on the cover very reminiscent of those seen on the covers of Whitley Streiber's books, particularly the picture on the cover of Streiber's *Communion*. He is one author who is considered to be the inspiration for Chung.

Mulder's character's name in the book is "Reynard Muldrake." Renard is French for "fox," and the term has become well-known in English as well.

When we see Mulder in bed, Chung says, "One shudders to think how he receives any pleasures from life." Mulder is watching a video, holding the remote in his left hand. His right hand is not seen, possibly under the covers, and he lets out labored breaths. There have been numerous references on the show (and, again, discussions on the newsgroup) regarding Mulder's fascination with pornography. However, the joke is, he is not watching porn at all; he's watching a video of the famous footage of Bigfoot, courtesy of Pat Patterson and Rene Dahinden, as it reads in the credits.

Chrissy sits at her computer in a darkened room, typing away at the end. This is probably how the show's producers see their fans on the Internet ... and, to a degree, they are probably dead on.

A brief reiteration of the melody line from *The X- Files* theme music is played at the end of the episode (after Chung's epilogue). The joke is that one note in the theme is altered in the reiteration, from a b-flat (which is actually called "the devil's note" in classical music) to a b-natural, thus transposing the tune from a minor key (spooky, sad, haunting) to a major key (happy, upbeat, friendly).

The entire episode has been viewed as the show's homage to the film *Rashomon* (1950), a film concerned with differing points of view of the same incident, which happens to be a rape and murder, both of which supposedly happened in this episode.

"Avatar": Skinner is haunted by an old woman wearing a red raincoat. This is a reference to the film *Don't Look Now* (1973), in which a figure in a red raincoat haunts the hero.

Apparently, Gillian's daughter, Piper, can be seen looking out of a window on the bus that speeds in front of Skinner as he tries to cross the street.

"Quagmire": Ever since Scully received her dog in the episode "Clyde Bruckman's Final Repose," there has been much discussion on the Internet newsgroup about what she does with it when she goes on assignment, what its name is, when she will get rid of it, and so on. The appearance (and dismissal) of her dog in this episode may have been a message to end the "name Scully's dog" threads. In fact, a fan posted the line "the poor dog must spend most of its life in kennels," and then in this episode Scully explains how she has sitters because "you know how I feel about kennels."

The dog is named after Queequeg, a character in *Moby Dick*, as Scully explains in the episode. In the novel, Queequeg was a cannibal. This is a reference to the fact that Queequeg's (the dog) original owner died and was partially eaten by Queequeg in "Clyde Bruckman."

The call numbers of the boat begin with GA. These are Gillian Anderson's initials, and how she is often referred to by her fans on the Internet.

The lake is named Heuvelman's Lake, after Dutch cryptozoologist Bernard Heuvelmans, who wrote *In the Wake of the Sea Serpents*, the definitive lake monster text.

Dr. Faraday (Timothy Webber) asks Mulder and Scully, "Has anyone ever told you two you have a great problem coming to the point?" Actually, this has been mentioned quite often on the Internet newsgroup.

Faraday is named after chemist and physicist Dr. Michael Faraday, who discovered the principle of electromagnetic induction, the basis for the generation of electrical power.

The photographer's name is Ansel, after famed photographer Ansel Adams.

The episode takes place in Millikan County, named for casting director Rick Millikan.

The boat *Patricia Rae* was named after writer Kim Newton's mother.

As he sets up the camera on the beach, Ansel hums Cyndi Lauper's song "True Colors" to himself. This song was used in commercials for Kodak film.

The two pothead teenagers from the episode "War of the Coprophages" (Tyler Labine and Nicole Parker) appear again in this episode, trying to get a buzz by licking the back of a frog.

"WetWired": In the home of the woman who shot her neighbor, Scully opens a trunk to find many neatly labeled videotapes. One of the tapes is labeled "Jeopardy," possibly a reference to the *Celebrity Jeopardy!* episode in which David Duchovny appeared.

When Mulder comes to visit Scully in the hospital, he turns off the television, which is showing footage of a plane crash. This is a reference to Gillian Anderson's hosting of the special *Why Planes Go Down*.

"Talitha Cumi": The mention of Quonochontaug, Rhode Island, may be a nod to Garrison Keillor's radio show *A Prairie Home Companion*. Keillor did a running series of jokes for two years or more featuring towns and lakes with Algonquin Indian names like Quogmocapidipog and Quontomocawoc and Quogwallimonowocomoc and Qonowantomaciwog. For a while, there was one of these towns or lakes mentioned almost every month. The scene with Assistant Director Skinner trying to say it and then Mulder rushing through it with practiced intonation is exactly the way Garrison Keillor has been doing it in his "Guy Noir, Private Eye" series on *A Prairie Home Companion*.

The conversation between Cancerman (William B. Davis) and Jeremiah Smith (Roy Thinnes) was taken from Dostoyevsky's *The Brothers Karamazov* with Cancerman as the Grand Inquisitor and Smith as Jesus Christ. In the book, Jesus comes back in 15th century France, performs some miracles, and is imprisoned by the Grand Inquisitor. The same argument comes up: "miracles, mystery and authority" vs. material needs. "Miracles, mystery, authority" is a direct quote from the book. In the end, the Grand Inquisitor lets Jesus go, with Jesus giving him a kiss (spark of faith). The Grand Inquisitor is struck emotionally but it does not change his thinking.

The name of the restaurant where this episode begins is Brothers K, another reference to *The Brothers Karamazov*.

The title of the episode is a biblical reference. In Mark 5:41, Christ heals a little girl by touching her hand and saying "Tal'itha cu'mi," which means "Little girl, I say to you, arise." Smith also heals this way and there are other Jesus Christ parallels as well. Before this season-ending episode was aired, however, many fans took the title to be a hint that Mulder's long-lost sister may be the little girl who "arises."

In this episode, Mulder must unscramble a word written by his mother. If you unscramble the letters in the title of the episode, you can form the words "I am a cult hit," which is how many have described *The X-Files*. Odds are, this is merely coincidence.

The Cancerman (William B. Davis) remarks that he and Mulder's father used to waterski together, and says that he was very good at it. Davis is one of Canada's top waterskiers in the 55–65 age group. He has placed first or second in many provincial and national championships.

There are two appearances of the time 11:21. It is the time when Mulder visits his mother in the hospital and also, on another day, the time when Scully finds the multiple pictures of Jeremiah Smith on her computer.

Among the extras in the opening restaurant scenes are cinematographer John Bartlet's daughter, first assistant director Tom (Frohike) Braidwood's daughter, key grip Al Campbell's daughter, and three of stunt coordinator Tony Morelli's children.

Jeremiah Smith is locked up in prison cell number B18. Building 18 is the location where many Roswell tourist items are supposedly housed.

"Herrenvolk": The title is a German word meaning "master race," popularized by Adolf Hitler's Nazis in World War II.

"Home": Mulder and Scully describe the town as being a lot like Mayberry, the rural town in the television series *The Andy Griffith Show*. It turns out that the sheriff of Home is named Andy Taylor and his deputy is named Barney. On *The Andy Griffith Show*, Griffith played a sheriff named Andy Taylor and Don Knotts played his deputy, Barney Fife.

Scully says she just recently watched *Babe* (1995) with her nephew and she uses the words "Baa Ram Ewe" to move the sheep. In the film, the old sheep tell Babe that the secret words to get any sheep, anywhere, to listen and move are "Baa Ram Ewe."

The inbreeding Peacock family was named after the neighbors of writer Glen Morgan's parents.

"Teliko": When Mulder glances at Aboah's resident alien card, we see that Aboah's birthday is 9/25/62. Gillian's daughter Piper was also born on 9/25.

"The Field Where I Died": Mulder's soliloquy at the beginning and end of the episode is from a Robert Browning poem titled "Paracelsus."

Vernon Ephesian, the character modeled after cult leader David Koresh, has Koresh's real first name, Vernon.

Sullivan Biddle and Sarah Kavanaugh are based on two real-life lovers who lived during the Civil War. A Civil War soldier named Major Sullivan Ballou wrote a now-famous letter to his wife, Sarah, in which he assured her that his love for her was "deathless" and that even though he might be killed in the war, he would always be with her, he would wait for her, and that "we shall meet again." Although the inference of his letter is that they would meet in heaven, it could be interpreted that they would be reincarnated, just as Biddle and Sarah were in this episode. One week after writing the letter, Sullivan Ballou was killed in the First Battle of Bull Run. His story was even chronicled in the PBS series *The Civil War*.

"Sanguinarium": Nurse Waite takes her name from Rider-Waite Tarot Cards, a long-time standard tarot deck.

Dr. Franklyn lives at 1953 Gardner Street. His street is named after British witch Gerald Gardner, who revived modern Wicca.

"Musings of a Cigarette Smoking Man": The CSM reads *The Manchurian Candidate* on his bunk. The book, which deals with government conspiracy and perception just as this episode does, was referred to (with a slightly different title) in the previous episode, "Jose Chung's 'From Outer Space.'"

James Earl Ray, who was arrested for killing Martin Luther King, Jr., maintains that during the time of the assassination he had a mysterious companion named Raul. This Raul told him to leave the rifle and disappear for a couple of hours, leaving Raul alone in the hotel room across from King's. Apparently, there is no proof of Raul's existence. The Cigarette Smoking Man, who assassinates King in this episode, uses the pseudonym "Raul Bloodworth" for his pen name.

Security Council Resolution #1013 says that any EBE caught by a national government must be immediately eradicated by that country's government. October [10] 13 is Chris Carter's birthday.

There are parallels to the film *Forrest Gump* (1994). Like Gump, the CSM takes part in various historical events, encountering and interacting with many historical figures (JFK, Martin Luther King, and so on). The CSM even has a speech reminiscent of Gump's "Life is like a box of chocolates" comment:

> Life is like a box of chocolates—
> a cheap, thoughtless, perfunctory
> gift that nobody ever asks for;

unreturnable, because all you get back is another box of chocolates. So you're stuck with this undefinable whipped mint crap that you mindlessly wolf down until there's nothing left to eat. Sure, once in a while there's a peanut butter cup or English toffee, but they're gone too fast and the taste is fleeting. So you end up with nothing but broken bits filled with hardened jelly and teeth-shattering nuts. If you're desperate enough to eat those, all you've got left is an empty box filled with useless brown paper wrappers.

"Tunguska": At the beginning of the episode, Krycek says that when one lives with the rats, one learns how to act like them. Krycek was earlier given the nickname "Ratboy" by fans of the show.

This episode contains a closed captioning in-joke. When Mulder takes the·cockroach out of his bowl of soup in the cell, he cannot be heard to say anything, but the closed captioning reads, "Bambi?" In the episode "War of the Coprophages," Mulder encounters some odd cockroaches with an attractive entymologist named Dr. Bambi Berenbaum.

The explosion that Mulder describes at Tunguska, U.S.S.R., actually happened. The explosion, which occurred on June 30, 1908, is most often considered to be the result of a large meteor or small comet (or UFO) colliding with earth. The blast leveled over half a million acres and was hundreds of times stronger than the blast of an atomic bomb.

The X-Men

In one episode, the villains drive around in a car with the licence plates THX 1138, after the groundbreaking George Lucas sci-fi film *THX-1138* (1970).

You Again?

This sitcom was based on the British show *Home to Roost*, and Elizabeth Bennett not only played Enid Tompkins, the housekeeper on this show, but simultaneously she played the same character on the British show.

The Young and the Restless

Killer David Kimball (Michael Corbett) plans to get himself a new face. To please his girlfriend, he demands that a plastic surgeon make him look like David Hasselhoff. Hasselhoff had starred on the show for many years as Dr. Snapper Foster.

In-Jokes
in Music Videos

**"Alternative Girlfriend"
by Barenaked Ladies**

The video is a parody of alternative music videos, and in one scene, the band can be seen destroying a bunch of pumpkins, a reference to the alternative group Smashing Pumpkins.

**"Amish Paradise"
by "Weird Al" Yankovic**

Yankovic and the other Amish erect a barn, a direct reference to *Witness* (1985), but the facing falls towards Yankovic. It ends up falling around him, with Yankovic standing in just a place where he will go through a window hole in the frame. This is a reference to Buster Keaton's film *Steamboat Bill, Jr.* (1928), in which Keaton has the facing of a building fall on him in a similar way.

"Back for More" by Ratt

Milton Berle makes a cameo appearance in this video (*see* "Round and Round").

**"Back Where You Belong"
by .38 Special**

This video starts off with a parody of the television show *Hill Street Blues*, and, partway through the clip, one of the band members is seen punching a side of beef like Sylvester Stallone did in the film *Rocky* (1976).

"Beat It" by Michael Jackson

Vincent Paterson, the video's choreographer, plays the gang leader in black.

The bartender is played by Jackson's bodyguard, and the man who peeks through Jackson's blinds is the video's assistant director.

"Big Me" by Foo Fighters

The video is a parody of the popular commercials for Mentos breath mints. The mints in the video are called "Footos."

"Borderline" by Madonna

The man on the street dancing with Madonna at the beginning of the video

253

is the clip's producer, DJ–record mixer John "Jellybean" Benitez.

"Discotecque" by U2

At the end of the video, the band dance around dressed as the Village People, who were big during the disco years.

"Do the Bartman" by Bart Simpson

Bart's prison number is A-113. This number, which appears frequently on *The Simpsons* in various locations, is animator Brad Bird's signature line. It is the number of the room in which he learned how to animate.

"Don't Answer Me"
by the Alan Parsons Project

This animated video was the first to use a variety of animation techniques within one clip. It is also unique in that it was created and directed under the supervision of a major advertising agency, Doyle Dane Bernbach. It even features a group of record company executives drawn into the video. They are the cartoon band behind the cartoon Parsons.

"Eat It" by "Weird Al" Yankovic

There are a lot of direct parodies of images and sequences in Michael Jackson's "Beat It." For instance, in the original, the six men who leap into the street howl like wolves. In this clip, they make noises like Curly from the Three Stooges.

The guitarist who blows up in the gang fight sequence is guitar virtuoso Rick Derringer. He takes the place of guitar virtuoso Eddie Van Halen, who played an identical part in the original video.

There is also a reference to Jackson's "Thriller." At the end of the video, Yankovic turns around ... and his eyes are yellow, just like Jackson's at the end of "Thriller."

"Free as a Bird" by the Beatles

Many references to former Beatles songs appear.

"Girls Just Want to Have Fun"
by Cyndi Lauper

Cyndi's brother, Butch Lauper, shows up in the wild party scene in Cyndi's bedroom.

Cyndi's mother, Catrine Lauper, plays her mother in the video.

"Gump" by "Weird Al" Yankovic

The video (and the song) parodies the film *Forrest Gump* (1994), and in the video Gump offers his chocolates to Ruth Buzzi, sitting beside him on the bench. She proceeds to whack him over the head with her purse, just as she did to the "dirty old man" (Arte Johnson) in the famous park bench scenes on the show *Laugh-In*.

"Headline News"
by "Weird Al" Yankovic

The man in the top hat and tails who leaves the theater at the end with the overweight woman in curlers is Yankovic's friend and mentor, novelty disk jockey Dr. Demento.

The red-haired man in Yankovic's band who makes the armpit noises with his hands is Mike Keiffer, who has contributed many sound effects to Yankovic's albums. He also works on *The Dr. Demento Show*.

"Hello" by Lionel Richie

Richie follows the blind girl and watches her in her dance class. A dance instructor comes from behind and dances with her. He is choreographer Michael Peters, who worked on Michael Jackson's "Thriller" and "Beat

It" and Pat Benetar's "Love Is a Bat-tlefield," among others.

Richie's wife, Wendy, also appears in this video. She is the woman in the opening scene in the white blouse sitting behind the blind girl.

"I Lost on *Jeopardy!*"
by "Weird Al" Yankovic

The man who turns around, winks, and drives Yankovic away at the end is actually Greg Kihn, who recorded the song that this one parodies, "Jeopardy."

The bearded technician with headset and glasses is comedy disk jockey Dr. Demento, who Yankovic was a huge fan of and who gave Yankovic his break on *The Dr. Demento Show*.

"I Love Rocky Road"
by "Weird Al" Yankovic

The top-hatted cashier who rings up "No Sale" and is also seen on the left in the group shot at the end is Dr. Demento (*see* "I Lost on *Jeopardy!*").

The red-haired man who rubs his hands in anticipation is Mike Keiffer, who has contributed many sound effects to Yankovic's albums. He also works on *The Dr. Demento Show*.

"I Saw You First"
by John Mellencamp

Matthew McConaughey has a brief cameo in the video as the man in the convertible. He asked Mellencamp for the opportunity because he was such a big fan of Mellencamp's.

"If Anyone Falls in Love"
by Stevie Nicks

Nicks's bandmate in Fleetwood Mac, Mick Fleetwood, appears in a cameo as Ivan the Terrible.

"If This Is It"
by Huey Lewis and the News

At the start of the video, the radio is turned on ... and Lewis's song, "I Want a New Drug" comes on.

"Let's Not Make Love"
by Robert Klein

Among the many cameos in this video by friends of Klein (including sportscaster Bob Costas as a referee), wrestling manager Captain Lou Albano appears on *The Joe Franklin Show* and says, "Girls don't really wanna have fun!" Albano is a good friend of Cyndi Lauper's and was in the video for her song "Girls Just Wanna Have Fun."

Klein also spoofs Robert Palmer's "models" videos, with long-legged women behind him with slicked-back hair in surgical masks and rubber gloves.

"Like a Surgeon"
by "Weird Al" Yankovic

There is a page for "Dr. Howard, Dr. Fine, Dr. Howard" at the start of the video. This is a reference to the classic Three Stooges bit in which Moe (Howard), Larry (Fine) and Curly (Howard) played doctors (see *Young Doctors in Love*, 1982).

"Love Is a Battlefield"
by Pat Benetar

Director Bob Giraldi's daughter, Maria Giraldi, has a walk-on as the girl on the left leaving the grocery store.

Producer Antony Payne can be seen standing in the shadows at the top of the long, dark staircase that Pat climbs. Beside him stands the video's choreographer, Michael Peters.

"Lucky Star" by Madonna

The man dancing on the street with Madonna is DJ and record mixer John "Jellybean" Benitez.

"Mediate" by INXS

This video features lead singer Michael Hutchence holding up placards with the words of the song on them, dropping them as the words are sung. This was originally done by Bob Dylan in his experimental video for the song "Subterranean Homesick Blues" from his movie *Don't Look Back* (1967).

"Money for Nothing" by Dire Straits

Sting appears, singing the opening lines, "I want my MTV..." Before the music channel became so widespread, Sting, Pete Townshend and Pat Benetar were among the rock stars who told their fans to scream this line from their rooftops to get the video channel installed in their communities.

"On Our Own" by Bobby Brown

Lori Singer appears in a cameo in the video, and she is seen playing and walking along with a cello. Singer's character played a cello on the series *Fame*.

"Only When You Leave" by Spandau Ballet

The surreal imagery in this clip was inspired by the "revenge" films of director Alfred Hitchcock. A Hitchcock look-alike even make a couple of cameos in the video. As the group performs, he crosses the stage in front of them carrying a bass fiddle (as Hitchcock did in *Strangers on a Train*, 1951), and later, he steps on a little kid's doll while smoking a cigar.

"Queen of the Broken Hearts" by Loverboy

Director Martin Kahan began to get a reputation as the Hitchcock of rock videos. Not because of his directing skills, but because he made a cameo in almost every video he directed, including this one.

The Video Star contest that ran on MTV advertised the chance for a fan to actually appear in a rock video. It was run just once, and this was the video that featured the contest winner.

"Ricky" by "Weird Al" Yankovic

The man in the top hat and tux dancing with the blond at the end is Dr. Demento, who gave Yankovic his first big break on his radio show.

The cheerleader in the group at the end is a reference to the original video for "Mickey" by Toni Basil, which this one is nothing like. It featured Basil and a group of cheerleaders in blue and white uniforms.

"Rock of Ages" by Def Leppard

The intro for the song is spoken by the band's manager, Peter Mensch—those are his teeth you see. He is also seen later in the video playing chess and looking very monk-like.

"Round and Round" by Ratt

Milton Berle makes a couple of cameo appearances in this video, one in drag. Berle's nephew, Marshal Berle, saw the group at the Whiskey A Go Go in Los Angeles and suggested to "Uncle Miltie" that he appear in a couple of their videos (*see also* "Back for More").

"Say Say Say" by Paul McCartney and Michael Jackson

The video is based on the Robert Redford/Paul Newman film *The Sting* (1973).

The big, burly black man Paul beats at arm wrestling is Sonny Barnes, who was Elvis Presley's bodyguard.

Director Bob Giraldi makes a cameo as the man McCartney hustles at pool.

The video's producer, Antony Payne, appears as the man who hands over McCartney's winnings.

Jackson makes eyes at a woman in a feathered headdress. She is played by his sister, La Toya Jackson.

The heroes pull up to an orphanage, followed by a horde of screaming kids. It is called Mrs. Ensign's Orphanage, named after Mary Ensign, who produced the clip.

One of the orphans is played by Heather McCartney, Paul's daughter.

"She Blinded Me with Science" by Thomas Dolby

The psychiatrist is played by British scientist–television personality Magnus Pyke, of *Don't Ask Me* fame. He ran a school that Thomas Dolby's sister attended, and Dolby managed to get him to appear in his video.

Dolby's dad, who is an archaeologist, appears in the video as well. He is the man on the jet-propelled rollerskates.

"She Bop" by Cyndi Lauper

Cyndi's mother, Catrine Lauper, and three of her aunts play the SWAT (Suburban Wives Against Transgressors) team of housewives with curlers on their helmets.

The spastic dancing partner who joins Cyndi Lauper for the grand finale is her boyfriend and manager, David Wolff. He also appears earlier in the video as the biker Lauper flirts with.

"She Don't Know Me" by Bon Jovi

Director Martin Kahan has a cameo (*see* "Queen of the Broken Hearts").

"Stand Up" by Def Leppard

In the video, a capitalist businessman with a baseball glove waits for a street person to hit a ball 50 stories up to him. The businessman is played by the group's manager, Peter Mensch, and the derelict by his partner, Cliff Burnstein.

"This Note's for You" by Neil Young

The song and video are a response from Young to advertisers who sponsor rock stars and use singers and their songs in their ads. The video parodies Michael Jackson's commercials for Pepsi (including Jackson's famous "burning hair" accident), Whitney Houston's commercials for Coca-Cola, pit bull terrier Spuds McKenzie's ads for Budweiser, and Calvin Klein's black and white ads for Obsession cologne.

"Thriller" by Michael Jackson

One of the zombies comes up out of a manhole, a reference to Jackson's previous "Beat It," in which gang members appeared out of the sewers.

John Landis directed the video, and he included a couple of trademarks:

The phrase "See you next Wednesday" is mentioned in lines of dialogue from the movie within the video: "...scrawled in blood...," "What does it say?," "'See you next Wednesday'..." (see *Schlock*, 1971). Also, there is a poster for Landis's *Schlock* in the lobby as Jackson and his date leave the theater.

Forrest J Ackerman, who Landis enjoys casting in his films, can be seen in the audience in the theater, eating a bucket of popcorn. In 1971, Landis cast Ackerman in Landis's first film, *Schlock*. He was sitting in the audience of a movie theater, eating a bucket of popcorn. Ackerman was the creator of the first successful sci-fi/horror magazine, *Famous Monsters of Filmland*.

"Time After Time" by Cyndi Lauper

Cyndi's mother, Catrine Lauper, plays her mother in the video.

"Tonight Tonight" by Smashing Pumpkins

The video is a parody-homage of the first ever science fiction film, *A Trip to the Moon* (1902), directed by the French magician George Méliès.

"UHF" by "Weird Al" Yankovic

In general, Yankovic's videos parody the video of the specific song that he is doing a spoof on (e.g., the video for "Smells Like Nirvana" spoofs the video for "Smells Like Teen Spirit" by Nirvana). For this one, however, he does a montage of spoofs of artists and videos unrelated to the song. They are, in order:

Guns n' Roses; "Faith" by George Michael; a Robert Palmer "models" video; Prince; "Once in a Lifetime" by Talking Heads; "Sledgehammer" by Peter Gabriel; ZZ Top; Billy Idol; Prince again; an early video by the Beatles (*see below*); "Mediate" by INXS (*see* "Mediate," *above*); "I Love L.A." by Randy Newman; Gabriel again; "When Doves Cry" by Prince; Idol again; Talking Heads' David Byrne in his "big suit," which Byrne wore in concert; Guns n' Roses again; ZZ Top again; the Beatles again; and Robert Palmer again. Yankovic took special care to lampoon Prince in this video because Prince once flatly refused to allow Yankovic to make a parody of one of his songs.

The Beatles video lampooned is from their television special *Magical Mystery Tour*. The song that the Beatles sang in the original was "Your Mother Should Know."

"Uptown Girl" by Billy Joel

As one of the mechanics dances by, the television in the background is playing one of Joel's earlier videos, "Tell Her About It."

"We're Not Gonna Take It" by Twisted Sister

Mark Metcalf plays the antagonist, the evil dad, in the video. He screams demeaning put-downs at his kid, including "You're worthless and weak!" and "A [Twisted Sister] pin?! On your uniform?!" These lines are from Metcalf's role as Doug Niedermeyer in the film *National Lampoon's Animal House* (1978). They are yelled by lead singer Dee Snyder at the end of the song as well.

"You Look Mahvelous" by Billy Crystal

The video begins with spoofs of singers Grace Jones, Prince, Tina Turner and Sammy Davis, Jr. Crystal plays all four.

Appendix:
Alan (Allen) Smithee
Credits

"Alan (or Allen) Smithee" is the pseudonym designated by the Directors Guild of America for those members who wish to remove their names from the screen and advertising credits of a particular film. Smithee is the only name (or "nonname") that the Directors Guild permits directors to use in place of their own on their films.

The Directors Guild generally does not permit directors to use pseudonyms. The Guild has been trying for years to build the impression that directors are the primary creative forces in motion pictures. The consequence of this is that when a film is really bad, it is usually seen as the director's fault. Therefore, the Directors Guild does not allow directors to get out of the responsibility for simply directing a bad film by hiding behind a pseudonym. Screenwriters, on the other hand, have been allowed to make use of many different pseudonyms.

If, however, a director does not have a reasonable amount of control over his or her film, usually because of studio or network interference, then the Guild will permit the use of the pseudonym "Alan Smithee." The name "Alan Smithee" in the credits of a film is an infallible sign that it did not turn out the way that the director intended it to.

Smithee first "replaced" Robert Totten and Don Siegel in 1967 as directors of *Death of a Gunfighter*, which was not released until two years later. In that instance, both Totten and Siegel alleged that star Richard Widmark had interfered with their creative control of the picture.

259

"Widmark had creative control, and he was running roughshod over everybody," Totten has said. "He spoiled the picture with his ego problems. I refused to have my name on the film, and Don didn't want his on it either."

Surprisingly, the Guild accepted Totten and Siegel's request to have their names removed from the film, but a name still had to be inserted. The guild board decided against the extremely obvious "Smith," also because there were real-life directors with the surname. Someone suggested adding a single "e" to the end, but the pronunciation of "Smithe" was rather ambiguous, so that idea was rejected as well. Veteran television director John Rich, who later became the executive producer of *MacGyver*, claims to be the one who thought up the second "e." The name would come back to haunt him when the director of the *MacGyver* pilot, unhappy with Rich's editing, took his name off the credits and replaced it with Alan Smithee. Rich has even admitted to using the Smithee pseudonym, on a film which he has yet to identify. "Suffice it to say," Rich has said, "that it was never released in the United States."

As for Smithee's debut, ironically enough, when *Death of a Gunfighter* was first released, a *New York Times* critic praised the fictitious director: "the film has been sharply directed by Alan Smithee."

Prior to the "Smithee Rule," director George Cukor had his name removed from the film *Desire Me* (1947) after the studio tampered with it. Mervyn LeRoy and Jack Conway also had a hand in directing the picture, but neither wanted credit for it. Its credits simply did not list a director. Director Joseph Losey also directed the film *Finger of Guilt* (1956) under the pseudonyms Alec Snowden and Joseph Walton, but this was because he was blacklisted at the time.

Michael Singer's *Film Directors: A Complete Guide* has a short biography for Alan Smithee: "Born 1969, Los Angeles, California. Contact: The Directors Guild of America, Los Angeles, 213/851-3671."

The 1998 movie *An Allen Smithee Film* stars Eric Idle as Allen Smithee, a director who is credited with directing some of the worst films in Hollywood. Ironically, the film's credits list "Allen Smithee" as director because Arthur Hiller had his name removed from the screen.

The Alan Smithee moniker has appeared in various other media as well. The Alan Smithee Band, based in Elon College, North Carolina, is a club favorite in the local venues, from Greensboro, North Carolina, to Norfolk, Virginia. An Alan Smithee wrote some issues of the Marvel Comics superhero *Daredevil* in 1995 after writer D.G. Chichester was unceremoniously fired.

Incidentally, "Alan Smithee" is an anagram for "the alias men."

In the listings that follow, the real filmmaker's name is shown following the film title and release date.

As director

Fade-In (released on video as *Iron Cowboy*) (1968): Jud Taylor.

Death of a Gunfighter (1969): Robert Totten and Don Siegel.

The Challenge (1970 TV): unknown.

Ruby (1977): Some prints of Curtis Harrington's 84 minute film run 85 minutes, with a hastily added epilogue featuring a *Carrie*-like shock ending. That version is credited to Smithee, and Harrington has his name on the original.

City in Fear (1980 TV): Jud Taylor.

Fun and Games (1980 TV): Paul Bogart.

Moonlight (1982 TV): Jackie Cooper, replaced by Rod Holcomb.

Dune (1984): David Lynch was the first to assign the directorial credit for the television version of one of his films to "Alan Smithee." The studio never asked Lynch to help when they recut his film for the small screen. Apparently, Lynch would have been happy to help, but because he wasn't asked, he angrily requested that his name be removed from the television version, which was expanded to 190 minutes from Lynch's original 141. Not only did Lynch change the director credit (and the possessory credit, which reads "An Alan Smithee Film"), he also requested that his name be removed from the screenwriting credit. The television version now reads: "Judas Booth," a reference to the traitorous implications of the biblical Judas and the assassination of Abraham Lincoln by John Wilkes Booth. There is no director's cut of the film, and Lynch has stated that he will never do one, due to the studio's tampering. The theatrical version is still credited to David Lynch.

Stitches (1985): Rod Holcomb.

Let's Get Harry (released on video as *The Rescue*) (1986): Stuart Rosenberg.

Dalton: Code of Vengeance II (1986 TV): unknown.

Appointment with Fear (1987): Razmi Thomas.

Riviera (1987 TV): John Frankenheimer.

Ghost Fever (1987): Lee Madden.

Morgan Stewart's Coming Home (1987): Terry Winsor, replaced by Paul Aaron.

I Love N.Y. (1988): Gianni Bozzacchi (also screenwriter).

Gunhed (1989): Masato Harada

Gypsy Angels (1989): unknown.

Backtrack (1989): This film was first released in Europe as *Catchfire*, which was 98 minutes long. Director Dennis Hopper disowned that version, and the film was restored to his cut (116 minutes) for its U.S. release on cable and video in 1991. The *Catchfire* version was also released on video, and it is credited to Alan Smithee.

The Guardian (1990): Television version. Theatrical version credited to William Friedkin.

The Shrimp on the Barbie (1990): Michael Gottlieb.

Solar Crisis (also known as *Starfire*) (1990): Richard C. Sarafian.

The Owl (1991 TV): unknown.

Bloodsucking Pharaohs in Pittsburgh (1991): The box of this direct-to-video horror comedy lists the director as "Alan Smithey," but the video's credits say that it was directed by the film's screenwriter, Dean Tschetter.

A Few Good Men (1992): Television version. Theatrical version credited to Rob Reiner.

Scent of a Woman (1992): Airline and television version. Theatrical version credited to Martin Brest.

Thunderheart (1992): Television version. Theatrical version credited to Michael Apted. Apted took the studio, TriStar, to court when his request to have the altered film credited to Smithee was denied. Apted had refused to participate in editing his film for television. "I have nothing against editing films for television, but massacring them, when you have to take 25% of the film out, is ludicrous," he said. "Much of the film's depiction of Native-American life and humor had been junked. It was just reduced to kind of a routine thriller." When the film was aired on FOX in 1995, 22 minutes were cut out and it was time-compressed (shown at a faster speed to take up even less time). An arbitrator ruled that the studio had to run the movie with a detailed disclaimer or with Alan Smithee as director. The studio reluctantly chose Smithee.

Fatal Charm (1992 TV): Fritz Kiersch.

Bay City Story (also known as *Deadline*) (1992 TV): Robert Butler.

The Call of the Wild (1993 TV): Michael Toshiyuki Uno.

Another Woman (1994 TV): This television movie's director is credited as "Alan Smythe."

Red Shoe Diaries 4: Auto Erotica (1994): Mary Lambert.

The Birds II: Land's End (1994 TV): Rick Rosenthal.

While Justice Sleeps (1994 TV): unknown.

The O.J. Simpson Story (1995 TV): Jerrold Freedman had his name removed after the FOX network made him take out a graphic scene showing Simpson beating up his wife.

Raging Angels (1995): unknown. This direct-to-video Christian rock demon political thriller has a director named Allan Smythe (see *Another Woman*, 1994 TV).

Hellraiser: Bloodlines (1996): Kevin Yeagher, replaced by Joe Chappelle.

Honorable mention: The opening scene of the film *Poetic Justice* (1993) consists of a drive-in theater showing a (fictional) crime drama called *Deadly Diva*. It stars Billy Zane and Lori Petty and, according to the theater marquee, it was directed by Alan Smithee.

As actor

Blades (1989): As "Engineer"

Flynn (1996): As "Man in Black"

As character

The First Nudie Musical (1976): Bruce Kimmel plays a character named "John Smithee."
An Allen Smithee Film (1998): Eric Idle.

As producer

Student Bodies (1981): Michael Ritchie. Ritchie even named the production company for the film "Alan Smithee Classic Films."

As second assistant director

Segment 1 of *Twilight Zone—The Movie* (1983): unknown. This was John Landis's segment. During the filming of this segment, actor Vic Morrow and two young Vietnamese extras, Renee Chen and Myca Dinh Lee, were killed in a helicopter accident. In the well-publicized case that followed, Landis was tried for manslaughter and, although he was acquitted, many actors and other filmmakers still refused to work with him. This would explain why someone even as low down the production line as "second assistant director" would want his or her name removed from this film.

As screenwriter

I Love N.Y. (1988): Gianni Bozzacchi.
The Nutt House (1992): Ivan Raimi and Sam Raimi appear here as Alan Smithee, Jr., and Sr.
The Horror Show (1989): Smithee gets rare coscripting credit on this film. The screenplay is credited to Alan Smithee and Leslie Bohem. Bohem is a gold record–winning country and western songwriter who also served as a member of the rock group Sparks and a group called Bates Motel. Bohem's script, his first to be produced, was rewritten by director James Isaac and possibly one or both of the directors who preceded Isaac on the project: Fred Walton (*When a Stranger Calls*, 1979) and David Blyth (*Death Warmed Up*, 1983).

As director (television)

Karen's Song: One 1987 episode
MacGyver: Series pilot
MacGyver: Fifth episode, "The Heist"
Omnibus: Special broadcast April 19, 1981
Paper Dolls: At least one episode
The Twilight Zone (new series): The 1985 Danny Kaye episode "Paladin of the Lost Hour": Gilbert Cates.
Tiny Toon Adventures: Episode #103, "Strange Tales of Weird Science" segments

"Pit Bullied" and "Duck in the Muck." The end credits of each episode of *Tiny Toon Adventures* contain a gag credit, and the credit in this episode reads "Number of Retakes / Don't Ask." The director apparently got fed up with the recutting of the Encore animators and didn't want his or her name on it.

Duckman: The clapboard for the April 21, 1996, episode, "The One with Lisa Kudrow in a Small Role," has the name "Raymie Muzquiz" (the episode's actual director) crossed out as the director and "Alan Smithee" written in.

As writer (television)

Eagle Riders: This animated series is the Americanized version of the Japanese anime *Gatchaman II*, the sequel to the popular series *Gatchaman*. *Gatchaman* was also Americanized twice, first in 1978 by Sandy Frank Syndication as *Battle of the Planets* and then in the mid-'80s by Turner Broadcasting as *G-Force, Guardians of Space*. The scripts of five episodes of *Eagle Riders* are credited to "R.D. Smithee." The episodes are "For the Global Good," "Temple Island," "Visit to Alcatraz," "Reunion" and "Old Friends, New Enemies."

As music video director

"Don't Let Go" by En Vogue
A Whitney Houston video

The theatrical equivalent of "Alan Smithee" is "George Spelvin." Traditionally, whenever an actor does not wish to be credited as appearing in a theatrical production, he has his name listed as "George Spelvin." The name goes back to the early days of theater. An adult film actress has taken the female equivalent for her stage name: Georgina Spelvin. Credits for George Spelvin have appeared in a number of films as well:

As a Magistrate in *Redemption* (1930)
As Gaston in *Suzy* (1936)
As Langston Hughes in *Pissoir* (1988)

Bibliography

Andrews, Bart. *The Official Cheers Scrapbook.* New York: Signet, 1987.

Armstrong, Richard B., and Mary Willems. *The Movie List Book: A Reference Guide to Film Themes, Setting, and Series.* Jefferson, N.C.: McFarland, 1990.

Asherman, Allan. *The Star Trek Compendium.* New York: Pocket, 1986.

Avallone, Susan. *Film Writers Guide.* Lone Eagle, 1991.

Beahm, George. *The Stephen King Companion.* Kansas City: Andrews and McMeel, 1989.

Bergan, Ronald. *Sports in the Movies.* New York: Proteus, 1982.

Bidd, Donald W. *The NFB Film Guide: The Productions of the National Film Board of Canada from 1939 to 1989.* The National Film Board of Canada, 1991.

Brautigan, Richard. *The Beatles Lyrics Illustrated.* Dell, 1975.

Brode, Douglas. *Once Was Enough.* Secaucus, N.J.: Citadel, 1997.

Brooks, Tim. *The Complete Directory to Prime Time TV Stars.* New York: Ballantine, 1987.

Clarke, Frederick S., ed. *Cinefantastique Magazine.*

Crenshaw, Marshall. *Hollywood Rock.* New York: Harper Perennial, 1994.

Farrand, Phil. *The Nitpicker's Guide for Next Generation TRekkers.* Volumes 1 and 2. New York: Dell, 1993, 1995.

Genge, N.E. *The Unofficial X-Files Companion.* New York: Crown Trade Paperbacks, 1995.

Guérif, François. *Clint Eastwood: The Man and His Films.* New York: St. Martin's, 1986.

Halliwell, Leslie. *Halliwell's Filmgoer's and Video Viewer's Companion.* Paladin Grafton, 1989.

Hogan, David J. *Who's Who of the Horrors and Other Fantasy Films.* San Diego: A.S. Barnes, 1980.

Horsting, Jessie. *Stephen King at the Movies.* New York: Starlog, 1986.

Jackson, Kenneth T. *The Encyclopedia of New York City.* Yale University Press, 1995.

Jakubowski, Maxim, and Malcolm Edwards. *The SF Book of Lists.* New York: Berkley, 1983.

Kieskalt, Charles John. *The Official John Wayne Reference Book.* Secaucus, N.J.: Citadel, 1985.

Lazell, Barry. *Rock Movers and Shakers.* Billboard Publications, 1989.

Lloyd, Ann, and Graham Fuller. *The Illustrated Who's Who of the Cinema.* New York: Portland House, 1987.

Lofficier, Jean-Marc, and Randy Lofficier. *Into the Twilight Zone.* London: Virgin, 1995.

Lowry, Brian. *The Truth Is Out There: The Official Guide to The X-Files.* Harper Paperbacks, 1995.

Lucaire, Ed. *The Celebrity Almanac.* New York: Prentice Hall, 1991.

McDonnell, David, John Sayers and Tim L. Smith. *The Starlog Science Fiction Trivia Book.* New York: Signet, 1986.

MacNeil, Alex. *Total Television.* New York: Penguin, 1991.

Maltin, Leonard. *Leonard Maltin's TV Movies and Video Guide.* Signet, 1989–1996.

Marill, Alvin H. *Movies Made for Television: The Telefeature and the Mini-Series, 1964–1984.* New York: Zoetrope, 1984.

Martin, Mick, and Marsha Porter. *Video Movie Guide.* Ballantine, 1992–1995.

Michael, Paul. *The Great American Movie Book.* Prentice-Hall, 1980.

The Motion Picture Annual 1990. CineBooks, 1990.

Naylor, Lynne. *TV Directors Guide.* Lone Eagle, 1990.

Nemecek, Larry. *The Star Trek: The Next Generation Companion.* New York: Pocket, 1995.

Premiere Magazine. K-III Magazines.

Quinlan, David. *The Illustrated Directory of Film Stars.* B.T. Batsford, 1984.

___. *The Illustrated Encyclopedia of Movie Character Actors.* London: Harmony, 1985.

Rees, Dafydd, and Barry Lazell. *The Illustrated Book of Film Lists.* London: Virgin, 1982.

Robertson, Patrick. *Movie Clips.* Guinness Superlatives, 1989.

___. *Movie Facts and Feats Edition 1 & 4.* Enfield, Middlesex: Guinness, 1988, 1991.

Schuster, Hal, and Wendy Rathbone. *Trek: The Unauthorized A-Z.* Harper Paperbacks, 1994.

Singer, Michael. *Film Directors: A Complete Guide.* Lone Eagle, 1997.

Sinyard, Neil. *The Films of Mel Brooks.* London: Bison, 1987.

Stanley, John. *Revenge of the Creature Features Movie Guide.* Pacifica, Calif: Large Press, 1988.

Starlog Magazine. Starlog Communications International, Inc.

Streebeck, Nancy. *The Films of Burt Reynolds.* Secaucus, N.J.: Citadel, 1982.

Trigg, Harry D., and Yolanda L. Trigg. *The Compleat Motion Picture Quiz Book.* Doubleday, 1975.

Waggett, Gerard J. *The Soap Opera Book of Lists.* Harper Paperbacks, 1996.

Weiss, Paulette. *The Rock Video Book.* Pocket, 1985.

Weldon, Michael. *The Psychotronic Encyclopedia of Film.* Ballantine, 1983.

Whitburn, Joel. *Top 40 Hits.* New York: Billboard, 1992.

White, Matthew, and Jaffer Ali. *The Official Prisoner Companion.* New York: Warner, 1988.

Willis, John. *Screen World Film Annual Volumes 34-37, 39, 42, 44.* New York: Applause, 1983, 1984, 1985, 1986, 1988, 1991, 1994.

Index